CONTENT AREA LITERACY
Strategic Teaching for Strategic Learning

Fourth Edition

ANTHONY V. MANZO

ULA C. MANZO

MATTHEW M. THOMAS

WILEY

JOHN WILEY & SONS, INC.

ACQUISTIONS EDITOR   *Brad Hanson*
MARKETING MANAGER   *Kate Stewart*
SENIOR PRODUCTION EDITOR   *Norine M. Pigliucci*
SENIOR DESIGNER   *Dawn Stanley*
PHOTO EDITOR   *Lisa Gee*
PRODUCTION MANAGEMENT SERVICES   *Pine Tree Composition*
EDITORIAL ASSISTANT   *Alec Borenstein*
COVER IMAGE   ©Images.com/CORBIS

This book was set in New Caledonia by Pine Tree Composition and printed and bound by Courier Westford. The cover was printed by Lehigh Press.

The book is printed on acid free paper.   ∞

Library of Congress Cataloging in Publication Data:
Manzo, Anthony V.
    Content area literacy : strategic teaching for strategic learning / Anthony V. Manzo, Ula C. Manzo, Matthew M. Thomas.
    p. cm.
    Includes bibliographical references (p.) and index.

    ISBN 0-471-15167-X (paper)
    1. Content area reading—United States. 2. Language arts—Correlation with content subjects. 3. Interdisciplinary approach in education. I. Manzo, Ula Casale. II. Thomas, Matthew M., 1940-III. Title.

LB1050.455.M36 2005

                                                                    2004040726

Printed in the United States of America

10 9 8 7 6 5 4 3 2

DEDICATION

To our parents—our first teachers
and
To teachers everywhere—guardians of the past and trustees of the future

"Bear in mind that the wonderful things you learn in your schools are the work of many generations. All this is put in your hands as your inheritance in order that you may receive it, honor it, add to it, and one day faithfully hand it on to your children."
—Albert Einstein

PREFACE

Face it: books and even newsprint are fixed tablets. Nonetheless, they have increased human ability to preserve and share thoughts, and therefore have accelerated the rate of human progress ten fold. Now we have entered an age where "Welcome, you've got mail," is as common as a telephone call. More astounding than getting e-mail and accessing light-speed search engines is the fact that you can offer, ideally, a gentle poke back to almost anyone, almost any time you wish. We are rapidly merging teaching, reading, writing, business, publishing, and telecomputing. The commerce taking place in *ideas,* while not winning many headlines, is far more vast and far-reaching than anything occurring in finance or product sales. Curiously, most people are showing a great deal of personal restraint. There's something about having to write that seems to induce self-reflection.

If communication is a major stimulus to brain development, what must be happening to our collective consciousness as these global messages whirl about our daily environments? Surely we all are becoming better informed, but our goal is not merely to have us become better mechanical "browsers," but better processors and interpreters. In this way, our students, and theirs also, might also become wiser, more literate, and more capable as thinkers and agents of stability and change, as the sometimes-ambiguous need requires. At the risk of sounding too dramatic, going to school is about the education of the soul, as much as it is about mere knowledge acquisition and career benefits. It is the place where human missions are grasped and life goals are set. Education may draw on the past, but it also charts the future. It requires human sentiment, but is best carried through without being overly sentimental. Thinking with the heart must be balanced with rigorous reading and critical-*constructive* thought—the 21st Century's enhancement of mere critical thinking.

The merging of the Internet, Education, and Commerce is amazing, exciting, and a wide-open frontier. So, don't just sit there reading your tablets. Learn and interact with your instructors, and if you like, let us hear from you. Maybe we'll be overwhelmed by your e-mails, but more than likely we'll answer many and incorporate others into our web sites, book revisions, and research. In any case, you have a chance to interact and influence thinking and teaching in ways that were never before feasible. Let's engage this latest revolution in communication and see where it takes us. Walter Lippman, an extraordinary 20th Century journalist said it best: "There is one bond of peace that is both permanent and enriching: the increasing knowledge of the world in which brave thoughts are welcomed, and experiment continues to occur." Let's educate as many people as we can to join this latest stage in social development and genuine human empowerment.

Anthony V. Manzo   avmanzo@aol.com
Ula C. Manzo   umanzo@fullerton.edu
Matthew M. Thomas   mthomas@cmsu1.cmsu.edu

CONTENTS

I

FOUNDATIONS OF CONTENT AREA LITERACY

The first three chapters introduce some of the basic ideas, goals, and frameworks for improving reading, writing, and thinking in almost any content area. Several practical methods are described and illustrated to anchor these foundational principals. By the beginning of the next section, you will have much of the knowledge base needed to begin to select specific methods based on student needs and your own style of teaching/learning.

CHAPTER 1

CONTENT AREA LITERACY'S BREAKTHROUGH ERA
Why and What Teachers Should Know

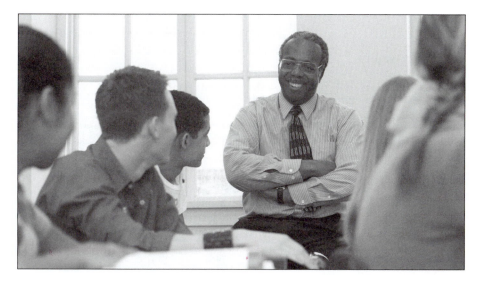

No one can reveal to you aught but that which already lies half asleep in the dawning of your knowledge.
—Kahlil Gibran

► FORE WORDS

This introductory chapter encourages teachers in all fields to reflect on their potential roles as content area literacy providers and facilitators of an enlightened twenty-first-century goal of fostering critical-constructive reading, writing, thinking, and responding across disciplines and in a multimedia world. The chapter is constructed around the emergence of the content area reading movement: the questions that impelled it, and its evolution into its currently highly formed state more accurately described as content area literacy. The underlying theme of the chapter is that teaching students to be self-teaching moves them toward becoming literate more than simply not being illiterate. This is illustrated in one broadly applicable and teacher-friendly method, called Listen-Read-Discuss, in this chapter and many other breakthroughs in teaching in the chapters that follow.

- ▶ FORE WORDS
- ▶ A DEFINITION OF A DEFINING FORCE
- ▶ ACCOMMODATING INCLUSION TO ENGLISH LANGUAGE LEARNING
- ▶ THE FIRST DAY OF SCHOOL
- ▶ BACKSTORY: FROM CONTENT AREA READING TO CONTENT AREA LITERACY
- ▶ THE WIRED CLASSROOM AND ITS AFFECT ON SCHOOLING AND LITERACY
- ▶ THE SECONDARY SCHOOL READING PROGRAM
- ▶ LISTEN-READ-DISCUSS: A SELF-INITIALIZING METHOD
- ▶ AFTER WORDS

▶ A DEFINITION OF A DEFINING FORCE

Content area reading (CAR) has become a defining force in contemporary education. A slightly modified definition (note brackets) from Moore, Readence, and Rickleman (1983) serves to introduce it:

> The specialty of content area reading instruction came about in recognition of the fact that readers [of varying ability levels] required various strategies when they study particular subject areas and read many kinds of materials for different purposes. Content area reading instruction is designed to deliver those strategies [and necessary accommodations]. To date, the primary mission of this instruction is to develop student reading-to-learn strategies. (p. 420)

With CAR as one of its mainstays, education today is successfully solving a multitude of problems and in some unexpectedly sound ways. One of the best-kept secrets of modern life is just how well we are delivering on ever-rising demands and expectations. Nonetheless, no one doubts that there is much more to be done. There are areas of crippling need, but we have moved past *crisis*. Education is a successful enterprise and a valuable and enriching way of life for career teachers. There are several chapters ahead that will bear testimony to this optimistic perspective.

▶ ACCOMMODATING INCLUSION TO ENGLISH LANGUAGE LEARNING

As further introduction to content area literacy (CAL), it is worth noting that this movement contains methods and options that to some substantial degree are adaptable to several contemporary needs. The basic methodology permits more practical levels of inclusion—that is, incorporating the needs of special education and learning disabled students in the regular classroom. It also shares a good deal of concern as well as instructional assistance with *sheltered instruction,* the most popular way to address the ongoing needs of English language learners (ELLs). The progress of ELL students in oral comprehension and even speaking may belie a continuing need for academic support in *reading to learn,* which often takes up to five years beyond conversational language. On a very positive note, CAL methods are equal to the challenge (Bean, 2000) and, by one impression, may be in a breakthrough era of progress. One of the authors of this text has referred to it as a *Cambrian Period* because it seems to parallel the wonderful warming period in the Paleozoic Era that gave way to a magical time when multiple life forms sprang into being on a previously lifeless planet (Manzo, 2003). But more on this in the chapters ahead; let's begin this journey where every teacher's heart, and in truth apprehensions, lies.

▶ THE FIRST DAY OF SCHOOL

New teachers often come away from their first classes feeling that they had wonderful lessons prepared, but the wrong students showed up. This mismatch in expectations happens largely because many teachers still feel that teaching is a process of transmitting information. This view is strengthened by the fact that some students can receive new information relatively effortlessly. They have sufficient background of information, appropriate independent learning strategies, and motivation to learn more about the subject. For many students in most subjects, however, merely presenting information is not enough. Most new learning is far from effortless and students will need help moving into, through, and beyond it. This requires some prior knowledge and, ideally, some concrete experience with the topic. Next, learners must somehow become engaged, or interested, in and attentive to the new information and ideas at hand. Further, learners must explore the information by questioning, comparing, and testing it against those elements of prior knowledge and experiences. Finally, learners must categorize and connect the new information with what they already knew—which often means adding to and even revising previously held ideas. For these reasons, learning has been called a *constructive* process. To initiate this process—to grab students' interest, and then maintain and focus it—teachers must start from where students are, socially, emotionally, and intellectually. This means that teachers need to have a good sense of what interests students, what background of information and experience they are likely to have, and what obstacles and misconceptions might prevent them from actively participating in the learning process. Students have been shown to sense when teachers show such caring and to respond positively to their strategies for reading and learning (Moje, 1996).

▶ BACKSTORY: FROM CONTENT AREA READING TO CONTENT AREA LITERACY

The field of content area reading evolved from an idea sparked in the 1920s into a movement that swept the nation by the 1960s. As previously noted, in recent years, the field has continued to evolve into the broader dimensions suggested by the label "content area literacy." Before the 1920s, education tended to follow a "survival of the fittest" model. Those who fell behind simply were permitted to drop from the system. A growing awareness of the need for an educated citizenry led to mandatory schooling legislation. It eventually became clear, however, that equal access to education meant more than requiring all students to stay in school until a certain age. If all students were to profit from staying in school, then schools would need to find ways to help them learn while they were there. In this context, educators began to believe that instead of simply presenting information, we could and should find ways to help students to *learn how to learn*—and especially how to learn through reading. This was a dramatic role change for schools and for teachers. It raised a host of questions. Just who was supposed to be responsible for figuring out why some students learn to learn and others do not? Who was supposed to help those who fell behind? And how could this be done? Some educators still question whether it really *can* be done, or even really *should* be done, given spiraling costs and competing priorities.

Nevertheless, this new concept of public education was an idea whose time had come. The need to equalize opportunities for all citizens was growing into a national priority that was fueled by the civil rights movement and the increasing skill demands of the job market. Today, most schools and teachers understand that they are not merely responsible for teaching a subject but for teaching all students to be flexible and independent learners. It is this shift in perspective that has driven the rapid development of the content area reading movement.

Early proponents of this movement laid the foundations for extending the definition and practices of reading instruction from an elementary grade focus on merely learning how to read to a new and broader focus on learning from reading. To meet this expectation, schools and teachers needed answers to immediate and pressing questions about how students learn and about how to help students to become better learners. They welcomed the answers that the field of study known as content area reading was beginning to offer. In many cases, however, these answers conflicted with teachers' attitudes and expectations. Changing teachers' views of their roles and responsibilities, like most change, has not been easy. It has been an ongoing process that continues to unfold within one teacher at a time, among both practicing and beginning teachers.

▶ THE WIRED CLASSROOM AND ITS EFFECT ON SCHOOLING AND LITERACY

You do not have to be the Delphic Oracle to realize that the Internet is changing the face and the functions of education at every level. Since this is one of those things that is still in progress, rather than historically analyzed and evident, our aim here is to set out some of the influences it seems to be exerting and the implications that are becoming evident. To date, it appears that the Internet is having unparalleled effects on daily life and learning.

- It is generating more reading and writing than ever before.
- It is, through *chat rooms*, *discussion boards*, and specialized Web sites, the ultimate niche maker and server to individual reading interests and tastes.

- It is, through the *surfing* option, the greatest means ever of promoting multiple literacies and broadened interests and tastes.
- It is more current and interactive than any prior media.
- It is a form of connection that ends much of the isolation that has characterized schools and classrooms to date.
- It is creating new communities of learners that are blind to a person's color, ethnicity, age, and background.
- It is blurring lines between services, business, entertainment, information, and education.
- It is democratizing the power of individuals to speak across political boundaries and be heard by a potentially wide audience.
- It is, through *homepaging*, producing some of the greatest wealth-making opportunities since free-land homesteading.

The authors are heavily involved in the evolutionary process that the Internet has set in motion. You will read about how we began in the early 1970s to create a reading-writing-teaching method (called REAP) that now serves as the vehicle for electronic sharing by readers and how we are now advocating for and extending it through what is being called *WebQuesting*, and social and economic entrepreneurism. However, we will proceed for much of the next two sections by preparing you with the knowledge base that content area literacy has provided to us for making the most of the connections and possibilities that telecomputing seems to be offering to education and contemporary life. See if you find the stories of CAL and the World Wide Web to be, as we do, a tale of two merging technologies.

▶ THE SECONDARY SCHOOL READING PROGRAM

Whose Job Is It?

In its early years, the slogan of the fledgling field of content area reading was "Every Teacher a Teacher of Reading." This slogan probably did the field more harm than good, since most junior high and high school teachers saw themselves as teachers of their subject areas and thought of reading as a basic skill that should have been mastered in the elementary grades. The following line of questioning represents the major points in the reasoning process that many experienced secondary teachers have worked through.

1. Haven't students learned to read by the time they finish grade school?

The answer to this question must begin with a basic definition of *reading*. Many people think of learning to read as learning to *decode*, or translate the little squiggles we call letters into the sounds we call words. Reading, however, means much more than this simple translation process. It means constructively comprehending, or making meaning from, print. Reading comprehension generally is defined as follows:

Literacy skills:

- *Understanding* the author's intended message (reading the lines);
- *Interpreting* the message's meaning and implications (reading between the lines);
- *Applying* the message in meaningful ways (reading beyond the lines).

Most children do master the decoding aspects of reading by about the fourth grade. At each higher grade level, however, the reading materials become more difficult. To express increasingly complex ideas and information, authors must use more technical vocabulary and more complex language forms. Thus, learning to read is a process that continues as long as one continues to learn.

Even children who master beginning reading in elementary school must continue to develop effective strategies for learning from more difficult materials and about increasingly specialized subjects. Some students acquire these strategies rather effortlessly, but many others do not. Even in elementary school, some children begin to fall behind their peers in comprehending what they read. As middle and high school teachers' expectations increase, these children begin to have more frequent unsuccessful experiences in attempting to learn from reading. And, of course, a few children fail to master even basic decoding.

For these reasons, content area teachers can expect to have several categories of students in their classes. A few students will still have basic decoding problems. Some will have fairly serious comprehension problems. Many will simply need assistance in acquiring the comprehension strategies appropriate to each higher grade and subject area. Finally, some students will continue to read and develop the needed comprehension strategies on their own. In the past, teachers could concern themselves primarily with presenting information and materials to the latter category of students. Learning to read content materials was treated as a "sink-or-swim" challenge: You figured out how to do it, or you failed to learn the subject.

Today, most teachers are willing to accept more responsibility for helping *all* children to learn to read and think. As they do so, they are accepting the challenge to teach in ways that don't simply *require* but that help students *acquire* the thinking strategies they need to actively construct meaning from print.

2. If some students acquire reading–thinking strategies naturally, simply by reading increasingly difficult materials, why do others fail to do so?

The fundamental premise of this book, and a large sector of the content area literacy movement, is that if all students did spend time reading and working at understanding in every subject through the grades, they all might continue to develop the reading–thinking strategies they need. However, for a variety of reasons, this does not always happen.

One simple reason why some students do not spend sufficient time reading and working at understanding every subject is that at each higher grade level students' personal interests begin to influence how much reading they do in different subjects. They read more in subjects they prefer and often avoid reading in subjects they do not like. Thus, they may continue to acquire the specialized vocabulary, language, and thinking strategies needed in some subjects but not in others.

Another reason why some students do not do enough reading to make so-called natural progress is related to their personal experiences with being taught to read. Reading instruction, even in the elementary grades, often is structured and conducted in ways that cause some children to see themselves as poor readers. For example, when children are grouped for reading, children placed in the low group know that they are seen as poor readers by their teacher and their peers and learn to see themselves as poor readers. The strength of this learning is evidenced in the fact that they seldom advance to a higher group. When children begin to view themselves as poor readers, for whatever reason, they read less and progress at a slower rate. By the time these struggling readers reach secondary school, they have had years of negative experiences with reading.

Thus, at each higher grade, in any given subject, there are students who have fallen behind in acquiring the necessary natural reading–thinking strategies: some simply because of stronger interest in other areas, and some because prior failures have caused them to stop trying. Secondary teachers, faced with increasing numbers of students who cannot or will not learn from reading, sometimes make the well-meaning but ironic attempt to present information in other ways that involve little or no reading. The irony in this approach is that it removes any possibility of students' acquiring greater ease and self-confidence in reading. Even those students who might have developed grade-level reading strategies through continued reading may fail to do so if no reading is required. The better alternative, and one of the most influential things a secondary teacher can do, is to use teaching methods that structure reading-based lessons in ways that enable more students to have more successful experiences with reading. It is only through repeated successful reading experiences that appropriate thinking strategies are acquired, and the effects of years of negative experiences can be counteracted.

3. Aren't there some students who just can't be taught to read better?

Since reading comprehension is almost synonymous with thinking, many educators once believed that there was a simple, one-to-one relationship between general intelligence and reading comprehension. It was assumed that intelligent students would acquire the ability to read and comprehend well and that unintelligent ones would not and could not be taught to do so. Today, few educators hold this simplistic view. We now know, for example, that intelligence is much more multifaceted than is measured by most conventional tests of intelligence. Several aspects of critical and creative thinking, in fact, appear to be only minimally related to conventional IQ test scores. In fact, some educators have proposed that poor reading comprehension may be a causal factor in low IQ scores rather than the reverse. In recent years, educational researchers have provided convincing evidence that thinking can be improved and that the methods for doing so are not terribly complex. Content area literacy is based on the premise that all students can be taught to read, learn, and think better, and that all teachers can share the challenges and rewards of helping them to do so.

4. Why can't reading be taught in a separate pull-out class?

Reading *should* be taught in a separate class by a reading specialist for those few students who have not acquired basic decoding strategies. Severe reading disabilities usually have multiple causes and may be accompanied by emotional and behavioral disorders. [You may have heard the media statements about how are prisons are filled with nonreaders, who, presumably, if they could read would not be there. These are exaggerations. Most people who can't read are decent, and by some estimates, quite able in many other ways (Manzo, 2003). It is best not to overstate an already serious situation. Professionals think and ideally speak in more balanced terms.]

Students who can decode adequately but simply do not seem to understand what they read are a different matter. At the beginning of the content area reading movement, and sometimes still today, separate reading classes were designed for these students. The problem with the separate-class approach is that, even though it seems to be the most logical solution, it simply doesn't work very well. Why it doesn't work seems to be related to at least three conditions. First, whenever students are grouped by ability, a multitude of negative factors tend to outweigh the logical advantage that might be gained by offering them instruction that is geared to their achievement level. Second, as discussed previously, most secondary students are stronger readers in some subjects than in others. Identifying which students are lagging in which subjects and trying to provide this level of individualized assistance is practically impossible. Finally, the pull-out approach assumes that students will be taught general reading–thinking strategies that they will then modify and apply when reading their various subject area assignments. This kind of transfer of training is a higher-order thinking process that is, almost by definition, what poor readers have difficulty doing.

Gradually, after years of trying various approaches, two things have become clear: (1) Pull-out programs are necessary for those students who have not mastered basic decoding. (2) However, all students, including those receiving separate remediation, need specific coaching in the particular grade-appropriate reading–thinking strategies of each subject. And who is more experienced in reading, thinking, talking, and questioning in the respective subject fields than the content teachers themselves?

5. How can content teachers be expected to find time to teach reading and thinking?

The fact that content teachers are being held responsible for the learning of *all* students is the strongest argument for all teachers to be prepared to coach students in the particular reading strategies relevant to their subject areas. Coaching reading and thinking need not be done *in addition to* teaching content. In fact, it is best done *while* teaching content. When such coaching accompanies the teaching of content, students (including mainstreamed students with learning disabilities) become more able to learn independently. Thus, in the big picture, teachers who help students to read on their own are able to teach more content rather than less.

Teaching methods that result in effective coaching of subject area reading and thinking have two important characteristics that make them appropriate for subject area teachers. These methods tend to be concurrent and interactive. *Concurrent* methods permit the teacher to teach toward several objectives at the same time. *Interactive* methods are designed to encourage what is called the *con-*

structivist side of education—that is, increasing student involvement in instructional exchanges and supporting the use of thinking strategies for making, or constructing, meaning. Many good teachers teach some reading without labeling, or even realizing, it as such. Teachers are teaching reading, for example, when they introduce a reading selection in a way that engages students' interest, or when they invite meaningful discussion following reading, or even when they just ask some questions to check comprehension following reading. Teachers who do these things naturally will want to know more; those who do not do so naturally need to know more.

6. Why should all subject areas be included in the schoolwide reading program?

Some content areas, such as English, science, and social studies, have an obvious connection with reading. Some content areas, such as foreign language, vocational and industrial technology, theatre, business education, and family and consumer science require moderate amounts of reading. Others, such as physical education, art, music, and mathematics, traditionally involve less reading. Yet most states require that all teacher certification programs include at least one course in the teaching of reading. This consensus is in part due to two concepts that are central to effective schools. First, schools are more effective when *all teachers accept responsibility for the overall goals of the school*, not simply for those of their own discipline and classes. Accordingly, every teacher is expected to contribute to the schoolwide literacy program. In some subject areas, this contribution may be as simple as including just a few reading-based lessons that are carefully designed to permit even poor readers to have more successful experiences as readers in that subject. Second, effective schools are organized not merely to teach a given body of information but also to develop interests and abilities that will allow students to continue to be reasonably well versed in their subjects in the future. In this information age, it is not enough to merely acquire information; students must know how to acquire it and, more important, to interpret and use it.

7. What level of reading achievement can content teachers expect students to have, and how can they evaluate their students' reading?

Naturally, the higher the grade, the higher the overall average reading level you can expect of a class. However, this fact tends to mask another more important one: The higher the grade, the wider the *range* of students' reading abilities from lowest to highest. This is because children who encounter difficulty in beginning reading often make far less than a year's progress for each year in school. Others, however, make more than a year's progress in a school year. Thus, a typical seventh-grade class may be expected to have reading levels ranging from the third- to the tenth-grade level, while a tenth-grade class is likely to range from the fourth-grade to the college level.

Some basic information about students' reading levels usually can be gathered from standardized test scores that are on file. Students with particularly low scores can be noted and observed during the first weeks of school to verify this test-based information. As discussed previously, however, students' reading abilities are likely to vary from subject to subject according to their personal interests, experiences, and prior knowledge. Subject area teachers can use a variety of techniques to cross-verify standardized test score information. These include observation, informal assessment procedures, and systems for portfolio collection, all of which are detailed in Chapter 10.

8. How can students of varying reading achievement levels learn from a single textbook or supplementary material that is written more or less on grade level?

Over the years, the field of content area reading has proposed and explored many solutions to this logistical question. Most of the early solutions were logical but not very practical. One popular suggestion, for example, was to collect a variety of reading materials on the same topic but at different difficulty levels and to match these with student reading levels. Individual students, or groups of students, could then explore the topic of study by reading at their own levels. Another suggestion was to prepare reading guides at different difficulty levels and to assign these based on student reading level. For example, lower-achieving readers were guided through acquiring the basic information, and more advanced students were asked questions that required more complex analysis of the information. These early attempts, while reasonable and still viable in some situations, tend to require an extraordinary amount of preparation and continuous monitoring. They also raise troublesome questions about how to evaluate students' work on these differentiated assignments and about whether lower-achieving students would be penalized rather than assisted by a steady diet of literal-level questions and easy material.

Content area literacy has moved to simpler, more manageable, and more equitable solutions. The basic approach is based on *interactive methods* for teaching reading–thinking *concurrently* with subject area knowledge and applications. Regular use of such methods from grade to grade and across subject areas supports student development of independent reading–learning strategies and empowers even relatively poor readers to read and learn from materials that they otherwise would find difficult.

Content Area Literacy

The research-supported answers and perspectives that have evolved in response to the preceding questions represent a fairly complete picture of the traditional field of content area reading. A substantial body of research now supports the propositions that teachers *can* teach reading–thinking strategies, that they *can* meet the needs of a fairly wide range of student reading levels in a single classroom, and that the most effective schoolwide reading programs are those that enlist the participation of *every* educator in the school. With that groundwork established, the field has begun to broaden its focus, viewing reading within the broader context of literacy. Whereas the term *reading* connotes acquisition of strategies needed to successfully complete schooling, the term *literacy* speaks more to the breadth of education needed to function in modern life, where ordinary citizens are given the executive power of the vote but also must live in a milieu of rapid technological change and job displacement.

In today's world, the acquisition of large amounts of information is less important than the acquisition of effective strategies for accessing and evaluating information, problem solving, and communicating and interacting with interested parties. We once assumed that learners must first acquire information before they could be challenged to critically analyze and apply it. Many frustrating hours have been spent in trying to teach/learn isolated history facts, math facts, grammar rules, and the like. These required so many hours that teachers often despaired of students ever acquiring sufficient information to enable them to operate at higher levels of evaluation and application. Research in the field of learning theory is refocusing our attention on what many effective teachers have long intuited: if students are initially engaged in an authentic, relevant problem, situation, or challenge, the relevant information is acquired almost effortlessly and in a fraction of the time.

Similarly, reading and subject area specialists are redirecting their attention toward creating educational environments in which students are challenged to analyze, reflect, communicate, and create. In such environments, effective strategies for reading, writing, speaking, listening, and thinking are more likely to develop more naturally and easily than when these are addressed as isolated elements. Thus, there is a growing trend to refer to this emerging field as *content area literacy*. This reorientation shifts the emphasis from reading as a somewhat isolated function toward its role in overall communication and higher-order thinking. Ironically, the need to write and to read highly technical information has been greatly intensified by telecomputing and related technologies that once were expected to reduce the demand for every citizen to be highly literate.

CAL is Enlightened Instruction, Every Teacher's Goal

So who, in conclusion, should have knowledge about content area literacy? In our judgment, everyone who teaches, and certainly anyone who will teach in a conventional school setting, should know about content area literacy. The interactive and strategic teaching methods of content area literacy permit students with a wide range of reading levels to learn from the same reading materials and in the same classroom. These methods offer practical ways to satisfy today's expectation that students of varied learning aptitudes and even those with special learning needs and from diverse cultural backgrounds should have the opportunity to learn in the traditional class setting. And, given the additions of new, electronic communication and computing systems, traditional class settings are now anything but traditional. Nonetheless, all teachers, including those who might think they have the least need for content literacy methodology, have the obligation to be informed about what constitutes enlightened instruction so that they can participate in the school's primary mission.

On a more personal career level, an understanding of content area literacy precepts and practices prepares all who work in a school setting to be ready to step in for their colleagues and to have sufficient flexibility and preparation in their education to be able to take on other related jobs, as often as is required over a typical lifelong career. It is not unusual today for those who originally prepared to teach in a conventional classroom to find themselves teaching in other settings: in adult basic and high school equivalency programs; in one of the burgeoning educational programs within business and industry; or extending their certification to work as school-based consultants or central office administrators. (See Appendix A for a sample portfolio system to help teachers better record and prepare for such varied career options.)

The Listen-Read-Discuss (L-R-D) method was created as a "starter" method for bridging from traditional instruction to a more interactive approach. Traditional reading-based instruction typically begins by having students read the assignment, listen to a brief lecture or overview by the teacher, and then discuss their responses to questions. The L-R-D simply inverts the first two steps.

► LISTEN-READ-DISCUSS: A SELF-INITIALIZING METHOD

Effective learning, including learning how to be an effective teacher, needs something to get it started, something to keep it going, and something to keep it from becoming random or misguided (Bruner, 1971). The L-R-D method (Manzo & Casale, 1985) tends to meet these requirements for both teachers and students. It is a simple lesson design that can be tried almost immediately and that offers several variations that can be phased in as a personal program of professional development. The L-R-D is a heuristic, or hands-on, activity designed to induce self-discovery about effective teaching by teachers and about effective learning by students. It is, in other words, a way to self-improve teaching that ideally helps students to self-teach in all the ways that their environments will allow.

Steps in Listen-Read-Discuss

Step 1. Review the reading selection, and prepare a brief, organized overview that points out the basic structure of the material, relevant background information, and important information to look for and generates interest in the topic.

Step 2. Present the summary orally to students. (See Figure 1.1.)

Step 3. Have students read the textbook version of the same material. Students will then be empowered to read material with which they have some familiarity.

Step 4. Discuss the material students have heard and read. Begin the discussion with the information and ideas students were directed to look for.

The following sample prereading script is based on the article"Dance and Sport: The Elusive Connection," which follows in this figure.

Did you know that football coaches sometimes have their players take ballet lessons? Can you see Frank over there in a tutu? (Frank is one of the school's star football players.) Well, this article tells about where this idea came from, and why it seems to work. Look for seven things dancers learn, and think about why these would be useful for football players. Write these down when you come to them—they're listed in one of the first paragraphs. Then the author tells how some sports are more like dance than others. In dance, it is the mastery over one's movement that is important. In sport, it is the result *of mastery over one's movement that is important. Look for the difference between "open skill" sports and "closed skill" sport, and how one type is more like dance than the other. The title of the article is "Dance and Sport: The Elusive Connection." Elusive means something that seems to keep slipping away. Read to see why the connection between dance and sport might keep slipping away.*

Students then read the following article, from the *Journal of Physical Education, Recreation, and Dance.*

DANCE AND SPORT: THE ELUSIVE CONNECTION

Techniques and principles effectively used in teaching dance can be applied to teaching sport.

Sandra Minton
Bradford Beckwith

(1)   What are the functional connections between dance and sport and the benefits that are derived from participation in both pursuits? This article presents ideas which are applied to both dance and sport in order to enhance performance and reduce injury.

(2)   Many well-known people have recognized a connection between dance and sport skills. It may have been this kinship that convinced Knute Rockne, famed football coach at Notre Dame, to require his players to enroll in dance classes. Maybe it was the similarity between dance and sport that caused Woody Hayes, former Ohio State head coach, to expect his players to take dance as part of their practice procedures (Lance, 1981). Lynn Swan, three-time Pro Bowl wide receiver while playing with the four-time World Champion Pittsburgh Steelers, studied dance for 14 years and attributed his graceful athletic abilities to dance.

Figure 1.1   Example of an L-R-D Prereading Script.

(3) It is possible that each of these individuals witnessed movement competencies shared by dance and sports. Some of these shared abilities include centering, balance, focus, breathing, transfer of weight, relaxation and the ability to use space, time, and energy with mastery. Such abilities are taught specifically in dance classes, while in athletics they are only alluded to as a part of skill instruction.

(4) The basic difference between dance and sport is that sport takes place within the conditions of a game, while dance is performed in other contexts. A game is a contest in which opposing interests are given specific information and are then allowed a choice of moves with the object of maximizing wins and minimizing losses. A game entails dominance over an opponent and the acquisition of some mutually coveted symbol. The athlete, by improving his or her movement abilities, will then improve sport skills.

(5) Dancers, on the other hand, are process-oriented rather than product-oriented. The goal in dance is the improvement of movement quality.

(6) Similarities between dance and sport outweigh their differences. Participants in both areas train to go faster and farther, while moving with increased control. The dancer and the sport participant both work to expand their movement vocabulary so they can use a particular action when the situation demands. Biomechanical analysis has been used for many years by physical educators to help their students learn. In recent years, dancers have also begun to use biomechanics to analyze movement with the goals of sharpening perception of movement, decreasing learning time, and enhancing performance (Laws, 1984). Dance and sport are similar in another respect. While some would say a dance was choreographed but a sport contest was not planned, further examination indicates that all the X's and O's used in game strategy simply represent another form of choreography.

(7) Some sport activities are more similar to dance training than others. The concept of open and closed skills helps explain this point. In a closed skill, one strives to master an effective and efficient motor program with the goal of being able to duplicate this program with each repetition. Environmental conditions remain relatively constant, and the performer attempts to be consistent in the execution of the skill. Sports such as the shot put, diving, and gymnastics are closed skills. Open skills exist in a changing environment, and the selection of appropriate movement responses is as variable as the environment itself. Baseball, football, soccer, and basketball are open skill activities (Sage, 1977). Both open and closed skill athletes can benefit from dance training. The abilities which are taught in dance classes used by both kinds of athletes are different, but are not less applicable to their sports' requirements.

Figure 1.1 *(continued)*

(8) The principle of relaxation can be used as an example. Dancers frequently talk about using the right amount of tension in one part of the body while allowing other body areas to remain relaxed. The main idea is to use energy efficiently and only where needed to perform a movement. Efficient movement is characterized by using the appropriate muscle groups in proper sequence. The use of the wrong muscle group at the wrong time can be deleterious to the skill and possibly to the performer. Another common word heard in dance class is "centering." Centering is finding the body's center of weight and manipulating it effectively in relation to gravity. It also brings the mind and body together to produce better concentration. Achieving a heightened perception of and facility with space, time, and energy is another principle used in teaching dance. Dancers are asked to look at the direction or level of a movement, its speed in relation to an underlying pulse, or the quality of energy used to propel actions through space. Such movement descriptions are provided in dance classes to help students see movement more clearly and to enhance understanding of the expressive aspects of each action (Minton, 1984).

(9) The point is that these principles are used in teaching dance, but generally not in teaching sport. In dance, these ideas are singled out in the classroom and used as learning tools. The examples given here are several of the techniques used in teaching dance that could be applied profitably to the teaching of sport.

REFERENCES

Lance, J. (1981). Practicing for touchdowns. *Journal of Physical Education, Recreation, and Dance,* 5, 38.

Laws, K. (1984). *The Physics of Dance.* New York: Macmillan, Inc.

Minton, S.C. (1984). *Modern Dance: Body and Mind.* Englewood, CO: Morton.

Sage, G.H. (1977). *Introduction to Motor Behavior: A Neuropsychological Approach* (2nd. ed.). Reading, MA: Addison-Wesley.

This article is reprinted with permission of the *Journal of Physical Education, Recreation and Dance,* May/June 1986, pp. 26 and 54. JOPERD is a publication of the American Alliance for Health, Physical Education, Recreation and Dance, 1900 Association Drive, Reston, VA 20191.

Sandra Minton is coordinator of the Dance Program at the University of Northern Colorado, Greeley, CO 80639. Bradford E. Beckwith is a doctoral candidate, psychological kinesiology, at the same school.

Figure 1.1   *(continued)*

Teachers See Text Differently, and Other Values and Benefits of Listen-Read-Discuss

Use of the L-R-D tends to benefit teachers, students, and the school program in ways that are not always immediately apparent. One such value emerges almost immediately in the lesson-planning stage. When teachers select textual material for use in an L-R-D lesson, they find themselves looking at the textbook more carefully and from more points of view than they might otherwise. They begin, quite naturally, to sense where students' comprehension is likely to falter and to better align the phrasing, facts, and organization of the lecture material they are preparing with the textbook material that students will read. With better alignment and organization, teachers automatically begin to heed a basic dictum of effective reading instruction: to stimulate active reading by preteaching key terms, pivotal questions, and new concepts before reading. Better organization and alignment also are likely to raise teachers' levels of tolerance for reasonable digressions in the form of comments about how the new information relates to real-life events and experiences. In so doing, teachers help students to better recall and develop relevant background information and appropriate anticipation, both of which have been shown to be natural to proficient readers and of great value in effective comprehension (Crafton, 1983; Harste, 1978; Stevens, 1982).

Careful preparation of L-R-D lessons actually raises students' ability to read a particular piece beyond their typical reading and thinking levels. This can be a positive and enabling experience for students and teachers. It tends to become a new benchmark for students to strive for in learning from text and for teachers to strive for in helping students to learn from text.

Following the lecture and empowered reading, the lesson design calls for discussion, providing a third repetition and elaboration of the material. This built-in redundancy factor is a most basic—and often overlooked—practice of effective teachers and principle of effective learning.

Finally, a teacher who follows the L-R-D guidelines will have begun to restructure class time and expectations from the typical 90% lecture format to one containing greatly increased proportions of purposeful reading and informed discussion. This achieves yet another important practice of effective teachers and precept of effective learning: increased time on task. Some have argued that the simple lack of attention to reading in typical content classes accounts for a great part of the current higher-literacy crisis in the schools. This conclusion seems justified by the fact that several observational studies of subject teaching at the postelementary levels reveal that virtually no purposeful reading goes on during class time (Feathers & Smith, 1987; Greenewald & Wolf, 1980; Mikulecky, 1982; Ratekin, Simpson, Alvermann, & Dishner, 1985).

Overall, the greatest value of the L-R-D seems to be its ability to provide a simple, hands-on way to introduce and initiate oneself to the principles and practices of content area literacy. The reapportioning of class time offers teachers with defensive teaching styles—who overuse either lecture or seatwork—an opportunity to experiment with reasonable alternatives. This tends to leave teachers with more energy and a greater willingness to try more sophisticated teaching methods and potentially benefit more fully from in-service workshops, consultations, and graduate coursework (Watkins, McKenna, Manzo, & Manzo, 1995).

A Self-Instructional Ladder: Strategic Learning of Strategic Teaching

To help teachers' self-discovery—that is, to ease their way into the actual use of more sophisticated, interactive teaching methods and to provide rich alternatives for different learning styles—we have developed a self-instructional ladder for trying variations and elaborations on the basic L-R-D procedure (see Figures 1.2 and 1.3). You can use L-R-D variations and elaborations to develop your sophistication as an interactive teacher and to explore possible diverse student learning style needs. Try ascending this ladder as your own readiness and students' needs suggest. It's a good idea to keep notes of your thoughts and questions as you try different variations. Your notes and thoughts will be useful in discussions with your instructor and coursemates and in processing your own teaching experiences.

1. Have students reread the information covered in the L-R-D format rapidly to increase their speed of reading and thought processing. Reading speed tends to rise as a result of increases in prior knowledge, although it can also be easily improved simply by systematic attention and practice.

2. Inform the class that you will lecture, intentionally omitting a few important details that they will need to read their texts to discover. This gives practice in recognizing what is not yet known and experience in careful reading and knowledge seeking.

3. Inform the class that your lecture will cover all the details of a lesson but that they will need to read to discover what questions these details answer. This is one way to teach students to actively seek an understanding of the concept base, or central question, around which an area of study is focused.

4. Inform the class that a quiz will follow the L-R-D sequence. Allow a short study period. This is recommended to activate a high level of focused attention, give practice in test taking, and set the stage for questions and discussion about how to study effectively.

5. Invert the core process occasionally by having the class R-L-D, or read (for about fifteen minutes), then listen, and finally discuss. This variation tends to focus and improve listening attention and the ability to learn from an effective lecture. This effect can be further heightened when joined with the other listening training and note-taking techniques covered ahead.

6. Watch a videotape, educational film, or multimedia presentation on a text topic *before* reading about it in the text. Such visual representations are compatible with the habits of contemporary youngsters and can help build new bridges to print. (See Figure 1.3.)

Figure 1.2   Ladder of variations and elaborations on Listen-Read-Discuss.

7. Ask students which portions of the text struck them as inconsiderate, that is, poorly written, poorly organized, or presuming too much prior knowledge. This activity can help students learn when to ask for help with textual and class material. It also helps the teacher become more aware of student learning needs. Analysis of the writing in texts is also a good way to informally teach some of the basics of effective writing.

8. Provide the class with a definitive purpose for reading and discussing that will require critical and/or creative expression or application. State that purpose clearly on the chalkboard for easy reference; for example, "As you read this section on the steam engine, try to determine why it was bound to be replaced by the gasoline engine." This will serve as a reminder to read actively and with reference to real-life problem solving.

9. Hold postreading discussions on teaching and learning strategies. Make the discussion positive by asking students what they or you may have done that resulted in solid learning. Such discussion gives credit to student intuition, develops reciprocity, and furthers metacognitive processing, or thinking about thinking.

10. Create research teams, and provide time for students to delve into a topic in greater depth. One group could simply see what other textbooks say on the topic. Another could check with other authoritative references—persons, books, and the Internet. Another could write a best estimate of which real-life problems the information learned might help solve or answer. Still another group, where appropriate, could try to identify and discuss theme-related stories, poetry, music, or art. Activities such as these provide links between text topics and nonprint resources and among school learning, artistic expression, multicultural perspectives, and the rest of the real world.

Figure 1.2 (*continued*)

Purposes for Viewing

Teacher: Today we are going to continue our study of Kenya by focusing on the Maisi tribe of Southern Kenya. First, we will watch a 20-minute National Geographic tape on this most unusual tribe of people. Listen carefully as you watch for two things, which you will then read about: the diet of the Maisi and the names of three other tribes of the north whom few people know of but who figure in Kenyan life in a big way.

Brief Review Following Viewing

Teacher: Okay, what were the two points we listened for?

Student: The Maisi basically live off their cattle, eating meat and drinking their blood and raw milk.

Teacher: And?

Student: Well, there were three other tribes mentioned, but I can't remember any of them.

Teacher: Okay, read pages 66 to 71 in your text now to learn more about the Maisi diet, and let's get the names of those tribes. If you happen to finish reading early, there are a few copies of a recent magazine report on cholesterol here on my desk that might help answer the question, "Why aren't the Maisi dying of clogged arteries and heart failure from their high-fat diet?"

Postreading Discussion

Teacher: What did you understand best from what you watched and read about?

Student: The names of the three other tribes.

Teacher: Say and spell them, and I'll write them on the board.

Student: Samburu, Turkana, and Hamitic.

Teacher: What did you understand least from what you watched and read about? [When students have understood what they have viewed and read, they will take this question to mean pretty much the same thing as the next one: What questions or thoughts did this lesson raise in your mind?]

Student: I pretty much understood what was said, but I don't understand why the Maisi don't raise things the way the other tribes do.

Teacher: The land they live on is not arable. There is poor topsoil and little water. But that really doesn't explain why they don't move to where there is arable land.

Student: I was wondering about their high-fat diet, so I read fast to get to the article you talked about. It seems that there are at least two reasons why they don't have high blood cholesterol. The raw milk has enzymes that break down fat in the blood. Also, they lead very active lives. They burn off the fat as fast as they put it on.

Teacher: If raw milk is so good for you, why do we homogenize and pasteurize ours, I wonder? Why don't you ask Mrs. Shell in science today if she can help us out with this?

Figure 1.3 Example of L-R-D elaboration 6: Viewing a videotape or film before reading in a world geography class.

▶ AFTER WORDS

Chapter 1 described the evolution of the field of content area literacy, and offered practical and research-based arguments for urging all teachers to become content area literacy providers. It offered a simple method, the Listen-Read-Discuss, as an example of this dynamic instructional technology. The chapter foretold of the great strides being made in professional education. Several chapters ahead will document these strides. The next chapter focuses on the theoretical bases for making reflective and effective instructional decisions.

CHAPTER 2

LITERACY CONCEPTS AND TERMINOLOGY TO HELP YOU GET STARTED

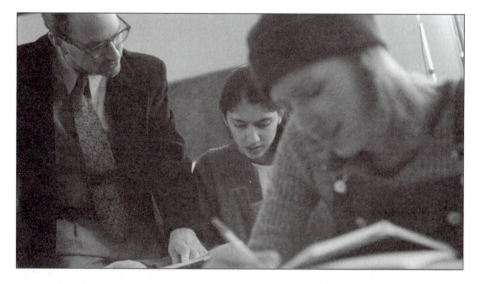

"Everyone who teaches has a theory of teaching,
even if they don't realize that they do."

—Harry Singer

▶ FORE WORDS

This chapter opens with a summary of what is known about the reading process, beginning with the three distinct levels of reading that can be identified for every person. Three theories, or models, of the reading process are analyzed, and the interactive/intervention model is interpreted in terms of what effective readers do as they begin, continue, and conclude a typical content reading task. The chapter concludes with an example of a simple teaching method, the Oral Reading Strategy, and how it facilitates learning from print.

- ▶ FORE WORDS
- ▶ READING TO LEARN: A CLOSER LOOK
- ▶ MODELS OF THE READING PROCESS
- ▶ HOW READERS ACTIVELY CONSTRUCT KNOWLEDGE FROM PRINT
- ▶ ALIGNING INSTRUCTION WITH THEORY
- ▶ AFTER WORDS

▶ READING TO LEARN: A CLOSER LOOK

Reading can be defined, simply, as unlocking and constructing literal, interpretive, and applied meanings from a coded message. What is not so simple is why some things are easy to read and others are hard or why one student can accurately decode a page and comprehend 95% of the information while another student accurately decodes the same page but comprehends only 60%. To answer these questions, it is necessary to consider what happens when one reads. The cognitive processes involved in reading are complex, and, for the most part, are performed subconsciously. Therefore, what we know about reading is in the form of various theories and findings from research designed to test the accuracy of these theories.

Because of the somewhat concentrated theoretical nature of this chapter, before we go any further, we feel that a brief aside is in order for some of our readers. We want to acknowledge that not all readers of this text are pursuing advanced reading specialization. As such, some of this material may seem at first to be somewhat literacy-theory heavy. However, our hope is that this chapter can serve as a fundamental knowledge base about literacy development that *all* educators will value, much like the ways in which most educators learn something about child development, psychology, nutrition, and substance abuse, even if those are not their primary areas of teaching. We would also like to encourage our readers by pointing out that as we progress through the text, the concepts, terminology, and theory of these initial chapters are made applicable in tangible, real-classroom reading, writing, and thinking activities.

One thing we know for sure about reading is that, for each of us, some things are easy to read, other things are more difficult, and still others are next to impossible. The next section introduces the terminology and specific criteria for categorizing and examining these levels of reading. To know these is to have the conceptual basis and the language for understanding and discussing much of what needs to be done instructionally in a content class to ensure that students will be able to learn from textual material.

Levels of Reading

The level at which materials are easy to read is technically referred to as the *independent level.* Reading feels effortless at this level, because we often know something about the topic and are familiar with the language, style, and vocabulary used. All we need to do is fit the new information into existing categories. At this level, we are able to read and comprehend without assistance. The independent level typically is defined as the highest level at which we can accurately decode 99% of the words and comprehend with 90% accuracy. For most people, independent-level reading—whether it is nonfiction, news, or novels—is enjoyable, relaxing, and entertaining. When a reading selection is at our independent level, we can begin at the beginning and read straight through without stopping. We literally can absorb the information without much active effort at all.

Most of us occasionally have had the experience of reading and suddenly realizing that we have not understood the last sentences, paragraphs, or even pages. What usually has happened is that we have been trying to read something that is somewhat difficult for us, using the same passive reading process that works for independent-level reading. When the topic, language, style, and/or the vocabulary are less familiar to us, we reach what is referred to as our *instructional level* of reading. To comprehend material at this level, we often need to create new categories or stop to decipher the meanings of unfamiliar words and/or language patterns. This is the level at which we probably would be able to read and comprehend with the type of assistance a teacher might provide in a classroom setting or by using a study-reading technique we have internalized. This level is defined as the highest level at which we can accurately decode 95% of the words and comprehend with 75% accuracy. Instructional-level reading cannot be done by reading straight through, passively, from beginning to end. It requires an active stance and can be painstakingly slow.

Beyond this point, some reading materials are so difficult for us that they are next to impossible to understand without an extraordinary level of effort and assistance. This *frustration level* is defined as the point at which decoding falls below 90% or at which we comprehend with less than 50% accuracy. It is next to impossible to learn from materials at the frustration level, even with the assistance a teacher could provide within a regular classroom.

Considering the reading process in this way, essentially as three *different* processes, helps to explain why many teachers fail to see the need for providing guidance in reading strategies. One reason is the frequent misinterpretation of the *grade-level* designation of textbooks. We tend to assume that this designation means that students at that grade should be able to use the book for independent study. In fact, it means that the book is intended to match the *instructional* level of the students' grade. It should be manageable for them, but only with a reasonable degree of guidance from the teacher. A second reason why teachers sometimes fail to provide reading strategy instruction is that they simply are uninformed about these levels and about the dramatic difference between passive, independent-level reading and active, instructional-level reading. Textbooks that are written at students' instructional level require the use of active thinking strategies for constructing meaning. Since these same textbooks will be at the teacher's independent level, the teacher can read them easily and passively and may be puzzled as to why students are not understanding what seems perfectly clear. This misunderstanding is probably the reason for the fact that many middle and high school teachers still rely on "round-robin" reading. In this familiar activity, students take turns reading aloud, a paragraph or two at a time. For this kind of straight-through reading to be comprehensible, it must be at the readers' independent level. Since this is seldom the case, few students gain much that is profitable from this activity. Better readers are bored, most others are occupied with looking ahead to the section they will be reading, and struggling readers are dreading humiliation.

Teachers' ability to provide guidance in instructional level reading strategies depends largely on their understanding of the nature of the reading process. What do teachers think *they* do when reading? Recent research related to the reading process suggests that many of our assumptions about the reading process may be inaccurate. This research is changing not only the way beginning reading is taught but how it is guided through the upper grades and even through professional school levels.

Comprehension as Guided Problem Solving

The scientific basis for the study of the comprehension process began around the time of World War I with a study designed to demonstrate that acquiring understanding from reading was far more than the simple act of reading words. Edward L. Thorndike (1917), one of the most eminent educational psychologists of the twentieth century, made the following observation:

> Understanding a paragraph is like solving a problem in mathematics. It consists in selecting the right elements of the situation and putting them together in the right relations, and also with the right amount of weight or influence or force for each. The mind is assailed as it were by every word in the paragraph. It must select, repress, soften, emphasize, correlate and organize, all under the influence of the right mental set or purpose or demand. (pp. 327–328)

In this single paragraph, Thorndike makes it clear that reading comprehension is a process of actively engaging text. It requires that the reader be attentive, analytical, purposeful, flexible, self-aware, world-aware, and emotionally sound.

Even as readers ourselves, it is difficult to identify the cognitive processes that yield such a complex product. Reading remains an unobservable act. We can see what goes in and test what comes out, but what goes on in between can still be known only in the form of theory. Theories of reading comprehension typically are presented in the form of models that attempt to describe or illustrate, in flowchart form, the sequence in which various elements of the process are activated and the ways in which they interrelate.

▶ MODELS OF THE READING PROCESS

Models of the reading process tend to be categorized as primarily bottom-up, topdown, or interactive/intervention. *Bottom-up models* assume that the reader builds upward from details and specifics toward a global concept. *Top-down mod-*

els assume that the reader begins with a sketchy grasp of the global concept and uses reading to build downward, filling in details and specifics. *Interactive/intervention models* concur with top-down model assumptions but add a strong dimension of direct instruction. Each of these three categories of models has distinct implications for how reading should be taught. Before looking at each of these three models in more detail, we would like to emphasize that these are only *models* that can help us *conceptualize* the reading process, but they are not, per se, *practices* that teachers would employ in the classroom. Some actual classroom practices that can be built from an understanding of these theoretical principles will be presented in the section that follows the explanation of the basic models themselves.

Bottom-Up Models

Bottom-up models define reading as a text-driven process that begins with perception and recognition first of letters, then of phonetic elements, then of words, then of word groups, and ultimately of sentence meaning and passage meaning. The reader's role is to process these units accurately and rapidly, building meaning from the smaller to the larger units—that is, from the bottom up. It is assumed that if children master each successive reading subskill, they eventually will attain overall reading competency (Gough & Cosky, 1977). Bottom-up theories of reading are the product of behaviorist learning theory, in which the learner was viewed as a blank slate to be inscribed by experience. Therefore, for educators who hold to bottom-up models of reading, the most important thing a teacher can do is to select and organize the information and skills to be taught and present these in a logical sequence. If this is done, and each child is permitted sufficient time to master each step, then all children will learn (see Figure 2.1).

Figure 2.1 Bottom-up (Behaviorist) models of the reading process.

Top-Down Models

Top-down models describe reading as a meaning-driven process. The learner is not seen as a blank slate but as an individual whose needs and interests drive attention and learning. Reading begins with the reader's incomplete perception of the whole and proceeds as an active process of recalling relevant prior knowledge and experience to reconstruct the author's meaning and construct related new meanings. Educators who hold to top-down models see education not as something done to the learner but as enriched environments structured for the learner (see Figure 2.2). For example, founders of the popular whole language movement (Goodman, Bird, & Goodman, 1991) state that if children are immersed in a literate environment, they do not even need to be taught to read but will acquire print literacy in the same way they acquire spoken language.

Interactive/Intervention Models

Interactive/intervention models of the reading process attempt to explain the complex cognitive activity of reading as involving both top-down and bottom-up reasoning. Here is how a very basic reading scenario for a younger student would be described from the perspective of an interactive/intervention model. While reading this, consider how many thousands of times a semester an older student might go through similar thinking processes through his or her content area reading assignments.

> A young student is reading the following: "Mary had a little lamb, whose fleece was white as snow." When the student gets to "fleece" this word may look unfamiliar, so s/he slows down to consider it. The student wonders, "Is it pronounced 'flees' or 'fleecy?'" Then, remembering the rhyme s/he has heard and recited before, realizes, "Oh, that's what that word is that I've been saying, and that's how it's spelled." In this process, sometimes called analytic phonics, the student deduces how to say a word by a combination of initial consonant sounds and context cues until the word is recognized as one already in the student's listening or reading vocabulary. Typically, the reader then continues with some related, human-experience-searching thoughts, such as, "Just what is fleece anyway?" Using the context again, the student seeks meaning: the context here suggests that it is another word for fur, because lambs

Figure 2.2 Top-down (Cognitive) models of the reading process.

usually have a white coat, and the student has seen storybook pictures of Mary and her little lamb.

In this apparently simple example, the student has conducted a complex interactive analysis. A top-down approach initiated the reading, as the student used what was known to enter the text. Then, on encountering an unfamiliar printed word, the student switched to a bottom-up approach, using some knowledge of phonics and sentence structure to predict and confirm the pronunciation of a word that had been, until that point, part of an incompletely comprehended string of language. Continuing this bottom-up analysis, the student noted and again visualized the printed form of the new word, and finally, switching again to a top-down approach, reflected again on the context to confirm and clarify its meaning. This view of the reading process strongly resembles Thorndike's early description of reading as problem-solving process (1917).

Source: From *Literacy Disorders: Holistic Diagnosis and Remediation,* 1st edition by MANZO/MANZO. © 1993. Reprinted with permission of Wadsworth, a division of Thomson Learning: www.thomsonrights.com. Fax 800 730-2215.

Addressing Real-Life Reading and Learning Challenges: The Recursive Model

When there is a pebble in your shoe and you must keep walking, you automatically turn your foot to one side and try to continue along. Of course, this is awkward, and more, the pebble eventually moves to whichever direction you might lean your foot. Soon it becomes evident that stopping to remove the offending annoyance is more efficient than living with it. This is pretty much what a reader does when encountering some obstacle to comprehension. First one tries every "quick" solution, usually more than once. This could be called a *recursive model*—or *default way* to easily fix most any comprehension difficulty with one's strengths. The chief, and probably best, *default function* is rereading—something every student eventually must learn to utilize. This generally gets us by for a given selection, especially if it is joined to class lecture and discussion and other such informational activities. However, ultimately, the reader who becomes expert is characterized by a resolve to fully grasp the challenging term, concept, or content connection. This generally combines *learning to read* and *reading to learn.* The *learning to read* aspect is keyed into several useful strategies. This book contains means and methods by which to teach many such strategies. However, each of us has a characteristic way of dealing with problems of most any type; reading problems or challenges are only one subset of these. When viewed in this way, most all models of reading essentially can be reduced to two functions: (1) how one faces an immediate challenge (we believe, *recursively,* using some *default option* such as rereading); and, just as importantly, (2) how one applies strategies that increase *determination* or a raised sense of consciousness about a topic that leads to, simply, thinking more fully about the topic at hand. This then, helps *no* knowledge and *static* knowledge to be converted into more *fluid* or curiosity-driven reading, listening, dialoguing, and questioning to learn. In this *reading–learning* model, content, syntax, orthography, semantics, and life experience are no longer component parts of successful reading but integrated parts of a single, though more complex, working system of knowledge acquisition, and something too, of a way of life—one that is more fact and discovery oriented. This worldview stage has been called the highest level of progress in reading. Of course, it really is not a stage or place that one arrives at but more a place from which one constantly departs in search of new knowledge built on prior knowledge and interesting perspectives. We must do this naturally; how else to explain humankind's constant and often life-risking quests into each crevice of possible knowledge, be it of the mysteries of space or those of the ultimately smallest possible particles of matter. As such, it seems that education should and could be much more interesting and engaging than many classrooms tend to make it; we hope that this next section of this chapter helps lay the groundwork for an understanding of how this improvement might happen.

Principles of Reading Models Applied to Classroom Practice

The bottom-up, top-down, and interactive/intervention models of the reading process have been shared here in this text for secondary teachers in order to build conceptualization of how reading happens more so than to be used as actual classroom practices. However, classroom practices can be derived that build on some of the extended principles found in these theoretical reading models. For example, a bottom-up foreign language teacher, in line with behaviorist learning theory, would begin an introductory-level class by requiring students to learn the alphabet and sound system of the new language and several sets of high-utilitarian words, such as days of the week, months of the year, numbers, and colors. Learning would be reinforced through a variety of drill and practice activities. Subsequent instruction would introduce the rules governing basic sentence structure, verb tense, and the like while continuing to practice vocabulary and add practice with short phrases. Most of the class would be conducted in the students' first language.

Behaviorist learning theory like this held sway in psychology until the early 1970s, but the seeds of change toward attention to top-down instruction were sown much earlier:

> In 1956, a group of psychologists, linguists, and computer scientists met at the Massachusetts Institute of Technology for a symposium on information science (Gardner, 1985). This three-day meeting was the beginning of a cognitive revolution in psychology. . . . That scientific revolution became a movement, and eventually a discipline, called cognitive science. Cognitive scientists study how our minds work—how we think, remember, and learn. Their studies have profound implications for restructuring schools and improving learning environments. Cognitive science—the science of mind—can give us an applied science of learning and instruction. (Bruer, 1993, pp. 1–2)

As such, a top-down foreign language teacher would begin an introductory-level class differently from the bottom-up teacher described previously. This teacher would enter the classroom speaking the new language, call the roll in the new language, begin to make simple requests and communications supported by reference to concrete objects and supported by gestures and expressions, and continue to conduct the class almost entirely without use of the students' first language.

While top-down models appear to align more closely with natural learning processes than bottom-up models, their limitation is that they tend to describe how learning occurs under ideal circumstances and without the physical and temporal constraints of classroom teaching and learning. *Interactive/intervention* models, however, accept all the tenets of top-down models but *add* direct attention to essential elements of the learning task: elements that might naturally be acquired over time but that, given the realities of classroom instruction, need to be identified and directly taught. These essential elements often are similar to the subskills that might be identified in a bottom-up model approach. However, interactive/intervention models are more than simply a combination of bottom-up and top-down theories. In the first place, learning *always* is initiated as a top-down process rather than as isolated skills practice. However, instead of relying solely on creating ideal learning environments (as would top-down theorists), interactive/intervention theorists begin with this and then move quickly to the identification of the essential bottom-up components of the learning task. While top-down teachers might argue that enthusiastic learners will, in most cases, deduce the underlying principles of an area of study, interactive/intervention teachers would place more importance on the fact that not *all* will do so in, say, a semester, largely because not all learners are enthusiastic. A second way in which interactive/intervention models are more than simply a combination of the other two is that in many cases the bottom-up components identified from an interactive/intervention perspective are different from those identified from a more purely bottom-up perspective.

With respect to reading comprehension, as an example, bottom-up theorists identify subskills such as identifying the main idea, identifying cause and effect, recalling events in proper sequence, drawing supportable conclusions, and so on. Interactive/intervention theorists, on the other hand, identify aspects of the reader's active self-talk about what the words are saying and what they seem to mean. The goal of instruction, from this latter point of view, is to have students internalize their interactions with the teacher and peers so as to improve their silent interactions with self in analyzing text.

Interactive/intervention models, then, are a real-world and research-based implementation of top-down models that incorporate a revisited and revised version of bottom-up components of learning. These models differ from top-down models primarily in their emphasis on identifying the bottom-up strategies for direct instructional intervention; they differ from bottom-up models in the *nature* of the strategies identified.

To return to the example of foreign-language instruction from the preceding sections, the *interactive/intervention* teacher would enter and begin the class in exactly the same manner as the top-down teacher, and most of the class would be conducted in the new language. However, initial instruction would focus on students' mastery of the same high-utility vocabulary words from the bottom-up teacher's lists (days, months, numbers, colors, etc.) to facilitate initial communication, and fundamental rules of grammar and syntax would be directly taught in the students' first language.

The interactive/intervention teacher plans instruction by considering how the material would naturally be learned in a top-down manner and providing as much of that environment as is reasonably possible. The teacher then analyzes the fundamental thinking strategies, principles, and concepts to be learned to determine which would best be taught directly (see Figure 2.3).

The interactive/intervention model views reading and learning as an active, strategic process of questioning, predicting, confirming, and self-correcting. The top portion of the triangle in Figure 2.3 is exactly the same as the top-down model in Figure 2.2, but a bottom portion has been added. Notice that the bottom portion is different in nature from the behaviorists' bottom-up model. Rather than emphasizing skills and facts, the interactive/intervention model calls attention to essential elements of the learning goal and emphasizes direct teaching of strategies for internalizing these. Interactive/intervention models acknowledge that these strategies can be acquired naturally, over time, but focus on the assumption that they also can and should be taught.

If being in a conducive environment and doing as others around you do were all that was natural and necessary for learning, no one enthusiastic for a sport such as golf would ever have to take lessons in how to play. Nor would there be the need for master classes in playing the violin or the piano. Of course, many children learn to read without being taught and continue to make developmental progress through the grades without much coaching. Most of us, however, with the exception of an occasional Tiger Woods type, need someone to lean over and say, "Tuck your elbow in when you swing" or, more to literacy and learning, "Turn that heading into a question and you'll get much more out of that selection."

For further information on models of reading, see Geyer (1972), Harker (1972–1973), Lovett (1981), Mitchell (1982), Ruddell and Ruddell (1995), Samuels (1977), Schell (1988), Singer (1976), Singer and Ruddell (1976), and Williams (1973).

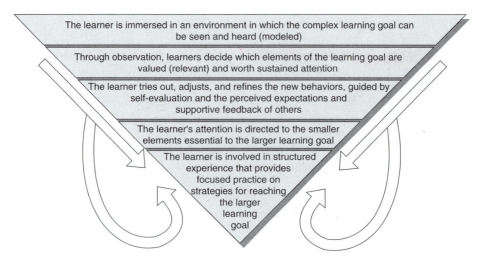

Figure 2.3 Interactive (intervention) models of the learning process.

► HOW READERS ACTIVELY CONSTRUCT KNOWLEDGE FROM PRINT

Interactive/intervention models of reading describe what readers do in three basic stages of the process: as they begin to read, while they are reading, and after they have read. The thinking strategies readers use in each of these stages are more or less automatic in independent-level, or easy, reading. For instructional-level, or study-type, reading, however, the strategies must be used much more actively and consciously. As such, the basics of the content area reading movement now involve paying specific attention to what teachers can do to help students during prereading, guided silent reading, and postreading (a sequence also sometimes referred to as into, through, and beyond reading). These three stages of the content area reading process are introduced now in this chapter and are then further developed in Chapters 4 through 6.

Prereading (Into)

Effective reading begins with readers quickly scanning some or all of the selection, consciously calling to mind what they know about the topic, and making some initial predictions about the content and the difficulty level of the selection. This process, in general, is called *schema activation.*

Schema is a term used in learning psychology to refer to an organization of information and experiences about a topic. *Schemata* (the plural form) are unique to each individual, both in content and in organization. A reader's schema for a topic can be thought of as a kind of net that screens incoming information and experience. The more information and experience that readers have related to a topic (the more finely woven the net), the better able they will be to learn, or catch, the new information (see Figure 2.4). This relatively passive process, which

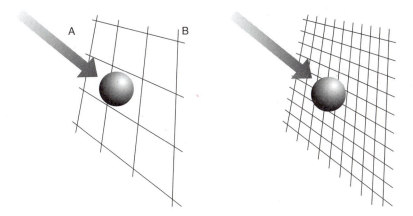

Figure 2.4 Schema theory.

Source: From *Teaching Children to Be Literate: A Reflective Approach,* 1st edition by MANZO/MANZO. © 1996. Reprinted with permission of Wadsworth, a division of Thomson Learning: www.thomsonrights.com. Fax. 800 730-2215.

simply involves adding to and refining information and categories within the existing net, was described earlier in the chapter as independent-level reading. When readers have an undeveloped schema for a particular topic (very few strands in the net), it is more difficult to read and to learn. At this instructional level, reading requires active construction or reorganization of the net to recognize, evaluate, categorize, and retain new information.

Put simply, the more you know, the better able you are to learn more. However, there is another important aspect of the function of schemata in learning. No matter how much one knows about a topic, it must be consciously called to mind in order to function effectively as a *learning net*. This process of consciously calling up related information and experience is called *schema activation*. It is the most essential element of the prereading stage. Thinking strategies for prereading involve

- Looking for organizing concepts
- Recalling related information, experiences, attitudes, and feelings
- Deciding how easy or difficult the reading selection is likely to be
- Setting a purpose for reading
- Trying to develop a personal interest in the reading

Active Silent Reading (Through)

Once the reader has an appropriate mindset for reading a particular selection, the general characteristic of active silent reading is referred to as *metacognitive monitoring*. Metacognitive monitoring is the continuous awareness of when one is understanding and when one is beginning to lose the thread of meaning. It involves continuous and active questioning: Is the author saying that . . . ? Is this like when . . . ? Does this really mean that . . . ? Or simply, What does this mean?

Metacognitive monitoring helps readers avoid lapsing into a passive, unproductive, independent reading mode. When comprehension begins to falter, active readers use a variety of *fix-up strategies* to construct meaning even from difficult text (Baker & Brown, 1984). Depending on the situation, these may include simply pausing to reflect and refocus, rereading, reading aloud, identifying problematic terms and using context to predict or confirm possible meanings, paraphrasing difficult sections, forming mental images, or even asking for help. Thinking strategies for active silent reading involve

- Translating ideas into one's own words
- Comparing ideas to personal experience
- Trying to identify main ideas—stop and question when this is unclear
- Noting important details
- Rereading whenever necessary for clarification
- Pausing to reflect whenever necessary to make relevant connections to prior knowledge and experience
- Consolidating ideas into meaningful groups

- Noticing unfamiliar vocabulary and predicting meanings based on context when possible
- Forming mental pictures
- Evaluating the author's purpose, motive, or authority when appropriate
- Inventing study strategies as needed
- Managing time to sustain concentration

Postreading (Beyond)

In the final stage of active instructional-level reading, readers check basic comprehension, appropriate interpretations, and decide on relevant applications of the new information. To do so, they may use any of a variety of strategies for *schema enhancement, schema building, or schema restructuring.* These terms correspond to the learning processes that developmental psychologist Jean Piaget called "assimilation" and "accommodation." The reader consciously compares the new information to existing schema categories and either adds it (assimilation) and constructs a new category or categorization system to incorporate it or alters existing schema structures to fit the new information (accommodation). This process is best done through review and reflection and can best be taught through some form of writing in response to reading and/or questions and activities that require discussion and application of the new information. Strategies for postreading comprehension development involve

- Checking basic comprehension by reciting ("What did I learn?")
- Organizing information into chunks of manageable size ("How can I remember it?")
- Deciding what is important ("How much should I understand this?")
- Trying to clarify ambiguous ideas ("Did I really understand this?")
- Evaluating new information in terms of previous knowledge and experience ("Does this make sense?")
- Developing study strategies according to class demands or personal purposes ("What should I do to remember this?")
- Reviewing material periodically ("How much do I remember now?")
- Relating what has been learned from reading back to real life experiences and related learnings ("How does this answer some question, issue or goal that I and/or others have been grappling with?")

Having provided an overview of the levels, theories, and stages of the reading process, we turn next to the more practical problems faced by teachers in translating this information into interactive classroom practice. This is followed by a simple interactive teaching method designed to help students acquire reading–thinking strategies by aligning instruction with what is known about the reading process. In doing so, it simultaneously causes teachers to discover many of the principles and guidelines for successful teaching.

▶ ALIGNING INSTRUCTION WITH THEORY

Problems Facing Students

Schooling and education cannot always be the same, but educators must continue to try to align them. The reason is simple. Students tend to have the greatest difficulty internalizing appropriate strategies for independent learning when classroom practices are markedly incompatible with natural processes for learning. Accordingly, the goal of effective instruction is to try to parallel our best understanding of natural learning processes, since such practices are more likely to put the wind at the students' backs as they try to learn and at the teachers' backs as they attempt to teach. Of course, even meeting this objective is no panacea for all possible problems since there are students who have differing and unique styles of learning.

Nonetheless, the interactive/intervention teaching approach advocated here intentionally tries to parallel the interactive, and presumably natural, model of the reading process described previously. In this way, both teacher practices and student learning processes move in the same direction. Ideally, too, each of these processes periodically should guide the other since the necessarily more contrived aspects of operating institutions called *schools* occasionally conflict with the more natural ways that humans learn.

Problems Facing Teachers

At every career stage, there are developmental problems to face and resolve in working toward ideal goals. For most new teachers, it is much easier to teach in the traditional manner they experienced as students than it is to acquire a more interactive/intervention teaching style. Most of us have had far fewer personal experiences with interactive/intervention teaching than with traditional methods. Furthermore, for new teachers who have been successful students, it can be difficult to realize the problems that many of their peers experienced in those more familiar instructional settings. These impediments are intensified by the fact that they must learn to use these new methods while standing before a class of students who have their own preoccupations, unique histories, and concerns. In a typical classroom setting, teachers must continually evaluate progress toward instructional goals and make many complex "in-flight" decisions based on their perceptions (Padak, 1986). The high potential for stress and job frustration that exists when students with growing pains are brought together with young professionals who are also feeling their own way suggests the need to support teachers so that they can effectively support students. Finally, the emerging reality of the high-stakes testing environment that is overtaking many of our schools may add further tension to teachers attempting to switch toward increased use of interactive/intervention teaching approaches. This probably should not be so, as the intervention aspects of the model could actually complement the assessment-driven curriculum frameworks that are emerging in many states. Nevertheless, tension remains high whenever trying something new under high-stakes conditions; this is particularly so for the cases where high-stakes testing rewards rote-level learning more than knowledge application and critical thinking (which can vary from state to state). For more information on this currently hot topic of assessment, please see Chapter 10.

Interactive Teaching Methods Benefit Students and Teachers

The interactive teaching (IT) methods of content area literacy parallel the needs of students and teachers during these difficult decision-making periods. They are fashioned around what research has revealed about what effective readers and teachers do. Interactive/intervention methods such as the Listen-Read-Discuss procedure, described in Chapter 1, are designed to produce a well-thought-out, but not confining, teaching–learning environment in which students can observe and try out a variety of thinking strategies. This is accomplished in several ways:

- Because IT methods are step-by-step guides, they help keep instruction and learning on course through most student disruptions as well as during teacher lapses resulting from inexperience. This structure helps to create a classroom environment that is conducive to the kind of cognitive and social risk taking that is essential to effective learning.

- Because IT methods are general enough in nature to be easily applied across grade levels, subject areas, and types of reading materials, they can reduce lesson-planning time. They can be drawn on to create a lively interaction in virtually any teaching–learning situation, freeing teachers to add as much subject-specific creativity as time and physical and mental resources permit.

- Because IT methods are designed to encourage greater student participation, teachers tend to be more responsive and empathetic. Teaching and learning become more interesting and engaging for both students and teachers.

In the next section, see how these characteristics are translated into a simple teaching method.

The Oral Reading Strategy: A Simple Interactive Method

The Oral Reading Strategy (Manzo, 1980) is a simple, direct way to model thinking strategies for prereading and active silent reading. The teacher reads a brief portion of the selection aloud to students while they follow along on their copies of the selection. While reading, the teacher makes a conscious attempt to think aloud; that is, to model the thinking strategies that proficient readers might use to focus attention, develop and maintain interest, and monitor comprehension. A similar method is called the "Think Aloud" (Davey, 1983). The Oral Reading Strategy calls for the teacher's oral reading to be *brief* so that students can maintain attention and have an immediate opportunity to emulate the model as they continue to read silently. (The literacy specialist or teacher with opportunity for individual tutoring may wish to have students attempt a "think aloud" while reading to get a sense of what students may or may not be saying to themselves while reading.)

Steps in the Oral Reading Strategy

Step 1. *Teacher preparation.* Preview the reading selection, trying to "see" it from your students' perspectives. On a photocopy of the first page or so (depending on print formatting), make notes of the thinking strategies that would be useful to model for students as you read the first few paragraphs aloud just before students' independent silent reading of the assignment. The prereading and active silent reading strategies listed above are a good place to start.

Step 2. *Teacher oral reading.* Tell students that you will read a little of the beginning of the reading assignment aloud to show them how to read actively when they are reading silently. Using the notes you have prepared, read and think aloud. Encourage students to answer your think-aloud questions.

Step 3. *Release responsibility to students.* At a reasonable stopping point (after no more than about three to five minutes), tell students to continue immediately to read silently, trying to use the same active thinking strategies you have just demonstrated. See the example in Figure 2.5 to get a sense of how the teacher can use this think-aloud process to demonstrate active reading strategies in a direct and interactive way.

The Oral Reading Strategy was used toward the end of class, to scaffold students' independent reading of a supplementary reading selection. In this example, the teacher has used the Oral Reading Strategy with this class several times before.

After distributing copies of the article, the teacher begins the interaction by stating, "Before you start to read this article, I will read the first part out loud to remind you of some of the ways we have to think actively when we're reading to learn something new."

The teacher then reads the first three paragraphs aloud (the boldface portions below), with the think-alouds inviting student responses as shown in parentheses.

DANCE AND SPORT—THE ELUSIVE CONNECTION

(*T:* Okay, when we read to learn something new, we start right off to do what?)

(*S:* Talk to ourselves.)

(*T:* Great, so, then, let's stop and think about the title, dance and sport— how *might* they be connected?)

(*S:* You have to learn to move in both.)

(*S:* You have to practice both.)

(*T:* Okay. Let's think some more about the title. If dance and sport are connected, how might the connection be *elusive*?)

(*S:* What does elusive mean?)

Figure 2.5 Example of the Oral Reading Strategy with "Dance and Sport—The Elusive Connection."

Source: This article is reprinted with permission from the *Journal of Physical Education, Recreation & Dance,* May/June 1986, pp. 26 and 54. *JOPERD* is a publication of the American Alliance for Health, Physical Education, Recreation and Dance, 1900 Association Dr., Reston, VA 20191.

(*T:* That's a good strategy question—what's the word culprit? Elusive means hard to hold on to or hard to pin down—in this case, it probably means hard to hold on to.)

(*T:* So, how might the connection be *elusive?*) (*after no immediate response, T:* Well, if we're not getting it, we could . . . ?)

(*S:* Read on a little bit.)

(*T:* Okay.)

Techniques and Principles Effectively Used in Teaching Dance Can Be Applied to Teaching Sport

(*T:* Let's stop and think about the rest of the title. Does this remind you of anything you've heard about?)

(*S:* I've seen how some football coaches make their players do ballet.)

(*T:* And how might that connection be elusive?)

(*S:* The guys probably feel kind of dumb doing it.)

(*T:* I think we've got a prediction about where the title is leading us; let's read on a little.)

1 **What are the functional connections between dance and sport and the benefits that are derived from participation in both pursuits? This article presents ideas which are applied to both dance and sport in order to enhance performance and reduce injury.**

(*T:* Let's stop for a second and boil that down.)

(*S:* By doing both dance and sport you can do your own thing better and not get hurt.)

(*T:* Any questions about this?)

(*S:* Do ballet dancers benefit from learning to play football?)

(*T:* Good question. Let's read on a little.)

2 **Many well-known people have recognized a connection between dance and sport skills. It may have been this kinship that convinced Knute Rockne, famed football coach at Notre Dame, to require his players to enroll in dance classes.**

(*T:* There's your football/ballet connection.)

Maybe it was the similarity between dance and sport that caused Woody Hayes, former Ohio state head coach, to expect his players to take dance as part of their practice procedures (Lance, 1981). Lynn Swan, three-time Pro Bowl wide receiver while playing with the four-time World Champion Pittsburgh Steelers, studied dance for 14 years and attributed his graceful athletic abilities to dance.

(*T:* What's the point of this paragraph?)

(*S:* Examples of people who have seen the connection between football and dance.)

(*T:* Let's read on a little bit.)

Figure 2.5 (*continued*)

3   **It is possible that each of these individuals witnessed movement competencies shared by dance and sports. Some of these shared abilities include centering, balance, focus, breathing, transfer of weight, relaxation and the ability to use space, time, and energy with mastery. Such abilities are taught specifically in dance classes, while in athletics they are only alluded to as a part of skill instruction.**

(*T:* What's important here?)
(*S:* Those look like the things that people need for both dance and sport.)
(*T:* The *"functional connections"?*) *(after nods, T:* Can we predict where this is going?)
(*S:* Maybe it's going to tell more about these things, like centering, and balance? Or tell about some other things that are the same in both?)
[Teacher writes on the chalkboard: "What are the functional connections between dance and sport?"]
(*T:* Any questions about this?)
(*S:* I still wonder whether any ballet dancers have tried to play football.)
[Teacher adds to the chalkboard; "Do the connections go both ways, or only from sport to dance?"]
(*T:* Do you have any other questions before you continue reading by yourselves?)
[No questions are raised.]
(*T:* Okay, continue reading to find answers to these questions. Remember to use the strategy phrases as you go.)

4   **The basic difference between dance and sport is that sport takes place within the conditions of a game, while dance is performed in other contexts. A game is a contest in which opposing interests are given specific information and are then allowed a choice of moves with the object of maximizing wins and minimizing losses. A game entails dominance over an opponent and the acquisition of some mutually coveted symbol. The athlete, by improving his or her movement abilities, will then improve sport skills.**

5   **Dancers, on the other hand, are process-oriented rather than product-oriented. The goal in dance is the improvement of movement quality.**

6   **Similarities between dance and sport outweigh their differences. Participants in both areas train to go faster and farther, while moving with increased control. The dancer and the sport participant both work to expand their movement vocabulary so they cular action when the situation demands. Biomechanical analysis**

Figure 2.5   *(continued)*

has been used for many years by physical educators to help their students learn. In recent years, dancers have also begun to use biomechanics to analyze movement with the goals of sharpening perception of movement, decreasing learning time, and enhancing performance (Laws, 1984). Dance and sport are similar in another respect. While some would say a dance was choreographed but a sport contest was not planned, further examination indicates that all the X's and O's used in game strategy simply represent another form of choreography.

7   Some sport activities are more similar to dance training than others. The concept of open and closed skills helps explain this point. In a closed skill, one strives to master an effective and efficient motor program with the goal of being able to duplicate this program with each repetition. Environmental conditions remain relatively constant, and the performer attempts to be consistent in the execution of the skill. Sports such as the shot put, diving, and gymnastics are closed skills. Open skills exist in a changing environment, and the selection of appropriate movement responses is as variable as the environment itself. Baseball, football, soccer, and basketball are open skill activities (Sage, 1977). Both open and closed skill athletes can benefit from dance training. The abilities which are taught in dance classes used by both kinds of athletes are different, but are not less applicable to their sports' requirements.

8   The principle of relaxation can be used as an example. Dancers frequently talk about using the right amount of tension in one part of the body while allowing other body areas to remain relaxed. The main idea is to use energy efficiently and only where needed to perform a movement. Efficient movement is characterized by using the appropriate muscle groups in proper sequence. The use of the wrong muscle group at the wrong time can be deleterious to the skill and possibly to the performer. Another common word heard in dance class is "centering." Centering is finding the body's center of weight and manipulating it effectively in relation to gravity. It also brings the mind and body together to produce better concentration. Achieving a heightened perception of and facility with space, time, and energy is another principle used in teaching dance. Dancers are asked to look at the direction or level of a movement, its speed in relation to an underlying pulse, or the quality of energy used to propel actions through space. Such movement descriptions are provided in dance classes to help students see movement more clearly and to enhance understanding of the expressive aspects of each action (Minton, 1984).

Figure 2.5   (*continued*)

9   **The point is that these principles are used in teaching dance, but generally not in teaching sport. In dance, these ideas are singled out in the classroom and used as learning tools. The examples given here are several of the techniques used in teaching dance that could be applied profitably to the teaching of sport.**

References

Lance, J. (1981). Practicing for touchdowns. *Journal of Physical Education, Recreation, and Dance, 5,* 38.

Laws, K. (1984). *The Physics of Dance.* New York: Macmillan.

Minton, S. C. (1984). *Modern Dance: Body and Mind.* Englewood, CO: Morton.

Sage, G. H. (1977). *Introduction to Motor Behavior: A Neuropsychological Approach* (2nd ed.). Reading, MA: Addison-Wesley.

Sandra Minton is coordinator of the Dance Program at the University of Northern Colorado, Greeley, CO 80639. Bradford E. Beckwith is a doctoral candidate, psychological kinesiology, at the same school.

Figure 2.5   *(continued)*

▶ AFTER WORDS

The concepts and theoretical background presented in this chapter, along with the Oral Reading Strategy for putting it all into practice, should have you ready, set, and able to continue your quest to be a competent content teacher and literacy provider. The next chapter outlines the elements of interactive instruction, and frameworks for selecting dynamic teaching methods. It is some of the schema that you will need to be a reflective practitioner.

CHAPTER 3

ELEMENTS AND FRAMEWORKS FOR INTERACTIVE INSTRUCTION IN CONTENT AREA READING AND WRITING

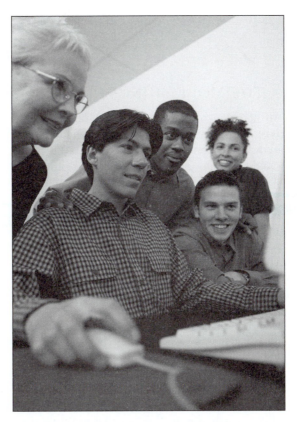

We have to change the way teachers interact with students in the classroom—and the changes must be grounded in an understanding of how children learn.

— John T. Bruer (1993, p. 7)

▶ FORE WORDS

This chapter provides an overview of the instructional elements that distinguish interactive teaching/learning from more traditional approaches. These elements are then translated into an instructional framework for planning and teaching any reading-based lesson in any subject at any level. The simple three-part framework described is rooted in the stages of the reading process described in Chapter 2: prereading schema activation, metacognitive monitoring of silent reading, and active postreading schema building. An example is given of how this three-step framework can be implemented using a method referred to as the Three-Phase Graphic Organizer.

- ▶ FORE WORDS
- ▶ THE MORE THINGS CHANGE . . .
- ▶ ELEMENTS OF THE INTERACTIVE CLASSROOM
- ▶ A THREE-PHASE FRAMEWORK FOR INTERACTIVE READING-BASED INSTRUCTION
- ▶ A QUICK WORD ABOUT WRITING: ENCOURAGING THE PROCESS AND THE PRODUCTS
- ▶ AFTER WORDS

▶ THE MORE THINGS CHANGE . . .

Recently one of us (A. Manzo) had occasion to visit Wyandotte High School in Kansas City, Kansas. This truly beautiful inner-city building was as pristine as it must have appeared at its opening in 1937. The pleasant feeling of nostalgia in being at this venerable site was interrupted by the realization that, in general, instruction here and at other secondary schools hasn't changed much since that time either. Students have changed, society has changed, and our understanding of the learning process has changed, yet life in many classrooms goes on much the same. The theory underlying robust, interactive instruction is not even very new. Its origins have been traced from a 1956, three-day symposium of psychologists, linguists, and computer scientists, to a full-blown movement by the mid-1970s. However, the movement has yet to make significant inroads into actual school practice:

> Cognitive science—the science of mind—can give us an applied science of learning and instruction. Teaching methods based on this research . . . are the educational equivalents of polio vaccine and penicillin. Yet few outside the educational *research* community [emphasis added] are aware of these breakthroughs or understand the research that makes them possible. (Bruer, 1993, p. 2)

> *Source: Schools for Thought: A Science of Learning in the Classroom.* By J. T. Bruer, 1993. © The MIT Press, Cambridge, MA. Reprinted by permission.

We believe that this is partly due to the fact that, until very recently, all of the component parts needed for practical school implementation were not fully developed or readily available to real teachers in real schools. But times have changed dramatically with development of specific teaching methodologies and widespread access to the Internet. Many, if not all, of the parts necessary for robust, interactive teaching and learning seem to be in place now. See if you agree as you review the following brief descriptions of the elements of interactive instruction and learning.

▶ ELEMENTS OF THE INTERACTIVE CLASSROOM

The Interactive Teaching Cycle

The broad goals of content area literacy are best achieved through interactive teaching methods that involve students in instructional conversations (Tharp & Gallimore, 1989) and hands-on experiences that cause them to be active learners. Interactive methods for teaching reading-thinking strategies mirror the three basic stages of the reading process:

- Prereading (into): teaching students to recall and use prior experience and knowledge about a topic, to identify and define difficult vocabulary words, and to set clear purposes for reading
- Guided silent reading (through): teaching students to apply a variety of active thinking strategies during reading
- Postreading (beyond): teaching students to check basic comprehension after reading and to apply information in a variety of ways

One way to conceptualize interactive teaching is as an ongoing, cyclical process that is characterized by the following elements: *assessment, engagement, scaffolding, modeling, reciprocity,* and *fading,* followed by reassessment to continue the cycle. Each of these elements is briefly described in Figure 3.1.

Another way to conceptualize interactive teaching is look at the three elements that distinguish interactive teaching from more traditional approaches. These are preassessment, use of authentic/evocative tasks and materials, and strategy instruction.

Preassessment Through Diagnostic Teaching

Preassessment refers to the knowledge about the particular group of students that a teacher draws on in lesson planning. Planning an interactive lesson must begin not only with the content to be taught, but also with knowledge and informed observations of students' information, abilities, and attitudes. Experienced teachers begin their planning with a rich background of informed assumptions about each new group of students. For beginning teachers and teachers new to a school, standardized test scores and prior grades in school can provide some basic information about students' general achievement and ability levels. Daily interactions during the first few days of school, and interactions before and after the bell rings each day, help teachers to begin to accumulate information about the nature and extent of students' prior knowledge and experiences, as well as their personal interests, talents, and possible areas of learning difficulty. As instruction progresses,

Assessment

Assessment of student needs is the starting point for effective classroom instructional interactions. Standardized test scores and prior grades in school provide information about students' general achievement levels. In addition, the teacher should begin to accumulate information about the nature and extent of students' prior knowledge and experiences, as well as their personal interests, talents, and possible areas of learning difficulty. This more specific assessment information can be collected from structured observations of students and from a variety of informal assessment techniques. For more on this essential topic of assessment, please see Chapter 10.

Engagement

Engagement is a concept derived from motivational and learning theories and simply means getting and holding students' attention during instruction. It is, logically, the single most essential element in teaching/learning: If the learner is not paying attention to the learning environment, none of the subsequent elements can be achieved. Whereas traditional instruction has tended to rely on external sources of motivation (such as grades) to encourage, or force, engagement, the interactive teaching approaches emphasize building internal motivation as the key to developing interested and lifelong learners.

Scaffolding

Scaffolding refers to elements of instruction that support the learner during the early stages of learning. Learning anything new involves an initial trial-and-error period that, in the social context of a classroom, can threaten the learner's self-esteem. Classroom interactions can be structured in ways that reduce this threat and encourage the learner to experiment with new ways of thinking and communicating. One of the best ways to build self-esteem and internal motivation is to provide lessons with sufficient scaffolding to build students' sense of their own competence as learners.

Modeling

Modeling is a means of teaching by showing. Although it has long been used to teach complex manual procedures, as in art and craft apprenticeships, only recently has it been applied to teaching *thinking* processes. This forward step in teaching came about with a simple realization. This realization was that just as toddlers first learn to speak by interacting with skillful language users, each of us continues to acquire more sophisticated language and thinking processes in the same way: by observing models of these behaviors, imitating those models, and self-evaluating our progress toward some personally desired level of competence.

Figure 3.1   Elements of an interactive teaching cycle.

Reciprocity

Reciprocity is a term used to characterize teaching situations that are structured so that students and teacher are encouraged to influence one another's thinking. This ingredient is necessary for effective modeling and interactive teaching. In reciprocal teaching situations, the teacher is still responsible for outlining and maintaining the general content and direction of instruction, but interactions are structured in ways that require the teacher to allow student response and encourage students to learn from one another. When teachers and students are connected reciprocally, they tend to create a communal learning spirit in which everyone, including the teacher, learns.

Fading

A final element of interactive teaching is fading of teacher support, in a gradual release of responsibility for learning from the teacher to the students. As each lesson nears its conclusion, the teacher returns to the beginning of the cycle by assessing students' developing competence, gradually removing the instructional scaffolding, and transferring control and responsibility for learning to the students. It is during this fading process that learners internalize new learning strategies by adjusting them into forms and formats for personal use.

Figure 3.1 *(continued)*

each lesson provides preassessment information for the next. This process of planning and implementing instruction in ways that intentionally provide ongoing informal assessments is referred to as *diagnostic teaching*. More specific assessment information can be collected from structured observations of students and from a variety of informal assessment techniques. Several of these techniques and instruments are described in Chapter 10.

Accessing Multiple Literacies Through Supplementary Reading Materials

There is a growing recognition that traditional school-based definitions of *literacy* represent a narrow strand of the broader, real-world literacies needed to function in today's complex society. Therefore, young adolescents need to be encouraged to engage in *multiple literacies:* reading, writing, and speaking in many arenas—fashion, sports, economics, interpersonal relationships, ethics—both in and out of school. This should not be so difficult to do since they encounter information and fictional events via television, movies, magazines, and the Internet. They communicate via telephone, through (forbidden) written notes, e-mail, discussion boards, and in chat rooms. The degree to which they make these literacy activities a public part of their public and private lives depends more on peer approval than on school sanctions. In fact, school sanction often equals peer disapproval and has the effect of driving many students' discovery of and interest in literacy activities "underground." In an article with the captivating title, "On Every Page Someone Gets Killed! Book Conversations You Don't Hear in School," Worthy (1998) describes her study of her middle school son and his friend, as "renegade readers." The study begins with a familiar scenario:

> Both Chase and Jared had followed a typical course of development in all academic and social areas and had been average to above-average students during their earlier school years. Each had grown up in homes in which literacy was valued and reading materials were abundant, and in which they had rich access to books, magazines, and comics of their choice. Both had enjoyed reading in their preschool and primary years, and both had begun to resist school reading in their upper elementary years and continued to do so." (p. 510)

> *Source:* Worthy, J. (1998). On every page someone gets killed! Book conversations you don't hear in school. *Journal of Adolescent and Adult Literacy, 41*, 508–517. © International Reading Association.

Chase and Jared were reluctant readers in school but had animated conversations about their self-selected reading outside of school. Another literacy researcher undertook a study with his two adolescent daughters to document the girls' various real-life literacy activities. Not unexpectedly, the report coauthored by father and daughters revealed differing patterns related to the girls' different ages and interests but very little overlap between in-school and out-of-school literacy involvement (Bean, Bean, & Bean, 1999).

Until recently, it was difficult to imagine an alternative to teacher-selected classroom reading materials: a single textbook or class sets of novels and supplementary books. Newspaper and magazine articles could not be reproduced easily until the cost of copying came down to practical levels. Simply locating materials related to an instructional unit was difficult. As schools and classrooms go online, these financial and logistical restrictions are dissolving. Search engines facilitate location of information on virtually any topic, by the teacher and/or students themselves. The use of high-interest, real-world online supplementary readings on unit topics has a number of benefits (Figure 3.2). We hope that you find Figure 3.3 thought-provoking as well.

Cognitive Modeling of Thinking Strategies

The third fundamental premise of interactive instruction is that "thinking" is not completely, or even primarily, a function of intelligence. Rather, it is a constellation of strategies and cognitive habits, or "habits of mind" that can be identified and taught through cognitive modeling.

Thinking strategies are *mental scripts used in active learning*. Thinking strategies for active study reading include, for example,

1. "Stop and think about the title."
2. "Where does this seem to be going?"
3. "How would I say this in my own words?"
4. "Maybe I'd better re-read that part."

1. High-interest non-textbook-type short online readings are an ideal way to provide top-down engagement for any subject at any level.

2. For classes with traditional textbooks, supplementary online readings can be selected to parallel, correspond to, or contrast with the textbook author's treatment of the topic to stimulate critical analysis.

3. Supplementary online readings can provide a simpler version, or a more detailed version, depending on the students' interest and prior knowledge for the topic.

4. Supplementary online readings can add currency in rapidly changing subject areas.

5. Supplementary online readings can link abstract new concepts to familiar real-world events.

6. In subjects where textbooks often are not available, occasional online reading-based activities can introduce students to sources for pursuing their interests outside of and beyond the classroom.

7. At the next level, WebQuest sites (*http://webquest.sdsu.edu* for example) make it easy for students to select from a wide range of potential sources of information on a given topic and to access these at their own pace.

8. Supplementary online readings allow for greater collaboration among students and schools that might not otherwise have the same text in common.

9. The online world is sometimes more "home turf" or "real world" to some students than might be our regular classrooms. So, using online reading resources may help some of these students see that our content is not just bound to the space of our classrooms and textbooks but indeed is a vibrant and real topic in their world too.

Figure 3.2 Advantages to using supplementary online reading resources.

These phrases should, of course, be worded in language that is comfortable to the individual teacher and appropriate to the age and level of the class.

Cognitive modeling is *thinking aloud to demonstrate a particular thinking strategy.* Although modeling has long been used to teach complex manual procedures, as in art and craft apprenticeships and in athletic coaching, it is only in relatively recent memory that it has been intentionally applied to teaching *thinking* processes that are otherwise hidden from view. The idea of cognitive modeling was sparked by the simple realization that each of us continues to acquire more sophisticated language and thinking processes by observing models of these behaviors, imitating those models, and self-evaluating our progress toward some personally desired level of competence. Another special value of cognitive modeling is based on the principle that "more is caught than can be explicitly taught." That is, when information is presented in ways that model relevant thinking strategies, students acquire not just the information in the day's lesson, but they begin to internalize the tools for acquiring similar information, as well as a host of other more holistic

A New Convergence Zone

The beginning of this next century is marked with transition between old and new: communism has faded out and democracy has grown; shopping can take place in the mall, in the old city farmer's market, or online, 24-7. So too, teaching is becoming a blend of the old and the new. Time-tested pedagogical practices are now being retried and refined using powerful new learning tools, such as the personal computer, the laptop, the growth of the Internet (including discussion boards, chat rooms, and wireless networks), personal digital assistant (PDA) devices, "SmartBoards," and even the new Tablet PC hybrid devices that are just starting to emerge as we write this text. These new tools hold the potential to act as catalysts, when they are combined with the highly validated teaching practices that we have known about for some time now. We don't know exactly what the future of teaching will look like, obviously, as we are currently too much in the middle of this time of transition. However, we do know that this reality is redefining what it means to be literate and what it means to be a content area teacher and a literacy provider. As such, we encourage you to keep watch out for some of the new teaching tools and learning devices that are emerging in our classrooms; please see below for a few recent references to get you thinking about the topic. We also invite you to read this text book with a mindset that always asks: "OK, so how might I add this teaching method to this new learning device that I might have in my classroom in five years? . . ." The combinations could yield a powerful impact on our teaching and our students' learning.

For Further Reading

Technology and Literacy, Comprehensive
Valmont, W. J. (2003). *Technology for literacy teaching and learning.* Boston, MA: Houghton Mifflin.

Internet Discussion Boards
Manzo, A. V., Manzo, U. C., & Albee, J. A. (2002). iREAP: Improving reading, writing, and thinking in the wired classroom. *Journal of Adolescent & Adult Literacy, 46*(1), 42-47.

Thomas, M. M., & Hofmeister, D. (2003). Moving content area literacy into the digital age: Using online discussion board interactions. *Journal of Content Area Reading* 2(1). 61-80.

Internet Chat Rooms
Albright, J., Purhohit, K., & Walsh, C. (2002). Louise Rosenblatt seeks QtAznBoi@aol.com for LTR: Using chat rooms in interdisciplinary middle school classrooms. *Journal of Adolescent & Adult Literacy, 45*(8), 692–705.

Figure 3.3 Literacy and technology—a powerful new convergence zone.

Wireless Networks
Flowers, R. (2003, April). Wireless technologies: A robust wireless LAN is within your reach—here's all you need to know. *ESchool News, eSN Special Report.* Retrieved from *http://www.eschoolnews.com/resources/reports/WirelessSpec403/*

Palm Pilots/Handheld Computing
Levin-Epstein, M. (2003, May). Handhelds in education: The answer to 1-to-1 computing? *ESchool News, eSN Special Report.* Retrieved from *http://www.eschoolnews.com/resources/reports/hhc/*

Tablet PCs
Murry, C. (2003, April). Tablet computing: The "next big thing" in school computing has arrived. *ESchool News, eSN Special Report.* Retrieved from *http://www.eschoolnews.com/resources/reports/TabletSpec403/*

Figure 3.3   *(continued)*

behaviors. These might include collateral factors such as body language, attitude, social poise, and even the civility with which something is spoken.

The essence of strategy instruction is intentional, frequent repetition of the strategy phrases and intentional, frequent cuing of students to use the strategy phrases. The intent is to help students to internalize the phrases to the point where they automatically occur in the appropriate contexts. Modeling and direct instruction in thinking strategies have the effect of enabling at-risk students while building self-awareness and confidence in developmental and advanced students as well.

This planned, structured interpretation of cognitive modeling may be one of the great discoveries of modern pedagogy. It has several interlocking features that have emerged from various quarters over recent years: engagement, scaffolding/fading, reciprocity, and structured peer interactions. Note how this next section elaborates on the linear presentation of the six aspects of the interactive teaching cycle, introduced earlier in Figure 3.1.

Engagement

Engagement, simply speaking, is *focused attention to the learning task at hand.* It is, logically, the single most essential element in teaching/learning: If the learner is not paying active attention to the learning task or challenge, none of the subsequent elements can be achieved. While traditional instruction has tended to rely on external sources of motivation (such as grades) to encourage, or force, engagement, the interactive approach emphasizes building internal motivation through top-down engagement with the essential principles and concepts.

Points to Ponder
What! No star, and you are going out to sea?
Marching, and you have no music?
Traveling, and you have no book?
What! No love and you are going out to live?

Translated from the French
(Author unknown)

The peceding poem represents the intent of top-down engagement. In traditional instruction, it is the teacher who presumably has the larger vision: the "star," the "music." The students' job is to be patient, cooperate, practice the parts as presented, and trust that at some point it will all come together. Failing to provide some top-down engagement is somewhat like trying to teach a child to speak without ever letting her or him hear spoken language or experience its value. One of the authors (U. Manzo) once observed a preschool classroom in which children, as they entered, were invited to come to the carpet, where they were given a black circle-shaped paper and shown how to punch holes of various shapes in the paper with special hole-punchers. Some children willingly began to punch holes and try out different shapes and patterns. Four or five others, however, didn't show much interest in the activity and wandered around the classroom looking for something else to do. After about ten minutes, all the children were asked to come to the carpet and sit in a circle. The lights were turned off, and an overhead projector was placed on the floor with the light projecting up to the ceiling. The teacher then began placing the children's hole-punched papers on the overhead screen to project the patterns of variously shaped "stars" onto the ceiling. There were audible rounds of awed "oohs" and "aah's," every teacher's dream response. Needless to say, the "wanderers" quickly found their unpunched papers and began enthusiastically to produce patterns of their own.

Many children will accept the teacher's authority and attempt seemingly aimless activities. But learning becomes more focused, animated, and rapid when students can see the "stars" before they begin. It is not always easy to work backward to the driving questions and fundamental issues of a discipline and then to translate these into classroom experiences. However, online activities and resources like WebQuests (pioneered by Bernie Dodge and Tom March at San Diego State University; see *http://webquest.sdsu.edu/*) are offering a rapidly growing collection of interactive resources for providing this kind of top-down engagement. Teaching and learning have never been so richly supported, responsive, exciting, and accessible "24/7"—24 hours a day, 7 days a week.

Scaffolding/Fading
Scaffolding refers to elements of instruction that support the learner during the early stages of learning. Any truly new learning involves the "burning-in" of some new pathways. This takes much more time than all subsequent learning and is characterized by a high-risk trial-and-error period that, in the social context of a

classroom, can threaten the learner's self-esteem. One of the best ways to build internal motivation and strengthen self-esteem is to design lessons with sufficient scaffolding to build students' sense of their own competence as learners. For interactive instruction to occur, learning situations must be structured in ways that reduce the social risks of active participation and encourage the learner to experiment with new ways of thinking and communicating. One important function of cognitive modeling is to externalize thinking in ways that honestly portray the initial awkwardness and increasing competence in acquiring new knowledge and skill.

As students attain confidence and automaticity in using a set of strategies with a particular content, the teacher *gradually removes the scaffolding*, a process referred to as *fading*. This happens to some extent within each lesson, and more obviously over the course of a semester or year. It is during this fading process that learners internalize new learning strategies by adjusting them into forms and formats for personal use.

Reciprocity

Reciprocity is the opportunity for students to influence the teacher's thinking and one another's thinking, as well as to be influenced. While this often happens by chance in many classroom interactions, interactive teaching intentionally structures situations that encourage it. In reciprocal teaching situations, the teacher is still responsible for outlining and maintaining the general content and direction of instruction, but interactions are structured in ways that require the teacher to allow student response and encourage students to learn from one another. When teachers and students are connected reciprocally, they tend to create a communal learning spirit in which everyone, including the teacher, learns.

Structured Peer Interactions. In the traditional classroom, any active participation can be a risky proposition. Yet genuine learning is virtually defined by active participation. By talking to others we discover what we think and feel; by listening to others we learn to consider other points of view. In recent years the early, complex versions of cooperative learning have evolved into more fluid, flexible cooperative structures for managing the complex social dynamics of the classroom. A cooperative structure is *an activity intended to produce active interactions among participants and create a sense of classroom community*. Kagan (1994) uses the acronym "PIES" to represent the elements of an effective cooperative structure:

Positive interdependence.	Interactions are structured in ways that students come to rely on their peers in positive ways.
Individual accountability.	Each student is, however, responsible for his or her own learning.
Equal participation.	All students are actively involved in the interactions for the same amount of time.
Simultaneous interaction.	A number of interactions occur at the same time.

▶ A THREE-PHASE FRAMEWORK FOR INTERACTIVE READING-BASED INSTRUCTION

Some subjects, such as social studies, science, and English, clearly are reading based; others traditionally rely far less on students' acquiring information from print. In either case, the range of student reading ability within any one class has tended to reduce teachers' expectations that students will complete reading assignments independently. Bintz (1997) details the problems that teachers face with reading-based instruction:

- Students who experience daily difficulties learning from text materials
- Students who regularly refuse to do required reading out of class
- Students who do read but fail to comprehend the most important information
- Students who are bored or uninterested in much of what they read

The fact is, in most middle and secondary school classes, most students need some guidance in reading, some need a great deal, and those who need little to no assistance benefit a great deal by becoming more aware of the strategies they are using. Following is a simple framework for structuring any reading-based lesson.

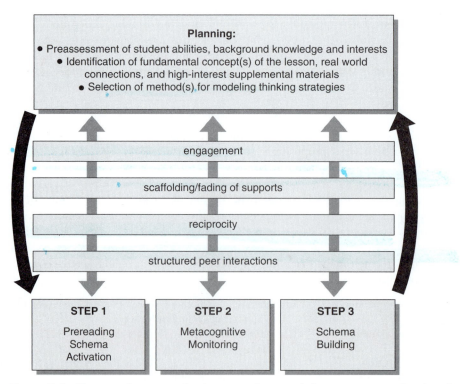

Figure 3.4 Planning elements and a three-step framework for interactive reading-based strategies.

See Figure 3.4 for an illustration of how the elements of interactive instruction should be woven into the reading-based lesson.

Planning

Lesson planning is a matter of finding a match between content to be taught and student readiness to learn. In most instruction, the basic content is a given; therefore, the task is in designing enabling learning situations that build on students' background information and experiences and engage them in exploring new ideas. Planning for any reading-based instruction should begin with envisioning students actually doing the reading. Then try to vision the essential concept(s) to be taught. Next address these questions: What is the range of abilities in the group? What do you know about student background knowledge, experience, and interests related to the topic? What real-world connections to the lesson topic can be drawn? In that context, what key terminology will students need in order to access the new ideas, and what basic questions will direct them toward the essential concept(s)? Considering where your students are and where you want them to go, what real-world connections might serve to engage their interest and attention? What authentic, real-world, reading, writing, viewing, listening, and/or speaking activities can be structured to provide these connections? If the core concepts are presented in a class textbook, how might these be brought to life through brief, high-interest supplemental reading materials, poignant video clips, and/or directed peer interactions? What online resources are available, and how can these be accessed and woven into the lesson planning?

The instructional framework described next provides a guide for designing reading-based lessons in which more students are likely to be more successful more of the time. This simple three-step framework parallels the interactive model view of the reading process. You might also notice that the three steps in this framework are the topics of the next three chapters of this book, as each one is expanded on considerably.

Step 1: Prereading Schema Activation

When the difficulty level of a reading selection is above the reader's independent level, good readers use a variety of active thinking strategies to consciously call to mind relevant schema for the general topic, including personal prior knowledge, experiences, and attitudes. This schema activation permits the reader to anticipate the structure, organization, and general content of the selection. Approaches to teaching prereading anticipation strategies may involve brainstorming, inquiry training, and/or guided prediction. The intent is to help students into the reading by engaging them in observing and practicing effective anticipation strategies for initiating study reading. General guidelines for structuring anticipation include the following:

1. Consider visual and aural prompts to aid in schema activation.
2. Model anticipation strategies such as:
   "I need to stop and think about the title."
   "What do I know about this already?"

"What are some categories that might be included in this topic?"

"I'll look over this quickly to . . . [see how detailed it is] or [see if I see any unfamiliar words]."

"What's the main thing that I might be able to learn from this?"

"After reading this, what should I be able to do with it or say about it?"

3. Generate clear purpose questions to focus student reading.

4. Provide low-risk, scaffolded opportunities for students to practice these anticipation strategies.

5. Consider preteaching any vocabulary terms that may be unfamiliar to most students and central to the meaning of the selection.

Step 2: Guided Silent Reading and Metacognitive Monitoring

Having anticipated the basic structure and something of the general content of the piece, the reader begins to attempt to reconstruct the author's basic meaning and to construct personal connections with and responses to it. In easy, or independent-level reading, this can begin as an almost autonomic process of moving the eyes across the print and passively absorbing the author's meaning. In more difficult, instructional-level materials, the reader must monitor comprehension more consciously and more continuously. Silent reading can be guided by asking students to do various things as they read. One traditional approach is to provide students with a reading guide—a set of questions to consider and answer as they read. Silent reading strategies can also be taught through various think-aloud methods that are modeled by the teacher and practiced aloud by students. Guidelines or exercises for teachers to use to help their students through the reading might include the following:

- Try reading the selection yourself as if you had only your students' background of information and their limited experience in reading material of this type. Anticipate possible misunderstandings and trouble spots, and alert students to these in whatever form of silent reading guidance is used.

- Use the Oral Reading Strategy occasionally to model silent reading strategies such as

   "How would I say that in my own words?"

   "What's the main point here, and why is it important?"

   "What would be an example of this?"

   "How could I cluster the ideas I've read about so far?"

   "Am I finding answers to the purpose question(s) yet?"

   "Where is this going next?"

   "Here's an unfamiliar word—what does it seem to mean in the way it's used here?"

   "Can I picture in my mind what is going on here?"

   "Does this make sense, according to my own experience?"

   "Can I trust this author's accuracy/authority/objectivity?"

- When using the Oral Reading Strategy, remember to also model "fix-up strategies" for when students *realize* that they have lost the train of thought:

    "Let me reread that last part, more slowly this time."
    "Let me think about that for a minute."
    "Is there a certain word here that is throwing off my understanding?"
    "Let me read ahead a little, to see if getting the larger picture helps."

- Incorporate these fix-up strategies into other forms of silent reading guidance provided to students. Occasionally ask them to think aloud as they read. Ask better students to do this first so that there will be some peer models from which to learn.

Step 3: Postreading Schema Building

Postreading strategies for connecting what has just been read with existing schema begin with a simple comprehension check to add new information to existing schema and include numerous strategies for analyzing and interpreting the author's message to add new schema structures or alter existing ones. Approaches to helping students beyond the reading by acquiring postreading strategies, as well as just correct answers, include peer discussion, writing, and traditional teacher-directed discussion. Peer discussion and writing activities help students to process and formulate their responses to reading in preparation for a larger group discussion. Guidelines for structuring the postreading stage of reading-based instruction include the following:

- Address all three levels of reading comprehension: basic or reconstructive comprehension (what did the author say?), interpretation (what did the author mean?), and application (how can this be used?). These do not always need to be addressed in sequence. Beginning with an interesting application question or activity can increase incentive to review and clarify basic facts and information.

- Model consolidation strategies, such as

    "Did we raise the best purpose question(s) for this selection?"
    "What were the main points made?"
    "Are there any parts/key terms that still are unclear? Do we need to reread any portions of this?"
    "How can this information be organized or 'chunked' to remember it better?"
    "Does this make sense when compared to my own experience and knowledge?"
    "How could we use this information?"
    "If what the author says is true, does it change what I thought before I read this?"
    "How could this be confirmed or challenged?"

- Structure writing prompts and cooperative group activities to engage students in practicing asking and answering the preceding strategic questions.

This three-step framework is not terribly different, on the surface, from one of the first published content area reading frameworks: Russell Stauffer's (1969) *Directed Reading-Thinking Activity*. Intuition and good sense often outrun theory and research. Stauffer's "DR-TA" recommended five steps for a reading-based content area lesson: Preparation for Reading, Reading the Material Silently, Developing Comprehension, Rereading, and Follow-Up. We have translated this generic framework into the version described above primarily to place a stronger emphasis on the type of thinking strategy instruction that has evolved into a powerful instructional technology over the 30 years since Stauffer's groundbreaking publication. We'd invite you again to look back at Figure 3.4 for a graphic illustration of the relationships among the elements of interactive instruction and the three-step framework. In addition, Figure 3.5 presents an updated version of a DR-TA approach rearranged into the three-step framework discussed here; you might also note the integration here of other more specialized/specific methods and strategies presented ahead in this text.

Using a Graphic Organizer to Plan and Teach a Reading-Based Lesson

A graphic organizer is a two-dimensional picture of the logical organization of textual material. In one standard format, called a *structured overview*, the main topic is placed in the center, subtopics are arranged around it, and details related to each subtopic are noted alongside each. Other forms of graphic organizers include Venn diagrams, flowcharts, and pyramid charts, and "herringbone charts" (see Figure 3.6 for examples).

Graphic organizers can be used in many ways to help students make concrete connections with abstract ideas and relationships. They can be used to structure brainstorming, to encourage active silent reading, or to prompt postreading reflective discussion or writing. In the following method, a graphic organizer is used to do all of the above.

Steps in the Three-Phase Graphic Organizer

Preparation: Analyze the reading selection to determine a graphic organizer format that illustrates its organization. Prepare a graphic organizer that includes all important information in the selection.

Step 1. *Prereading Schema Activation.* Without showing the prepared graphic organizer to the class, announce the topic, and ask students what they think they will read about in the selection. As students make suggestions, begin a rough construction of the graphic organizer on the board or overhead while students copy it on their papers. Typically, the first suggestions made will be details rather than major subtopics. For example, in a selection about spiders, one of the students' first suggestions would likely be that "they have eight legs" rather than the subtopic "body parts." For some selections, students will be able to generate the needed subtopics or anchor information; for other selections, the teacher will need to supply some if not most of these. During this inter-

Background

This version of the DR-TA is a comprehensive method that address all three phases of the reading process: prereading, guided silent reading, and postreading. It includes addressing vocabulary and word recognition, together with comprehension, and critical, creative, constructive reading, writing, and thinking. For some settings, the multiple aspects of the DR-TA may be challenging to implement. However, it does provide a comprehensive framework for fostering robust interactive content area literacy instruction. It also seems well suited to block-scheduling arrangements and allows opportunities for thematic and interdisciplinary activities.

Steps in the DR-TA

Step 1: Prereading—Schema Activation and Scaffolding (to help students *into* the reading)
- (a) Discuss students' background experience and knowledge related to the selection.
- (b) Preview the material by discussing the pictures and other graphics that accompany it.
- (c) Preteach key vocabulary terms and concepts (see Chapter 7 for a number of creative approaches for doing this).
- (d) Have students make reasonable predictions about what the reading selection is likely to be about.

Step 2: Guided Silent Reading—Metacognitive Monitoring (to help students *through* the reading)
- (a) Provide silent reading guidance by reminding students to read to check their predictions. Have students read silently, and check their predictions as they go. Where student predictions are correct, ask for verification from the material; where predictions are incorrect, have students ask themselves why.
- (b) Consider providing additional silent reading guidance by using strategies provided by such as: Guiding Questions, or About-Point, or a Comprehension Monitoring System (see Chapter 5 for details about these strategies).

Step 3: Postreading—Schema Solidification and Application of New Learning (to help students *beyond* the reading)
- (a) Check basic comprehension of material, using recognition and recall sorts of questions (see Chapter 6) and/or by using Reconstructive Response Types listed for the REAP Strategy (see Chapter 8). Also, discuss prereading predictions.
- (b) Refine understanding by seeking verifications for comprehension questions that require silent and/or oral rereading and citing of the material.
- (c) Consider having the students and/or the teacher read orally some favorite parts of the reading selection.

Figure 3.5 Modified Directed Reading-Thinking Activity (DR-TA).

Updated from versions developed in Stauffer (1969), Manzo & Manzo (1997), and Manzo & Manzo (1995).

(d) Relate the information in the text to other materials that have been read or to common experience.

(e) Engage in some follow-up activities that promote critical, creative, and/or constructive thinking and writing. These may include the following:

   • Write a personal reaction or a different ending, with the goal of a higher-order literacy response being the result. See the Constructive Response Types listed for the REAP Strategy (in Chapter 8).

   • Outline or summarize the text in a graphic organizer format.

   • Build or create some artistic expression, dramatization or other unusual perspective on the text. This is the best place for far-reaching critical, creative, constructive postreading activities.

(f) Build anticipation of something to be read at a later time by connecting it to some relevant aspect of the text and postreading discussion.

Figure 3.5 *(continued)*

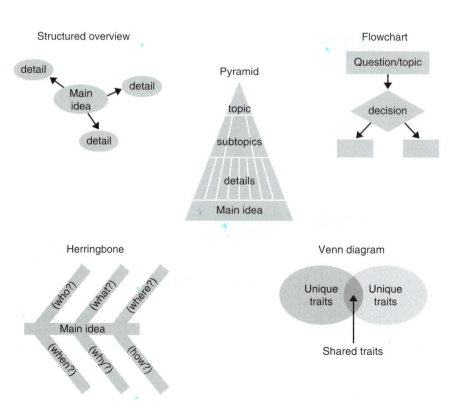

Figure 3.6 Graphic organizer formats.

action, the teacher should be open to modifying the planned structure of the graphic organizer if students make reasonable alternative suggestions. For maximum support, the teacher may show students where to draw blank lines for information to find in their reading. By the end of the prereading session, students will have an incomplete graphic organizer that they have helped to develop (see Figure 3.7).

Step 2. *Metacognitive Monitoring.* Students read silently to complete the graphic organizer. While they read silently, students add information to their graphic organizers as they find it in the selection. The incomplete graphic organizer produced in Step 1 provides a ready-made reading guide, reminding students to read actively, question their understanding, and note important points, details, and relationships.

Step 3. *Schema Building.* Once students have read, the teacher guides a discussion based on students' additions to the prereading graphic organizer, or students are directed to compare their work in cooperative groups. Optionally, the graphic organizer may be used as a writing prompt. For example, the graphic organizer may be divided into sections, with each section assigned to a small group of students. Each group then works together on their portion of the organizer to "retranslate" it from pictorial form into a connected paragraph (see Figure 3.7 for another variation on this idea) or to add some deeper level of understanding and research on the topic.

Notes on Graphic Organizers

Many content textbooks now include graphic organizers at the beginning or end of each chapter. Recent research indicates, however, that graphic organizers have little influence on reading comprehension if they are simply *given* to students before or after reading. Their effectiveness lies in students' participation in creating them. For this reason, in the prereading portion of the Three-Phase Graphic Organizer, the teacher uses the prepared graphic merely as a reference for guiding a brainstorming session on students' background knowledge about the topic.

Graphic organizers have been found to be especially useful in helping readers deal with what has been called *inconsiderate text;* that is, textual material that is too difficult because of poor writing and/or faulty assumptions about the reader's level of familiarity with the topic (Alvermann & Boothby, 1983). They do this by visually highlighting important ideas and playing down irrelevant and potentially distracting points. In the example shown in Figure 3.7 the description of creativity is not clearly laid out in the article: Part of the description is toward the beginning, and part at the end.

Notice that in the three-phase graphic organizer lesson example, students spend a good deal of time speaking, listening, and writing, as well as reading. Cooperative groups are used to encourage students to talk about what they have read and to develop points for an argument. After they have predicted, read, taken notes, compared notes with peers, and discussed an arguable position, they are asked to write a summary of what they have discussed. This intermingling of

This example is based on a short article entitled, "How Do I Know if I Am, or Could Be, Creative?" as used by high school art teacher, Jeanette. Working from notes for a complete graphic organizer, Jeanette wrote the topic *"Are Some People More Creative Than Others?"* in the center of the chalkboard. She told the class, "I found an interesting article on the Internet about creativity. Before I have you read it, let's think together about some of the ideas you have about creativity—who is creative and who isn't." As I put your ideas on the chalkboard, each of you should copy them onto your own paper. This will make a kind of worksheet for you to use as you read the article. Now, what is something you would expect to find in an article on this topic?" [Note: Jeanette reworded the topic for the graphic organizer because she thought that the title of the article would lead the prereading brainstorming down the wrong paths.] The next interactions went something like this:

Student:	Well, sure. Look at Sheila. She always comes up with ideas for her projects that no one else would have thought of. [Sheila jokingly replies, "Maybe I'm just weird."]
Jeanette:	So, one answer could be "yes." Creativity is something you're born with—something innate. [Jeanette adds the word "yes," followed by the phrase "Creativity is innate" to the GO, indicating that students should copy these terms and their placement on their papers.] Is that what you think?
Student:	Yes. [Several students nod.]
Jeanette:	Okay, then, think about creativity: what kind of mental process is it? How do you know it when you see it? [She adds "Define creativity" to the GO.]
Student:	I don't know about that, but some people might be kind of creative but not, like, show it—because they don't want to be different or something.
Jeanette:	Ah, so there may be people who are *potentially* creative? [adds the word "no", and the phrase "Some just have unrealized potential?" to the GO]. Anyone could be creative, but for some reason some people just don't use their potential. Maybe because they don't want to be different [adds the phrase "looking different" to the GO]—can you think of any other reasons why someone might not realize their creative potential?
Student:	Well, like you said, what do you mean by "creative"? Some people might be creative in some things that they're interested in, but not in other things that don't interest them as much.

Figure 3.7   Example of a Three-Phase Graphic Organizer.

Jeanette: Good, so, "motivation" would be a reason for not realizing creative potential [adds "motivation" to the GO], and we're back to trying to define "creativity." Let's stop here and go to the article. Add a few lines to your graphic organizers to show where there is information to look for [adds lines]. While you're reading, look for how the author describes creativity—be sure to put these into your own words—and two other reasons why some people may have unrealized creative potential. Also look for what the author says about testing creativity.

By the end of these exchanges, Jeanette and the students had created the following incomplete graphic organizer. Its structure and contents follow the one Jeanette had prepared, with one point ("looking different") added from a student's contribution. Jeanette also added a few points to direct students to key points in the article.

Prereading Incomplete Graphic Organizer:

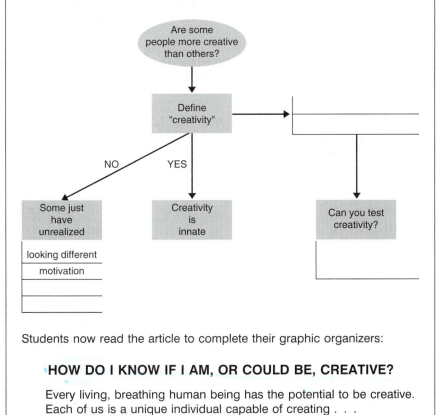

Students now read the article to complete their graphic organizers:

‣HOW DO I KNOW IF I AM, OR COULD BE, CREATIVE?

Every living, breathing human being has the potential to be creative. Each of us is a unique individual capable of creating . . .

Figure 3.7 *(continued)*

it comes with the human territory. We are, simply, quite a creative species.

All people can be creative but those who are recognized as being creative have an awareness that others don't. Creative people seem to be able to tune in more to their thought patterns and glean great ideas. People who do not use their creative potential don't know how to do this or aren't even aware it is possible. Creative people can start thinking about something, then forget it.

Meanwhile, their brains are still thinking about it. Later on, the person will start thinking about whatever it was again and their brain will say, "Excuse me, I've been thinking about this while you were off doing other things and I have a few ideas. Care to hear them?" Noncreative people don't know that their brains are working for them off-shift—they don't know what they don't know!

This is not to say that people tremendously fluctuate in their creativity day to day and hour to hour; the opposite is often believed—that some individuals are generally more creative most of the time than others. The reasons why some people are more creative, however, are many.

1. Without the abilities needed to do the creative act, it is highly unlikely the individual will do the act. Just because a person has the ability to do something, however, does not necessarily mean that the person will do it. This is why researchers examine people's motives.

2. Without the motivation to do so, it is unlikely that a person would complete an act, regardless of the person's abilities.

3. Lastly, opportunities in the environment can affect the creativeness of individuals and groups of individuals.

If you've ever generated a novel response to a problem or challenge then congratulate yourself as being creative. If you do this on a regular basis, say every day, then put the "creative person" badge on yourself. With practice, your ability to generate novel and useful responses to problems and challenges will greatly improve.

One aspect of a creative personality is the fluency with which he/she generates a number of new ideas. Not only does the creative person think of good ideas, but he/she can think of many ideas, explore them, and record them. If you feel a need to quantify your creative ability, go to a local psychologist and ask about taking a test to measure your creative ability. If you live near a college or university approach their psychology department with this request. But recognize that creative ability can be learned, improved upon, and increased over time.

Source: Am I Creative? © 1999, Creativity Web http://www.ozemail.com.au/~caveman/creative. E-Mail:charles©mpx.com.au. Reprinted by permission.

Figure 3.7 (*continued*)

> After students have read the article and completed their graphic organizers, students are directed to go to their home groups (four students each), compare what they have written, and make corrections or additions as needed. They are then asked to number off within groups. Students 1 and 2 are directed to develop the strongest arguments they can for the position that some people are naturally more creative than others. Students 3 and 4 are directed to develop their strongest arguments for the alternate position. They are given about 5 minutes to complete this discussion, and then students 1 and 3 are asked to relate their arguments to the other pair in their group. As a final step, students are asked to write, on the back of their graphic organizer, one paragraph stating and defending the position of their own choice.

Figure 3.7 *(continued)*

listening and speaking, reading, and writing is a key characteristic of interactive teaching and learning.

It should also be noted that computers, personal digital assistants (PDAs), and tablet PCs in the classroom can also be used in new ways to facilitate the process of using three-phase graphic organizers. For instance, many word-processing and common drawing software programs can be used to build sophisticated and visually pleasing graphic organizers that the students design themselves. Also, new specialty software such as Inspiration (*www.inspiration.com*) is getting enthusiastic reviews from classroom teachers for the ways it helps facilitate visual learning and graphic organizer creation. Finally, assigning online discussion board responses as a three-phase graphic organizer postreading activity could be one more (yet brand new) way to encourage student thinking, writing, and interaction regarding the content area material they have read (c.f. Thomas & Hofmeister, 2003).

► A QUICK WORD ABOUT WRITING: ENCOURAGING THE PROCESS AND THE PRODUCTS

The process of simply writing something down—a note while reading, an item on a "to-do" list, a message to a friend, or an answer to a study guide question—adds a slight but significant element of commitment to that thought that it previously did not have. It becomes more real, more concrete, more likely to be remembered. Any form of writing prior to reading or listening tends to activate prior knowledge and experience and heighten the reader's anticipation of the author's focus and key points. This could be called engaged reading and listening. It is a more active, interactive, and memorable mode of operating than is the passive, or disassociated reading and listening that tends to occur in school. Additionally, each effort to write *after* reading also provides considerable benefits to learning. It requires active reconstruction of text and thereby increases sensitivity to the text's content, logic, and organization. Further, each effort to write in reaction to or evaluation of text constitutes that invigorating plunge into the unknown where language and thought trigger one another to discover and organize the "inchoate lump of meanings" (Henry, 1974) that we often are left with following typical passive reading.

Simply put, a routine requirement to write something—almost anything—before or after reading ignites more active thinking before, during, and following reading. In spite of these benefits, writing tends to be an underused tool in content classrooms. This topic will be developed more fully in Chapter 9 in the section called "Writing to Learn," but we wanted to be sure to introduce it briefly here, as you will see suggestions for using writing as a thinking tool throughout the following chapters.

▶ AFTER WORDS

Now you've had a chance to enrich your schema and understanding of the elements and frameworks for powerful content area literacy instruction. The concrete examples offered are extended in the next section of the text (Chapters 4, 5, and 6) into a rich menu of teaching methods from which to choose and plan daily instruction and units of study.

II

READING AND LEARNING FROM TEXT

The next three chapters that you are about to engage contain the research-based and experiential core of content area literacy instruction. Knowledge of the content of these chapters will place you among the most technically competent of teachers. Skill in *delivering* a representative group of the methods in the chapters ahead will cause you to be among the most competent and influential of teachers. Read now about the best means available by which to guide reading and learning before, during, and following encounters with content-rich textual material.

CHAPTER 4

INTO—PREREADING METHODS FOR DIRECTED SCHEMA ACTIVATION, PURPOSE SETTING, AND LIFE-LONG LEARNING

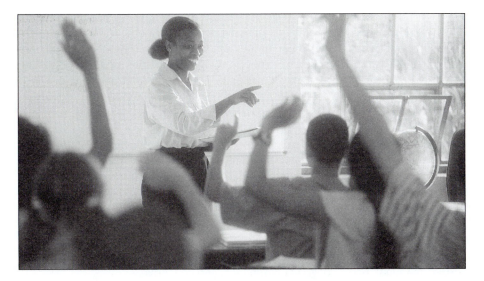

The whole art of teaching is only the art of awaking the natural curiosity of young minds for the purpose of satisfying it afterwards.

Anatole France

► FORE WORDS

This chapter explains the importance of the objectives, goals, and practices of prereading instruction. It explains why and how you find educational value in reading a chapter introduction such as this one. It does so by focusing first on the role of teacher questioning and its impact on student self-questioning and curiosity. It then discusses the process of *mental modeling*, which is the fundamental technique employed in several prereading methods. Finally, it describes a variety of other research-supported methods for providing this frontloading element of content area literacy instruction.

- ▶ FORE WORDS
- ▶ IMPORTANCE OF PREREADING
- ▶ GOALS OF PREREADING INSTRUCTION: READER ENGAGEMENT, DIRECTED SCHEMA ACTIVATION, AND ACTIVE MEANING-MAKING
- ▶ MENTAL MODELING: A FORM OF APPRENTICESHIP TRAINING
- ▶ PREREADING METHODS FOR READER ENGAGEMENT, SCHEMA ACTIVATION, AND ACTIVE MEANING-MAKING
- ▶ AFTER WORDS

▶ IMPORTANCE OF PREREADING

Minds never rest; they don't really need to be activated as much as aimed. Effective comprehension depends largely on the reader's *readiness* for entering the page with an appropriate mental set, or orientation. In a survey of teaching practices, professors specializing in content area literacy ranked prereading methods as the most important action content teachers could undertake to help students learn from their reading of text (Gee & Rakow, 1987). Prereading instruction helps students to establish an appropriate orientation to the reading task. It is especially important in today's diverse linguistic and cultural circumstances. Its purpose includes inviting multiple perspectives and reducing social inhibitions to *critical literacy*—or identifying possible false assumptions. It also builds strategic, independent learners (c.f. Pressley 2000). There are essentially three types, or dimensions, to such prereading orientation. Often these overlapping needs are served by one or two teacher actions. Seldom do all need to be done. In fact, to do so could be counterproductive since it would tend to overweight the warm-up and underweight the time remaining for engaged reading and postreading discussion. Ultimately the best warm-up for reading is what has been previously read, digested, and made part of one's living thoughts and concerns.

Taking Aim: Prereading Orientation

Attitude Orientation: For Reader Engagement

- Focus attention and reduce distractions. This twofold goal often can be accomplished by setting a compelling purpose for reading, since clear focus on an objective automatically tends to take the focus off of competing stimuli or possibilities.

- Pique interest in the topic and the task by relating it to a possible parallel (analog) in students' lives and sphere of interests.

- Motivate for sustained effort by eliciting and explicitly stating how the textual material may shed light on adolescent interests.

- Provide a conceptually relevant organizing principle, concern, or purpose, and where possible tie it to a basic human need. (For example, "Most everything you will read about these explorers and discoverers was due to their efforts to find an all water route through the new world. This would allow them to continue their trade with the eastern world without having to pass through the Barbary coast of North Africa, where they were easy prey for pirates. They didn't set out to claim or develop the Americas, but rather to figure out how to get through them. It seems that sometimes our best opportunities are right in front of us.")

Background Orientation: For Activation of Relevant Schema

- Activate appropriate schema: relevant background knowledge and experiences.
- Preteach key concept terms and unfamiliar allusions.
- Correct possible misunderstandings.
- Provide necessary new ideas and information.
- Establish a sense of the organization and sequence of the reading selection.

Reading Strategies Orientation: For Active, Pointed Meaning-Making

- Preview text to establish a sense of the structural organization and sequence of the selection.
- Identify reading aids such as headings, graphics, pictures, and terms in italics.
- Predict possible outcomes based on prior knowledge and experience.
- Raise factual and evaluative-type questions that can serve as purposes for reading and thinking.

Of course, these components are not taken up in a tedious, step-by-step fashion. Rather, they should be addressed selectively, depending on the particular needs of students and the challenges presented by the materials to be read. The methods in this chapter each address some combination of these elements, but in a focused, brisk, and interactive manner.

▶ GOALS OF PREREADING INSTRUCTION: READER ENGAGEMENT, DIRECTED SCHEMA ACTIVATION, AND ACTIVE MEANING-MAKING

Reader Engagement

Successful reading begins with genuine attention to the task: the reader must be actively *engaged* in the process (Rosenshine, 1984). Thus, one goal of prereading instruction is to help students develop the attitudes and interests that build the habit of quick and lively engagement as an initial step in study-type reading. This could be called *active anticipation*. When done well, this can produce a fundamentally positive feeling that can excite minds about reading and learning much like an energetically wagging tail accompanies the sound of food being poured into a pet's bowl.

Directed Schema Activation

In a previous chapter, schema was defined as the sum of one's prior knowledge, experience, sensory-motor learning, and inclinations. In this section, we will focus on its functional value in focusing and organizing reading. The primary role of schema is to provide the grid for receiving and organizing information. However, simply having a broad background of information and experience about a topic may not ensure effective comprehension. To read with comprehension, the reader must consciously recall the schema structures that are relevant to the reading selection so that he or she can actively form connections between this personalized organization of facts, perspectives, and experiences and the new information from the text. Thus, directed schema activation, or how readers *use* what they know, can be as important as how *much* they know.

The final goal of prereading instruction is to demonstrate and build strategies for constructing meaning from print. Most such strategies, beginning with formulating appropriate purposes for reading, are grounded in inquiry and expressed through questioning.

Active Inquiry: Meaning-Making through Questioning and Purpose Setting

Interest and motivation are driven by, expressed in, and organized around questions. New knowledge is built by means of identifying these organizing questions and converting them into an intentional purpose to guide our initial incursion into print. Nonetheless, students in most traditional content classrooms ask very few lesson-related questions. One of the primary reasons for teacher burnout, in fact, is teachers' perception that students lack interest and motivation. For the most part, however, lack of interest and motivation is only a secondary symptom. Inquiry and learning are natural human inclinations. The primary cause of what appears to be apathy, in most cases, is that students simply do not know what it is they don't know, and more, even when they do, they don't quite know how to convert this itch-they-can't-seem-to-scratch into questions that elicit a satisfying response. This can be especially true in the classroom environment, which can be layered with subtle inhibitions to student inquiry. Noting the inhibitions to inquiry is one way to begin to remedy this common problem. Let's convert this concern now into a question that should serve as an organizing purpose, or net for catching much of the information and methods in this text:

Why Don't Students Ask More Questions?

The first thing to grasp is that it is not one thing that inhibits inquiry but several layers of social, personal, and cognitive factors. One layer of inhibitions is composed of peer-related issues. Asking a question in class amounts to making a public proclamation, and, because it is a question for which one obviously doesn't know the answer, it amounts to something of an admission of ignorance. It also is a public acknowledgment of the teacher's expertise and, therefore, authority—something many adolescents tend to resent having to state, even implicitly. Another layer of inhibitions is composed of the cognitive aspects of inquiry. Each subject area is, in a way, a foreign language, with its own, peculiar, terminology, ways of thinking, and style of discourse.

Each of these come into play in formulating a question that sounds sensible. Moreover, research and intuition suggest that rather than encouraging and supporting student questioning, teachers too often behave in ways that inadvertently teach students to avoid asking questions. Figure 4.1 elaborates on the most common of these. See if these sound familiar. As illustrated in this figure, the way in which teachers ask *and answer* questions can do much to overcome the inhibitions to active curiosity and questioning that seem to become thick and invisible plasma in the typical classroom.

Teaching students to ask as well as answer questions is what Aristotle was explaining when he said, "these, then are the . . . kinds of questions we ask and *it is in the answers to these questions that our knowledge consists"* (McKeon, 1947, p.73, as quoted by Ciardiello, 1998). The simple goal of teaching students to engage in active questioning is to put them into an intelligent, ongoing search mode, to use an Internet metaphor. In this way, the quest to learn is more likely to continue after a particular lesson is over, the book is closed, and the classroom lights are dimmed.

Of further aid in teaching with questions is to know more about the types of questions that can be posed and the cognitive demands that each involves.

The Squelch.
Teachers sometimes respond to questions with sarcastic replies. Often, the questions that receive these replies are the kind of passive-aggressive questions that students raise when they are fearful or defensive. Before a test, for example, teachers often hear this flurry of questions: "Do we have to skip a line after every answer?"; "Do you want last names first?"; "Can we use notebook paper?"; "Can we use pencil?" Faced with these irrelevant, time-consuming questions, teachers sometimes get *too* skilled at squelching student questions with responses like, "Is today any different from yesterday?"; or "Are you new here?" Students, however, don't always see the distinction between relevant and irrelevant questions. If they come to expect sarcastic replies, they will be less likely to raise genuine, on-task questions. Overuse of the squelch is partly a matter of personal style, in which case it should still be used sparingly and in good humor. In general, we find that where a good rapport is established in a classroom, the passive-aggressive questions that deserve a squelch seldom occur.

The Sting.
As teachers, we occasionally *use* questions as a kind of "weapon" against student misbehavior. When we suspect that a student is unprepared, or is not paying attention, we may call on him or her to answer a question. Or when a student persists in talking while we are trying to explain a point to the class, we might use a punishing question like, "John, will you please explain this to the class?" When students feel and observe the sting of punishing questions, they often overgeneralize, and become fearful of asking and being asked *any* question. They fear that to ask a question is to challenge the teacher, and that to be asked a question is to be suspected of some misdeed. Even worse, more aggressive students begin to intentionally use questions to undermine the teacher's authority.

Figure 4.1 Why students stop asking questions.

The Void.
"Any questions?" is a popular teacher tool for encouraging students to raise clarifying inquiries. When students are asked this question in an inappropriate context, however, they quickly lose confidence in their ability to ask good questions. They often don't know what it is that they don't know; and/or, don't know how to articulate a vague thought into a clear question; and/or are unsure of how to frame the question so as not to annoy the teacher or alienate their classmates. Ironically, the more one knows about a topic, the easier it is to ask questions about it. With this in mind, it is important for the teacher to anticipate points of the lesson that may be unclear, and guide student questioning into those areas: "Can someone ask a good question to clarify when we need to change signs in an equation?"; then "What other questions could be asked about signs?"; and finally the more general question, "Any other questions about anything discussed today?"

The Volley.
Teachers too often fall into the habit of answering a question with a question, like the classic approach of indirect psychiatry. While there is a place and a time for this technique, if students expect that they will be put on the spot with a return question, they will grow reluctant to ask questions. Admittedly, this technique can be useful in "buying time" to think of an answer to a question that has come seemingly out of the blue. However, even in these instances, the more helpful teaching strategy is to think aloud through the processes needed to come up with an answer. This provides a perfect opportunity to demonstrate the teacher's role as a coach, rather than an encyclopedia.

Figure 4.1 *(continued)*

Question Types and Cognitive Load

No discussion of questioning can be complete without reference to how questions can be classified by cognitive levels. The rationale for knowing this is fundamental to teaching because the types of questions that teachers ask influence the nature of the thinking and discourse that follows. The types of questions also influence the thinking patterns that students will anticipate and likely internalize. The type and focus of the question asked becomes the agenda for what will be discussed and hence valued.

The most widely used systems for characterizing questions is based loosely on a hierarchy of difficulty called the *Taxonomy of Educational Objectives: The Cognitive Domain* (Bloom, 1956). There are eight basic types of questions that we have derived from this and several other authoritative sources (Aschner, Gallagher, Perry, Afsar, Jenne, & Farr, 1962; Barrett, 1967; Manzo & Manzo, 1990b; Sanders, 1969). See Figure 4.2 for a description of each.

The most effective way to help students develop the complex cognitive and affective elements of effective questioning is *not* simply to teach them about the various types of questions, although arguably there could be some small benefit to

1. **Recognition questions.** Recognition questions require identifying the answers from available choices (e.g., multiple-choice questions).

2. **Recall questions.** Recall questions require remembering the answers with little prompting and no clues ("When was the Battle of Hastings?").

3. **Translation questions.** Translation questions entail transferring something from one symbolic form to another ("Can you describe this picture?"; "Can you tell in your own words what the author said in this paragraph?"; "Can you say what you just heard in your own words?").

4. **Inference questions.** Inference questions have the reader combine available textual information to reach an answer that is compellingly logical but not explicitly stated in the text ("What is the relationship between Jack and Joseph in this story?").

5. **Conjecture questions.** Conjecture questions involve an inferential leap, because all the information is not yet, or may never be, available ("As we read ahead, do you suppose that Jack's life will rise above his father's?").

6. **Explanation questions.** Explanation questions require verification of a previous point. They may involve reference to the text and/or to other sources ("Why do you think Jack's life will rise above his father's?").

7. **Application questions.** Application questions require critical and constructive thinking and problem solving ("In similar circumstances, how might a person like Jack avoid hurting his father?").

8. **Evaluation questions.** Evaluation questions are a specialized type of application question that requires critical thinking, aesthetic sense, and personal judgment ("How do you feel about the story? the characters? the style of writing? the moral to be drawn?").

Figure 4.2   Question types.

this as well (Ciardiello, 1998). In general, questioning may be too complex, both cognitively and affectively, to be guided by a set of simplified rules. It appears best to address *questioning* as *inquiry* and to provide opportunities for students to interact with models of effective questioning in real and simulated reading-thinking situations. This life experience–based approach is necessary because inquiry and questioning can be mind numbing or mind expanding with the slightest difference in the way they are conducted.

Higher-Order Questions Can Be Reduced to a Lower-Order of Cognitive Functioning

While evaluative-type questions are listed as having a very high level of cognitive demand, they can be reduced to the lowest level of thought if the question of what one holds to or believes is not accompanied by an explanation-type question requiring one to say why a certain belief is held; a third grader explained this to us when she said " I've been waiting to get to third grade, where you have to say not only whether you like something or not, but you have to tell and even show why you do." Ideally, this type of higher-order teaching is done through an *instructional conversation*, a hands-on way to establish a mental *apprenticeship* relationship between the best minds on each matter discussed. Of course, this ideally needs to be designed to overcome the social inhibitions previously noted and is likely to be led by the teacher, but it can, and must, include peers, since few are likely to go off the high dive before they have seen someone else their age and size do so successfully. In the case of invisible acts such as higher-level thinking, a special kind of demonstration is necessary. It is called "mental modeling" (Manzo & Manzo, 2002), and while it may now seem obvious, it was not until the late 1960s that it became an explicit and intentional educational practice.

▶ MENTAL MODELING: A FORM OF APPRENTICESHIP TRAINING

Modeling of a certain act or skill is a form of teaching in which the instructor demonstrates a desired outcome and encourages the learner to imitate and then emulate it. It is the traditional means of apprenticeship training in trades and crafts, where the objective is to teach complex motor skills. It is only fairly recently that learning psychologists and educators have begun to recognize and explore the power of this form of teaching when applied to cognitive, rather than motor, learning (see Figure 4.3).

The human inclination to observe and imitate one another is the most familiar and frequently used mode of human learning outside of school. A prime example of its use is in natural language acquisition. Only a very small percentage of the words and language forms we know did we acquire as a result of direct instruction. A mother may teach her child to say some important words like "mommy," "hot," "chair," and so on, but the child picks up an enormous number of other words on his or her own. A parent or teacher may remind the child to say "he ran" instead of "he runned," but the majority of what the child learns about word order and language structures is learned incidentally. This does not mean that it isn't intentional. On the contrary, children actively decide much of what they will learn based in great measure on who appears to be doing best in that environment.

Model Selection

The way we speak, the words we use, and the way we feel when using these words are the direct result of the speech patterns and concerns of the models to whom we were exposed and with whom we have interacted. From the models we select to emulate, we learn motives and attitudes as well as words and actions. Thus, *inquiring minds beget inquiring minds*.

In any situation, however, there are various models available from whom to choose. Selection of the model to be emulated is based on subjective assessments

Figure 4.3   Cognitive modeling and apprenticeship training.

of the degree to which those around us appear to have mastery over a given environment or situation. In school settings, the student does not automatically choose the teacher or the good student as a model. There is an ongoing competition with other influential peers and adults in the home and community. *Instructional strategies that employ modeling must include devices for winning students' attention to the desired models and behaviors.*

Social and Imitation Learning Theory

Modeling of mental operations has its rational basis in *social and imitation learning* theory (Bandura & Walters, 1963; Miller & Dollard, 1941; Vygotsky, 1978). Simply put, the idea is that we tend to copy and internalize *a larger* array of a model's character and behaviors than merely those traits that are essential to the task at hand. By taking advantage of this additional, (seemingly) incidental learning dimension, it becomes possible to teach very complex and subtle behaviors along with key target behaviors, and in a much shorter period of time. Further, the mental image of the model serves as a mental template, or set of guidelines, that the novice can use to monitor and evaluate subsequent attempts to apply and refine the new thinking strategy in different situations. In short, internalization of the target strategy is most likely to occur only after youngsters have used a cognitive operation in situations where adults and other peer experts have modeled and given them some form of feedback on their performance (Camperell, 1982; Manzo, 1969a, 1969b; Vygotsky, 1978).

Conditions Conducive to Effective Mental Modeling

Modeling is a very *efficient* means of teaching complex tasks; however, its *effectiveness* is likely to vary depending on the management of certain conditions. Six conditions that have been identified (Manzo & Manzo, 1997a) seem to be particularly relevant to the content area classroom:

1. When the student's attention is drawn to a desired model;
2. When the impression can be made that the model is doing something masterful and desirable;
3. When there is a reduced social risk entailed in imitating a desired behavior;
4. When the new behavior appears "doable," as when a student observes someone from his or her peer group engaged in the behavior;
5. When students are permitted to interact with the model in an affective (feeling) manner as well as in purely cognitive, or, "school-like" ways;
6. When *reciprocity* is used to help students develop a sense of *agency* or the feeling that they have some reasonable level of influence over the instructional environment.

The last element, *reciprocity*, serves other critical purposes in effective teaching and learning. It creates an otherwise difficult to achieve *rotation* between the teacher and students (Manzo & Manzo, 2002). In so doing, it tends to raise student competence while inviting the student's individuality to emerge. In this way, students come to learn generalized strategies for effective learning that are *personalized* and owned by them rather than continuing merely to *copy* the behavior and objectives of the model alone.

Search and Learn Mode

As you study the teaching methods ahead that feature social and mental modeling, remember to look for the specific action(s) of the teacher that might generate *rotation*, and active student participation; and attract students' attention and desire to emulate available models of question asking, reflecting, and answering. Initially, this is likely to be the teacher, but eventually it will include peers, and, finally, a personal quest to ask and puzzle about things some of which may never be known. It is at this point that a student can be said to be fully engaged, or in an active *search and learn mode*. Ideally, this mode becomes internalized as a life quest as much as a momentary or textbook-bound reading and learning strategy.

▶ PREREADING METHODS FOR READER ENGAGEMENT, SCHEMA ACTIVATION, AND ACTIVE MEANING-MAKING

The short article, "Vaulting Vampires," in Figure 4.4 is used for examples of the prereading methods in this section. Skim through the article before beginning to read about the ReQuest Procedure.

---

(1) On most nights a vampire bat tries to drink about half its body weight in blood. After feasting, the blood-bloated bat launches itself into the air. But unlike other bats, which simply drop from their perches to initiate flight, vampire bats jump from the ground into the air. How do they manage their takeoffs?

(2) "They can't run to get up a head of steam like a swan or a goose does," says William Schutt, a zoologist at Bloomfield College in New Jersey. Schutt recently managed to give biologists their first detailed look at the dynamics of a vampire bat takeoff.

(3) Of the world's 900 or so bat species, only the common vampire bat, Desmodus rotundus, is able to maneuver as well on the ground as it does in the air. "They can hop, move backward, side to side—like little spiders," says Schutt.

(4) To study how the bats launch themselves, Schutt put them on a force-measuring platform and recorded their movements with a high-speed camera. The animal begins with all four limbs on the ground. Then it extends its hind knees and tips itself forward, so the center of mass is over the forelimbs. For the actual jump, it extends the fore-limbs and pushes itself off the ground with the tremendously large pectoral muscles," he says. Schutt found that the pectorals are the major flight muscles in bats, just as in birds. The triceps muscle and the bat's very long thumb also generate some force. The thumb is the last part of the body to leave the ground and helps steer the bat's takeoff.

(5) The entire jump lasts a mere 30 milliseconds, but during that time the bat catapults itself three to four feet off the ground. The transition from jump to flight is almost seamless, says Schutt. At the end of the jump "all the limbs are pointed toward the ground, which is the equivalent of a downstroke. So now it just has to bring the forelimbs into an upstroke position and it can begin to power itself in flight."

(6) Since vampire bats do most of their feeding on level surfaces, their deftness is a definite advantage. "If they are feeding on a cow's foot, and the cow takes a step back, they need to be quick to get out of the way," Schutt says, "and they also need to be fast on the ground to get away from predators."

Figure 4.4 Sample Reading Selection "Vaulting Vampires" (*Discover*, March 1998, 19:3).
Source: Kathy A. Svitil © 1998. Reprinted with permission of *Discover Magazine*.

ReQuest Procedure

The Reciprocal Questioning or ReQuest Procedure (Manzo, 1969b) is a well-proven and robust method that introduced the idea of "mental modeling" to educational intervention. It is a constructivist method designed to permit the teacher to model good questioning and question answering (Ciardiello, 1998). It encourages students to *focus on the teacher and competent peers* as effective models of question asking and answering. However, while the teacher is the initial focus, ReQuest emphasizes *strategy* more than mere *skill* learning by teaching students how to set their own purposes for reading. Just as important, the *reciprocal* step creates *procedural rotation* that gives students a good deal of control and makes a learner of the teacher as he or she grows in understanding of students' different constructions of what they have read.

ReQuest can be used to introduce an in-class reading activity or at the end of a class period for a home reading assignment. It has been used from the primary grades to the graduate school levels.

Steps in the ReQuest Procedure

Preparation: Teacher and students should have copies of the reading selection. ReQuest is best used by directing students to look only at one sentence at a time, without reading ahead. When possible, it is useful to have the first portion of the selection on a PowerPoint slide or an overhead transparency, so that it can be shown one sentence at a time (title and first sentence together first, then the second sentence, the third, etc., to about the fifth sentence). Ideally, the teacher should prepare at least four questions for *each*, over: the title and first sentence, and the second through about the fourth sentences. These should be questions that students would probably *not* ask, since students are given the chance to ask questions first.

Step 1. The first time the method is used the teacher should explain its purpose; for example, "Before you read this selection, we will look at the first few sentences together and ask each other some questions. The purpose of this activity is to improve your ability to set a sound purpose for reading."

Step 2. The teacher guides the students through as many sentences of the selection as necessary to formulate a logical purpose to guide silent reading. This is done in the following way:

    a. Students and teacher read the title and first sentence. Students are told that they may ask the teacher as many questions as they wish about the title and first sentence only (see Figure 4.5). Students are told that they should try to ask the kinds of questions a teacher might ask, *in the way a teacher might ask them* (this is one way to subtly urge students to mentally note the teacher's mental processes).

    b. The teacher answers each question fully, but without excessive elaboration and without asking questions back. How much to "tell" in answering a question will be a judgment call in any lesson. The objectives at this stage of the lesson are to encourage and reinforce questions that activate relevant schema; to fill in needed background information (but only in answer to questions); to stay focused on setting a sound purpose for reading; and to *model good question-answering behaviors*.

   c. Once students have asked all their questions about the title and first sentence, the teacher follows up with a few additional questions. Some question types to consider include basic information, translation, inference, personal experience, and evaluation. The purpose in this follow-up questioning is to model the kinds of prereading questions that activate schema and help to set good purposes for reading.

   d. The pattern used to review the first sentence—silent reading, followed by student questions, followed by teacher questions—is continued through the second, third, and fourth sentences, and/or continuing until enough information has been generated to form a sound purpose for reading.

Step 3. After *about* the fourth sentence, the teacher should conclude his or her questions on the sentence by asking students what they think the rest of the selection will *mostly* be about (few things are written with only one focus and one solitary purpose). Briefly note student responses on the chalkboard, and then ask students to form one or more of these ideas into a question. Write the purpose question(s) on the board. If students are to read the remainder of the selection outside class, have them copy the purpose question(s).

Step 4. Following silent reading, the teacher's first question should be, "Did we set a good purpose for reading this selection?" If so, discussion can begin with what was learned in answer to this question; if not, a better purpose question should be stated and then answered (Manzo, 1985).

Notes on ReQuest: Tips on Implementation

- The first time you use ReQuest with a group, it is likely that when you direct them to ask questions over the title and first sentence, they will respond with blank stares. Be calm. Count to 10. Take confidence from the fact that you know *why* you are making this seemingly strange request, and you know *where* the lesson is going. You know that the purpose of spending time at the beginning of a difficult reading selection is like initializing a computer disk: it helps the brain to recognize and process the information that is coming. You also know that while there are only a handful of fact questions that can be asked about a single sentence, there are many more inference and beyond-the-lines questions that would be helpful in recalling prior knowledge and experience in order to set a good purpose for reading. Most important, you know that pupils have been conditioned *not* to ask questions in the classroom and that you are willing to try to counter this conditioning. Much of this counterconditioning is accomplished simply by setting up the game-line ReQuest situation, in which students are *procedurally rotated* to the position of asking as many questions as they can over a single sentence at a time. So don't despair in waiting for that first question. If wait time isn't enough, you can say something like, "This is a different kind of lesson, I know. Any question you can come up with is fine. It will help to try to think of the type of questions teachers might ask. You've heard a few questions asked, I take it." When the first question or two come, answer them respectfully: Another important element in counterconditioning students' reluctance to ask questions is the way the teacher *responds* to the questions that are raised—discussed next.

- When students take you up on your offer to answer any questions on a sentence, in ReQuest, you can expect a few unexpected questions: ones for which you do not know or cannot quickly formulate answers. Be ready for this. It's your chance to show students that you *aren't* threatened or frightened by questions you can't answer and that you won't respond with sarcasm or by asking a question back. Instead, you will give the question a thoughtful, measured response. If it is a relevant, schema-activating question, you will say so and give an honest explanation as to why you can't answer it, if only to say you just can't remember: "That's exactly the kind of question we're trying to bring up here. It is information the author assumes the reader knows. And, do you know, I can't remember that fact myself." At this point, another student may know the answer. Since it's not your turn to ask questions, turn to the person who asked the question, and tell him or her that another student is willing to help you out . . . a wonderful and practical way to build toward the ideal of a *community of learners*. If, on the other hand, the question that stumped you is clearly off the subject, you might say something like, "Because of the way the title was worded, I didn't think the author was going in that direction, so I haven't tried to remember what I might know about that. It's an interesting point, but I don't think I'll get myself off the subject with it right now." This too can demonstrate the concept of a *community of learners*.

- When calling on students to *ask* you questions, keep an eye on students who typically do not participate in discussion. With the ReQuest structure, you've given all students, even the most shy and reticient, a much more possible situation for involvement. They don't have to answer a question—they only have to ask one. Call on them, and be supportive in your answers.

- When it is your turn to ask questions, you will need to have several questions prepared for each sentence that students probably won't ask. Prepare four or five such questions for each sentence, even though you may not use them all. How many questions you ask on each sentence will depend on how many and what kind of questions the students ask. In general, you should ask at least two questions when it is your turn, trying to ask questions of different types than the students have asked. Basic facts will probably be covered by student questions. In fact, the reason ReQuest uses single sentences for questioning is that this places a natural limit on the number of fact questions that can reasonably be asked. Once these are covered, both teacher and students are challenged to ask schema-connecting beyond-the-lines questions.

- While it is somewhat gamelike in the back-and-forth rotation of questioning, ReQuest shouldn't take on a *stump-the-teacher/stump-the class* tone, which tends to get off the track of a clear focus on setting a sound and sensible purpose for reading a specific selection. This can happen if the teacher asks questions that the class clearly cannot answer—students will begin to ask the same types of questions back. Be careful to ask questions that *can* be answered by prediction, inference, judgment, evaluation, and experience.

- ReQuest should move along briskly, taking no more than about 15 minutes. If it is extended too long, it can become tedious and lose focus. This can be difficult to keep in mind. While student questions can be intimidating at times, it also can feel satisfying to be asked the questions by students to which we are obliged to teach them the answers. Be careful, though; it is easy to go into too much detail in answering or to use technical terms that extend beyond students' *zone of proximal development* (ZPD).

- The questions generated from the first three or four sentences usually yield enough context for students to form a sound purpose question or two. When preparing your own questions, you usually can predict a good stopping point. You should have a possible purpose question in mind in order to help guide students' suggestions.

See Figure 4.5 for an example of the ReQuest Procedure with "Vaulting Vampires," from *Discover* magazine.

Further Backstory and Wider Uses of ReQuest

You may wish to know a bit more about ReQuest due to its role in advancing several different areas of social learning and cognitive psychology and in interpreting constructivist theories into practice, before they were known as such. Again, ReQuest pioneered the use of cognitive modeling to teach mental processes. It first was developed for one-on-one teaching. However, it proved equally effective in content classrooms with heterogeneous groups (Manzo, 1973), in programs to promote personal-social adjustment in juvenile delinquents (Kay, Young, & Mottley, 1986), in mainstreaming learning-disabled students (Alley & Deshler, 1980; Hori, 1977), with second-language students (McKenzie, Ericson, & Hunter, 1988), and as a significant part of an instructional program to improve social studies education (Ciardiello, 1998; Ciardiello & Cicchelli, 1994). It also has become the basis for a larger movement in education called Reciprocal Teaching (Palincsar & Brown, 1984). A survey of over 450 teachers revealed that based on descriptions of ten leading comprehension improvement methods, teachers would most like further information and training on ReQuest (Spor & Schneider, 1999).

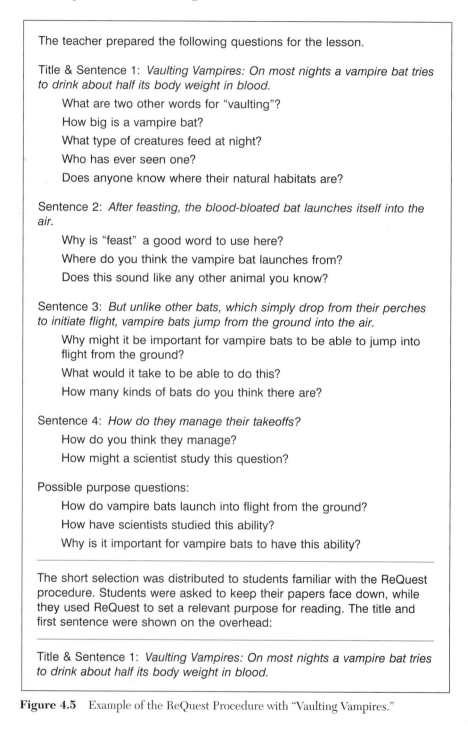

The teacher prepared the following questions for the lesson.

Title & Sentence 1: *Vaulting Vampires: On most nights a vampire bat tries to drink about half its body weight in blood.*

What are two other words for "vaulting"?

How big is a vampire bat?

What type of creatures feed at night?

Who has ever seen one?

Does anyone know where their natural habitats are?

Sentence 2: *After feasting, the blood-bloated bat launches itself into the air.*

Why is "feast" a good word to use here?

Where do you think the vampire bat launches from?

Does this sound like any other animal you know?

Sentence 3: *But unlike other bats, which simply drop from their perches to initiate flight, vampire bats jump from the ground into the air.*

Why might it be important for vampire bats to be able to jump into flight from the ground?

What would it take to be able to do this?

How many kinds of bats do you think there are?

Sentence 4: *How do they manage their takeoffs?*

How do you think they manage?

How might a scientist study this question?

Possible purpose questions:

How do vampire bats launch into flight from the ground?

How have scientists studied this ability?

Why is it important for vampire bats to have this ability?

The short selection was distributed to students familiar with the ReQuest procedure. Students were asked to keep their papers face down, while they used ReQuest to set a relevant purpose for reading. The title and first sentence were shown on the overhead:

Title & Sentence 1: *Vaulting Vampires: On most nights a vampire bat tries to drink about half its body weight in blood.*

Figure 4.5   Example of the ReQuest Procedure with "Vaulting Vampires."

Teacher:	Who has a question about just the title and first selection of this article?
Student 1:	What does "vaulting" mean?
Teacher:	Good vocabulary question. It means leaping. Springing or jumping high.
Student 2:	How much do vampire bats weigh?
Teacher:	Hum, I'm just guessing here, maybe 3 pounds.
Student 3:	Whose blood do they drink?
Teacher:	Large animals, like cows. That's a good question, because it gets at why it's important for them to be able to vault.
Student 3:	Why is that?
Teacher:	To get out of the way if their prey tries to shoo them off.
Teacher:	No other questions? Okay, my turn. Has anyone ever seen a live vampire bat?
[Several students raise their hands]	
	Jake, you have? Where was it?
Student 4:	At the zoo, they make a big show out of the vampire bats' "feeding time."
Teacher:	Has anyone seen them in the wild?
[No hands]	
	Why does it say "on most *nights*"?
Student 4:	Bats sleep during the day, and feed at night.
Teacher:	Yes, and what's another name for creatures that do this?
Student 2:	Nocturnal animals.
Teacher:	Good. Let's go on to the next sentence. After you've read it, you can ask me questions.
Sentence 2:	*After feasting, the blood-bloated bat launches itself into the air.*
Student 5:	Do they jump off the cows' backs?
Teacher:	Not usually.
Student 5:	What do they jump off?
Teacher:	The ground.
Student 2:	Can they fly?
Teacher:	Yes.
Student 6:	Can they walk on the ground.
Teacher:	Yes, they can move very easily and quickly on the ground. No more questions? Okay, my turn. Why is "feasting" an especially good word to use here?
Student 1:	Because they eat, or drink I guess (yuck) so much.
Teacher:	If you picture yourself as a bat, what muscles do you think you would use to launch yourself into flight?
Student 7:	My leg muscles.
Teacher:	Maybe. Do you think other kinds of bats launch into the air in this way?

Figure 4.5 *(continued)*

Student 5:   Maybe other ones just drop off the branches they're hanging from.

Teacher: Okay, let's look at the next sentence.

Sentence 3: *But unlike other bats, which simply drop from their perches to initiate flight, vampire bats jump from the ground into the air.*

Teacher: So that was a good prediction, John. What questions could we ask now? Remember, we're trying to predict what the rest of this article is about, and write a purpose question.

Student 8:   How many kinds of bats are there?

Teacher: Actually, this article says that there are over 900.

Student 1:   So they have to jump into the air to get out of the cows', or whatever's, way. Is this going to explain how they do that?

Teacher: That's a good prediction. Let's put it up here.

[Writes "How vampire bats vault" on the board]

Student 7:   Is it about what muscles they use?

Teacher: Another good prediction.

[Writes "What muscles?" on the board]
    Any others?

[No hands]

Teacher: Okay, well, how do you think a scientist might try to find out how the vampire bat launches itself from the ground?

Student 9:   Take a video?

Teacher: Good idea. What if it's too fast to really see on the tape?

Student 9:   Put it in slow motion.

Teacher: Good prediction. [At the risk of creating a digression, the teacher may occasionally wish to add other sidebar information, such as "By the way, when something is filmed for slow-motion the film/tape often needs to move much faster, except if it is 'time-lapse' photography."] In any case, how can you tell how hard it has to push off?

Student 6:   What if you put a scale, like you weigh yourself on, under it. Would that show how hard it was pushing down to jump?

Teacher: Good idea. Let's see what we have.

[Writes "Use videotape & scales to study?" on board]
    Can we put these predictions into one or two purpose questions?

Student 2:   What muscles do vampire bats use to vault, and how did scientists find out?

Teacher: Terrific.

[Writes prediction question on board:
"What muscles do vampire bats use to vault, and how did scientists find out?"]

Teacher: Okay, turn your papers over, and let's go ahead and read to see if we find answers to this question.

Figure 4.5 *(continued)*

[Students read article]
Teacher: Was this a good purpose question for the article?
Student 2:   Yes, it told what muscles, and how scientists found out.
Student 3:   But it seemed like the point of the article was the part at the
              end, about why it was important for this kind of bat to be
              able to do this.
Teacher: To get out of the way if the cow started kicking! That came
              up in our discussion before we read. So, just from the title,
              we might have added another purpose question:
[Writes, "Why is it important for them to vault?"]

Discussion continues with what students learned about how one scientist
studied these bats, and what he learned.

Figure 4.5   (*continued*)

Cooperative-Collaborative ReQuest

Even with ideal participation, if four different students asked a question about
each of the first four sentences of a selection, only sixteen students, half a traditional classroom, would have actively participated. Once students have become
familiar with the method, try this Kagan-like, cooperative structure variation
(Spencer Kagan is a popular cooperative learning expert). Our sense is that it increases active involvement of more students. Several of these suggestions also add
more of the elements of what Ciardiello (1998) calls TeachQuest, or explicit
teaching about and cueing of question types to students.

Preparation

- Prepare an overhead transparency with the title and first four sentences
  or so of the selection, or write these on the chalkboard, with strips of
  paper taped over each sentence to be removed to uncover one sentence at
  a time; for even more cueing of the type recommended by Ciardiello
  (1998), prepare a worksheet for each group, with space after each sentence for questions to be written.
- The teacher should prepare questions over the title and first four sentences, as described for ReQuest (personal experience, translation, inference, background information, evaluation, and prediction questions).
- Form groups of four. A good way to form heterogeneous groups for the topic
  of a given reading selection is to have students form a Kagan-type "Lineup"
  from "no knowledge or experience with the topic of xxx" at one end, to "lots
  of knowledge and/or experience with the topic of xxx" at the opposite end.
  Then count off by the number of groups needed to form groups of four. Have
  students, in groups, number off or self-select roles such as recorder, speaker,
  discussion starter, and encourager. Roles can be rotated for each sentence.
- Have copies of the reading selection available for each student.

Step 1. Assuming that students are familiar with ReQuest, show the title and first sentence, and tell students that they have two minutes in their groups to come up with as many questions as they can over that portion of the reading. Tell students that even though they may not use all of their questions, you will collect all of their questions at the end of the lesson.

Step 2. Proceed as with ReQuest, calling on the speaker in one of the groups to begin. Not every group needs to be called on for each sentence.

Step 3. At a reasonable point, have groups write possible purpose questions for the selection. Have the writer from each group write his or her group's purpose question(s) on a designated spot on the chalkboard. Review these together with the class and select from or combine these to form the best collaborative purpose question(s).

Step 4. Have students read silently to answer the purpose question(s).

Step 5. Ask whether a good purpose was set, and continue discussion based on what students learned in answer to the question(s).

Now let's gather some details about another *rotation* and modeling teaching method. It, too, has been carefully researched.

Reciprocal Teaching

Reciprocal Teaching (RT) (Palincsar & Brown, 1984) is an attempt to amplify and elaborate the fundamental elements of the ReQuest Procedure into a more broadly based educational approach (Gipe, 1998). To raise students' sense of *agency,* or involvement in the process, RT begins, as does Ciardiello's (1998) TeachQuest, with a class discussion of why we sometimes experience difficulties in reading text. The processes of *questioning, summarizing, clarifying,* and *predicting* are introduced as helpful strategies for attending, understanding, and remembering.

The next phase in Reciprocal Teaching is direct instruction in each of these four seminal processes. This is done in isolation but through teacher modeling and examples based on a meaningful text. When students are comfortable with the four processes of questioning, summarizing, predicting, and clarifying, they and the teacher begin to take turns assuming the role of teacher. The one playing the role of teacher is responsible for leading the dialog examining the reading selection. Figure 4.6 presents an example of the questioning, summarizing, and predicting aspects of Reciprocal Teaching. This script is taken from an actual classroom dialog with a group of children that Palincsar and Brown trained in this strategy.

In this content area version of Reciprocal Teaching, students are grouped by twos in "peer dyads" and are instructed to ask each other questions about the material to be read. The content area variation has the following steps:

1. Students convert subheadings in the text into two written predictions of what they think they will read about.

2. The class discusses these.

3. Following reading of a segment of material (usually four paragraphs), students write two questions and a summary reflecting the information in that segment.

4. Students write examples of any information that requires clarification.

5. The class discusses their written questions, summaries, and clarifications.

Positive outcomes have been reported from studies using Reciprocal Teaching with students who were classified as good decoders but poor comprehenders (Reeve, Palincsar, & Brown, 1985). *Time* magazine (circa 1988) called Reciprocal Teaching the most important development in instructional theory in the twentieth century. Bruer (1993) further referred to it as a primary example of the cognitive psychology revolution that has taken place in instruction and that few outside education are aware of. Ironically, Reciprocal Teaching has appeared in fewer and fewer textbooks for teachers in recent times. A possible reason for this diminished interest may be found in the fact that Reciprocal Teaching requires considerable

---

Student 1 [in role of "teacher"]: My question is, what does the aquanaut need when he goes under water?

Student 2: A watch.

Student 3: Flippers.

Student 4: A belt.

Student 1: Those are all good answers.

Teacher: Nice job! I have a question too. Why does the aquanaut wear a belt? What is so special about it?

Student 3: It's a heavy belt and keeps him from floating up to the top again.

Teacher: Good for you.

Student 1: For my summary now: This paragraph was about what aquanauts need to take when they go under the water.

Student 5: And also about why they need those things.

Student 3: I think we need to clarify *gear*.

Student 6: That's the special thing they need.

Teacher: Another word for *gear* in this story might be *equipment*— the equipment that makes it easier for the aquanauts to do their job.

Student 1: I don't think I have a prediction to make.

Teacher: Well, in the story, they tell us that there are "many strange and wonderful creatures" that the aquanauts see as they do their work. My prediction is that they'll describe some of these creatures. What are some of the strange creatures you already know about that live in the ocean?

Student 6: Octopuses.

Student 3: Whales?

Student 5: Sharks!

Teacher: Let's listen and find out. Who would like to be our teacher?

Figure 4.6 Illustration of Reciprocal Teaching.

teacher and student training prior to use, whereas its predecessor ReQuest, which Palincsar and Brown (1984) credit as RT's theoretical platform, ideally is used by uninitiated students and teachers to learn how to interact reciprocally. The only other reservation that we once had about RT was that findings on its efficacy were based exclusively on investigator-made tests based on the subject matter read. Now, however, there are findings to suggest that overall reading comprehension can show improvement on standardized tests as well (King & Parent Johnson, 1999), as is the case with primary research on the ReQuest Procedure (Manzo, 1969a, 1969b). In other words, if you are looking for *evidenced-based methods*, both of these qualify.

The next few methods have the simplicity of a straight piece of wire twisted into the now ubiquitous paper clip: evident once seen and said, but apparently not so easy to imagine without prompting. See if any of these instructional ideas have ever occurred to you in some form. The first such method for facilitating the prereading stage of comprehension arose from earlier studies on the rise and decline of curiosity in school age children. The method that evolved from these studies is very robust and slightly unorthodox.

Question Only

To follow this simple instructional idea, it is useful to review some prior points on inhibitions to questioning. Whenever students read or listen in school, questions are being answered. The problem is that students often don't know what those questions are and hence cannot read or listen actively. Even when they have some level of awareness of an important organizing question, students tend to be inexperienced in framing their question in such a way as to allow focused reading, or to invite appropriate help from a speaker/teacher when they are listening. In due course, natural curiosity begins to suffer and soon most inquiry grinds to a halt. Question-Only (Manzo, 1985) can almost instantly reverse this trend.

Question-Only is designed for nonfiction materials and does not work particularly well with fiction or poetry. It can be used for a selection to be read in class or as preparation for an outside reading assignment.

Steps in the Question-Only Method

Preparation. Review the reading selection to write several quiz questions covering important information and including at least two questions that students are not likely to ask about before they read. Decide whether to use the title of the selection to introduce the lesson or a more general statement of the topic.

Step 1. The teacher announces the title or topic of the reading selection to the class and explains that *before reading* the selection, they will have a chance to learn about it by asking questions. Then they will be given a quiz over the content of the selection. The quiz will cover all the information the teacher considers important, whether or not the students actually extract the information with their questions.

Step 2. The class questions and the teacher answers fully but without going beyond the answer to the question as asked.

Step 3. The teacher gives the quiz.

Step 4. Do *not* "grade" the quiz yet. Ask students to raise their hands if they think they got most of the questions right. Ask which question(s) they had trouble with.

Step 5. Have students read silently to double check their answers to the quiz questions and to find the answer(s) the question(s) they did not ask about. If the selection is to be read as a homework assignment, write the purpose question(s) on the board or overhead for students to copy.

Step 6. After students have read, begin discussion or other follow-up with their answers to the purpose question(s).

Tips on Implementation of Question-Only

- The Question-Only quiz should be given orally. If it is prepared on a handout ahead of time, you can't adjust it based on the questions students asked. Remember, the objective is to have as many students as possible get the correct answers to all but one or two questions. Therefore, you should prepare more quiz questions than you probably will use.

- When answering student questions during Step 2, it is a good idea to write a *brief form* of each question and a *brief form* of the answer on the chalkboard and leave this in view during the quiz. When students ask why you are leaving it up, you have the perfect opportunity to explain that the object of the lesson isn't really to get the quiz questions right but to learn to ask good questions. All the information students got from questioning, therefore, is theirs to use during the quiz. It is very important, though, to use abbreviated forms and write quickly, or the lesson will get bogged down and boring.

- Keep an eye on students who did not typically participate in class discussion. Question-Only gives them an excellent opportunity to participate. They don't have to answer a question, only to ask one.

- Many questions are likely to be about information not covered in the reading selection. To keep the lesson on track, simply tell students when this is the case. Say something like, "That's not included in this selection, but you're using good logical thinking processes to eliminate possibilities." You can also answer in ways that subtly direct students toward important questions and follow-up questions (see the example in Figure 4.7).

- Research and field experience have revealed that Question-Only helps students from kindergarten (more on this in Chapter 9) through medical school to raise incisive and systematic questions on difficult and mundane topics (Legenza, 1978; Manzo & Legenza, 1975). The enthusiasm students have shown for this method probably arises from the fact that it offers them an assertive but nonbelligerent means of "poking back" and reciprocally influencing lesson activity. It also helps students to develop a sense of agency or to incidentally discover and provide for their own learning needs, in an upbeat and ego-protective atmosphere, by stimulating them to ask questions about the things that most befuddle them.

The teacher prepared the following topic and quiz questions:

Topic: Vaulting vampire bats

Quiz Questions:
[Underlined questions are questions the teacher expects that students may not *ask—one should be included in the quiz, to serve as a purpose for reading]*

- Do vampire bats really drink blood? (yes)
- How much blood do vampire bats drink? (half their weight per night)
- How do vampire bats launch themselves into flight? (jump from the ground)
- How high do they jump? (3–4 feet)
- How many types of bats are there? (about 900)
- What is unusual about the vampire bat's ability to move on the ground? (It is the only bat that can move as well on the ground as in the air.)
- What is the major muscle the vampire bat uses to launch itself from the ground? (the pectorals)
- How have scientists studied the vampire bat's vaulting? (force measuring platform and high speed camera)
- Why is "vaulting" an important ability for vampire bats? (they do most of their feeding on level ground)
- What are two ways in which other creatures launch themselves? (dropping from branches, and running to build up speed)

Teacher: For tomorrow, your assignment will be to read an article called "Vaulting Vampires." Right now, I'll give you a chance to find out everything you can about it just by asking me questions. Then, I'll give you a quiz over what's in the actual article.

Student 1:   You mean, we have a quiz before we read it?

Teacher: Yes, but you have 20 minutes or so, right now, to get all the answers you can.

[Writes "Vaulting vampire bats" on the chalkboard—see below for information eventually written on the board]

Student 2:   Oh, vampire *bats*. You didn't say that before.

Teacher: Yes, *vaulting* vampire bats.

Student 3:   Why do they vault?

Teacher: They vault, or jump, to launch themselves into flight.

Student 1:   Will that be on the quiz?

Figure 4.7   Example of the Question-Only with "Vaulting Vampires."

Teacher:	The questions can only be about what might be in the *article*.
Student 1:	Can they really fly?
Teacher:	Yes.
Student 4:	Are there other kinds of bats?
Teacher:	Yes, and the article tells how many other kinds.
Student 1:	How many?
Teacher:	About 900.
Student 2:	Where do they live?
Teacher:	Good question—about a whole category of information—but the category of their habitat isn't included in this article. Now you've narrowed it down a lot. I'm going to use the abbreviation "NI" to mean that there's no information about the vampire bat's habitat in this particular article.
Student 5:	Do all bats vault?
Teacher:	Good question! No, vampire bats are the only ones that launch themselves into flight from the ground.
Student 6:	How do the others do it?
Teacher:	They begin their flight by dropping down from a tree branch.
Student 7:	How high does the branch have to be?
Teacher:	Ha. Good detail question, but this article is about the vampire bats, remember.
Student 8:	Do vampire bats really drink blood?
Teacher:	Yes, they certainly do; you might be surprised at how much.
Student 8:	How much do they drink?
Teacher:	They try to drink half their body weight every night.
Student 9:	How much is that?
Teacher:	Well, they're kind of small. The article doesn't say how small, but I'll guess about 3 pounds. So that would be a pound and a half of blood a night.
Student 4:	What kinds of animals do they drink blood from?
Teacher:	The article mentions cows, as one of their prey.
Student 1:	How do they hang onto the cow's neck?
Teacher:	The article doesn't mention the bats drinking from the cow's *neck*.
Student 4:	Where, then?
Teacher:	It mentions the bats drinking from the cow's *foot*.
Student 7:	Don't they get kicked?
Teacher:	They would, if they couldn't move around pretty well on the ground.
Student 9:	Can they?
Teacher:	Can they what?
Student 9:	Can they move around pretty well on the ground?

Figure 4.7 *(continued)*

Teacher: Yes, in fact they're the only kind of bat that can maneuver as easily on the ground as in the air.
You've asked some good questions: Take out a sheet of paper now, and number from 1 to 7. You can use the information you got from your questions [on the chalkboard].

Information recorded on the chalkboard:

Vaulting Vampire Bats

Why do they vault?	To launch into flight
Really fly?	Yes
Habitat?	NI
Other kinds?	Yes, about 900
Do all vault into flight?	No—drop from branches to launch
Drink blood?	Yes—1/2 body wt.—about 1/1/2 lbs.? a night
Prey?	Ex: cows
How?	Not from the neck—from the foot
Move on the ground	Yes—only kind of bat that can

The teacher then gives this oral quiz:

1. Do vampire bats really drink blood? (yes)
2. How much blood do vampire bats drink? (half their weight per night)
3. How do vampire bats launch themselves into flight? (by jumping)
4. How many types of bat are there? (about 900)
5. What is the major muscle the vampire bat uses to launch itself from the ground? (the pectorals)
6. How have scientists studied the vampire bat's vaulting? (using a high-speed camera)
7. What is unusual about the vampire bat's ability to move on the ground? (it is the only bat that can move as well on the ground as in the air)

Teacher: How many of you think you answered at least 5 questions correctly?
[Most students raise their hands]
Which ones did you have trouble with?
Students: Numbers 5 and 6.
Teacher: Okay, copy these two questions on the back of the article, to read for tomorrow:
[Teacher writes questions 5 and 6 on the chalkboard]

Figure 4.7 *(continued)*

- Ironically, the only time this highly analytical activity may go stale is when the teacher becomes overwhelmed by the rapid pace with which material is covered. The teacher may react by slowing down the lesson and, in the process, taking the winds of enthusiasm out of the students' sails; therefore, be prepared to cover a good deal of information quickly and with considerable depth.

Cooperative Question-Only

To increase student participation in Question-Only, try this Cooperative Question-Only (CCO) variation. Children's knowledge construction has been significantly enhanced by guided cooperative questioning (King & Rosenshine, 1993). There also is logical and anecdotal support for certain types of *Facilitative Role Play* in learning situations (cf. Manzo, Manzo, & Albee, 2004), the other ingredient in CQO.

Preparation

- Prepare the quiz questions as for the regular Question-Only lesson and decide whether to use the title of the selection or a reworded version.
- Form heterogeneous groups of four students each. Assign roles such as recorder, speaker, clarifier, and encourager.

Step 1. Introduce Question-Only in the same way as previously, but tell students that they will have three minutes, in groups, to write as many questions as they can to get the information in the reading assignment.

Step 2. Call on each group in turn to ask one question, continuing around the groups until all questions have been asked. A group may only ask a question if they have it written down. If all their questions have been asked, they must "pass." Tell students that they will have one more opportunity to compose follow-up questions, so each group's writer may want to make some notes of ideas for these.

Step 3. Give groups an additional two minutes to form and write as many follow-up questions as they can.

Step 4. Call on groups in turn to ask their follow-up questions, again accepting only questions they have written, and continuing until all have been asked.

Step 5. Give the quiz.

Step 6. Have students read silently to check their answers to the quiz questions and look especially for the question or questions they did not ask.

Anticipation-Reaction Guide

The Anticipation-Reaction Guide (A-R Guide) (Duffelmeyer, 1994; Duffelmeyer, Baum, & Merkley, 1987) is a teacher prepared worksheet that students use to respond to carefully crafted statements before reading and again after reading.[*] The primary purpose of an A-R Guide is to alert students to currently held ideas and attitudes, which may differ, from those presented in the reading selection. Thus, the effectiveness of the method depends on the teacher's knowledge of the particular group of students' background of information and experience. So this method not only teaches anticipation, but it requires some from the teacher, who may need to revise his or her perceptions following this very interactive lesson.

[*]Excerpt from "Maximizing reader-text confrontation with an Extended Anticipation Guide" by F. Duffelmeyer, D. Baum, and D. Merkley, *Journal of Reading, 31.* © 1997 by the International Reading Association.

Steps in the Anticipation-Reaction Guide

Preparation. Review the reading selection to identify information or attitudes that may differ from those currently held by students. Write statements to which students will be asked to agree or disagree with before they read, and again after they have read. Use these statements to create an A-R Guide worksheet such as the one shown in Figure 4.8.

Step 1. Distribute the A-R Guide to students, with directions to write their responses (agree or disagree) to each statement.

Name: _____   Date: _____

Hour: _____

Directions: Read each statement below, and in the left-hand column labeled "Before Reading," write an "A" if you Agree with the statement, or a "D" if you Disagree. After you have read today's assignment, you will be asked to reread each statement, and respond in the right-hand column labeled "After Reading."

Before   After
Reading   Reading

_____   1. Vampire bats really drink blood.   _____

_____   2. Bats can jump very long distances,   _____
                but they don't really fly.

_____   3. Bats are unable to move easily   _____
                on the ground.

_____   4. Studying animal behavior would be   _____
                an interesting and challenging
                occupation.

Figure 4.8   Example of an Anticipation-Reaction Guide for "Vaulting Vampires."

Step 2. Students then are directed to read, and, after reading, respond again to the A-R Guide statements.

Step 3. Begin discussion by asking whether anyone changed their responses to any of the A-R Guide statements after they had read the selection.

Notes on Writing Statements for an Anticipation-Reaction Guide

- A-R Guide statements are based on your knowledge of your students. The statements must be written so that students have a reasonable basis for agreeing or disagreeing with each statement.

- Statements can be based on facts which can be verified in the selection; however, consider attitude-type questions as well, since these are more likely to elicit experience-based schema connections with the new information.

- As a variation on the basic A-R Guide, have students write the page number on which they found confirmation for or a difference from their prereading belief, or have students select one of the statements as the topic for a brief postreading essay.

- A-R Guides can be used with fiction as well as nonfiction.

Using Cooperative Structures with the Anticipation-Reaction Guide

Anticipation-Reaction Guides can be used as the content for a number of cooperative structures, after students have individually completed the postreading step.

- Use "Find Someone Who" to structure peer comparisons. Give students a short time limit (about 30 seconds) to move around the classroom until they have found a classmate who agrees with their response to the first item. These pairs of students should initial each other's worksheet for that item. Call on a few students to explain their reason for agreeing or disagreeing with that statement. Continue in the same way with each of the statements.

- In "home groups" of four students, appoint these roles: Writer, Pro, Con, and Arbitrator. Distribute an extra copy of the A-R Guide to the Writer in each group. Give students a time limit of about two minutes, in which Pro attempts to convince the Arbitrator that one should agree with the statement, Con attempts to convince him or her to disagree with it, and the Arbitrator attempts to document "proof" for one position or the other or to state a compromise position. The Writer records the Arbitrator's conclusion. Continue in the same way with each statement, *shifting roles* one person to the right each time.

Prereading Graphic Organizer

The Prereading Graphic Organizer described in Chapter 3 is another way to help students activate schema prior to reading. See Figure 4.9 for a prereading Graphic Organizer a teacher might help students create for the "Vaulting Vampires" article.

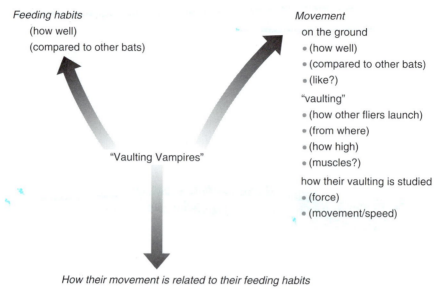

Feeding habits
   (how well)
   (compared to other bats)

Movement
   on the ground
     • (how well)
     • (compared to other bats)
     • (like?)
   "vaulting"
     • (how other fliers launch)
     • (from where)
     • (how high)
     • (muscles?)
   how their vaulting is studied
     • (force)
     • (movement/speed)

"Vaulting Vampires"

How their movement is related to their feeding habits
(why "vaulting" is important)

Figure 4.9 Prereading Graphic Organizer for "Vaulting Vampires."

Reading-Before-Reading

The idea of *reading-before-reading* started as a popular movement in the 1950s with *Cliffs Notes*, or book digests. In due course, comic-book versions of the classics became familiar underground means of making the classics more palatable and giving readers a head start on reading unabridged versions. Not surprisingly, these mechanisms received a black eye when many students began using them as substitutes for, rather than supplements to, the original books. Open resentment against digests and abridged materials was reversed shortly thereafter, however, when a theory called *Advance Ideational Organizers* restored credibility to the intuitive value of some type of reading-before-reading.

Advance Organizers

In a now classic study, learning theorist David Ausubel (1960) had college students read a "prestructured" statement (500 words), or Advance Ideational Organizer, before reading a longer (2,500-word) selection in science. The Advance Ideational Organizers clearly and significantly improved student comprehension. Subsequent studies by several other researchers produced results that sometimes replicated this finding but at other times did not. The difference in these outcomes was traced primarily to the quality of the prereading passage. Ideally, an organizer had to impart a sense of structure but not be too abstract. There also were some findings to indicate that short literal accounts, usually used by the "control group" treatment, had a positive effect on comprehension as well.

    Accordingly, we recommend combining abstract and literal organizers. One way to do this is to paste an *abstract organizer* to the inside front cover of a book and a *literal organizer to* the inside back cover. Then encourage students to use both organizers as a prereading strategy and as frequently as they wish while reading the larger work. Figures 4.10 and 4.11 provide examples of each type of organizer for *The Old Man and the Sea.*

Notes on Advance Organizers: Teacher and Peer Supported

Apart from this more literary use, abstract and literal Advance Organizers also can be made and provided for difficult content textbook chapters. Students can be encouraged to read these and ask questions about them before reading the text and reminded to refer to them as needed during reading.

The Old Man and the Sea tells of an extremely poor old fisherman, SANTIAGO, who fishes along in the Gulf stream, and of MANOLIN, a boy who had fished with him until the man's luck had gone bad. The boy still had deep respect and affection for him, however, and brought him food and other things he needed.

The book opens in September as the old man decides to go far out into the Gulf Stream to take advantage of a strong current. He rowed out in the dark, lowered his bait, and began drifting with the current. When the sun was high, the bait was taken by a large fish. The man tried to pull the fish up, but it was too big and simply began towing the boat out to sea. All afternoon and all night the fish pulled the SKIFF, with the old man resolutely straining against the line to ensure that the fish did not break it.

About sunrise, the fish gave a lurch, which cut the man's hand. Santiago ate strips of raw tuna to keep up his strength, and he wished the boy were with him. Finally, the fish surfaced, and it was the biggest fish the man had ever seen—longer than the skiff. But it dove again and continued towing the boat the rest of that day and into the night.

The old man was suffering greatly by now but was still resolved to bring the fish in. He tried to sleep, still standing and holding the line, but woke as the fish again surfaced and pulled him down into the boat, where the line cut into his hands and his back. He got up and fought the fish to try and tire it. As the sun rose on the old man's third day at sea, the fish began to circle, and the man was able to pull in some line. After several hours, feeling dizzy and faint, the old man pulled the fish near enough to the boat to harpoon it. Since the fish was larger than the boat, the man lashed it alongside, rigged the sail, and, exhausted, set sail for home.

But it was too good to last. Sharks had caught the scent. From sunset until after midnight, the old man fought the sharks, first with his harpoon, then his knife, and finally a club. But it was no use—they had cleaned his fish, and he was beaten.

He arrived in the harbor and managed to reach his shack before he collapsed with fatigue. In the morning, the fishermen were astounded at the 19-foot skeleton lashed to the boat. When the old man awakened, the boy heard of his ordeal and tried to console him.

Figure 4.10 *The Old Man and the Sea*: Literal organizer.

> *The Old Man and the Sea* tells of a fisherman's struggle with the elements while trying to hook and kill a huge fish, only to have it eaten by sharks.
>
> The story is a testament to humankind's unconquerable spirit—to our ability to achieve dignity in the face of defeat. Humans are shown to be noble because of their willingness to struggle and preserve against the hardships in life. The man tells the fish, "I will show him what a man can do and what a man endures" [p. 66] and "Man is not made for defeat . . . a man can be destroyed, but not defeated" [p. 103].
>
> The book also shows the author's view of humankind in relation to the physical universe. The fisherman refers to both the stars and the fish as "my brother." This is taken to mean that we should respect and love our natural environment even as we strive to carve existence out of it and conquer it.

Figure 4.11 *The Old Man and the Sea:* Abstract organizer.

In a later chapter (Chapter 8), a reading-writing exchange method called REAP is described that teaches students how to prepare an annotation-like facsimile of prereading help for one another, and through the Internet, on a system-wide basis.

Reiterative Reading

Reiterative Reading (Crafton, 1983) is based on the proposition that students can independently acquire relevant background information through the reading process itself.° In one study of this approach, it was found that simply having eleventh graders read two different articles on the same topic "dramatically improved students' comprehension of the second article and the cognitive level at which they processed it" (Crafton, 1983, p. 587). The researcher went on to say that her study supports three assertions: (1) "the common view of reading as a natural knowledge-generating activity"; (2) the belief that "text on an unfamiliar topic can serve as cognitive preparation for the next"; and (3) the observation that experimental subjects who read two forms of the same material "were more *active* during the reading process and personalized information to a greater degree than did subjects who read unrelated materials" (1983, p. 590). Interpreting this finding into practice has been demanding, since it has not been easy to find two selections on the same topic at the same level, let alone different reading levels. However, that is being changed by the Internet.

Notes on Reading before Reading: Supported in Terms of Efficacy, Logistics, and Online Resources

Search engine products are fun to track down before or after a conventional reading assignment, and can be counted on to provide preparation for reading, and practice and elaboration following from it. An anecdotal validation of this idea is illus-

---

°Excerpt from "Learning from reading: What happens when students generate their own background information?" by L. K. Crafton, *Journal of Reading, 26.* © 1983 by the International Reading Association.

The first author once taught world geography to a difficult, sometimes unruly class of low-achieving ninth graders. We had a new, slick, black-covered text that was impossible in almost every way: the print was small, information was dense, and sentence structures were complex beyond reason. In short order, we found 20 copies of a very old geography text in the districtís attic. We read both books, alternating the order according to fancy more than to any deep analysis of textual value. In addition to the obvious benefits of seeing most things twice, and in different words, we often were challenged and amused by diverse perspectives, sometimes-contrary information, and changing and often bewildering facts. For example, we puzzled over how a then-obscure and backward Iran could have been the seat of the great Persian Empire. There were many times when we wished we had a third or fourth text to explain some things in even greater detail. We never could quite get a conceptual fix, for example, on how maps were made in times past when map makers could not get up high enough to see.

Figure 4.12 Anecdotal evidence for reading-before-reading.

trated in Figure 4.12. The Internet provides round-the-clock, Sunday-through-Saturday (24/7), content-rich electronic text on most any topic. As more and more classrooms have at least one online computer in them, using the Internet for reading-before-reading is not only much easier than ever before but also becomes one more simple, quick, and valuable way to effectively use the technology in which so many resources have been invested. Without very much preparation time, teachers can now use their online computers (or assign students) to quickly search the Internet for material relating to their core topics for the day. In your own classroom, you will probably find some favorite portals or search engines that can be called up regularly to help with this in the search for reiterative reading materials. Many have found *www.encarta.com* (Microsoft's online encyclopedia) and *www.google.com* (a popular search engine) to be especially helpful in this process. A monthly look at public and cable television offerings provides numerous opportunities for nontextual reiteration or previewing and reviewing of films, documentaries, and programs on topics in literature, science, social studies, and the arts.

▶ AFTER WORDS

This chapter presented some important ideas regarding frontloading or helping the reader to optimize prior knowledge and experience before reading. It advocated teaching students to do this for themselves through several inquiry-based methods and by reiterative methods, such as parallel texts and computer- and multimedia-based supplementary assistance. The next chapter discusses several means of keeping interest and attention focused during independent silent reading and viewing. See if you can find a method for guiding silent reading that suits your subject area and teaching style.

CHAPTER 5

THROUGH—METHODS FOR GUIDING SILENT READING

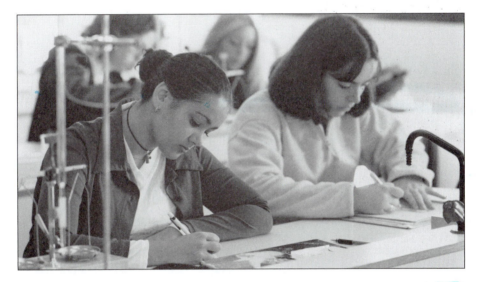

Reading taste and ability are always tethered to past experience. But reading itself is one way of increasing this capital fund of past experience.
—Edgar Dale

▶ FORE WORDS

Of the three phases of reading instruction recently referred to as Into, Through, and Beyond, it is the Through—or guiding students while they read silently—that we know least about. This chapter presents the techniques, prompts, and methods now available for doing so. These range from methods that attempt to teach readers to internalize reading strategies that resemble antiviral software, to various types of reading guides, to restructuring or reformatting the text to readers' needs. No doubt you will find some method(s) that suit your subject specialty and personal style of teaching. For a professional experience in constructive-creative thinking, read ahead as a pioneering partner in the quest to better understand the act of silent reading-thinking and what educators might do to further facilitate it.

▶ FORE WORDS
▶ TEACHING STUDENTS TO THINK WHILE THEY READ
▶ METACOGNITIVE MONITORING AND FIX-UP STRATEGIES
▶ ENTERING STRATEGY INSTRUCTION THROUGH A SIDE DOOR
▶ PROMPTING AND SELF-PROMPTING ANTIVIRAL TECHNIQUES FOR FOSTERING COMPREHENSION MONITORING AND FIXING
▶ READING GUIDES (PLUS)
▶ BUILT-IN (COACHES' GAME) GUIDES TO SILENT READING
▶ TEXT STRUCTURE: HISTORICAL FOOTNOTE AND LUKEWARM SUPPORT
▶ AFTER WORDS

▶ TEACHING STUDENTS TO THINK WHILE THEY READ

The aim of effective content area literacy instruction is not so much to teach *reading skills* as to build the habit of *skilled reading*. This is not just a play on words. It is the difference between teaching how to use a skill and teaching understanding of a skill's purpose and role, and then offering the supportive scaffolding needed as a learner struggles through the arduous process of trying it out, adjusting, and mastering it as an intentional, and flexibly applied strategy.

In one study, students were interviewed about their understanding of this metacognitive process:

> When Susan, a seventh grade student, was asked to talk about what she had been thinking as she read a portion of text she responded: "Oh, I don't usually think while I read." Clearly, Susan misunderstands the purpose of reading and can not be successful." (Lipson & Wixson, 1997, p. 581)

For Susan, like many students, all reading is the same. She makes no distinction between the easy, passive process of independent-free instructional-level reading and the challenging, active process of assigned and perhaps assisted instructional-level *study reading*. Helping students to make that distinction is the point of the silent reading stage of the three-phase framework for content area literacy. Even with the best Into, or prereading instruction, at some point each student goes to the printed page alone. At this point, they need something to keep the process going and something to keep it focused and productive.

In silent reading, students must sustain attention, draw on prior knowledge and experiences, translate new information into familiar terms, identify main ideas and relevant details, monitor comprehension, use fix-up strategies when they are not understanding, and, most of all, sustain these efforts in a sea of other competing interests, needs, and distractions. There seems to be a rather complex art required to do this well, which could be called "reading savvy." Reading savvy can be hard to teach—teachers cannot physically follow students on their silent incursion into print. They can, however, provide support in the form of various types of reminders to read strategically; that is, actively and purposefully.

▶ METACOGNITIVE MONITORING AND FIX-UP STRATEGIES

Most people, adults and students alike, do more reading of independent-level than instructional-level materials. Therefore, passive reading becomes a strongly imbedded habit, and we tend to enter any reading act as if it were easy, independent-level reading. Metacognitive monitoring is like a little red flag that goes up, saying, "Uh oh, I don't think I'm getting this," and prompting the realization that something more needs to be done here. The "something more" is the active thinking strategies for continuous comprehension monitoring, and the fix-up strategies that act like an antiviral software program that automatically steps in as the need is detected. See Figure 5.1 for a review of the active reading strategies introduced in Chapter 3.

Strategies for Monitoring Silent Reading Comprehension

   "How would I say that in my own words?"

   "What's the main point here, and why is it important?"

   "What would be an example of this?"

   "How could I cluster the ideas I've read about so far?"

   "Am I finding answers to the purpose question(s) yet?"

   "Where is this going next?"

   "Here's an unfamiliar word—what does it seem to mean in the way it's used here?"

   "Can I picture in my mind what is going on here?"

   "Does this make sense, according to my own experience?"

   "Can I trust this author's accuracy/authority/objectivity?"

Fix-Up Strategies

   "Let me reread that last part, more slowly this time."

   "Let me think about that for a minute."

   "Is there a certain word here that is throwing off my understanding?"

   "Let me read ahead a little, to see if getting the larger picture helps."

Figure 5.1   Review of metacognitive monitoring and fix-up strategies.

▶ ENTERING STRATEGY INSTRUCTION THROUGH A SIDE DOOR

Engagement or focused attention was introduced in Chapter 3 as the single most essential element in teaching/learning. Textbook material, almost by definition, tends not to be immediately engaging. One alternative means of securing engagement long enough to provide effective strategy instruction is to *supplement* curriculum materials with interesting, real-world reading selections (such as from newspapers, magazines, and Internet resources) that help students link abstract concepts and distant facts to the context of their own lives, concerns, and conversations. These supplemental reading selections are more likely to get and keep students' attention. More important, they usually are written at a level closer to students' independent level, thereby increasing the likelihood that *more* students will have a *more successful* reading-based experience. With more content of this type, more students are more likely to pay focused attention to the teacher's modeling of active reading/thinking strategies with content of this type. More students are also more likely to participate in trying out these strategies for accurately reconstructing an author's meaning and creatively constructing personal reactions to and applications of the new information, ideas, and/or attitudes.

The short newspaper article reprinted in Figure 5.2 was used by an area social studies teacher to introduce a unit on the internment of Japanese citizens early in World War II. It is used for the examples in this chapter.

▶ PROMPTING AND SELF-PROMPTING ANTIVIRAL TECHNIQUES FOR FOSTERING COMPREHENSION MONITORING AND FIXING

Pausing

Impulsivity, distractibility and unreflective reading are comprehension killers. The wise teacher is always on the lookout for ways to counter such unseen and unheard student needs. One way to counter these is with activated and self-monitored reading. To build such active, near study-type reading habits simply require students to pause periodically while reading and use some type of self-monitoring strategy. This approach can be highly structured at first, fading to greater student independence as they gain familiarity with the technique. Three variations on this quintessential *prompting* technique are described below, other possible variations are limited only by the individual teacher's imagination and creativity.

Strategic Guiding Questions

The wise teacher always looks for the easiest way to meet student needs. Several research findings suggest that students can easily be taught to ask strategic questions while they read (Baker & Brown, 1984; Meichenbaum & Asarnow, 1979;

(1) Early in 1942, amid the mood of rage and fear following the Japanese attack on Pearl Harbor, the U.S. government interned more than 110,000 Japanese-Americans living on the West Coast. The great majority of those internees, some of whom were held as long as three years, were native-born American citizens.

(2) At the time, few outside the Japanese-American community had the courage or foresight to protest what many now consider one of the most shameful acts in American history. But one man who did speak out was a Presbyterian minister named William Lindsay Young, then president of Park College in Parkville, just across the river from Kansas City.

(3) Young happened to be in Los Angeles when the internment process began. And he was horrified to see thousands of people herded into a holding area behind barbed wire at the Santa Anita Racetrack. He was even more distressed to discover that the internees, rounded up solely because of their ancestry, were being shipped off to hastily constructed internment camps in Wyoming, Colorado, Arizona, Arkansas, and other states. What he was witnessing, Young thought, was frighteningly similar to fascist doctrines espoused by the nations that the United States was fighting in the name of democracy. "If we are not careful," Young said in a speech to Park students, "we are apt to do damage to those very values which we are now anxious to preserve."

(4) When he learned of a government program allowing some interned students to attend colleges away from the West Coast, he immediately set out to recruit as many as possible. "Would you like to study at Park College? All expenses provided?" he wired to prospective students. In all, he enrolled nine second-generation Japanese-Americans, or Nisei, each of whom had to be cleared by six federal agencies, including the FBI, before they could travel to Missouri.

(5) But the federal bureaucracy was not the only obstacle facing Young. His recruitment policy aroused an anti-Japanese furor in the community around his school. The response grew so intense that local newspapers called the debate the "Battle of Parkville." And into that heated atmosphere came the nine Nisei students, already traumatized by the sudden upheaval in their lives.

Dreadful Journey

(6) One of them was Masaye Nagao Nakamura, who came from East Los Angeles. She left for Park College as her family was being sent to an internment camp in Wyoming. She began her college journey

Figure 5.2 Sample supplementary reading selection: "Embracing the Persecuted: Park College Kept Japanese-Americans out of Detention Camps during War," by Joe Popper.

Source: Kansas City Star, Saturday, February 20, 1999. Metropolitan Edition, page A1. Reprinted by permission of The *Kansas City Star.*

in an Army truck. "I sat on my suitcase in the back of that open truck surrounded by three soldiers," she said. "I was going to Union Station in Los Angeles, but I felt like I was going to the guillotine." After boarding the eastbound train, she was denied a seat and forced to crouch on her suitcase in the front of the passenger car among the baggage. "You could hear a pin drop when I got on," she said. "And then, behind me, all I could hear were whispers of 'Jap, Jap'." After the conductor disdainfully snatched her ticket, he leaned down and spit in her face. "I was so shocked, I couldn't raise my arm to wipe it off," she said. "I felt his spit running down my face. I wanted a hole to open up so that I could drop through and vanish."

(7) For two days she sat alone and terrified. She did not move. She did not eat. She did not go to the lavatory. Arriving in Kansas City, though, she was encouraged by Young's warm greeting. "The students and faculty of Park College all welcome you," he said. But then he added a warning. "You must be careful when you leave the campus," he said. "Some people in Parkville have threatened to lynch any Japanese-American student they catch."

A Hostile Town

(8) Young had good reason to be wary. The mood in Parkville, already hostile to the Park College Nisei program, was further fueled by the Mayor, Herbert Dyer. "If the FBI is so sure that these Japs are loyal citizens, why didn't it let them remain on the West Coast instead of sending them to a concentration camp?" Dyer told the *Kansas City Star*. It was outrageous, he added, that the government chose to "dump them" on Parkville. He threatened legal action. Anonymous calls to the college threatened worse.

(9) Dyer was supported by the City Council and by local chapters of the American War Mothers and the American Legion. Two Parkville merchants, saying they spoke for many others, announced they would not serve any Japanese-Americans.

(10) But Young stood his ground with calm dignity. The opponents of his plan, he told the *Kansas City Times,* "apparently have lost sight of exactly those things for which this nation is now fighting." He sent a letter to 1,000 residents of Parkville and adjacent towns pointing out the irrational and racist nature of the internment policy. "What about the thousands and thousands of young men and women already in our colleges whose parents were born in Germany?" he wrote, "Is war hysteria making us lose sight of our democratic ideals?"

(11) In September 1942, at the college's opening convocation, Young addressed the student body. "The Axis (powers) are not the only danger to our liberties as we know them," he said. "There are

Figure 5.2 *(continued)*

those who, because of their intolerance and bigotry, would deny to a fellow American citizen his just rights. . . . What makes this spurious loyalty so dangerous is that it is cloaked in the garb of patriotism."

(12) His words inspired students and alumni alike. "I am proud of you and proud to be a graduate of your school," wrote one alumnus living in Chicago who had read a news report about the Battle of Parkville. "What a stirring speech it was," said Harold Smith, who graduated from Park College in 1944. He later became the college's librarian, and his research was a major source for this article.

(13) "Dr. Young had already met with us in small groups," Smith said. "He told us that when the Nisei students arrived, they would need our help. And we were all receptive to the idea. I don't think there was a doubt in our minds that what was being done to the Japanese-Americans was wrong." Echoing Young, a headline in the campus newspaper proclaimed: "Welcome Nisei."

(14) But off campus, Nisei students faced threats of violence several times that year. When Nagao Nakamura walked into Parkville alone, she was harassed by a crowd that followed her through the streets. Two other Japanese-American students were chased by a mob brandishing a rope. In response, the Park College students formed groups to escort and protect their classmates. Gradually, the mood in Parkville changed. Within two years, the town, having seen reality rather than stereotypes, had embraced the Nisei students.

"You took me in"

(15) After she graduated in 1945, Nakamura returned to California, where she became an honored teacher in the Oakland school system. Retired now, she often speaks to student groups about the internment period. "It was a long time ago, but it is vivid to me yet," she said recently. "And I will remember Dr. Young's courage until the day I die."

(16) One of her classmates, William Yamamoto, became a physician and a professor at the University of Pennsylvania Medical School. In 1991, he sent a large contribution to his alma mater along with a letter. "I was declared a stranger in my own land, and you took me in . . . from behind the barbed wire that surrounded the Santa Anita Racetrack," he wrote. "At Park, many befriended me and became my campus family. All the modest success I have enjoyed, and the fullness of my days since, I owe them, the people who made up Park College."

Figure 5.2 (*continued*)

Singer & Dolan, 1980). For example, there are three simple questions that have been shown to guide students in story-type reading:

1. What is the main idea?
2. What are the important details?
3. How do the characters feel, and why? (Meichenbaum & Asarnow, 1979)

The first two questions also can be used to guide the reading of expository textbook material. This simple approach can be structured initially by having students pause after a few minutes of silent reading and asking them these questions aloud. Depending on the content of the reading material, other strategic questions might be added, such as

1. Where is the author going next with this?
2. How might you organize the information you have read so far?

Students reading the newspaper article in Figure 5.2, for example, might be given about a minute and a half to read silently. This should put most students up to about the first subheading, "Dreadful Journey," a good point to pause and model strategic questioning: "Turn your papers over for a few minutes. A good first *strategic question* to ask about anything we read is, 'so far, what seems to be the main idea here?' Can someone say, in your own words, the main idea of what you have just read?" Students should be encouraged to respond with more than single words or facts and helped to shape a main-idea statement that the teacher records on the chalkboard or overhead. They should not look back to the article while trying to recall the information. The main-idea statement might eventually read something like this:

> The president of a college near Kansas City saved Japanese-Americans from being put in detention camps during World War II by offering them a special full scholarship and helping them qualify for a government program that would allow them to attend a college away from the West Coast.

As students suggest ideas for the main-idea statement, the teacher should ask, when necessary, "Is that part of the main idea, or is it a supporting detail?" Ideas that students decide are supporting details can be written to the side of the main idea statement. After the main idea has been formulated, the teacher might permit students to look back at the article for a very brief, timed, period—in this case about 10 seconds—in order to locate the more important details to add to the list that has been started on the board or overhead. The list for the opening section of this article would reasonably include the following:

1. This happened in 1942, after the Japanese attack on Pearl Harbor.
2. Over 110,000 Japanese Americans on the West Coast were interned.
3. The camps were in Wyoming, Colorado, Arizona, Arkansas, and other states.
4. Few other Americans protested.
5. The college president's name was Lindsay Young.

6. The college was Park College.

7. Young enrolled nine Japanese-American students.

8. To qualify for the special program, prospective students had to be cleared by six federal agencies.

9. The local community was against the students coming to the college.

Then the teacher might say, "Now, before you turn your papers back over, where do you think the author is going next with this?" Likely responses might include the following:

1. Real stories about some of the Japanese-Americans who went to Park College

2. How the town responded

3. How the college responded

4. What eventually happened to those students

Finally, the teacher might ask whether the five-W's of a newspaper article (*who, what, where, when, and why*) have all been answered. In this example, the teacher might emphasize what they have learned so far about the "why" question: Why did President Young put himself and his college on the line to go against public opinion? Students may recall reading in the introductory section that Young had been in Los Angeles when the internment began and seen people herded into one of the camps. But this doesn't fully explain why he decided to personally undertake to do something to change what was happening. Urged to consider this question further, students will be more likely to take note of the message of Young's speech, which is quoted later in the article.

After several lessons in which silent reading questioning has been modeled in this way, the teacher can begin to fade out the supportive scaffolding. For example,

1. Direct students to make small pencil checks on the reading assignment at given points. When they come to these points during reading, they are instructed to write out a clarifying question of any type and briefly record their answers.

2. Direct students to select three points on their own, while reading, and to stop and write clarifying questions and answers.

Each of these variations also is ideal for structuring student collaboration in pairs or groups of four.

About-Point

About-Point (Martin, Lorton, Blanc, & Evans, 1977) is an easy-to-remember formula for strategic reading. Students are taught to pause at logical points, such as at the ends of paragraphs or text subsections, and complete the following two phrases:

This section is about _____; and the point is _____.

The simple About-Point prompt reminds readers to translate the basic meaning of the section and then to ratchet up their comprehension to the interpretive level in order to state the author's probable intent for presenting just this information in just this way. Teach students the basic About-Point format using several short sample paragraphs. Explain that an *about* statement should be more than a single key word but less than a summary. A *point* statement should include the most important elements of the section. It is useful to demonstrate a few examples and talk through the process of expressing good *about* and *point* statements. Here are two possible About-Point statements from the newspaper article in Figure 5.2:

Paragraph 6

This paragraph is about one Japanese-American woman's trip from Los Angeles to Park College, and the point is that, having done nothing wrong, she was treated worse than a criminal.

Paragraph 11

This paragraph is about President Young's opening of school speech in September 1942, and the point is that bigotry is a greater threat to freedom than an invading army.

Once students have the idea, the simple format can be used in at least two ways.

1. For a structured beginning, have students put pencil checks beside particular paragraphs in a reading assignment. Direct students to write About-Point statements on these paragraphs.

2. For decreased structure (fading), instruct students to select their own paragraphs for About-Point statements.

Like the Guiding Questions technique described earlier, About-Point statement writing is an ideal activity for student pairs or cooperative groups.

Comprehension Monitoring System

The *Comprehension Monitoring System* was field tested with high school teachers in home economics, social studies, and biology (Smith & Dauer, 1984). In this self-prompting technique, teachers create a coding system for students to use to record their *cognitive* and *affective* responses while they read. The code will vary according to the characteristics of the material and the curriculum objectives. A coding system for social studies reading might be as follows:

B	=	Bored
C	=	Confused
D	=	Disagree
MI	=	Main idea
Q	=	I've got a question about this (Note the question, because you are not likely to remember it.)

A coding system for science reading might be:

C = Clear
D = Difficult
I° = Important
S! = Surprising

Not every paragraph needs to be marked, but initially, the teacher should assign a minimum number of paragraphs for marked responses. If students are permitted to write in their reading materials, they can note the letter codes in the margins while reading. If not, 2-inch-wide strips of paper (or sticky-notes) can be distributed to insert in the assigned pages for recording responses.

Sample markings for the article in Figure 5.2 might be as follows:

Coding System:

ID = Important detail(s)
R = Reminds me of something
MI = Main idea
S = Surprising

Paragraph 1	ID	(Sets out the basic newspaper requirements for "who, what, when, where")
Paragraph 2	R	(Reminds me of how people don't have the courage not to laugh at crude ethnic jokes)
Paragraph 3	MI	(We were doing the same thing the Nazis were doing to the Jews)
Paragraph 4	S	(Nine students doesn't sound like many, when 110,000 were arrested)
Paragraph 6	R	(Reminds me of movies I've seen about the time when blacks were supposed to sit in the back of the bus)
Paragraph 11	MI	(This seems to be the main point so far—that we were doing the same thing to these people that the Nazis were doing to the Jewish people.)
Paragraphs 15 & 16	ID	(Important to note what became of these two people.)

After students have been introduced to the basic technique of coding their responses to sections of a reading selection, students can work together in cooperative groups to compare their responses, and/or to create their own custom and self-prompting coding systems.

K-W-L Plus

Know-Want to Know-Learned, Plus (Carr & Ogle, 1987; Ogle, 1989, 1996) is a popular method for implementing the full three-step framework for active reading-based instruction. It is placed in this chapter on *silent* reading because of the unique way in which it facilitates this step of the framework. In K-W-L Plus, students are guided in generating their own anticipation-based reading guides to prompt active silent reading. This helps them to read with greater awareness of what they already knew, what they need to know, and *with the charge to carefully process and restate what they learn from reading.*

Steps in K-W-L Plus

Step 1. *Know.* Students make or are given a three-column worksheet with the columns headed *Know, Want to Know,* and *Learned.* The teacher leads a brainstorming session on what students already know about the topic. As ideas are given, students write them in the *Know* column of their individual worksheets. (See Figure 5.3 for an example of a worksheet that might be generated with a class for the reading selection on World War II Japanese-Americans that we have been using for illustrations in this chapter.)

Step 2. *Want to Know.* The teacher then moves the discussion toward aspects of the topic that students do not know. Students are helped to state these as questions and write them in the *Want to Know* column of their worksheets.

Step 3. *Learned.* As they read, students locate and write their answers to the *Want to Know* questions in the *Learned* column of their worksheets. New questions and answers can be added as they read and find information they did not anticipate. The teacher leads a discussion of what was learned in answer to the original questions and what additional information was learned.

Step 4. *Plus.* The teacher leads students in categorizing the information that was learned and in creating a graphic organizer to represent this. (See Figure 5.7 for a graphic organizer format that might be used for this article in the *Plus* step.)

Notes on K-W-L Plus

The early version of a K-W-L that did not contain the *Plus* step of creating a graphic organizer did not fare well in research comparisons with other methods. The *Plus* version, however, has been uniformly supported; it is a tail that now wags the dog. Teachers especially like this method because it is well structured

Know	Want to Know	Learned
Japanese-Americans were imprisoned during World War II even if they were American citizens	How did a *college* keep them out of the camps?	
Some of the prison camps were in California	How many people did the college help in this way?	
There was a lot of negative public opinion about German-Americans at that time, too	Was everyone in favor of this, or did some object?	
	How did those who were helped feel about it?	

Figure 5.3 Example of a K-W-L Plus worksheet for the article "Embracing the Persecuted: Park College Kept Japanese-Americans out of Detention Camps during War."

and students respond well to reading to answer questions that they themselves have raised.

The next section describes several types of guides that teachers can prepare for students to complete while they read. Teachers' understanding of the specific active reading processes they are attempting to encourage significantly enhances this fairly traditional form of reading assistance.

▶ READING GUIDES (PLUS)

When coaches shout commands during an athletic event, they are attempting to remind the athletes of what has been taught and practiced in a less competitive situation. Such coaching from the sidelines would be distracting were it not for extensive prior training. The same general principle applies to written aids to text comprehension or adjunct aids. These aids work best when students have been explicitly taught to use them and are given ample opportunity for guided practice. This specific Plus practice step has been missing from prior uses and research evaluations of the effectiveness of reading/study guides. Its addition is analogous to a "Coach's game"—one played in basketball where the coach comes on the court during a scrimmage for the purpose of prompting strategic moves and critiquing live play.

The idea of *reading guides*, according to Herber (1978), their chief contemporary proponent, is to simplify difficult material. Reading guides are designed to teach reading processes as well as to improve information acquisition. Students are expected to refer to the guide while reading, then back to the text, then back again to the guide (Manzo & Garber, 1995). Often, a guide amounts to an attempt to create a written-out version of the *three-step framework*—or *into*, *through*, and *beyond*—described in Chapter 3. It can contain vocabulary and concept preparation as well as guiding purpose questions. Ideally, reading guides serve as supplementary aids in the independent processing of heavily content-dense text. The most significant advantages of guides, in our judgment, are that (1) they permit the teacher to focus student attention on key information and concepts in a passage, and (2) they require *every* student to attempt some type of active and reflective response to at least the points referenced.

Despite mixed findings on guides, (we suspect for lack of the Plus step noted above) their popularity is evident in the numerous versions that have been developed. Some of the most traditionally used formats for reading guides and some recent innovations are described next.

Three-Level Guides

A *Three-Level Guide* is designed to lead students from basic to more advanced levels of comprehension of textual material (Herber, 1978). Part 1 of a Three-Level Guide contains questions at a literal level: What did the author say? Part 2 contains interpretive questions: What did the author mean? Part 3 contains application questions: How can you *use* this information?

Guidelines for Constructing a Three-Level Guide

1. The Guide should alert readers to the information and ideas needed to respond to the questions or activities in Part 3. Therefore, begin by deciding which Part 3 *applications* are appropriate to the material. This will help you to select which details and inferences to focus on in writing Parts 1 and 2 of the Guide.

2. Next, determine what information is needed to make these applications and whether it is explicitly stated in the text or must be inferred. Information that must be inferred to make the level-three applications is used to develop questions for Part 2 of the Guide.

3. Finally, write questions for Part 1 of the Guide, directing attention to the necessary literal information in the reading selection (Vacca & Vacca, 1986).

Typically, students are directed to answer the literal questions in Part 1 while they are reading and to complete the interpretive and applied questions in Parts 2 and 3 after reading. A useful variation is to have students complete Part 1 independently and then form cooperative learning groups to complete Parts 2 and 3. See Figure 5.4 for a simple example of a Three-Level Guide for the short article used for examples in this chapter.

Directions: Answer questions in Part 1 as you read. After you have read, go on to Parts 2 and 3.

Part 1: Literal Understanding

1. Who did the U.S. government imprison early in 1942?
2. Who protested this, and why?
3. What did Young do to help some of the Japanese-Americans?
4. What was the response of the townspeople?
5. What was the response of the college students?

Part 2: Interpretive Understanding

6. Why did Parkville merchants refuse to serve the Japanese students?
7. What did President Young mean by his statement that "what makes this spurious loyalty so dangerous is that it is cloaked in the garb of patriotism"?

Part 3: Applying your Understanding

8. You are a Park College student in September 1942. You have just listened to President Young's opening of school address. Write a one-page script in which you and a friend argue about the President's decision to offer scholarships for Japanese-American students to attend your college.

Figure 5.4 Example of a Three-Level Guide.

Process Guides

Typical teacher-made reading guides focus on product or fact identification and basic inference. A *Process Guide* is intended to teach the active thinking strategies needed to construct meaning by combining text with experiences and learnings beyond the text. There is no single format for a Process Guide. The sections and questions need to be matched to students' background information and experience related to the topic and difficulty of the particular reading selection. The best way to learn how to construct one is simply to try it. Following are a few suggestions for preparing this type of guide. See an example of a simple Process Guide in Figure 5.5.

Guidelines for Constructing a Process Guide

1. Pick an important selection. Process Guides are time-consuming to construct, so you will want to spend your efforts on something of conceptual value.

2. Read the selection carefully, putting yourself in the students' place: "If I didn't know much about this, what would I need to do?"

3. Construct questions that engage the reader in setting a purpose for reading and in reading actively to reconstruct information and examples.

4. Construct questions that engage students in considering possible interpretations, implications, and applications of new information.

---

1. Read paragraphs 1 and 2. Record as briefly as possible the answers to the 5-W questions:

   Who?
   Did What?
   Where?
   When?
   Why?

2. Imagine that you are a Japanese-American in 1942, and have just learned that your family is to be sent to one of the internment camps. Write five words to describe your feeling.

3. As you read the remainder of the article, jot down your thoughts about these two general questions:

   a. What was the mood of the country that permitted this to happen?

   b. What can one person do to change the minds of an entire campus, or town, or country?

4. What more current examples of discrimination came to mind as you read or reflected on this article?

5. What parallel did Young see between internment of Japanese-Americans and the events leading to U.S. involvement in World War II?

Figure 5.5 Example of a Process Guide.

The next type of reading guide breaks with traditional routines. It departs from the usual expectation that students need to begin at the beginning and read every word through to the end.

Advanced Guidance Activity

An Advanced Guidance Activity, originally called "Reading Guide-O-Rama," (Cunningham & Shablak, 1975) is a set of written prompts to students as to the best way to read and think about a given reading selection. It is a form of *cognitive apprenticeship teaching* at the workbench of the traditional content textbook. In constructing such Advanced Guidance prompts, teachers should determine which concepts and information they expect students to learn from the reading. Next, teachers should consider how they, as an expert reader, would approach the selection. An effective Advanced Guidance Activity points out unimportant as well as important information and forewarns readers about what to expect in class discussion. It may direct students to read portions of the material out of sequence, such as reading a final summary first. It may instruct students to read a short section of the assignment and then summarize the key points or facts. As such, an Advanced Guidance Activity uniquely serves as a scaffolded or structured way to help students increase their craft or "reading savvy," as it is modeled and represented through the teacher's creation of the activity and then practiced by the students in the completion of the activity. See Figure 5.6 for an example of an Advanced Guidance Activity.

Directions: Reading for information is not like reading a story. In study reading, it often helps to skip around, looking for a "hook," instead of reading straight through from beginning to end. Use this Guide to show you how this process works. Notice that you are to read paragraphs 6 and 7 first.

Read paragraphs 6 & 7	Write some brief predictions about *why* this might be happening. Briefly describe something this reminds you of.
Read paragraphs 1–5	Stop and put in your own words why the young woman in paragraphs 6 and 7 was traveling to Park College.
Read paragraphs 15 & 16	How does the story turn out?
Read paragraphs 8, 9, & 14	Briefly describe ways in which the Japanese-Americans faced "a hostile town" in 1942.
Read paragraphs 10–13	Briefly describe the strategies used by President Young to encourage acceptance of the new students.

Figure 5.6 Example of an Advanced Guidance Activity.

Graphic Organizers as Reading Guides

As described in Chapter 3, graphic organizers provide another way to guide silent reading comprehension. These may be partially constructed through a whole-class brainstorming session as described in Chapter 3, or included as part of a structured reading guide. See Figure 5.7 for an example of a Graphic Organizer used to guide fact acquisition, interpretation, and application.

Additional Notes on Creating and Using Reading Guides

Composing any type of reading guide can be a powerful *heuristic,* or insightful experience for teachers. It draws one into a careful analysis of the textual material and a deeper understanding of the processes that students must call on to read in a given discipline. It also can get the creative juices flowing; teachers often are surprised at the insights into students' reading and learning needs that can be gained in this way. Furthermore, former limitations related to producing, revising, and storing guides have been virtually eliminated with the increasing availability of computers with word processing, graphics, and storage capabilities.

The next and final section of this chapter describes a way to give students ready access to another kind of guidance for silent reading. These are guides that are built directly into the reading selection and optimistically are a harbinger of things to come.

▶ BUILT-IN (COACHES' GAME) GUIDES TO SILENT READING

A logical alternative to teacher-prepared reading guides is a textbook with *built-in* guides. These are coaches' games. Again, as in one played in basketball where the coach comes on the court during a scrimmage for the purpose of prompting strategic moves and critiquing live play. These are electronic or are hard copy versions of what now is called *hypertext.* These internal guides have been called *imbedded aids* (Manzo, 1977) and *marginal gloss* (Otto & Hayes, 1982). Both typically include help with word analysis, word meaning, basic comprehension, remembering, and even thinking beyond the text to greater depth, elaboration, and critical analysis. Aids can lend timely prompts and assistance at all levels of reading and to readers at all levels.

The idea of built-in guides is that they are woven into the actual textbook itself during the production stage. A. V. Manzo produced the "imbedded aids" prototype shown in Figure 5.8 for a chapter from a high school world history text, *Man's Unfinished Journey* (Perry, 1971), as part of a research and development project more than two decades ago.

Despite the high marks that the built-in guides received from teachers and students, it was a hard sell to publishers at the time to assume the additional costs involved in producing such books on a regular basis. However, books with imbedded guides are beginning to appear quite regularly now (note how similar

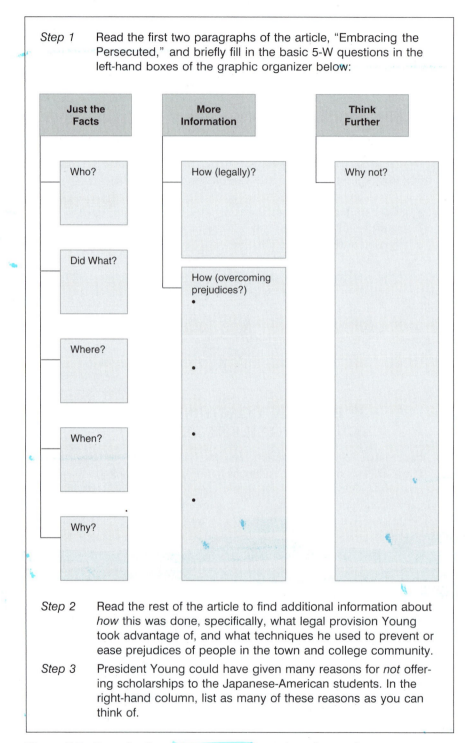

Step 1   Read the first two paragraphs of the article, "Embracing the Persecuted," and briefly fill in the basic 5-W questions in the left-hand boxes of the graphic organizer below:

Just the Facts

Who?

Did What?

Where?

When?

Why?

More Information

How (legally)?

How (overcoming prejudices?)
•

•

•

•

Think Further

Why not?

Step 2   Read the rest of the article to find additional information about *how* this was done, specifically, what legal provision Young took advantage of, and what techniques he used to prevent or ease prejudices of people in the town and college community.

Step 3   President Young could have given many reasons for *not* offering scholarships to the Japanese-American students. In the right-hand column, list as many of these reasons as you can think of.

Figure 5.7   Example of a graphic organizer for guiding silent reading.

many news magazines and new high school textbooks are to Figure 5.8). This may be due to significant advancements in desktop publishing software and to our growing collective exposure to hypertext. This latter software innovation, which permits additional explanatory detail by clicking on an idea or sentence, seems to be increasing our expectation that such things can be achieved in some measure with conventional print. Relatedly, a field of study called *text technology* (Jonassen, 1982, 1985a, 1985b) first grew rapidly, but now seems to have stalled out. It seems that the delight that many of us are having in accessing vast amounts of information through intelligent search engines on the Internet has at least temporarily distracted efforts to help people better read, process, and critique the content of this 24/7 medium. It is our hope (and anticipation) that improvements will be made in this area soon. Such progress in support of cross-disciplinary comprehension seems assured with the growth in popularity of e-textbooks increasing, along with other student-friendly computer tools like the Tablet PC, which are starting to be integrated into literacy research studies and classroom practices (c.f. Murry, C. 2003, Thomas, 1998, Thomas, King, & Cetinguc, 2004).

▶ TEXT STRUCTURE: HISTORICAL FOOTNOTE AND LUKEWARM SUPPORT

Some reading educators contend that teaching students to identify text structure and expository patterns is an effective way to improve silent reading comprehension (see Figure 5.9 for a listing of the twelve most common paragraph patterns). This belief is based on a frequent research finding that there is a strong *correlation* between reading comprehension and knowledge of text structure (Meyer, 1975). This was thought to imply that teaching poorer readers about the structure of writing would result in improved comprehension. Those who interpret the research in this way propose that recognizing the form and format of a communication are integral parts of understanding its message. However, a study of the views of reading specialists had them ranking text structure instruction fourteenth of twenty-three teaching practices for comprehension improvement (Gee & Rakow, 1987), a very lukewarm level of support. Recent research in related fields, such as grammar and phonics, has concluded that elaborate instruction in classification schemes is not only unnecessary but potentially counterproductive. The reason is simple: In human learning, applications generally are acquired *before* rules. In short, when students are taught to read for meaning, their awareness of text structure increases, but when they are taught to identify text structures, comprehension growth does not follow to the same extent. That said, there is a difference between belabored isolated instruction in any system of rules and incidental teaching of these rules as they apply in a given meaningful context. Teachers of beginning reading should know phonics rules; all teachers should know something of English grammar; and all teachers should know something of the basic paragraph patterns that lend both variety and predictability to written language.

The lines of the main text are numbered to provide easy reference.

Notes in the right-hand columns summarize the information in the text. Use them to preview and review the main ideas presented.

The notes in the right-hand columns should be read both before and after you read the main list.

Liberal Responses to Industrialization

1   Liberalism emerged in England in the seventeenth century during the struggle
2   between parliament and kings. By the end of the eighteenth century British
3   liberalism stood for religious toleration, parliamentary government and the rule
4   of law, freedom of the press, natural right of individual to life liberty, and
5   property, and the right to resist arbitrary and tyrannical government seeking
6   to interfere with these natural rights. □British liberals had confidence in human
7   intelligence, supported science, and attacked superstition.□ In the seventeenth
8   and eighteenth centuries British liberals had been mainly concerned with
9   protecting the rights of the individual against the dangers of oppressive
10 government. But by the beginning of the nineteenth century a new set of
12 problems had arisen in Britain. These problems focused around the plight of
13 the working class and the impact of industrialization.

(a) T or F: Liberalism first appeared in England in the 19th century. *(page IV, line 1)*

(b) *Against what dangers were the liberals first concerned with protecting the rights of individuals? (page IV, lines 9-10)*

14 *British liberals advocate a laissez-faire policy.* British liberals had come to
15 support the doctrine of *laissez-faire* (leh-sey fair')—the notion that
16 government should not interfere with business. They based their thinking
17 largely on the writings of Adam Smith. In The Wealth of Nations, published in
18 1776, Smith stated the following: (1) Only when a man is free to operate his
19 business in the way that brings him the most profit can a healthy economy be
20 achieved. (2) By acting in his ownself-interest— by trying to achieve a
21 maximum of profit— the businessman benefits the entire community, for his
22 actions lead to increased production, distribution, and consumption of goods.
23 (3) The government harms business and the community when it interferes with
24 the activities of businessmen. (4) The duty of government is to maintain peace
25 and order within the community and not to meddle with the affairs of business.

17th century liberalism in England stood for
(a) religious freedom,
(b) freedom of the press,
(c) natural rights of individuals,
(d) the right to resist oppressive government,
(e) confidence in human intelligence.

By the 19th century, liberal concerns turned to the plight of the working class.

British liberals supported a laissez-faire form of government.

This idea was developed by Adam Smith in The Wealth of Nations written in 1776.

Vocabulary:
Terms likely to be unfamiliar are defined in the left-hand columns. The number in parentheses points out the text line where the term is first used.

(1) Liberalism
tolerance of the views of others and the willingness to challenge traditions and established institutions.

(5) Tyrannical
cruel and unjust use of governmental power

TO RESEARCH
Check in an encyclopedia or economics book for further information on Adam Smith's theories.

These □ symbols mark the beginning and ending of phrases or statements that are especially well written.

To Research
are suggestions for independent research on related topics.

Figure 5.8 Sample textbook passage with imbedded aids.

Occasionally a word is missing from the text. You should be able to fill in the missing word with little trouble. Failure to do so may mean your attention is drifting. The correct word can be found in the lower left-hand margin.

Reader Helper Notes: stimulate you to think beyond the basic information covered in the text. Notes at the end of the chapter (pages 32-34) provide additional information and suggest possible answers to the questions raised.

To Think About: are questions which have no correct answer. They are intended to raise broad generalizations or to provide topics for discussion and debate.

Mini Notes: provide enrichment information related to the text.

Was the liberal ideas of laissez faire limited to business? See reader helper Note 78.

TO THINK ABOUT
What possible connections can you see between the growth of liberal thinking in Britain and the success of the American Revolution?

MINI NOTE
Adam Smith and T. R. Malthus each had the ability to see things differently from others around them. This is called divergent thinking.

(3) laissez faire

---

1 The supporters of _____ insisted that poverty is natural. Since some are
2 meant to be wealthy and some poor, government can do nothing about
3 poverty. Any governmental reforms might hurt business and make things
4 worse.

5 *Malthus blames poverty on overpopulation.* Another English thinker who
6 helped shape the liberal attitude in the early days of the industrial revolution
7 was T. A. Malthus. In his Essay on the Principle of Population (1789), Malthus
8 declared that the population always increases faster than the food supply. As a
9 result mankind is always threatened with starvation. The real cause of poverty,
10 according to Malthus, is overpopulation. Until the poor learn to keep down the
11 size of their families, poverty will never be eliminated, Malthus concludes:

13 When the wages of labor are hardly sufficient to maintain two children, a man
14 marries and has five or six. He, of course, finds himself miserably distressed. . .
15 He accuses the greed of the rich. . .He accuses the [prejudiced] and unjust
16 institutions of society. . . The last person that he would think of accusing is
17 himself.

18 Malthus had also argued that as the population increases, the supply of
19 workers becomes greater than the demand. This leads to unemployment, low
20 wages and perpetual poverty. For Malthus lowering the birth rate was the only
21 effective way to combat poverty.
22 In effect Malthus was saying that, since the misery of the worker is his own
23 doing, no law passed by the state can eliminate poverty. Factory owners were
24 delighted with Malthus' view. It soothed their consciences to be told that they
25 were not responsible for the suffering of workers.

26 *Democratic liberals propose reform legislation.* The problems of the
27 working class persisted. Convinced that a laissez-faire policy was not
28 acceptable, a growing number of liberals in England and elsewhere urged the
29 government to introduce reforms to aid the working man. They wanted
30 legislation that would improve conditions of work in the factory, allow the
31 growth of labor unions, eliminate property requirements for voting, and
32 increase educational opportunities for the poor. Whereas the older liberals

---

Another idea popular with British liberals came from T. R. Malthus in Essay on the Principle of Population (1798).

Malthus said excessive population growth was the real cause of poverty, not greedy business practices.

Figure 5.8 (*continued*)

123

1. Introductory
2. Definition
3. Transitional
4. Illustrative
5. Summary
6. Main ideas supported by details or examples
7. Chronological order
8. Comparison/contrast
9. Cause and effect
10. Problem/solution
11. Descriptive
12. Narrative

Figure 5.9 Paragraph patterns.

▶ AFTER WORDS

Several options for guiding silent reading were presented in this chapter. To help yourself to decide on the one or two that you might use in your own teaching, go back, right now, and select one or two that you will try using as you read the next chapter. Chapter 6 focuses on options for making the most of the postreading—or Through—phase of learning from text.

BEYOND—METHODS FOR POSTREADING SCHEMA BUILDING

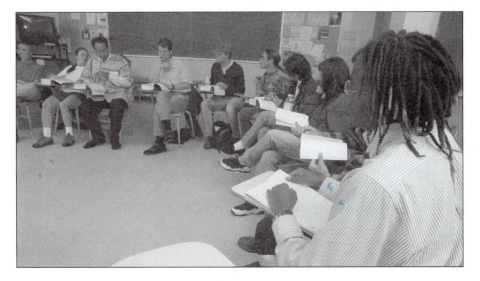

*Great discoveries and improvements invariably
involve the cooperation of many minds.*

—Alexander Graham Bell

▶ FORE WORDS

Successful silent reading sets the stage for reflective verifying, clarifying, exploring, and elaborating the information and ideas encountered in print. Teachers can help students develop active postreading habits in a variety of ways. Traditional class "discussion" is probably the most familiar way, but orchestrating a "good" discussion—one with high participation and that rises above factual recitation—is an arduously acquired skill. Discussion, by nature, is an unpredictable and sometimes unwieldy event. It depends on the group's willingness to pursue unplanned avenues of thought and the leader's accompanying ability to bring those avenues together toward some meaningful hub of conclusions and insights. This chapter begins with an analysis of discussion and then lays out a variety of whole class and small group methods that can help both students and teachers to increase their competence and grace in this artful and elusive form of interacting, reflecting and transforming.

- ▶ FORE WORDS
- ▶ CLASS DISCUSSION: WHAT IT IS AND HOW TO GET THERE
- ▶ TEACHER-DIRECTED RECITATION FOR CHECKING COMPREHENSION
- ▶ PEER RECITATION FOR INCREASED STUDENT INVOLVEMENT
- ▶ BRIDGING TO REFLECTIVE DISCUSSION AND APPLICATIONS
- ▶ FULL CIRCLE TO DISCUSSION
- ▶ AFTER WORDS

▶ CLASS DISCUSSION: WHAT IT IS AND HOW TO GET THERE

In postreading, prior knowledge is combined with recently encountered information and transformed into usable new knowledge and opened thoughts that are likely to have the process continue in students' minds and in class. The postreading, or beyond, step of most three-phase content-area literacy lessons is the point at which teachers help students to (1) check basic comprehension, (2) develop concepts, (3) connect new ideas with existing schema, and/or (4) identify misconceptions to restructure existing schema. The most familiar means of doing this is through teacher-directed class discussion. You can probably recall class discussions that helped you to see an idea more clearly or caused you to look at something in a different way or perhaps even transformed your entire outlook on a topic. There is little done in school that is quite as "mind moving" as a good discussion, but there also is little that can be quite as numbing as a really dull one. Good, revelationary discussions are always going to be few and far between. Think how few you have heard on television or even on radio discussion programs. This is because conducting a memorable discussion is more like leading an improvisational music group than it is like conducting an orchestra that has great music on a stand. Of course, even improvisation only *appears* to be unplanned. Much unseen work has gone into "jamming." Keeping this in mind, let's take a closer look at some of the elements of an effective teacher-led class discussion. In this analysis, it becomes evident that teacher-directed discussion is more a culminating achievement than an inspirational moment.

Analysis of a Memorable Class Discussion

In a memorable class discussion, the teacher takes and releases control through several classical moves that are rooted in cognitive and social psychology—that is, in the way the mind works in learning and the way people feel while they are learning and thinking out loud. Here is a quick summary of this byplay.

- The teacher usually begins by asking questions to determine whether students have basic comprehension of the topic.

- The teacher maintains a low-risk environment by rephrasing questions that students cannot answer and through skillful handling of students' incorrect responses.

- The teacher uses various strategies to ensure that most students are engaged and following the discussion most of the time.

- Once it appears that most students have a basic understanding of the information, the teacher's questions become less literal and more conjectural. It is the degree to which these questions are compelling and evocative that moves the interaction to the next levels.

- At some point, the lines of communication shift from the pattern of teacher asks/student answers to a much looser pattern resembling informal conversations. Students interact with each other as well as with the teacher.

- Different points of view are welcomed, but there is a soft press to keep them relevant.

- Responses are longer and more elaborate than in recitation.

- The teacher encourages students to explore different avenues of thought but again tries to ensure that the discussion does not wander too far astray of intended educational objectives.

- As conflicting perspectives emerge, a dynamic tension is created within as well as among individuals.

- Discussants, including the teacher, are expected to be willing to change their minds or be transformed in response to points made.

- Passions are allowed to find expression, but incivility is not permitted.

Good class discussion tends to externalizes the thinking strategies that characterize the internal conversations of effective learners of a given subject area. Students hear and find themselves trying out new ways of questioning and commenting that they ideally will internalize and independently employ (Calfee, Dunlop, & Wat, 1994; Tharp & Gallimore, 1989). This is more likely to happen in classrooms where there is rapport among students and between student and teacher. And to be realistic, just one constitutionally–grouchy or conflicting–agenda student can be disquieting and disruptive . . . which is one of the reasons why teachers shy away from this format.

Clearly, leading a "common" class discussion is a worthy goal but an uncommonly difficult one to achieve. Consider now some of the guidelines and methods for providing quality discussion and a developmental plan for achieving greater mastery of these as a teacher.

A Developmental Plan for Fruitful Class Discussion

Following is a sequence of guidelines for emphasis and practice as you plan and implement postreading instruction.

- Begin on safe ground with conventional recitation-based approaches. Students have all done this before and will recognize the drill.

- When you anticipate that students will *not* need a great deal of review of literal meaning after reading, use teacher-directed recitation, taking these opportunities to practice pacing, questioning techniques, and tactful handling of incorrect responses.

- When you expect a greater need for basic understanding, heighten the impact of recitation-based activities by implementing them through cooperative structures in which more students are more actively involved more of the time.

- Use writing based methods to engage students in reflective thinking, building schema connections, and self-evaluation.

- Use cooperative structures to engage students in activities that raise higher-order comprehension and build students' confidence in offering and accepting constructive criticism.

- Teach students explicit listening strategies, including the subtle nonverbal signals that indicate listening involvement (Barton, 1995).

- Use teacher-directed class discussion sparingly at first, selecting topics and crafting questions that are likely to engage student interest and lead to lively interactions.

- Use known and tested methods and strategies designed to teach students *how* to engage in "instructional conversation" type discussion.

- Alter the class discussion routine occasionally, using the guidelines for a Socratic Seminar (described later in this chapter).

▶ TEACHER-DIRECTED RECITATION FOR CHECKING COMPREHENSION

Traditional teacher-directed recitation, or old-fashioned drill, has gone from being overvalued and overused to being undervalued and occasionally derided. Some educators believe that postreading drill should not be thought of as teaching at all but simply as another form of testing (Durkin, 1978–1979). We respectfully disagree. Simple literal-level questioning following reading is a reasonable way to reinforce and model several essential elements of effective reading, most particularly

- The need to quickly check basic comprehension of what has just been read, and

- The specific *kinds* of recitation questions that are useful for a given type of material.

Haven (1999) describes the importance of postreading recitation even as it applies to reading fiction:

> The heart of student learning comes after the story is over and they have a chance to review and assess why the story was structured as it was and how the story achieved

its effect. Before real analytical work can begin, however, it is important to cement each student's experience and version of the story in his head. Once they take full ownership of their images and interpretation of the story, evaluation and dissection of the story and of the associated writing techniques will be easier and more beneficial. (p. 12)

With nonfiction, there is even less room for variance in basic comprehension. After reading a nonfiction selection, it is not "each reader's experience and version of the story" that must be fixed in mind, but the basic facts and information the author has presented. This does not exclude challenges to material presented, but it does presuppose a certain amount of clarity of understanding of what has been presented.

Guidelines and Formats for Teacher-Directed Recitation

Recitation, as defined here, consists of three general types of literal level questions: *recognition, recall,* and *translation*. Recognition questions require *finding* information; recall questions require *remembering* information; and translation questions require *paraphrasing,* or putting the new information into one's own words. When it is used as a postreading comprehension check, it typically is not an end unto itself but a bridge to further, less fact-based explorations, reflections and applications of the new information.

There are several variations on the basic teacher-led recitation routine. Here are a few reminders for conducting this segment of postreading in the most effective way:

1. *Help students to differentiate recitation from discussion* by telling them that the object of the recitation is to check and encourage their basic understanding.

2. *Keep it short*. About ten to twelve minutes is a good rule of thumb for most classes.

3. *Keep it moving*. The point is to review the facts, not to overly elaborate on them.

4. *Don't forget "wait time."* Students need to process the question and formulate a response; yet, the typical "wait time" is one second or less (Rowe, 1974, 1986). Try counting to five after asking a fact question, and to ten after a translation question.

5. *Watch who you call on.* Try to call on all students as equally as possible.

6. *Avoid using recitation as punishment*. Rather than calling on students who clearly are unprepared or not attending, try calling on them to answer a question you're fairly sure they can answer. This will have the effect of pulling them in rather than pushing them out.

7. *Try versions of "Every Pupil Responds."* For example, ask yes/no questions to which, at a given signal, all students respond with thumbs up or thumbs down.

8. *Don't forget verification-level recitation.* Ask students to find and point to the place in the text, which answers the question raised. Try using a timer; students like to race the clock.

9. *Don't forget translation (including vocabulary).* Read aloud a short section, phrase, or key term, and ask the class to put it in their own words.

10. *Try open-ended recitation.* Following reading, call on a student to tell any *one* thing he or she remembers from what was read. Continue to call on students to offer information, in any sequence, but without repeating any item previously stated. A variation is to permit the student who offers an item to call on another student to offer the next item. This begins to build the habit of intrastudent interaction that will support discussion.

Teachers can use these recitation routines to build their own expertise in two important elements of group leadership: modeling listening behaviors and handling incorrect responses to questions. Think of different ways to say, "Sorry, that is incorrect." You will need all of them. Compare them to suggestions you will find later in the chapter.

Modeling Active Listening

Listening to one another is an important ingredient in a lively discussion. Modeling effective listening to your students goes a long way toward teaching them to listen to one another. During recitation, teachers can model active listening and an appreciation for students' contributions in several ways (Barton, 1995):

- Moving toward students as they speak
- Occasionally writing students' ideas on the board in their own words
- Returning to something someone said earlier

Handling Incorrect Responses in Teacher-Led Recitation

Given that one of the primary purposes of recitation is to get things straight, it does present some nagging social problems in how to handle incorrect responses. There are several other research-based means of turning incorrect answers into positive learning experiences (Collins, 1987; Rakes & Smith, 1987). You probably use or would use several of these techniques intuitively, but it is good to have your intuition validated when teaching is your profession.

1. *Think again.* The most common reason for an incorrect answer is a too-hasty or impulsive response. If you think this might be the case, simply ask the student to think again. Keep in mind that those moments between the time that the question is asked and an answer is given may be the most instructionally valuable time in the school day. These are the moments in which the students are engaged in active thinking, self-talk, and rehearsal for their public response.

2. *Give a prompt*. When a student gives an incomplete answer or needs you to provide more structure, offer a small piece of information: e.g., "The person whose name we are looking for also died prematurely in a duel with Aaron Burr."

3. *Differential reinforcement*. Tell what part of the answer was correct: "You're right, bears are mammals. Do you recall whether mammals are warm blooded? Are human beings warm blooded?"

4. *Rephrase the question*. If no one seems to know the answer yet you think that they have learned the information, change the wording of the question: "When you go west, do you gain or lose time?" "Well is it earlier on the East coast or the West coast?"

5. *Provide help but make students accountable*. If a student gives two incorrect answers to the same question or if two students answer incorrectly, give the answer and tell them they will need to remember it. Return to the student(s) again before the period is over, and ask the same question, "Now, before you go, who can tell me again one state that borders New Hampshire?"

6. *Permit clues*. Ask fellow students to give clues, or ask the student who missed the question to call on a classmate to help by giving either a clue or the answer, "Charlie, who would you like to ask for help in naming the other three Great Lakes?"

7. *Incorrect "if" statements*. If you recognize why the answer was wrong, supply the question for which the answer would have been correct. For example, if you asked, "What is the capital of New Zealand?" and the student answered "Canberra," you could respond, "Canberra would be the answer if someone asked what the capital of Australia was. How about the capital of New Zealand?"

8. *Examples of possibilities*. If students are drawing a blank, translate the question into a multiple-choice format: "Who was the first European to see the Pacific Ocean? Balboa, Cortez, or Cabeza de Vaca?"

9. *Nonexamples or opposites*. When students have difficulty answering, tell them what the answer is not: ("Which country in South America has the oldest tradition of democracy?") "The answer is not Brazil or Chile."

Teacher-led recitation can raise attention and engagement and lay the foundation for further, more reflective discussion. This is no small accomplishment, since one of the biggest problems in any group discussion, at any level, is just getting everyone on the same page.

▶ PEER RECITATION FOR INCREASED STUDENT INVOLVEMENT

To get more students more actively involved in checking their basic understanding of what they have read, it helps to add a certain measure of peer involvement. Several means of structuring these interactions are described here. These methods tend to support the important element of quality teaching that has been previously referred to as "fading," or withdrawing ancillary assistance so that pupils may assume more responsibility for guiding their own learning.

Recitation Led by Home Groups

Have "home groups" of four students each take turns leading postreading recitation sessions, using structures such as the following:

- *Five-question format*: A team leads the class in filling out a "who-what-when-where-why-how" outline.

- *Peer questioning and The BUZZER!*: One team, designated as the answer team, tries to learn everything they can on a given section of text. The class then questions the answer team, and they try to answer as best as they can, with a short time limit for conferring when necessary. For fun a beeper or buzzer can be added. We observed one eighth-grade science teacher who gave the questioning group a child's toy that made a deep buzzing sound when a button was pushed. The class used it to signal a wrong answer. No one seemed disturbed by the competition, and several otherwise low-participating students were quite caught up in the "in-your-face" humor that young teens seem to enjoy.

- *Written questions*: Everyone prepares a few questions on the material. Going around the room in a certain order—up and down rows or across aisles—students read one of their questions that has not been asked and call on a volunteer to answer. The teacher might collect the questions and use some on a future test. This enhances students' motivation to write good questions and to listen carefully to the answers.

- *Have student groups work together to complete a graphic organizer*, on a large sheet of newsprint (or using a desktop computer, PDA, Tablet PC, or other such technology when available), based on the text material. This may be the final version of a graphic organizer generated as a prereading activity and filled in individually by students as they read. Groups may be encouraged to use design elements that represent the content, or other creative twists. When finished, each group presents and explains their graphic organizer to the class.

- *Numbered Heads Together* (Kagan, 1994°): Have students number off within groups. The teacher asks a recitation-type question, and each group briefly confers to agree upon their answer. The teacher calls a number at random (1–4), and the student with that number in each group stands. The teacher calls on one of these students to answer, then asks the other standing students if they agree, students sit and the next question is asked.

- *Find the Fiction* (Kagan, 1994°): Seated in groups of four, students work individually at first to write three statements: two true statements, based

°This material has been adapted from the following book with permission from Kagan Publishing & Professional Development: Kagan, Spencer. *Cooperative Learning*. San Clemente, CA: Resources for Teachers, 1994. 1(800) 933-2667; www.KaganOnline.com.

on the reading, and one fiction. Within groups, students take turns reading their three statements and challenging their partners to "Find the Fiction." Optionally, each group may be asked to select the best set of statements from their group to challenge the rest of the class.

- *Act it out* (Haven, 1999): Developed by Kendall Haven for fiction and some nonfiction, a team is assigned to act out the story for the class. One team member tells the story as the other three enact each story element, providing sound effects, actions, and setting elements. Following the group's presentation, discuss whether the enactment helped students picture scenes, events, and characters better, and whether it changed their first impressions of the story in any ways.

Jigsaw

One of the most well-known cooperative learning activities, the Jigsaw approach (Aaronson, Blaney, Sikes, Stevan, & Snapp, 1975; Aaronson, Stephan, Sikes, Blaney, & Snapp, 1978) is particularly useful for postreading recitation.

1. Divide a reading assignment into four numbered sections.

2. Set up four-student groups, have students number off, one to four, and distribute the four-part reading assignment. Each group has the entire reading assignment, with each student having a different one of the four sections.

3. Give time for students to read their section silently.

4. Have all students who read the first section of the reading (one student from each group) meet in one corner of the room, all who read the second section meet in another corner, third section in another, fourth in another. In these groups, they are to check their recall and understanding of what they read, so they will be prepared to share it with their home group members. Depending on the nature of the reading selection, you may wish to have a worksheet for students to complete in these section groups.

5. Students return to four-member home groups and share, in order, the important information from their sections of the reading.

This method is especially useful for bridging to further analyses or applications in another cooperative group structure, since students already are in groups and each group member is an expert on some portion of the material.

Paired Recitation

Another approach to structuring peer recitation is to have students work in pairs. Kendall Haven (1999) suggests three "verbal reprocessing activities" for fiction; these are reworded as follows to extend their usefulness to nonfiction material.

°This material has been adapted from the following book with permission from Kagan Publishing & Professional Development: Kagan, Spencer. *Cooperative Learning*. San Clemente, CA: Resources for Teachers, 1994. 1(800) 933-2667; www.KaganOnline.com.

- Allow each student about one minute to tell their partner about what went through their mind while they read the assignment. What were they thinking about and picturing while they read? Hold a general class discussion in which students share with the class what they told to their partner (or each student summarizes what his or her partner said). Show students that most of their comments fall into the following three categories:
  1. Evaluation of the reading assignment (form, content, style, etc.)
  2. Comparison of the information to other versions
  3. Relating the information to their own life and experience.

- Give students about a minute to draw a quick sketch of the main point of the reading assignment. The time limit means that students can't worry about the quality of their drawing. Have student pairs compare and choose one of their drawings to share with the class. In the general discussion, help students to categorize the text elements represented in their drawings.

- Have each student pair retell the information in the reading assignment. One student begins and tells for 30 seconds. The other student continues for the next 30 seconds, then the first takes over again, and so forth. The teacher times the tellings, and calls "Switch!" at 30-second intervals. If students can't remember what comes next, they are not excused from telling. Instead of moving forward, they repeat the last information told by their partner during their 30 seconds. If students are truly stuck, they can ask their partner for a hint. However, it is recommended that this be discouraged. Part of the value of this exercise is for each student to remember and claim his or her own version of the material.

▶ BRIDGING TO REFLECTIVE DISCUSSION AND APPLICATIONS

Examples of techniques and methods in this section are based on the short article, "Pollution of the Caesars," found in Figure 6.1. Take a moment now to read it, then study the original Guided Reading Procedure.

Guided Reading Procedure

The Guided Reading Procedure (GRP) (Manzo, 1975) is a highly structured method that begins with basic postreading recitation and concludes with a test designed to convince students that they can read with much greater comprehension than they may have thought themselves capable of. This can be a transformative experience with a considerable impact on metacognitive monitoring and an increased feeling of empowerment and self-regulation. It teaches students how to harness their own will and self-determination to instantly improve comprehension. In the course of the GRP lesson, students retrace and restructure a reading assignment in several ways, thus providing a great deal of support for understanding, organizing, and recalling the information. See Figure 6.2 for an example of a GRP lesson.

The ancient Romans, for all their knowledge, didn't know that lead was poisonous. They used it to preserve food and to halt the fermentation of wines. Lead glazes coated drinking vessels and cookware. Some historians have speculated that the brain-damaging effects of lead poisoning contributed to Rome's downfall. Rome's leaden legacy survives in pottery, pipes, and other artifacts. It also survives, a physicist has now found, in Greenland's ice sheet. Kevin Rosman of the Curtin University of Technology in Perth, Australia, has detected traces of lead in Greenland's ice, evidence of large-scale pollution of Earth's atmosphere two millennia ago. And some 70 percent of that pollution can be pinned to Roman mining in one region: Rio Tinto in southwestern Spain.

Rosman wanted to trace the source of the lead found in a Greenland ice core studied by two of his colleagues. The lead concentrations in that 3,300-yard ice core peaked between 150 B.C. and A.D. 50. This matched historical records of Roman mining activity at Rio Tinto. Lead pollution levels during the Roman era were about four times greater than natural background levels of lead but were still low by modern standards. Between the 1930s and 1970s, the lead concentration in the ice was 25 to 50 times higher than during Roman times, due in large part to leaded gasoline.

Rosman was able to trace the Greenland lead to the Spanish mine because of the unique ratios of lead isotopes in the Rio Tinto ore. Lead and its isotopes form over billions of years from the decay of uranium and thorium. The ratio of two isotopes in particular—of lead 206 to lead 207—generally increases in crustal rocks over time. (The numbers refer to the total of protons and neutrons in lead nuclei.)

Unlike lead in crustal rocks, lead at Rio Tinto was trapped in a vein of silver ore and was isolated from uranium and thorium. So Rio Tinto's lead still has the lower ratio of lead 206 to 207 that it had when it became trapped in the ore billions of years ago. When Rosman found this low ratio in pieces of the Greenland ice sample dating from 600 B.C. to A.D. 300, he consulted historical records to determine which mines were active during ancient times and compared lead isotope fingerprints taken from them in recent years to isotope ratios from the Greenland core. Rio Tinto captured much of the blame.

"Greenland is quite a way from Spain, so the lead that went into the atmosphere affected the entire Northern Hemisphere," Rosman says. He also notes that hard scientific facts show the history books were right. "It's a beautiful example of the application of science using sophisticated instruments to really understand the past."

Figure 6.1   Sample reading selection: "Pollution of the Caesars" (*Discover*, March 1998, 19:3).

Source: Jessica Gorman © 1998. Reprinted with permission of *Discover Magazine.*

Steps in the Guided Reading Procedure

1. Preparation. Select a reading assignment that is fairly short but information-rich. Prepare a short-answer test of ten to twenty items on the reading assignment. (As the lesson proceeds, make sure that the test items are given fair coverage.)

2. Purpose for reading. Give the topic of the reading assignment, a brief purpose for reading, and tell students to read to remember *everything they can* about the reading assignment. Tell students that as soon as they have finished reading, you will write everything they remember on the chalkboard (or overhead, whiteboard, or SmartBoard). Tell them that if they finish reading early, they should reread to identify the most important information in the selection.

3. Reading and recalling. Give students ten to fifteen minutes to complete their silent reading, and then ask them to tell anything they remember, without looking back at the reading selection. Record all information on the board in the order given. If students question the accuracy of anything that is offered, simply record the information, and place a question mark beside it.

4. Self-monitoring/self-correcting. Instruct students to go back to the reading selection to correct any inconsistencies that arose in their attempts to recollect and/or to add information previously overlooked. Record all changes and/or additions on the chalkboard or overhead.

5. Restructuring. Guide students in organizing the information from the board into outline form to be recorded in their notebooks, again without referring back to the reading selection. The outline can be as simple or elaborate as age and grade level permit. Use nonspecific questions, such as "What was discussed first?", "What was brought up next?", and "What seems to be the main idea?" Avoid overly specific and leading questions.

6. Teacher monitoring and correcting. If students appear to have overlooked any critical ideas or inappropriately equated them with other ideas, raise guiding questions about these points, such as "What do you suppose is the most important of these five points made by the author?" and "How does this information relate to what we studied last week?"

7. Evaluation. Give the test prepared in Step 1. A score of 70% to 80% should be required to pass the test.

8. Introspection. After the test, ask students whether they have learned anything about their own learning as a result of the GRP experience. *The point to be made is that accuracy in comprehension and recall can be greatly improved by an act of will.*

9. Optional study step. Several days later, give a second test on the same material. Allow students about fifteen minutes before the test to review material from their notes.

1. **Preparation**
   "Pollution of the Caesars" is used in a ninth-grade Physical Science class. Before the lesson, the teacher prepares the following test items:

   > What is the effect of lead poisoning? (brain damage)
   >
   > Why have historians thought that lead poisoning was one of the reasons for the downfall of the Roman Empire? (evidence of lead in pottery they ate and drank from)
   >
   > Where was the Roman lead mine? (Rio Tinto, Spain)
   >
   > Where did Rosman find evidence of pollution from the Roman lead mine? (in the ice in Greenland)
   >
   > How did the Roman lead get to the place where Rosman found it? (in the air, as pollution)
   >
   > How did Rosman know the lead he found in the ancient ice was from the Roman mine? (it had a different chemical structure from most lead)
   >
   > What two lead isotopes were compared to determine the type of lead Rosman found? (206 and 207)
   >
   > Which lead isotope is present in a higher proportion in most lead? (206)
   >
   > Why was the Roman lead different? (it had been trapped in a silver vein and not exposed to uranium and thorium)
   >
   > What was part of the cause of the lead pollution Rosman found in the ice dating from 1930–1970? (leaded gasoline)

2. **Purpose for Reading**
   A. "Read this article to find out how one scientist has used chemistry to find out about air pollution in ancient times."

   B. "Try to remember all that you can about this selection. You have ten minutes to read, and then I'll ask you to turn your papers over and tell me everything you remember, so I can write it on the chalkboard."

3. **Recitation and Recalling (Following Fifteen Minutes of Silent Reading)**

Teacher:	Who can tell me one thing you read about?
Student:	A scientist found lead from a Roman mine in the ice in Greenland.
Student:	It's called "Pollution of the Caesars."
Student:	The lead mining in Rome caused major pollution.
Student:	No, the lead mine was in Spain.

   [teacher records the information on the chalkboard or overhead, and places a question mark above the words "in Rome"]

Figure 6.2 Guided reading procedure: sample dialogue.

Student:	The Romans used lead in the dishes they ate from.
Student:	And drank from.
Student:	The lead from the Roman mine had different kinds of isotopes.
Student:	Not different ones, different amounts of them.

[teacher places a question mark above the words "different kinds"]

Student:	The lead he found was different because it came out of a vein of silver and didn't get exposed to the air.
Student:	It had different amounts of the isotopes 206 and 207.
Student:	They think lead makes you brain damaged.
Student:	They know it does.

[teacher places a question mark above the words "they think"]

[interaction continues; teacher records information on chalkboard, putting question marks beside any items that are challenged]

4. **Self-Monitoring/Self-Correcting (Sample Student Responses)**

Teacher:	You remembered a lot. Now turn your papers over and reread the article to see if we need to change or add anything to what we have on the board.
Student:	The mine was in Rio Tinto, Spain.
Student:	The lead had the same isotopes, but more of the 206 than 207.
Student:	Lead poisoning does cause brain damage, and more people than the Romans must have had it because the lead was in the air all the way to Greenland.
Student:	We said what made the lead different was it wasn't exposed to the air, but this says it wasn't exposed to uranium and thorium.

[interaction continues, with the teacher noting corrections and additions on the chalkboard]

5. **Restructuring**

Teacher:	Turn your papers face down again and let's organize our information into an outline. Take out a sheet of paper, and copy this down the way we reorganize it, so you'll have it for your notebooks. We have about ten minutes to get this all down, and then I have a short test for you. Now, what would be a good title?
Student:	It's called "Pollution of the Caesars." Maybe it should be called "Rosman Rats Out the Romans."
Teacher:	Okay, that will be easy to remember; now, what's the first thing the author talks about?
Student:	How they think lead poisoning made the Romans brain damaged.

Figure 6.2 *(continued)*

Teacher: Okay, the first topic will be "Lead poisoning in ancient Rome caused brain damage." Will that work?

Student: Then under that, they got it from their dishes.

Student: And it caused the downfall of the Empire.

[Teacher records the outline on the chalkboard:]

Rosman Rats Out the Romans
  I. Lead poisoning in ancient Rome caused brain damage
    A. Source
      1. dishes
      2. ?

[Teacher continues recording the outline for students to copy, leaving space where information or topics are missing]

6. **Teacher-Guided Correcting and Completing**

Teacher: Turn your papers face up now, and reread quickly for the information that we are still missing, and let's fill it in.

[Teacher completes outline on chalkboard from students' contributions]

7. **Evaluation**

Teacher: Put away the articles and your notes, now, and I will pass out the test.

[Students complete the test]

8. **Introspection**

Teacher: What did you learn from this lesson about how to "read smarter"?

Student: I remembered a lot more than the first time we did this, just by really trying to concentrate and remember.

Student: I still missed a lot the first time I read it, but then I knew what to look for the next time we got to look at it.

Student: Rereading and focusing really helps. I got 100% this time. I had only 40% the first time.

9. **Optional Study Step (one week later)**

Teacher: Today we're going to see how we are progressing in developing effective study habits. Take out your notes on *Rosman Rats Out the Romans,* and use the next five minutes to study them. Then I will put some questions on the board on that topic, and let's see how well you do. After our little quiz, we'll discuss how you studied and how to "study smarter."

Figure 6.2 *(continued)*

Notes on the Guided Reading Procedure

1. In a typical GRP lesson, students may say little or nothing on the first invitation to recall and recite what they have read. As teachers, we tend to have great difficulty with silence. If you can force yourself to wait silently for a few (seemingly interminable) seconds, the flow of language and thought will begin. The first few, hesitant student responses will spark other recollections, which will lead to other connections, suggested corrections, and associations. This spiraling effect tends to draw in even the most reticent students. See the sample dialogue in Figure 6.2 for examples of this.

2. When writing on the board, take the opportunity to model good notetaking. Write as quickly as you can, and use as many logical abbreviations as you can. If you write slowly and painstakingly, the lesson loses its focus: While you're writing, students are forgetting. Depending on the age and level of the class, consider selecting one or two reliable students to do the writing in the first part of the lesson.

Efficacy of the Guided Reading Procedure

The GRP has been studied by several researchers and has collected strong empirical validation (Ankney & McClurg, 1981; Bean & Pardi, 1979). Its effectiveness has been most clearly demonstrated at upper elementary and middle school levels with science and social studies material. It also has been shown to be an effective way to improve active listening (Cunningham, Moore, Cunningham, & Moore, 1983) and a particularly effective method for adolescents with learning disabilities (Alley & Deshler, 1980; Maring & Furman, 1985).

Note Cue

Note Cue (Manzo & Manzo, 1987, 1990b) is another highly structured method to scaffold students' participation in a focused class discussion. It helps to *get* discussion going, *keep* it going, and keep it *on target*. It builds the behavioral and social learnings that come from actually doing something. More specifically, it teaches students to *ask* questions and, more important, to confidently *comment* on the text as well as simply *answering* questions. It does this by relieving students of the complex burden of having to think about what to say and how to say it, leaving them only to think about *when* to say it.

Note Cue, as its name suggests, provides *cues* to students, in the form of written *notes*, that guide them through participation in a *model* discussion—model because it is prescripted by the teacher. Initially, almost the entire discussion is prescripted. Enactment of these *early* Note Cue discussions is a form of *strategic parroting* in which students are paradoxically expected to participate with relatively little thinking. The potential value of strategic parroting was discovered separately by two sets of researchers working with reluctant learners (Manzo & Legenza, 1975; Palincsar & Brown, 1984). You will be pleasantly surprised to see how this opportunity for class participation through simple parroting can provide a form of instructional scaffolding that can gradually be removed as students begin to internalize the many complex aspects of effective classroom discussion. As you read about Note Cue, notice its particular suitability for use with ELL students (English Language Learners) and others who may have underexposure to typical social and language conventions.

Steps in Note Cue Postreading Discussion

Preparation. Prepare a set of cue cards for discussion of the material. These should be prepared as follows:

a. Write several questions on 3 × 5-inch index cards (one question per card), based on information from the reading selection. Include questions that go beyond the facts, such as translation, interpretation, inference, evaluation, and application questions.

b. Write complete but brief answers to each question on separate cards (one answer per card). When writing answer cards, use complete sentences that include enough context to make it clear what question it answers (see sample below).

c. Write several comment cards (one comment per card)—relevant thoughts that might be sparked by the reading selection.

d. Label each card at the top as appropriate: Question, Answer, or Comment.

Sample Note Cue cards for postreading discussion.

Question	Answer	Comment
How did the lead from the Roman mine get to Greenland?	The lead from the Roman mine got to Greenland by getting into the air, as pollution.	I wonder what kind of brain damage lead poisoning causes.

Step 1. After students have read, the teacher places one or more of the prepared *prereading* cards on each student's desk. *A few students may be given blank cards.*

Step 2. Students are instructed to read the card(s) they have been given and think about *when* they should read it (them) during the discussion; *students with blank cards are instructed to try to think of their own question or comment* related to the material they are surveying, and write it on the blank card.

Step 3. The teacher begins the discussion by asking who has a question or comment card to read that seems to be a good place to begin the discussion. If a question is read, the teacher asks who has an answer that seems to fit it. This process continues until most or all students have had a chance to participate. At this point, the teacher should ask, "Who has other personal reactions or comments?" This last question is intended to encourage personal-evaluative thinking and responding apart from the statements on the cards but modeled after them in terms of relevance to the topic.

Step 4: (Optional) Within the same or the next class period, give a test of five to ten questions that require brief written responses. Questions should be taken directly from the Note Cue cards and relevant comments made during the discussion. This builds appreciation of the value of reading one's card so that all might hear and learn, and respect for independent commenting.

Fading. As a group of students becomes familiar with Note Cue (as they quickly do), subsequent lessons should include *fewer teacher-prepared cards* and *more blank cards* for students to generate their own questions, answers, and comments. In this way, responsibility is gradually turned over to students as they become more equal to the expectation.

Notes on Note Cue

The Note Cue system can be used to structure prereading as well as postreading discussion, guiding students into and beyond the reading. For a prereading discussion, questions should be written that will elicit students' background of information about the topic of the reading selection or that urge predictions that could be made from a quick preview of the selection. Similarly, write comment cards that contain relevant thoughts that might be sparked by previewing the reading selection.

The second author (U. Manzo) piloted Note Cue in an inner-city middle school with low-achieving minority youngsters who had an established pattern of low participation, poor oral reading, and ineffective participation in pre- and postreading discussions. Although these early trials of the strategy were not objectively measured, when these students' participation was prompted with Note Cue lessons, their behavior seemed to be more on task for longer periods of time, and their written responses on short tests showed higher levels of comprehension than they typically demonstrated. In a set of field-based studies for Education Specialist Degree projects at the University of Missouri–Kansas City in 1986–87, three out of four teachers obtained similar results.

There are some other incidental benefits in using Note Cue. The cards youngsters write offer insight into their thinking. Collections of student cards, and their placement in students' individual portfolios, can offer an overview of student progress in writing and oral communication.

A number of whole-class cooperative structures are useful for achieving optimal student involvement while checking and building on basic comprehension. Four such structures are described next: Inside-Outside Circle, Find Someone Who, Stroll Pair Share, and Postreading Three-Minute Write. These structures can be implemented in a variety of ways. The descriptions are tailored from Kagan (1994) for use as postreading recitation techniques.

Inside-Outside Circle[*]

1. <u>Preparation</u>. Write half as many basic comprehension questions on cards as you have students in class (30 students = 15 question cards). The answer should also be included on the card. Opinion and evaluation type questions may also be included.

2. Move desks toward the walls to clear a large space in the center of the classroom. Have students count off by 2s. Have the 1s form a circle in the middle of the room, facing *out*. Have the 2s form a circle *outside* the 1s, facing *in*. There now should be a double circle, with student pairs facing one another. Students are asked to greet one another by name and shake hands.

3. Distribute question cards to students in the inside circle. The inside student reads the question to his or her outside circle partner. The outside circle student answers, or attempts to answer. If the student cannot answer or gives an incorrect answer, the inside circle partner is to tell him or her the answer.

4. At your signal (a switch of the lights, or a beeper), the outside circle students are to take a step or two to their left, so that they now are with a new partner. They are to shake hands and greet their new partner, who reads them a new question.

5. The outside circle continues to shift to the left until students are back with their original partners. The inside/outside students then trade places, and the question card is traded to the new inside circle person. The new outside circle students take a few steps to the left to greet a new partner and continue until they are again back to their original partners.

Kagan (1994) recommends adding "gambits" to structures such as this. A gambit is a phrase students are instructed to say at a certain point in the interaction. For example, you might tell inside circle students that if their partner answers the question correctly, they are to say, "What a terrific answer!"—and sound like they mean it. Or outside circle students might be instructed that if they have to be given the answer, they are to tell their partner, "I appreciate your help with that!" Gambits sound awkward at first, and students say them jokingly, but don't be surprised to hear them again when you might least expect to, and spoken appropriately and sincerely.

Find Someone Who[*]

1. <u>Preparation</u>: Prepare any type of worksheet to check students' understanding of a reading assignment. The questions and worksheets in teacher's guides for textbooks are usually perfect for this.

[*]This material has been adapted from the following book with permission from Kagan Publishing & Professional Development: Kagan, Spencer. *Cooperative Learning.* San Clemente, CA: Resources for teachers, 1994. 1(800) 933-2667; www.KaganOnline.com.

2. Have students clear their desks, keeping out only a pencil. Distribute the worksheets and give students five to ten minutes to complete as much as they can individually (tell them they are not expected to complete the worksheet during this time, but to skim through the questions and answer those that seem "easiest" first).

3. Have students stand, and tell them that they are to take their worksheets and pencils and walk around the classroom without talking until you give a signal. At the signal they are to stop where they are, find a partner, shake hands, greet one another by name, and find the nearest two seats together. They are to compare the information they have written on their worksheets, and each should try to give an answer to the other. They are to write their partner's initials beside information they got from him or her.

4. At your next signal, students are to thank their partner, stand, and mill around again, quietly, until you signal again. They greet a new partner, find seats, and share information again.

5. The milling-and-pairing continues until most students have completed their worksheets.

Stroll Pair Share*

1. Preparation: Write several discussion-type questions based on the reading assignment (again, teacher's guides usually provide questions of this type).

2. Clear the outside perimeter of the classroom and have students form a double parade line—each student with a partner, facing forward.

3. At the teacher's signal, students are to begin walking forward, casually, while talking to their partners. Beginning with the person on the inside, they are to tell everything they remember about what they have just read. After about two minutes, the teacher signals for the outside partners to speak. After about two more minutes the teacher signals for the line to stop, and the inside partners to move up to a new partner in the outside line (the front person on the inside goes to the back).

4. The process continues through several shifts of partners.

Postreading Three-Minute Write*

Several of the methods and techniques described above have included some form of writing. Writing is an especially useful ingredient in postreading instruction for several reasons:

*This material has been adapted from the following book with permission from Kagan Publishing & Professional Development: Kagan, Spencer. *Cooperative Learning*. San Clemente, CA: Resources for teachers, 1994. 1(800) 933-2667; www.KaganOnline.com.

- It is another way to ensure involvement of more students.

- Writing something down forces it into a linear string of thought—this often helps students see when they may have been fooling themselves into thinking they know something they do not yet know.

- Writing induces a greater sense of agency or ownership and commitment that can be a useful lead-in to lively discussion.

The Postreading Three-Minute Write is a simple way to structure postreading writing. After students have read, provide them with a prompt for writing about what they have read. The prompt may be as broad as "write everything you re-member," or a specific question requiring analysis and/or evaluation. Let them know up front that their writing will not be collected or graded for spelling or other mechanics but that it will be useful to them later in the lesson. Some guide-lines for this technique as follows:

- It works best when everyone writes at the same time (ideally, including the teacher).

- The only rule is that everyone must be *writing something* for the entire three minutes, even if they are writing "I can't think of anything to write," over and over.

The three-minute write can also be structured as a "write-pair-share," in which, following writing, students are placed in pairs and take turns, within a specific time limit, telling (not reading to) their partner what they have written.

Group Reading Activity—A Legacy Method with Modern Values

The Group Reading Activity (GRA) (Manzo, 1974) predates most all coopera-tive structures, including the Jigsaw Approach. Its goal is to structure postread-ing recitation in a way that helps culturally and psychologically diverse students learn to collaboratively *offer and receive constructive criticism.* The GRA meets these fundamental requirements for effective learning as well as merely encour-aging greater social interaction. It tends to be quite transformative of student classroom decorum and capacity to work toward common learning goals. It is ideal for today's heterogeneously grouped classrooms that mirror the diversity of the real world.

Steps in the GRA

Step 1. The teacher selects the reading assignment and writes a purpose ques-tion on the chalkboard.

Step 2. The teacher divides the text into subsections of a few pages each and as-signs each subsection to a small group.

Step 3. Students read silently and write their individual responses to the purpose question.

Step 4. Each group is given a worksheet to complete together. The worksheet should contain general, open-ended comprehension-check questions such as the following:

a. What question does this section answer?

b. Write a statement of the main idea(s) of this section. Support it with direct quotes or paraphrased facts and points found in the text.

c. Comment on the quality of the ideas and supporting statements: Do these seem true? Complete? Biased?

d. What other things, ideas, and facts have you learned in the past that seems to relate to what you have read here?

e. Using the information from the worksheet, the group works together to prepare a brief presentation for the rest of the class. They should choose who should present what information, in what order, and in what way.

Step 5. As each group becomes ready, a student critic chosen by the teacher from one of the other groups is sent to see and hear the group's presentation. The student critic is expected to react with constructive criticism, such as "That sounds fine," "That doesn't seem to make much sense," "Perhaps you should have. . . "

Step 6. The group is given time to revise their presentation, drawing on the feedback provided by the student critic.

Step 7. The teacher consults briefly with each group to review their presentation plan.

Step 8. Presentations are made, and the class and teacher comment and question as relevant. The teacher or a designated student lists important information from each presentation on the chalkboard (or overhead, whiteboard, or SmartBoard).

Step 9. Finally, students are directed to "rapid-read" the *entire* reading assignment, watching for main points and important details.

Notes on GRA: Induces Civility and Constructive Responding

Anecdotal reports (Manzo & Manzo, 1990a) indicate that students involved in the GRA tend to assume required roles in a surprisingly adult manner. Their language, thinking, and even social graces seem to rise to the occasion. The keenest benefit seems to be that students tend to criticize each other in constructive and intelligent ways, probably to reduce the likelihood of being treated sharply when they are critiqued in turn.

▶ FULL CIRCLE TO DISCUSSION

The preceding sections presented a variety of teacher-directed and peer-group approaches to checking and extending comprehension after, or beyond, reading. Structured experiences with these approaches help to prepare students to participate in more sophisticated forms of classroom discussion. Before turning to the next methods for scaffolding discussion, however, let's further consider some of the ways in which teachers can anticipate and handle student questions, answers, and comments that can lead a discussion off track or otherwise diminish its impact.

Further Girding for Nonproductive Questions, Answers, and Comments

There are numerous ways for students to question, answer, and comment during classroom interactions. Some of these are facilitating and productive, and others are quirky and difficult to handle. Some typical problem situations that tend to arise, and some techniques we have seen veteran teachers use to deal with them, are described next. Consider starting a personal journal of "useful verbal protocols," or "things to say when . . .".

Problem

The student who can't seem to think without talking. They are not really disrespectful but garrulous or irrepressibly talkative. They begin to answer every question whether or not they know the answer.

Remedies:

- Avoid eye contact with them.
- Occasionally turn your back to them and ask a question while walking away from them so that they can't quite hear it thus preventing them from answering before others can.
- Call a name or a row before asking a question.
- Strictly enforce a rule of raising a hand before talking.
- Find a reason to talk about the different ways people think and talk. Be sympathetic, but point out that "compulsive talkers" tend to disrupt the teacher, dissuade others from speaking up, overly dominate a discussion, close out opportunities to listen and learn, appear boorish, and anger others. Stress that this is a problem that can plague a person for the rest of his or her life if not curtailed early.

Problem

The student who raises the same question that has been raised and answered.

Remedy:

Ask, "Does anyone recognize this question?" If no one responds, you have strong evidence that you need to raise and probably answer the question again. If the question or the answer has more than one part, write out key words on the chalkboard.

Problem

The student who characteristically speaks too low to be heard.

Remedy:

Begin walking to the other side of the room so that the student must project to you, and in the process speak loudly enough for others to hear.

Problem

Disruptive sounds, such as heating or cooling systems, prevent class members from hearing one another.

Remedies:

- Have students arrange desks so that they face one another.
- Repeat students' questions and answers (despite the usual prohibition against doing so).
- Explain the problem to the class, and say that you frequently will be calling on someone else to repeat questions and answers to ensure that everyone hears. This also can keep students more alert the first time.

Problem

Students who fail to participate in responding to recitation-type questions.

Remedies:

- Examine your questions. You might be asking "guess what I'm thinking" questions. All teachers occasionally lapse into this routine.
- Provide more "wait time": Count to five mentally before saying another word, then ask students if they want the question repeated or explained further.

Problem

Students who do not pay attention or participate in discussions or other class activities.

Remedies:

- Reassess what you are asking students to do. Is it meaningful, clear, and "doable" in the time you are allowing?
- Use a polling technique to warm up your audience and get them involved. The most popular method is to ask questions that require one of two choices, such as those asked in television polls in which one calls a given phone number for each choice. You can also offer more elaborate, content-related choices. Here is an example: "Some people think *The Merchant of Venice* is a put-down of Jews, others think it is a put-down of Christians. Who thinks it is a put-down of Jews? Who Christians? Who is undecided? Who has no idea? Let's continue to analyze this play and see whether Shakespeare tips his hand one way or the other."

Problem

The student who asks a question, gives an answer, or makes a comment that is "out in left field."

Remedies:

- Simply say, "I don't quite see the relevance of that. Can you explain further?" Where such responses clearly are characteristic of a certain student and it is clear to the class that you are not being arbitrary, omit the request for further explanation.

- Ask if another student can help explain or clarify the question, answer, or comment.

- Try to get things going in another direction by simply accepting the response and saying, "OK, does anyone else have a different point of view or way of answering this question?"

- When such a response seems to be intentionally irrelevant, don't forget the power of a stare or simple silence in response.

The following techniques and methods provide further scaffolding to assist students in actively participating in more traditional forms of class discussion.

Fine-Tuning Discussion

When you are ready to further fine-tune your discussion strategies and techniques, you will want to consider some additionally effective gambits—or playful ways to elicit reflective discourse. It is wise not to try to master more than one or two of these methods at a time. Both you and the class will appreciate the orderliness of learned routines.

Fishbowl*

The Fishbowl technique (Baloche et al., 1993) is a useful way to raise students' awareness of their own and others' classroom discussion behaviors. Students are seated in two concentric circles (both circles facing inward), with approximately the same number of students in each ring. Students in the inner circle are given a discussion topic and a given time limit. Students in the outer circle are given an inner circle member to observe and a teacher-designed worksheet for recording their observations. When the discussion time is up, outer circle members each give constructive feedback to their "fish." Feedback should focus on discussion behaviors rather than the topic of the discussion or specific points made.

---

*Baloche, L., Mauger, M. L., Willis, T. M., Filinuk, J. R., & Michalsky, B. V. (1993). "Fishbowls, Creative Controversy, Talking Chips: Exploring Literature Cooperatively." *English Journal*, 82. Copyright (1993) by the National Council of Teachers of English. Reprinted with permission.

This technique should be structured according to the sophistication level of the group. For optimal structure, assign students to one of the two circles; provide specific discussion prompts for the inner circle and very specific items on the observation worksheet provided to the outer circle. For more sophisticated groups, and as students become familiar with the technique, participants can be permitted to choose which circle they will be in, and discussion and observation prompts can be more open-ended. Some ideas for structuring the observation checklist include:

- Place a check beside the appropriate item each time the person makes a verbal contribution to the discussion: states a new idea, paraphrases another person's idea, supports or agrees with another person, states an opposing or alternate point, summarizes, makes a humorous remark.
- Place a check beside each nonverbal behavior observed: smile, laugh, nod, frown, disinterested expression.

U-Debate*

Some postreading discussion lends itself naturally to a debate-type format. The U-Debate (Athanses, 1988) is a useful structure for teaching students to engage in this type of discussion. The technique begins by the teacher stating two opposing ideas. Classroom seats are then moved into a "U" shape, with one side representing each opposing idea, and seats in the middle representing a neutral position. Students are directed to find a seat that best represents their opinion. The teacher facilitates the discussion in a typical way, with the difference that participants' views are readily observable to the teacher and one another. Students who select seats at the top of either side of the "U" usually are the most willing to begin the discussion. A lively camaraderie springs up among students seated in each of the opposing positions, and they begin to defer and/or appeal to one another as they attempt to express their points. As students change their opinions or the strength of their views, they are permitted to change their seating position.

Socratic Seminar

The Socratic Seminar is the primary instructional tool of Mortimer Adler's Paideia Proposals for educational reform (1982). Its intent is to engage students in meaningful postreading discussion by minimizing the teacher's direction and maximizing student participation. This is done by laying out a set of specific guidelines for participants and by the teacher/discussion leader following another set of guidelines for opening the discussion and moving it along. Any text selection may be used, including standard textbook selections. It is helpful to number the lines in

*Athanses, S. (1988). "Developing a Classroom Community of Interpreters." *English Journal*, 77. Copyright (1988) by the National Council of Teachers of English. Reprinted with permission.

the text for easy reference. After everyone has completed the reading, the group is seated in a circle (or around a large table) and the basic ground rules for the discussion are explained (or reviewed). It is helpful to have students prepare name cards for themselves that they place in front of them so that during the seminar, participants can refer to each other politely by name.

Socratic Seminar: Guidelines for Participants

1. The purpose of the Seminar is understanding of the author's message and the group's interpretations and analysis of it.

2. Every comment or question must be based on a specific portion of the text. The discussion leader may open with a text section to respond to, or may ask for a volunteer to identify a starting point.

3. You do not need to raise your hand; simply take turns as in a casual conversation.

4. Talk to each other, not the teacher.

5. You may make comments, ask questions of the group as a whole, or ask a question of a person by name.

6. You may "pass" when called on.

7. At any time, you may ask participants if they are ready to move to a different portion of the text. If they agree, identify the section you wish to respond to, read it aloud, and then ask your question or make your comment.

8. Stick to the point. Make notes of ideas you want to come back to.

9. Listen carefully, and ask for clarification when needed.

Socratic Seminar: Guidelines for Teacher/Discussion Leader

1. Identify a portion of the text to begin the discussion. Read the selection aloud, and ask a relevant clarifying question. With experienced groups, you may ask for a volunteer for this opening step. (For longer reading selections that may elicit more complex discussions, you may wish to assign the reading ahead of time and develop a plan for double-checking that the students have read and comprehended the basics of the text prior to class. For instance, you could require a "ticket" for admission to participate in the seminar. The ticket could be, as an example, a brief graphic organizer over the reading material that you could quickly scan from each student as they took their seats in the seminar circle.)

2. Maintain an unintrusive role, communicating through body language the expectation that participants should share responsibility for moving the discussion along. It may help to avoid eye contact with the person speaking to encourage them to look at and speak to the other participants, rather than you.

3. Watch participants' body language to invite them in ("You don't seem to agree. Can you explain why?" "Can you give an example to support what he or she is saying?"). Remember that those who aren't speaking are thinking.

4. Correct all misreadings on the spot.

5. Supply key factual information when needed (but attempt to keep this to a minimum).

6. Coach students on seminar behaviors when needed.

7. Model effective discussion strategies, such as asking for clarification of a question or statement, paraphrasing the text, distinguishing between fact and opinion, identifying conflicting views, and drawing out the reasons for or implications of an answer or a comment.

8. If overly argumentative or nonparticipating members fail to respond to subtle approaches, speak with them privately after the discussion.

9. Conclude the seminar by going around the circle asking each participant to comment briefly on the seminar.

The final step in the Socratic Seminar is a writing prompt based on the text and the points raised in the discussion (steps and guidelines amalgamated from Paley, 1986; Gray, 1988; Sizer, 1994; and Zola, 1998).

In our view, "Socratic Seminar" is an unfortunate misnomer. The method just described bears scant resemblance to the method practiced by Socrates and his student, Plato, in which the teacher's role was that of a "grand inquisitor," posing a question, and responding to questions and answers with ever more sharp and stinging questions intended to expose faulty assumptions and misinformation. This latter, more genuine version of the Socratic Method, as it has been most familiarly practiced in schools of law, has been referred to as "ritualized combat" (Guinier, Fine, & Balin, 1997).

▶ AFTER WORDS

This chapter underscored the importance of postreading recitation when this traditional practice is part of a program that includes other additional means of comprehension development and application. These additional means include a number of teacher-directed and cooperative group activities for bridging to and conducting "traditional" discussion, which is perhaps better referred to as "instructional conversation."

III

COMPLEMENTS TO CONTENT AREA READING: VOCABULARY, HIGHER-ORDER LITERACY, WRITING TO LEARN, ASSESSMENT, AND STUDY SKILLS IN THE DISCIPLINES

You have now been exposed to the rudimentary tools for helping students to *read the lines* and in some measure to *read between the lines*. The next section addresses the knowledge and skills that teachers will need to also promote the essential aspects of vocabulary acquisition, for *reading and thinking beyond the lines*, and for study skills and life-long learning. Chapter 7 addresses a variety of ways to assist students with their vocabulary development. Chapter 8 focuses on critical-constructive reading, writing, and thinking. Chapter 9 addresses emergent content area literacy, the use of literature and trade books to teach content, and the use of writing to enhance student learning. Chapter 10 introduces assessment techniques for achieving the objectives of the previous chapters, and Chapter 11 is designed to reground us in one of the more inescapable elements of school life—the development of powerful reading/study habits.

CHAPTER 7

STRATEGIC METHODS FOR VOCABULARY AND CONCEPT DEVELOPMENT

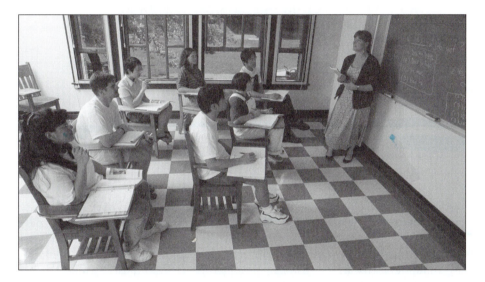

The most powerful thing that can be done is to name something.
—Albert Einstein

▶ FORE WORDS

From the first time you behold a beach at sunset to the next time your computer or your aspirations experience a "megaflop," new images get formed into clearer ideas, ways to think, write, and speak. Improving a youngster's access to this communication source code or mental software does not merely facilitate learning, it is learning. This chapter is about increasing expertise in teaching the "software" language with which we organic computers interface, store, feel, express, and self-transform.

There are many, many more teaching ideas in this chapter than any single teacher can reasonably be expected to master. It would be wise to select a very few that meet your current situational needs and to strategically implement just these. The others will be here waiting for you when you are ready and/or your situation changes.

- ▶ FORE WORDS
- ▶ HOW MANY WORDS CAN WE AND DO WE NEED TO KNOW?
- ▶ WHAT'S IN A NAME?
- ▶ VOCABULARY LEARNING IS DISCIPLINE LEARNING
- ▶ WHAT WE KNOW ABOUT VOCABULARY LEARNING AND TEACHING
- ▶ STRATEGICALLY SELECTING METHODS FOR VOCABULARY INTRODUCTION
- ▶ STRATEGIES FOR RAISING WORD CONSCIOUSNESS AND HANDLING UNFAMILIAR VOCABULARY DURING SILENT READING
- ▶ METHODS FOR POSTREADING VOCABULARY/CONCEPT DEVELOPMENT
- ▶ AFTER WORDS

▶ HOW MANY WORDS CAN WE AND DO WE NEED TO KNOW?

Word learning can actually improve one's *capacity* to learn, it is literally an IQ booster (Manzo, Manzo, & Albee, 2004). It is comparable to the modern marvels of engineering that can make a four-cylinder engine behave like an eight cylinder on a highway, and a small, personal computer function like a large desktop.

Estimates vary widely on how many words we need to know at each grade level and, therefore, at what rate they should be learned. But a few things are clear: Children must learn at least 2,000 words per year through the fifth grade (Nagy, 1988); many learn over 3,500 per year. Words with the lowest frequency of occurrence also are the ones that count for the most in school learning. Additionally, youngsters who are English language learners (ELLs) must learn new words in English at about twice the rate of those who are native speakers of English. Fortunately, there is no detectable upper limit to the numbers of words that most of us can learn, especially if we are properly taught and the words occur—or are made to occur—with some frequency in daily experience.

The challenge to teachers is relatively clear: We must identify ways to enable students to acquire the low frequency words that permeate content area teaching and learning (Unrau, 2004). It has long been understood that the major contributing factor to the impoverished learning of disadvantaged students has been inadequate vocabulary knowledge. Ironically, the teaching of vocabulary has not been considered a "hot" topic in recent years (Cassidy & Cassidy, 2001–2002, 2003–2004). On the plus side, it has been a known fact, though not one always implemented, that almost any attention to vocabulary would result in some vocabulary growth (Manzo & Sherk, 1971–1972). Further, there is considerable evidence cited throughout this chapter that excellent instruction can result in extraordinary gains, and not only in words learned but in the concepts and content that they embody.

As a conceptual "heads-up" for the remainder of the chapter, here are two critical ideas for teaching and improving vocabulary: (1) Raise student *word consciousness*, or sensitivity to the new words in their school and life experience; and (2) increase your own interest in, knowledge of, and excitement about words because this alone is contagious—words used in class become part of an elevated community of language and, hence, of human experience, the most natural means by which new words are learned.

▶ WHAT'S IN A NAME?

Einstein's comment aptly captures the power of vocabulary acquisition and development. As children learn the words that name the basic elements of their environment, they gain the power to express their needs and wishes. As we learn the words for the more abstract and subtle aspects of experience, we gain the power to reflect on these and to begin to shape our personal value systems and worldview, or life filters. The power of words is deeply engrained in culture. In Judeo-Christian and Muslim cultures, for example, words such as the following are intended to slow the heart and evoke a sense of reverence: "And out of the ground the Lord God formed every beast of the field, and every fowl of the air; and brought them unto Adam to see what he would call them: and whatsoever Adam called every living creature, that was the name thereof."

Words are the brain's shorthand system for *encoding* experience—or exchanging a meaning from a code—without having to turn its full attention to every item and nuance of sensory experience. Try looking around you, wherever you are at this moment. Imagine that you are experiencing (seeing, hearing, smelling, feeling) every aspect of your current environment for the first time, and try labeling everything you can. Would it be difficult to come up with 100 words? With 500? The brain doesn't have to be conscious of each of these things, because it has words for them: The words we know form a lens through which we see (and hear, and read, and sense) the world. Thus, every person, whether scientist, historian, artist, musician, or new age candlestick maker, experiences the world in a unique way, through a lens fashioned out of a system of naming called *vocabulary*.

▶ VOCABULARY LEARNING IS DISCIPLINE LEARNING

Clearly, mastering the information and ideas of any discipline is largely a matter of mastering its vocabulary. Some approaches to vocabulary instruction, however, are based on faulty, more minimalist, assumptions about word learning and fail to hook into the enormous innate word-learning capacity of the human brain. This chapter tells of several traditional and modern methods of introducing new vocabulary in ways that teach words and strategies for word learning. The chapter is divided into five main sections: (1) What we know about vocabulary learning and teaching; (2) introducing new words in ways that teach strategies; (3) building silent reading strategies for vocabulary development; (4) postreading vocabulary/concept development; and (5) practice formats for long-term retention.

▶ WHAT WE KNOW ABOUT VOCABULARY LEARNING AND TEACHING

The standard approach to teaching vocabulary is one of the most consistent things about school. On Monday, a list of words appear on the chalkboard. Students copy the words, use a dictionary to look up and write the definition of each word, and write a sentence using it. (The quality of these sentences is fodder for oft-repeated humor: "My father sings in the cascade.") The words are then to be studied for a test on Friday. While this approach does work for some students some of the time (Tan & Nicholson, 1997), better vocabulary instruction proves more effective for more students more of the time (c.f. Rhoder & Huerster, 2002).

A Metaphor for the Process

Earlier in this text, we introduced the image of a fishing net as a metaphor for schema—the intricate web of information and experience each person has constructed from his or her unique history of experience. Think of vocabulary as the substance from which that net is constructed. Ideas, information, and experience are coded in words, represented by the knots in the fishing net, each connected to all the others by cords of meaning. This is a useful metaphor to keep in mind as we consider the following summary of what is known about the process of vocabulary acquisition, or exchanging print and voice code for possible meanings.

How We Learn Words

To examine the process of word learning, consider the following characteristics of an expert word learner, comparing these to characteristics of a novice word learner. Keep in mind that each of these is a learned habit or strategy. Expert word learners

1. notice new words when listening and reading—they have high word consciousness;

2. are interested in learning new words—have a positive disposition toward vocabulary enhancement;

3. are especially likely to learn words that are encountered in situations marked by strong emotion—this is really true of most all of us;

4. are active word builders—use the situational or textual context to predict possible meanings of the new term, and make a mental note of the word and its predicted meanings to check against future encounters with the word;

5. relish nuances in language—connect shades of meaning with personal experiences, images, and examples;

6. are self-reliant and strategic learners of new words—use their knowledge of elements of word meaning (prefixes, suffixes, root words) to predict, confirm, and anchor new word meanings;

7. engage in self-teaching—mentally rehearse the personal connections they have created to link a new word with its meaning.

Now consider the extent to which even the traditional word list approach—which, you will recall, works to some degree, despite its shortcomings—helps to teach these habits and strategies. This minimalist approach to word learning is worth dwelling on because it a makes a few critical points: It shows that humans seem to like and to be able to learn words fairly easily and, therefore, if you feel overly burdened with other curricula demands, that you should do at least this much. But, as you will see, there is much more that you can do fairly easily that can convert "singles" into doubles, triples, and home runs. In the traditional word list approach

1. The teacher provides the words for study: Students are not helped in recognizing and noticing new words.

2. There is typically an overreliance on the extrinsic motivation of the weekly test rather than building intrinsic motivation and interest in words and word learning.

3. There is typically an overemphasis on dictionary work that rarely generates excitement, enthusiasm, or emotion.

4. Words are often presented in isolation, so there is no opportunity to learn to make use of context.

5. While some students may expend the extra effort to compose sensible sentences that accurately use the assigned words, for the most part students' sentences are vague or inaccurate applications.

6. Although word histories are included in the dictionary, few students pay attention to them, and such work is not usually required.

7. When students study word lists for an upcoming test, they usually do so by memorizing the word-for-word definitions and spellings they have looked up rather than trying to make any personalized, meaningful connections to the ideas represented by the words.

On this view, it is fairly clear that the traditional word list approach does relatively little to teach students how to learn words (c.f. Rhoder & Huerster, 2002). Its purpose is to have students memorize definitions. Its expectation (usually unfulfilled) is that students will, on their own, make the comparisons, connections, evaluations, applications, and exclusions that will firmly affix the words as solid elements of operational schema—tight knots in their own personally constructed net. But will they?

Do We Need to Do It Better?

It could be that vocabulary instruction comes under the category of "if it ain't broke, don't fix it." However, sound research indicates that the vocabulary level of college-bound 18-year olds has dropped sharply in recent years. In 1940, these students typically knew the meanings of 80% of the words on a standardized reading test. By the mid-1990s, the typical student scored only 30%, which is just a little better than random guessing (Johnson O'Connor Research Foundation, in Dortch, 1995). These figures are likely due, in large measure, to self-selection, the fact that there are far more students today than in 1940 who have declared themselves to be "college bound." Be that as it may, it is evident that students are not being well served by whatever approaches to vocabulary instruction they have experienced. This picture is even more distressing when one considers the implications for thinking, reading, writing, and learning. A measure of a person's vocabulary provides the single best prediction of general (academic) IQ, scholastic aptitude, level of reading comprehension, and grade point average.

Vocabulary acquisition, like improvement of reading comprehension, is an ongoing, lifelong process. To teach someone effective vocabulary learning strategies is indeed a "gift that keeps on giving." Unlike most factual knowledge, vocabulary terms are like self-generative energy packs that unlock doors, offer insights, and automatically grant interesting perspectives when heard, read, thought, or expressed in speech or writing.

Principles to Guide Vocabulary Instruction

There is an extensive body of research on how words are learned and how to best promote that learning. The next section provides a summary derived from several reviews of this research (Baumann & Kameenui, 1991; Harmon, 2002; Kibby, 1995; Manzo & Manzo, 1990a; Manzo & Sherk, 1971–1972; Mountain, 2002; Nagy 1988; Nilsen & Nilsen, 2003; Ruddell & Shearer, 2002; Stahl & Fairbanks, 1986).

- Students develop a lifelong interest in learning new words primarily through observation and interaction with others. Intentionally or unintentionally, teachers communicate their personal attitudes about the importance of word learning and their interest in words.

- It is far more beneficial to show students how to use strategies for learning word meanings than to require rote memorization of definitions. Only about 20% of an average adult vocabulary of approximately 20,000 words is learned through direct instruction. The rest is learned incidentally, through reading and listening.

- Vocabulary is best taught at the "teachable moment;" that is, when the need to know arises. However, it also must be taught regularly and systematically for significant growth to occur.

- When a student encounters a new word in everyday experience, he or she will remember the word by associating its meaning with the actual or vicarious experience in which the word was encountered. The most effective word learning strategies to teach students are those that most closely resemble natural word learning strategies.

- The familiarity of vocabulary in text is one of the most important determinants of students' ability to comprehend. Preteaching selected words from a reading selection before students read greatly improves their comprehension of the material.

- Simply noticing unfamiliar words in print and oral language is a fundamental vocabulary learning habit, one that can be developed during silent reading.

- Transformation of superficial word knowledge into concept knowledge requires multiple encounters with a word and analysis of its shades of meanings in a variety of contexts.

- Once a student learns a word at the definition level, repeated practice and use of the word will solidify its meaning.

- The meanings of many unfamiliar words can be predicted based on knowledge of morphemes—prefixes, suffixes, and roots. It is useful to teach word learning strategies based on morphemes, the meaningful elements that constitute words. Just as words combine to form sentences and sentences combine to form paragraphs, morphemes (mainly prefixes, roots, and suffixes) combine to form words. Word = prefix + root + suffix is the general formula for a word in English.

- The most important step in improving students' vocabulary is to foster a rich "community of language" within each classroom and across the school to encourage continued vocabulary reinforcement and use outside the classroom.

Selecting Words for Instruction

How many words should you teach each week/month/year? Which words should you teach? The answers, of course, depend partly on your students, partly on your subject, and partly on your instructional emphasis. In general, as they plan each course unit, teachers should identify key terms for concept development. Then, in previewing materials students will read during the unit, vocabulary for preteaching should be identified. Of course, there will be more words that *could* be taught than there will be time. Ruddell (1999, pp. 148–149) offers suggestions for selecting words for prereading, guided reading, and postreading instruction:

1. Select a word for prereading instruction when it is central to the meaning of the selection and you anticipate that many of your students do not know the meaning of the word as used in this context and the context does not convey the meaning.

2. Select a word for emphasis in a silent reading format when students are likely to know the word in general, but not in this specific context, or when the context clearly conveys the meaning.

3. Select a word for postreading emphasis when it is central to the knowledge and concept base of the unit, and, because of students' limited background knowledge related to the word, small group and/or whole class discussion is needed to connect the new ideas to prior learning and experience.

▶ STRATEGICALLY SELECTING METHODS FOR VOCABULARY INTRODUCTION

Introducing key terms from a particular reading selection often is an essential element of prereading instruction. When a word is judged to be needed, vocabulary preteaching should meet three basic criteria:

1. introduce students to words that are likely to be unfamiliar to them;
2. do so in ways that not only provide the word meaning but permit the teacher to model strategies for learning new words (in doing do, the teacher also models an interest in words and word learning);
3. establish a low-risk environment in which students can try out and experiment with these word learning strategies.

We know of only few methods that satisfy these criteria. Before we introduce these methods, consider some of the general components that they have in common.

1. They introduce a maximum of five words for a given reading selection.
2. They limit this part of the lesson to a maximum of 15 minutes.
3. Each method puts the words on display as each is introduced (not the entire list at once).
4. In each case, the word is spoken, written, and defined. This is a crucial component of vocabulary preteaching for several reasons. First, the meaning is given in the simplest terms possible. To see the importance of this translation step, look at the dictionary definitions of these words, and try translating them into "student" language:

   Potential: "Capable of being but not yet in existence; latent."

   Expansion: "The act or process of expanding."

   This component is also crucial because it is contrary to one of the most basic teacher scripts we have internalized through years of traditional classroom experience: After the teacher writes a word on the board, she or he next asks, "can anyone tell me what this word means?" What this question does, in effect, is eliminate a large portion of the class—all those who don't have a clue as to the word's meaning. When the teacher says instead, "This word is ____, and it means ____," everyone is still able to participate.
5. The teacher then introduces a strategy for connecting the new word with its meaning, and invites volunteers to try out the strategy. At this point, the teacher should watch for and encourage contributions from students who might not have known the meaning of the word and who might not otherwise have been able to participate.
6. As suggested, the teacher tries to keep the interactions brief and to the point.
7. When possible, time should be given for students to at least begin the reading immediately following the vocabulary preteaching. When it is

not possible to have them do the entire reading in class, be sure to have students write the pretaught words and keep them with the reading assignment to be done later.

The word learning strategies used in the methods in this section represent strategically different ways of connecting the new word with some schema element that is related to the new word meaning. In the Keyword Method, the schema element is a visual image; in the Subjective Approach to Vocabulary, it is an image of a personal experience; and in Motor Imaging, it is a symbolic gestured pantomime that suggests the new word meaning. The fourth method in this section, Incidental Morpheme Analysis, is different in nature from the first three. It is a kind of guided guessing game that teaches students to draw on what they already know about the structural elements of words (prefixes, suffixes, and roots), in the form of other words they know, and to apply this knowledge to predict the meaning of the new word. Incidental Morpheme Analysis, as its name implies, can only be used incidentally when the word to be used is composed of familiar word elements. It will be used fairly infrequently, but when the opportunity for a teachable moment arises, it is a powerful way to teach students an important independent word learning strategy.

Incidental Morpheme Analysis: Using Known Word Parts as Analogs to Unlock New Word Meanings

Eighty percent of the words in the English dictionary contain Greek or Latin prefixes, suffixes, or roots. The proportion probably is much higher for discipline-specific words, which tend to be more scientific and less likely to change with high frequency and casual language usage. These word parts, called morphemes, are units of language that cannot be further divided without losing meaning. Some morphemes have meanings only when attached to other word parts. Examples of such bound morphemes include *ed*, *ing*, *tele*, and *cide*. Other morphemes, such as *cover*, *graph*, and *stand*, called free morphemes, can stand alone, that is, are words in themselves.

Most expert readers and language users employ these word parts, or morphemes, to make sense out of and remember new words (c.f. Nilsen & Nilsen, 2002). The Incidental Morpheme Method (Manzo & Manzo, 1990a) teaches students to apply existing knowledge of morphemes to new words encountered in content reading. It also offers a way to teach new morphemes by raising sensitivity to word parts and providing casual, or "on-the-spot," instruction in a set of morphemes with a high-frequency of occurrence in "school" words.

Generally speaking, students with a weak orientation toward words, and therefore the greatest needs, are the ones least likely to warm to direct instruction in morphemic study. Hence, it is best to make these lessons brief, frequent, and spaced. A bulletin board display with space for adding examples can help to keep the project ongoing and the students able to participate as they come across new words containing meaningful word parts. (A similar strategy is used at the elementary level very successfully for teaching children how to decode "new" words phonetically from a list of familiar "sight words.") This approach is especially recommended in classes with English language learners. Speakers of Romance languages, such as Spanish, actually could have a considerable advantage in learning and utilizing such word parts because Romance languages are derived in even greater measure from Latin root words that these students know from common native language usage.

Steps in Incidental Morpheme Method

As preparation for using the Incidental Morpheme Method, watch for words in reading assignments that probably are unfamiliar to students but contain familiar word parts, or morphemes. Use the following steps to *preteach* these terms.

Step 1. Write the term on the chalkboard or overhead, and underline meaningful word parts, or morphemic elements, that might help students understand the word's concept base.

> *Example:*   <u>seis</u>   <u>mo</u>   <u>graph</u>

Step 2. Ask students if they can use the underlined parts to grasp the word meaning, and why. If the word meaning is predicted correctly, write the meaning under the word and proceed with steps 3 and 4 as reinforcement.

Step 3. Tell students you will give them additional clues for predicting (or remembering) the word meaning. Beneath the underlined word parts, write "Level 1" clues, which are other, easier words using those morphemes. If students have not yet correctly predicted the word meaning, continue to ask for predictions.

> *Example:*   <u>seis</u>   <u>mo</u>   <u>graph</u>
> *Level 1 clues:*   seizure   telegraph
>   graphic

Step 4. Beneath the "Level 1" clues, write "Level 2" clues, which are word part meanings, and continue to ask for predictions until the correct definition is reached and written below the clues.

> *Example:*   <u>seis</u>   <u>mo</u>   <u>graph</u>
> *Level 1 clues:*   seizure   telegraph
>   graphic
> *Level 2 clues:*   to shake   written
> *Meaning:*   An instrument that records the direction, time, and intensity of earthquakes.

See Figure 7.1 for a sample listing of common Latin roots. Many dictionaries will provide lists of Latin and Greek prefixes, suffixes, and roots.

Keyword Vocabulary Method

The Keyword Vocabulary Method is based on an ancient memory technique that dates back to the time when unschooled messengers had to recall long and explicit details. In this application, a new word is linked to a mental image that it suggests, and that in turn is connected in some logical way to the actual meaning

Root	Meaning	Derivatives
-aud-, -audit-	hear	auditorium, audio,
-avi-	bird	aviation, aviary
-caput-	head	capital
-ced-, -cess-	move, yield	recede
-clar-	clear	clarify
-clin-	lean	incline
-clud-, -claud-, -clus-	shut	seclude
-cord-	heart	cordial
-corp-	body	corporal, marine corp
-cred-	to believe	credible
-curr-, -curs-	run	current
-dic-, -dict-	say	predict
-domin-	master	dominate
-duc-, -duct-	lead	conduct
-fac-, -fic-, -fact-, -fect-	to make, do	factory
-fer-	bear, carry	transfer
-fin-	end	finish
-fort-	strong	fortitude
-jun-, -junct-	join	junction
-laud-, -laudat-	praise	applause
-let-, -lect-	gather, read	lecture, collect
-legis-, -lex-	law	legislate
-lux-, -luc-	light	elucidate
-magn-	great	magnificent, magnify
-mal-	bad	malevolent
-man-	hand	manual
-mit-, -miss-	send	missile
-mov-, -mot-	set in motion	motor
-nov-, -novus-	new	renovation
-pac-	peace	pacific, pacify
-pel-, -puls-	urge, drive	propel
-pend-, -pens-	hang, weigh	pensive
-plic-, -plex-	bend, fold	plexiglass
-pon-, -pos-	place, put	postpone
-sci-	know	science
-scrib-, -script-	write	describe
-solv-, -solut-	loosen	solution, solve
-spec-, -spect-	look	spectator
-sta-	stand firm	stable
-stru-, -struct-	build	construct
-tend-, -tens-	stretch	tendency
-tort-	to twist	distort
-ven-, -vent-	come	convention
-ver-	true	veritable
-vert-, -vers-	turn	reverse
-viv-, -vit-	live, life	vitality
-vid-, -vis-	see	evident
-voc-	call	vocation

Figure 7.1   Common latin roots and derivative words.

of the word. The object is to create mental images that are easy to recall because they are easy to visualize, and even odd or amusing.

Steps in the Keyword Vocabulary Method

Step 1. Write the word on the chalkboard, pronounce it, and tell what it means.

Step 2. Ask students to come up with a visual image that will help them remember the word meaning. For example, *plateau* (a large grassy flatland) could be linked to the image of a huge upside-down green dinner plate. *Collage* (an artwork created by random combination of bits and pieces of other pictures and/or objects) could be linked to the image of a bulletin board filled with pictures of different colleges. *Amulet* (a charm worn around the neck to ward off evil forces) could be linked to the image of an arm bracelet with an odd charm on it.

Step 3. As an optional step, students can be directed to write each word, its meaning, and draw a simple line drawing or stick figure to represent their visual image connector. Another option is to have students record the words in a form that can be used for later review by writing the word and drawing their picture representation on the front of a note card and writing the meaning on the back. This is a useful technique for studying lengthy word lists in preparation for standardized tests such as the SAT (Scholastic Aptitude Test).

Notes on Keyword Vocabulary

The Keyword Vocabulary Method has been reported to be effective in learning content material (Konopak & Williams, 1988; Levin, Morrison, McGivern, Mastropiévin, & Scruggs, 1986) and with learning disabled students (Condus, Marshall, & Miller, 1986; Guthrie, 1984). Those who have studied Keyword the most extensively maintain that it helps students to learn how to form connections and to develop elaborations on concepts (Pressley, Johnson, & Symons, 1987; Pressley, Levin, & MacDaniel, 1987; Pressley, Levin, & Miller, 1981).

A Keyword Vocabulary lesson usually sparks an interesting instructional conversation in which the teacher and students come to the "word workbench" together in an attempt to capture and represent word meanings in memorable ways. It also tends incidentally to reveal students' thought processes, thus making it a useful diagnostic teaching tool. Its only drawbacks are that many words do not lend themselves to such imaging, but this merely suggests that this is not the best strategic approach for those words.

The next method has long been popular for concentrated vocabulary study. It is shown here for use on those occasions when key subject area vocabulary terms are composed of familiar prefixes, suffixes, and/or roots.

Subjective Approach to Vocabulary

The Subjective Approach to Vocabulary (SAV) (Manzo, 1983) builds on what students already know by urging them to find personal experiences or other associations with which to anchor the somewhat ethereal definitions of new terms found in dictionaries. The method helps students remember meanings of important content-related terms while illustrating how they might use the same strategy in self-directed word learning. In the Subjective Approach to Vocabulary, the teacher engages students in a highly interactive "talk-through" designed to have them learn how to use their *own and other students' experiences* and tales as a foundation for acquiring new word meanings. In this way, the biographies of individual lives become connected to the stories of the words and ideas offered in school. SAV can be particularly useful for providing multicultural outlooks and for working with second-language students. It gives teacher and students access to the alternative ways students may be processing and interpreting the world around and within them.

Steps in the Subjective Approach to Vocabulary

Step 1. Write the word on the chalkboard, pronounce it, and tell what it means. Direct students to write the word and its objective, dictionary-type meaning on their own paper.

Step 2. Ask students to try to think of a personal experience they are reminded of by the word meaning. (The teacher should have an example or two in mind for each word, in case students are especially slow in coming up with their own. Usually, once they have heard one example, they will quickly begin to come up with their own). Call on several volunteers to tell their "subjective" associations. Tell students to try to picture their association as clearly as they can, and to think about how it connects to the new word meaning.

Step 3. Tell students to record their subjective association for the word underneath the objective meaning. They can record an association they volunteered in class, or one that they thought of but did not state, or one offered by another class member. See Figure 7.2 for a Sample SAV lesson.

Step 4. *Optional:* Distribute or guide students in preparing a worksheet consisting of a large square divided into four smaller squares. There should be one four-section square for each word introduced. Have students write the word in the top left section of a larger square, its objective definition in the top right section, their subjective association in the bottom left section, and a line drawing or stick figure illustration in the bottom right section.

Notes on the Subjective Approach to Vocabulary

It is hard to tell how readily a class will take to an SAV lesson on its initial presentation. Group size may be an important factor. For example, the second author once used SAV with a tenth-grade English class of only nine students. When asked for associations with five words (*adipose, adage, accrual, agape, alimentary*), the students stared at me blankly. The very next hour, with a little trepidation, I trotted out the same five words and another tenth-grade class of 15 students was off and running. Soon they were composing as well as associating: "I

The word "arboreal" was in a seventh-grade science text. The teacher wrote the word on the board and gave the meaning: "The word *arboreal* means 'having to do with trees or living in trees.'" A few examples were given: "Monkeys are arboreal animals; the word *arboreal* comes from the word *arbor,* as in Arbor Day, the day put aside to plant trees." The subjective-based aspect of the lesson began at this point. Explaining her question, the teacher added, "It will be easier for you to learn and remember this new term if you can think of some personal images or experiences which you can picture with it."

One student suggested, "The word reminds me of how my mother killed my peanut tree that we brought home from Georgia by overwatering it." To this, another student added, humorously, "That sounds like a 'tragic arboreal' experience." In that same humorous vein, another student asked, rhetorically, "Did you say that *arboreal* means 'living and swingin' in trees(?),' cause I think my little brother is arboreal!"

The teacher then asked if anyone had formed a new meaning for *arboreal.* "It sounds to me like 'anything to do with trees,'" one student volunteered. The teacher then directed the class to record the word *arboreal* in their notebooks with the objective meaning she had provided and a parenthetical note on their initial and subsequent personal associations with the word.

Figure 7.2 Subjective Approach to Vocabulary—sample lesson.

picture Royal Stadium [home of the Kansas City Royals] when we were down but not out and came back to win the pennant and the Series; it's not over 'til the 'adipose' lady sings." A large group sometimes may be necessary to increase the chance of at least one extrovert stirring the class's imagination and responding.

In a study with sixth-grade subjects (Casale & Manzo, 1983), SAV was found to be considerably better than traditional (dictionary "look-up" and sentence writing) approaches to vocabulary instruction. However, it was slightly less effective than the approach described next, which urges teacher and students to employ physical, or symbolic motor, associations to a greater extent than is usual in the sedentary context of schooling.

Motor Imaging

Motor Imaging (Casale [now Manzo], 1985) draws on the physical-sensory as well as cognitive and affective domains of learning. The underlying principle of this method is akin to an expression that says, "Nothing is in the intellect which was not first in the senses."

Developmental psychologists have observed that infants learn to represent meaning with gross motor movements. Over time, these motoric representations, or "motor meanings" are increasingly refined until they are internalized as "symbolic meanings," in Piaget's terminology. Apparently our initial ways of learning consist almost exclusively of tactile and sensory-motor experiences. While this is no great surprise, since that is all babies can do, we seem to have overlooked the fact that this aspect of learning may remain active and viable long into human development.

Steps in Motor Imaging

Step 1. Write the word on the chalkboard, pronounce it, and tell what it means.

Step 2. Tell students to imagine a simple gesture, or pantomime, for the word meaning that you might use to show the word meaning or that you might use when speaking the word in context.

Step 3. On the teacher's signal, students do their gestures, or pantomimes, simultaneously.

Step 4. While observing the student's pantomimes, choose one of the most common ones, show this gesture to all the students, and tell them that when you point to the word, they are to do the selected gesture while saying the word aloud.

Step 5. Introduce each of the words to be pretaught in this way. As words are added to the list, when you point to the word for students to say and pantomime, go back to earlier words to review these word/pantomime connections.

Step 6. Now that each of the new words has been connected to a pantomime, tell students that this time, when you point to a word, they are to do the pantomime and say the meaning. Practice the words in this way, in mixed up order, for several minutes.

Figure 7.3 presents some examples from a Motor Imaging lesson.

New Word	Language Meaning	Motor Meaning
Appropriate	Right or fit for a certain purpose	Both palms together, matching perfectly
Convey	Take or carry from one place to another	Both hands together, palms upward, moving from one side to the other
Woe	Great sadness or trouble	One or both hands over the eyes, head tilted forward
Dazzle	Shine or reflect brightly	Palms close together, facing outward, fingers spread
Utmost	The very highest or most	One or both hands reaching up as far as possible
Abode	Place where you live	Hands meeting above the head in a triangular "roof" shape

Figure 7.3 Motor imaging examples.

Notes on Motor Imaging

The same comparison study cited previously, of a cognitive (dictionary), affective (subjective association), and this physical-sensory, motor approach to vocabulary, showed the Motor Imaging method to be significantly better on four of five vocabulary measures (Casale [now Manzo] & Manzo, 1983). It appears that the highest forms of learning have a most humble, if not primitive foundation.

The promising implication of this point is that students at every level of intellectual ability seem to share a common capacity for physical-associative learning. This makes Motor Imaging, and possibly other motor-based methods yet to be devised, especially promising possibilities for heterogeneously grouped students. The next method can power the effects of the previously described Incidental Morpheme Method, and vise versa.

Explicit Morpheme Analysis

Morphemes, again, are the smallest units of meaning within a word, and they are sometimes themselves a word, such as *auto*. In the Explicit Morpheme approach, a teacher identifies core concept words in the text—words like *ecology* in science, *quadrangle* in math, *millennium* in social studies, *participle* in grammar, or *prologue* in literature—that are composed of elements likely to be familiar to students.

A graphic organizer for vocabulary acquisition such as that shown in Figure 7.4 is helpful for analyzing the morphemes from which unfamiliar words are constructed. The target word, correctly spelled, is written in the center of the graphic by the teacher and copied by the students. The teacher asks the students to use their knowledge to identify possible prefixes, roots, and suffixes that are embedded in the word. Students then define the target word as best they can, using clues from their knowledge of the parts of the word. Next, they share their definitions with a partner or in a small group. To conclude this first step, the pair or group composes one definition and writes it on the chalkboard. Groups compare their definitions and begin to discuss similarities and differences. When the root of the target word begins to emerge in the discussion, the teacher shares the dictionary etymology with the students, inserting this in the section of the graphic labeled roots.

Then the teacher writes the prime dictionary definition in the appropriate space on an overhead transparency copy of the graphic. The students compare their definitions with that written by the teacher. They discuss similarities between definitions, with emphasis on why the word means what it means and why it is spelled as it is. Often, the students are very close in their definitions, and since learning what a thing is *not* can be very helpful in understanding what it *is*, the discussion of differences between the conventional and unconventional definitions helps everyone get closer to actually knowing the word.

The teacher and students create an exemplary sentence using the target word, based on what they've found together to that point. The teacher refers the students to the actual definition as the context of the discussion requires. This keeps the focus on the actual target of the lesson.

Next, students brainstorm synonyms for the target word. If a word can be substituted in the sentence and still make the same sense, it must be a synonym.

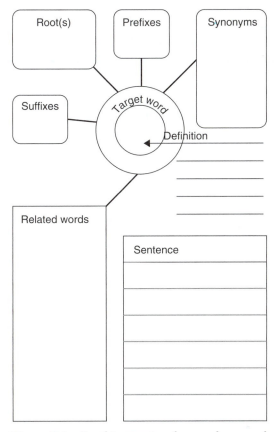

Figure 7.4 Graphic organizer for morpheme analysis.

Sometimes slight changes in the sentence are necessary to retain sense, but often the substitute word will not fit at all. Then the question becomes, "Is this a related word or a discard?" (Related words are words similar in meaning, though not synonymous, or words with the same root.) When the morpheme graphic is complete, students have a picture of the meaning of a word and, more important, a clear idea of how the word means what it does.

▶ STRATEGIES FOR RAISING WORD CONSCIOUSNESS AND HANDLING UNFAMILIAR VOCABULARY DURING SILENT READING

An important goal of vocabulary instruction is to teach students to notice unfamiliar words when they are reading and to develop a variety of strategies for predicting and confirming the meanings of these words. One way to do this is the straightforward strategy approach represented in the name of the Context, Structure, Sound, Reference method described first in this section. The next method in this section, Contextual Redefinition, focuses on the process of using context to predict word meanings. The next two methods, the Community of Language Approach and the Vocabulary Self-Collection Strategy, focus on developing the habit of realizing that a word is unfamiliar when it is encountered in print or oral language.

Context, Structure, Sound, Reference: The Basic Strategy

Context, Structure, Sound, Reference is a good basic strategy for handling unfamiliar words encountered while reading (Gray, 1946; Ruddell, 1997).

1. Read to the end of the sentence. Can you guess the meaning? Are there any clues in the surrounding sentences or paragraphs that help you? Now do you have a pretty good idea of the meaning? Does it make sense? If so, keep right on reading.

    If not,

2. Look at the parts of the word. Are there prefixes or roots that you know? Do the suffixes or inflections (plurals, past tense, etc.) help you? Combine this information with context information to arrive at a meaning. Does it make sense? If so, go right on reading.

    If not,

3. Try to pronounce the word. When you hear it, does it sound like a word you already know? If not, are there letters or letter combinations that help (e.g., the "ct" in "tract" as opposed to the "ck" in "track")? Combine this information with information from context. Does it make sense? If so, go right on reading.

    If not,

4. Look for footnotes or margin notes. Check the glossary or a dictionary. Ask someone for help: a friend, or me, or anyone else. Combine this information with information from context. Does it make sense?

Contextual Redefinition Strategy: Using Context to Predict Word Meanings

Typically, new words are encountered in the following sequence: context, isolation, context (Putnam, Bader, & Bean, 1988). This means that when readers encounter an unfamiliar word in context, they try to figure out its meaning from the context, and then, if unsuccessful, seek meaning from another source, such as a dictionary or another person. Finally, they return to the original context to make better sense of both the word and the context. The Contextual Redefinition Strategy (Cunningham, Cunningham, & Arthur, 1981) applies this natural process to a simple format for classroom instruction (Tierney, Readence, & Dishner, 1990). Although this method is used before reading, its goal is to model and provide practice in an important "during reading" vocabulary strategy.

Steps in Contextual Redefinition

To prepare for using this method, first select target words from the reading selection. Then, for each word, write one or more sentences that provide reasonable clues to the word meaning. The sentences may come from the selection itself, if these provide reasonable clues.

Step 1. Write each target word on the chalkboard or overhead and ask students to guess the word meaning. Students should be encouraged to discuss their ideas and try to come to a reasonable consensus on their predicted meaning for each word.

Step 2. Present each target word in the context sentence(s) you have prepared. Have students revise their predictions for each word meanings, again encouraging them to provide the reasons for their ideas and building on one another's thoughts to come to a consensus.

Step 3. Ask a volunteer to look up the word in the dictionary and to compare the dictionary definition with students' predictions. This step can stir a very productive instructional conversation, since dictionary definitions can sometimes be too abstract for easy interpretation, or the word could have been used in some unusual or ironic way.

Notes on Contextual Redefinition

This method teaches youngsters that context can provide clues to word meaning (Gipe, 1978–1979), but cannot be relied on to reveal word meanings in all cases. Teaching students to overrely on context clues is one of the great errors that tends to be made in vocabulary strategy instruction. A less structured approach to calling student attention to context clues is to provide a list of words for students to watch for while reading an assignment. When they come to each of the words, they are to write a predicted meaning and tell what clues they used to make the prediction.

Community of Language Approach: Utilizing the School Experience

One of the most effective things that can be done to improve reading, word learnings, and oral written language is to elevate the vocabulary used in a class, subject, or, ideally, the entire school. This is not easily done since it does require a good deal of cooperation and leadership. We know of at least one situation in which all of the teachers in a junior high school adopted a list of 30 very difficult words from a test preparation manual. Rather than teaching these words explicitly or assigning them to students, each teacher made a conscious daily effort to use the words whenever and wherever possible. Teachers watched for opportunities to use the words in appropriate contexts and sometimes even created contexts as an excuse to use the words. Throughout the spring semester, students heard these 30 words in math class, science lab, shop, art, gym, and even on morning announcements. In only a few weeks' time, students could be heard using the words in casual conversations in the hallways and cafeteria. The teachers effectively had created an elevated community of language (Manzo & Manzo, 1990a).

The impact of a simple *intentional-incidental* learning plan such as this one cannot be exaggerated. It builds student respect for teachers as models of language, reinforces reading vocabulary, raises word consciousness and precision in thinking, and boosts standardized test scores. This seemingly incidental approach can have an even more important and far-reaching effect: Students will take their new oral language home and, in turn, incidentally share it with their family and friends. This can elevate the levels of language and precision in thinking in students' families and in the community at large, *thereby reaching children who have not yet started school and among parents who have long since left it.*

The Secret Language Police: Weaving New Words into the Environment

The *Secret Language Police* (Baines, 1998, pp. 209–210) is another approach to teaching students to pay attention to words around them.° It is compatible with the Community of Language approach and, in some ways, easier since it can be initiated with students with little prior commitment from others.

Steps in the Secret Language Police

Step 1. Designate two students in class to serve as the secret language police.

Step 2. The secret language police have the job of communicating the words and definitions of two bonus vocabulary words to other members of class.

Step 3. The secret language police cannot directly state, "These are the bonus words and they mean . . .," but they should use the words in their own comments during class.

Step 4. The secret language police are encouraged to spread the words around to the principal and to other teachers. If the secret language police convince the principal (or whoever makes the school announcements) to use their words over the public address system, they receive five extra points on the exam of their choice. If they spot one of their words in a newspaper, magazine, book, or Web site and highlight it for the class before the day of the exam, they receive another five points.

Vocabulary Self-Collection Strategy: Developing Independence in Identifying Unfamiliar Words and Predicting and Clarifying Meanings

The Vocabulary Self-Collection Strategy (VSS) (Haggard [now Ruddell], 1982; 1986) is a cooperative structure that provides practice in identifying important

°Excerpts from "The Future of the Written Word," Simmons, John S., & Baines, Lawrence (Eds.). (1998). *Language Study in Middle School, High School, and Beyond* (pp. 207–209). Newark, DE: International Reading Association. Reprinted with permission of John. S. Simmons and the International Reading Association. All rights reserved. © 1998 by the International Reading Association.

terms and using context to predict meaning.° Although it takes place after students have read, its goal is to teach students to identify important key terms as they read and to access appropriate sources—from context, to dictionary, to other people—to obtain meaningful definitions.

Steps in Vocabulary Self-Collection

Step 1. *Preparation:* Use this method with concept-rich reading selections that contain several important vocabulary terms. Identify the terms you would expect students to have difficulty with. When using VSS for the first time with a group of students, prepare an example to use in introducing the method. After students have completed the reading assignment and some type of comprehension check, form small groups (nominating teams) of two to five students.

Step 2. *Small Group Work:* Each group's task is to identify and nominate one vocabulary word from the reading assignment for further emphasis. When the team has agreed on a word, they prepare the following information for the team spokesperson to present to the rest of the class. (When this activity is new to a group, the teacher gives a pre-prepared example.)

Step 3. Read the word in context.

Step 4. Tell what the group thinks the word means (they may use context and/or any other resources available in the classroom).

Step 5. Explain why the group thinks the word should be emphasized.

Step 6. *Whole Class Reporting:* Each group's spokesperson provides the information his or her groups have prepared. The teacher facilitates by writing the words and meanings on the chalkboard, along with any additional information and clarifications provided by the class.

Step 7. *Recording:* Students record the information from the chalkboard in their vocabulary notebooks or journals.

Research has provided support for VSS as an effective means for increasing student vocabulary and for developing student abilities to be strategic, independent word learners, including with at-risk readers (Ruddell & Shearer, 2002). This method provides a natural link to the next level of postreading vocabulary/concept development.

▶ METHODS FOR POSTREADING VOCABULARY/ CONCEPT DEVELOPMENT

Once a new word has been noticed and its meaning has been either predicted or superficially determined, it can be thought of as clinging lightly to the appropriate schema location. To learn the word, it needs to be more tightly affixed. This is

°Adapted from: Ruddell [formerly Haggard], Martha Rapp. (1982, December). The vocabulary self-collection strategy: An active approach to word learning. *Journal of Reading*, 26 (3), 203–207. © 1982 by the International Reading Association.

achieved through cross-referencing it with numerous other bits of information and experience and through repeated exposure. Word knowledge is transformed into concept understanding by means of inclusion, exclusion, subordination, and superordination.

1. *Inclusion.* What other words belong in the same category with this word? What are its relevant characteristics or properties? What are some specific examples/applications of the word?

2. *Exclusion.* What similar words do not belong in the same category with this word? What are some related but inappropriate examples/applications? What are some nonrelevant characteristics?

3. *Subordination.* What are some words that would fall into subcategories of this word?

4. *Superordination.* What broader category does this word fall under?

This section deals with the deepening of understanding that converts word meanings to concept knowledge. The following section provides activities for repetition and practice.

Typical to Technical Meaning Approach

Common words often have special, technical applications in a particular content area. For example, the word *true* is used in mechanics to indicate that gears are well synchronized; hence, *not-true* means "poorly synchronized." Today this phenomenon occurs most with tech terms like *cookies* and *spam*. In the Typical to Technical Meaning Approach (Welker, 1987), the teacher prepares a worksheet exercise that provides practice in using a term in both its typical and its technical meanings. While these practice sheets require considerable preparation time, once students have become familiar with the format, the teacher simply can ask, "Do we have any terms in today's material for which there is a common as well as a technical meaning?" and the rest of the lesson will unfold from previous practice.[°]

Steps in the Typical to Technical Meaning Approach

Step 1. Discuss a term's common meanings and then introduce its technical meaning.

Step 2. Have students complete a word-to-meaning exercise, matching each term with both its common and its technical meaning (see Part 1 in Figure 7.5). Then have students complete a cloze-type exercise, filling in the blanks where the terms are used in either the typical or technical sense (see Part 2 in Figure 7.5).

Step 3. Briefly discuss students' responses prior to presenting information based on technical uses of the terms.

[°]Excerpt from Welker, William A. (December, 1987). Open to Suggestion: Going from typical to technical meaning. *Journal of Reading* 31(3), 275–276. Reprinted with permission of William A. Welker and the International Reading Association. All rights reserved. © 1987 by the International Reading Association.

Part 1

Directions: For each term below, write the letter of its common meaning, and its technical meaning under the headings given.

Terms **Common Meaning** **Technical Meaning**

acute
supplementary
complementary
angle

Meanings

A. A person's point of view

B. Making whole, or completing something

C. Something additional to the basic requirements

D. Space between two lines or surfaces that meet

E. Having a sharp point

F. Either of two angles that combine to equal 90 degrees

G. An angle which is less than 90 degrees in value

H. Either of two angles that together form exactly 180 degrees

Part 2

Directions: Select the best word from the word bank to complete each sentence below. Each word will be used twice.

Sentences

1. The sword had a very _____ cutting edge.

2. The _____ angle for a 50-degree angle is a 40-degree angle.

3. Our reading textbook comes with _____ materials such as workbooks and ditto sheets.

4. If an angle is 53 degrees, it is called an _____ angle.

5. A black tie with a white shirt would be considered a _____ match.

6. Now that I have gotten my thoughts on the subject, what is your _____ (or opinion) on the matter?

7. A pie can be sliced into pieces with many different _____.

8. Two angles that together equal 180 degrees are _____ angles.

Word Bank

complementary   acute   angle   supplementary

Figure 7.5 Typical to Technical Meaning Exercises.

Source: Welker, William A. (December, 1987). Open to Suggestion: Going from typical to technical meaning. *Journal of Reading* 31(3), 275–276. Reprinted with permission of William A. Welker and the International Reading Association. All rights reserved. © 1987 by the International Reading Association.

Subject Area Vocabulary Reinforcement

Learning is a process of placing new information into existing categories until a special feature that does not fit is encountered. Then a new category must be created to expand schema. Semantic Feature Analysis (Johnson & Pearson, 1984) is a method designed to permit students to engage in this process in a conscious and focused way. A variation on this method, called SAVOR, or Subject Area Vocabulary Reinforcement (Stieglitz & Stieglitz, 1981), is designed specifically for content area use.

Steps in SAVOR

Step 1. Identify a category of words. Then have students brainstorm words that fit in this category, and list these examples in a column on their own paper.

Step 2. Then have students brainstorm specific features of the words they have listed. These features are listed as column headings across the top of their paper (see Figure 7.6 for an example of how the chart is constructed).

Step 3. Next, have students fill in the charts individually, using plus (+) or minus (−) signs to indicate whether each word has a particular feature.

Step 4. After students have completed their charts, the teacher encourages discussion about the patterns of pluses and minuses and to discover the uniqueness of each word.

As students gain experience with the Semantic Feature Analysis format, the teacher may wish to switch from a plus/minus system to a numerical system (0 = none, 1 = some, 2 = much, 3 = all). The method is viewed as a culminating activity for reinforcing and expanding concepts introduced in the conventional content

Shapes	Four Sided	All Curved or Rounded Lines	Line Segment	Sides Equal in Length	Right Angles
Triangle	−	−	+	+	+
Rectangle	+	−	+	−	+
Parallelogram	+	−	+	+	+
Circle	−	+	−	−	−
Trapezoid	+ −	−	+	−	−
Semicircle	−	+	+	−	−
Square	+	−	+	+	+

Figure 7.6   SAVOR Example in Mathematics.

Source: Chart (p. 48) from Stieglitz, Ezra, & Stieglitz, Varda. (1981, October). SAVOR the word to reinforce vocabulary in the content areas. *Journal of Reading,* 25(1), 46–51. Reprinted with permission of Ezra Stieglitz and the International Reading Association. All rights reserved. © 1981 by International Reading Association.

area lesson or following reading. It is particularly suitable for clarifying frequently confused terms.

Notes on SAVOR

Semantic Feature Analysis has been found to be significantly more effective than traditional methods for this purpose (Johnson, Toms-Bronowski, & Pittelman, 1982). It also has been shown to improve content area reading vocabulary and comprehension in learning-disabled adolescents (Anders, Bos, & Filip, 1984).

Cultural-Academic Trivia

The Cultural-Academic Trivia, or CAT, game (Manzo, 1970b, 1985) refers to common cultural learnings and associations that are found in our language as frequently used metaphors and allusions to explain feelings, facts, and concepts. In initial field tests of this method, students felt it was appropriate that the word *trivia* appeared in the title. In time, however, as their connections and fund of academic information, vocabulary, and allusions grew, they concluded that it is minds that can be trivial, not information. This prompted the idea that the game should be called "Cultural-Academic Treasures." CAT is an *intentional-incidental* approach that builds a fund of knowledge, or schema (the best single predictor of comprehension) as well as vocabulary.

Steps in Cultural-Academic (Treasures) Trivia

Step 1. The class is divided into two groups. A chairperson is assigned to each group and given a set of index cards initially prepared by the teacher. On the front of each card is a word or phrase with a number from 1 to 3 designating its relative difficulty. On the reverse side is an explanation or definition of the word or phrase.

Step 2. The chairperson of one group chooses and writes a word or phrase on the chalkboard and then asks students in the other group if they know that word or phrase. All the information gained from the members of a group constitutes that group's total response. If that information amounts to merely an identification or recognition of the word or phrase, only the number describing the level of difficulty (from 1 to 3) is awarded to the group. If any worthwhile elaboration, as determined by the teacher, also is contributed, the score is doubled. Conversely, if the students on one team cannot respond successfully, the opposing team is given the opportunity to win points.

Example

In a high school class, the word utopia *might be assigned a difficulty level of 2. If one team volunteers that the word means "a perfect political and social system," they gain the two basic points. If team members add that utopia is also the title of a book by Sir Thomas More, or that it came from Greek, they receive two additional points. After the first round of the game, students are asked to submit terms they have selected from their reading, viewing, and living environments.*

Notes on Cultural Academic Treasures

Students' contributions are essential if students are to be re–sensitized to the language they encounter around them but tend to block out because the unfamiliar can cause undue dissonance. In the particular setting in which this game was first played, the first author treated the cards as "admission tickets" to class. Students who arrived without one were sent scurrying to the library to find an appropriate term. Today, we would urge students to browse the Internet for new and poignant terms. See Figure 7.7 for some indications of this phenomenon.

Of course, not all words are created equal. The success of this game hinges on the terms used. Well-selected words and phrases should key students to central, or schema-enhancing, academic ideas and allusions (e.g., hieroglyphics, Communist Manifesto, citizen's arrest, Chaucer). If the teacher intends to develop students' sophistication in just one area, the name of the game can be altered accordingly; for example, BAT (Biological-Academic Trivia/Treasures) or HAT (Historical-Academic Trivia/Treasures).

Themed Vocabulary, Webbing, and Semantic Clustering

One of the most rational means of vocabulary enrichment is based on grouping words by themes. *Themed Vocabulary Study*, also called *Webbing* and *Semantic Clustering* (Marzano & Marzano, 1988), permits students to take well-known,

Technology is the language du jour. It permeates our style of speaking/writing and is an analogical, or metaphorical means of thinking and hence communicating. Vocabulary knowledge itself could be likened to a computer's random access memory (RAM). The human equivalent of RAM pretty much defines the type and sophistication level of the learning software, or content and concepts, that a mind will be easily able to recognize and run. Of course, this need not be the case. RAM is mechanical, fixed, unreflective, and indeed bogs down with demand. Minds are organic, have no apparent limitations, and can reflect on and, with proper stimulation, restructure themselves in ways that actually permit them to grow greater, wiser, and more efficient with each additional word and concept that is strategically added. If there is a limit to the mind's capacity to learn, we have yet to discover it; thus far it seems to expand further with each breakthrough means of teaching it.

In any case, once it was trains that captured human imagination with images like "building up a head of steam"; now we speak of someone's "bandwidth" to describe their capacity, or ask ourselves if we have enough "cycles" to get something done. New dictionaries are listing between 300 and 400 new and new-meaning words.

By the way (or BTW, in e-mail lingo), if you need a dictionary before one is available for terms like *digerati* or *cookie* or *Netiquette,* try www.whatis.com.

Figure 7.7 Tech Talk—new members to our community of language and allusions.

partially-known, and barely recognized words and link them together into a semantic web that will catch and hold yet newer words as well as nuances of meaning and connotation for familiar words. Paradoxically, it helps students understand that words do not always have precise, distinct, and unchanging meanings (Anderson & Nagy, 1989). Most important, themed vocabulary study imparts an effective strategy for lifelong word learning. The act of categorizing terms also is one of the most fundamental forms of human thinking and, therefore, no doubt contributes to improved cognitive processing.

Steps in Themed Vocabulary Study

Step 1. Identify a theme. For example, the theme "talk" is used in Figure 7.8. As shown in this example, the inner cluster reflects words as might be known by a second grader, the outward cluster words known by most sixth graders, and the outer cluster as should be known by college students.

Step 2. Ask students to state words they think are related to the theme.

Step 3. If necessary, use dictionaries to check word meanings and to find additional synonyms, antonyms, and subtly different meanings.

Step 4. Link the relevant words to one another (with brief definitions) in the form of a semantic map or web as shown.

Step 5. Reinforce and evaluate by testing students' recall of word meanings and distinctions by having them write sentences or descriptive pieces designed to elicit the new words.

Notes on Themed Vocabulary Study

Themes for vocabulary study can be selected based on the guiding concept of instructional units: The possibilities are as broad as one's imagination. Here are some themes to consider for general word study that we have found to be of particular interest to middle and senior high school students:

- Noncomplimentary but nonvulgar terms (pesky, brusque, prissy, scattered, antsy, bawdy, addlebrained)
- Behavior-related terms (manners, antsy, comportment, deportment, inappropriate, maladaptive, poised, irascible)
- Character traits (endurance, restraint, perseverance, reflection, tolerance)
- Thinking terms (abstract, concrete, rational, irrational, creative, critical, cognitive, diffusive, constructive, coherent)
- Temperament labels (sanguine, industrious, hyper, choleric, mercurial, pensive)
- Attitudes (positive, negative, hostile, aggressive, assertive, constructive)

The impact of Themed Vocabulary Study can be greatly amplified by combining it with other vocabulary methods previously described. It also can be linked to the next method as an incidental means of building word power.

Figure 7.8 Themed Vocabulary Study—semantic cluster web for *talk*.

Source: From *Teaching Children to be Literate, A Reflective Approach,* 1st edition, by MANZO/ MANZO © 1996. Reprinted with permission of Wadsworth, a division of Thomson Learning. *www.thomsonrights.com* Fax 800-730-2215.

Multimedia Vocabulary Review

Two formats are suggested by Baines (1998) for transforming vocabulary work-sheets into a multimedia experience.° The first has students working in pairs to create word posters.

1. Place students in pairs.

2. Give each pair of students the responsibility for one vocabulary word.

3. Give students 10 minutes to illustrate their word. Students may draw pictures, cut out pictures in magazines, use computer clip art, or use images from the Internet. After the images have been selected (printed and cut out), students should paste them on a large piece of posterboard and beside it write their own brief definition in large letters. Encourage students to use mnemonic devices.

4. Have the students explain their posters and then perform a live 30-second skit that illustrates the meaning of their word.

5. Give an extra point on the next vocabulary test to the first student each day to use one of the vocabulary words in class in "everyday conversation."

6. If more than one class has the same vocabulary words, place all the posterboards with the same words in the same area. Hang the posterboards conspicuously around the room until the exam is given.

The second format is the *Vocabulary Chain E-Mail* (Baines, 1998, pp. 208–209).°

1. Create a flowchart with PowerPoint, Persuasion, or another presentation software package. If you do not have access to these, use a ruler. Draw a flowchart in which one green box is at the top, five red boxes are under the top green box, and five more blue boxes are under each of the red boxes. This is a flowchart for 31 students that is easily modifiable for more or fewer students.

2. Give the student whose name is in the top green box the vocabulary list a day before you hand it out to the rest of the class. The student should write definitions of the words, be able to pronounce them correctly, and use them in a sentence.

3. The next day, speak individually with the student whose name is in the top green box. Answer any questions he or she might have about the vocabulary. Then hand out the list of vocabulary words to the rest of the class.

4. A day or two before the vocabulary test, the student whose name is in the top green box e-mails or calls the students whose names appear in the five red boxes and helps them in review for the vocabulary test. Then

each of the students whose names appear in the five red boxes e-mails or calls each of the students whose names appear in the five blue boxes. By the day of the exam, everyone in class has received an e-mail message or a telephone call and has reviewed for the exam.

5. Shift responsibilities weekly. At the end of the term, give a prize to the individual whose name was in the top green box when the class scored the highest on the exam.

QuestMagnet for Pioneering Minds—Join the Revolution

Where vocabulary/concept development is concerned, there are two interacting issues. First and foremost, few educators seem to understand just how important vocabulary acquisition is (not one school principal in a recent literacy leadership institute expressed any interest whatsoever in the topic, nor in a doctoral level literacy course did any student choose it for a focus topic). Relatedly, while there are solid methods, there are no integrated, wrap-around approaches to ensure that it occurs—that is, "surroundsound" strategies that are equal to the several different and overlapping ways by which kids acquire concepts, content, and language proficiency. Each of the methods discussed in this text has strengths, but individually they have some weaknesses as well. Weaknesses range from methods that some teachers would find too mechanical, to others that may be too much of a digression from the content, to yet others that require school or department leadership, planning, and cooperation. See if you can envision a cohesive, wrap-around program that would make school a place where vocabulary and concept acquisition occurs more soundly, systematically, and effectively. Since we already know a good deal, much of what needs to be done may require little more than skillful synthesis of off-the-shelf parts and procedures.

► AFTER WORDS

This chapter laid out a technology for building better thinking—one word and concept at a time. Methods were described for teaching potentially difficult words before students begin to read a selection. Other methods were described for helping students deal with unfamiliar words encountered while reading. Follow-up methods were outlined for helping students revisit, practice, and reflect on new word meanings. The next chapter tells how to create active, expressive ways to use new words and concepts in writing to further build critical/constructive thinking in the disciplines.

CHAPTER 8

BEYOND THE LINES: CRITICAL-CONSTRUCTIVE READING, WRITING, THINKING, AND INTERNET COMPUTING

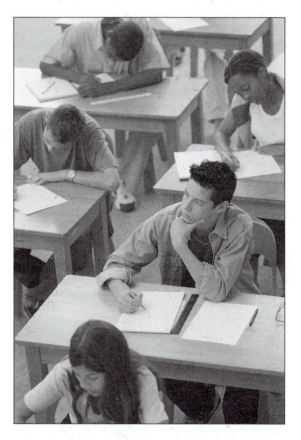

Izzy, did you ask a good question today?

—From D. Sheff's account of the life of Isodore I. Rabi, Nobel laureate in physics

▶ FORE WORDS

Parallel to pre-, during-, and post-reading functions are the expressions *Into, Through* and *Beyond.* This chapter is more akin to reading (way) *Beyond* the lines. The ideas presented in this chapter are aimed at the heroic and evolving 21st-Century goals of improving critical-constructive thinking and problem solving at all levels of reading proficiency. This chapter is about raising new targets for fertile minds. This type of teaching has been given lip service in the past but little real support in school or common culture. Achieving this aim implies the need for instructional approaches designed to *transform* rather than merely inform. The chapter focuses on three interlocking approaches to transformation. One is aimed at converting inert knowledge to dynamic knowledge, an objective that has been described as moving the simple thinking of "ungeared minds" to the more complex thinking of connected minds (Chase, 1926). This is accomplished largely through brief, multiperspective writing and exchanges with other reader-writers. The second approach is to stress knowledge making or original thought as well as the more traditional goal of knowledge taking. Ironically, this is accomplished by reeducating minds to patterns of thought that could make creative thinking part of school tradition (Manzo & Manzo, 1997b). The third approach is to connect students to virtual communities of learners whose knowledge quests and idea exchanges match the most idealized campus environments of the past.

- ▶ FORE WORDS
- ▶ WELCOME TO THE 21ST CENTURY—AIMING HIGHER TO CONSTRUCTIVE THINKING
- ▶ CRITICAL READING-WRITING-THINKING: A TRADITIONAL AND EVOLVING GOAL
- ▶ WRITING-BASED METHODS FOR GUIDING CRITICAL-CONSTRUCTIVE READING
- ▶ A FORMULA FOR PROMOTING CRITICAL-CONSTRUCTIVE THINKING
- ▶ CRITICAL-CONSTRUCTIVE DISCUSSION TECHNIQUES
- ▶ AFTER WORDS

▶ WELCOME TO THE 21ST CENTURY— AIMING HIGHER TO CONSTRUCTIVE THINKING

Chances are that you already know something about *critical* reading-thinking. However, your own schooling and teacher education probably have not tended to address issues in *constructive-creative* thinking. It is a fairly new development in school programming. Despite its newness, teaching for constructive-creative outcomes does have some lore associated with it. Knowing some of this will help you be ready to learn more. So here is a quick summary of some of the key ideas that should make your reading of the content area literacy contributions to constructive thinking more profitable. First, we briefly address the role of text in construc-

Constructive/ Creative (generative, *productive*)	*Both* Metacognitive reflection	Critical (Analytical/ *evaluative*)
Flexible thinking	Use of past knowledge	Precision
Fluent thinking	Communication Skills	Accuracy
Wonderment	Transfer	Ability to critique reference criteria
Inquisitiveness	Accessing Information	Prioritization
Curiosity	Problem solving	Tolerance for ambiguity
Ingenuity	Decision making	Organizing
Originality		
Insightfulness		
Elaborative thinking		

Figure 8.1   Cognitive map of similarities and differences between creative-constructive and critical thinking.

Source: From Fogarty, R., & McTighe, J. (1993). Educating Teachers for Higher-Order Thinking: The Three-Story Intellect. *Theory Into Practice*, 32(3), 161–69. Copyright by the College of Education, The Ohio State University. All rights reserved.

tive reading, then the relationship of constructive reading to constructivism and conventional critical thinking, then the affective side of this process, and, finally, some general guidelines for promoting constructive-creative thinking outcomes in the classroom. Think of this initial information as *frontloading* for reading the remainder of this chapter, which in turn is front material for personally joining this very exciting 21st–Century development in professional education and hope for the future. See Figure 8.1 for a cognitive map of similarities and differences between creative-constructive and critical thinking.

The Role of Text

An English teacher in Brookline, Massachusetts, wrote an article on her remarkable three-month effort to teach to students *To Read Beyond the Plot* (Metzger, 1998). She used her own variations on Socratic Seminars and other elaborate techniques to foster such in-depth thinking. Along the way, in reading *Romeo and Juliet, The Great Gatsby*, and the poem *Ozymandias*, the class she led and tutored in discussion techniques did something else that can be easily forgotten when reaching "beyond the lines": They read "the lines" again, and again.

At the beginning of each discussion, we read the passage two or three times, each time more slowly. Therefore during a single class period, the same page was read four to six times . . . The act of re-reading helped students focus and notice details . . . (and) words . . . It was no longer enough to skim over an assignment and consider it finished.

(From "Teaching Reading: Beyond the Plot," by Margaret Metzger,
PHI DELTA KAPPAN, November, 1998, p. 246.
© 1998 Phi Delta Kappa International.)

This teacher's words and experience tell how important the words are in teaching thinking beyond the text. Literal understanding is essential, although it need not all be achieved before there is any discussion; which is to say that it is necessary but not sufficient for promoting higher-order literacy.

Constructive-Creative Thinking and Constructivism

By constructive thinking, we mean thinking that is grounded in *critique more than criticism,* and critique is pointed toward building alternative perspectives and options. This approach is not quite the same as *constructivism,* a sometimes overly subjectivist philosophy advocating the importance of learners figuring things out for themselves. Unlike constructivism, teaching for constructive-creative outcomes does not contradict the value of old fashioned lecture, recitation, and factual learning—three potentially powerful forms of "verbal learning" (Ausubel, 1960). What it does do is emphasize the greater good, inquiry, and personal responsibility for one's own knowledge and for the state of human knowledge. It raises this seemingly abstract responsibility to a conscious goal for teachers and students. In so doing, it should help to increase internal motivation, grasp of larger concepts, and appreciation for existing "knowledge" that has been painstakingly accumulated. Done properly, efforts to teach about the limits of knowledge can implicitly impart ways to respond to the irritation of uncertainty, that ever-present feeling that can either immobilize the will or stir its quest for new knowledge. This is almost a definition of a higher purpose and, of itself, can help balance a worldview based on self-interest.

Disposition

The way in which a person typically deals with life-problems foretells whether and how he or she will address problems in reading, writing, thinking, and knowledge acquisition. There are five characteristic dispositions for responding to a barrier, conflict, or paradox:

1. Ignoring it
2. Saying it is unsolvable
3. Working harder at the same solution hoping for a different result
4. Trying for more inventive solutions
5. Considering the possibility that the wrong questions are being asked

The first three tend to be counterproductive. The latter two—looking for inventive solutions and reconsidering the question—are the prime movers of human progress and lives well lived. As such, these are chief aims of this chapter, and as you will see, not merely the hope, but well within the scope of most any classroom. Teaching for creative outcomes is not a tedious new challenge, it is a pragmatic solution to the tedium of schooling.

Guidelines for Teaching Creative Outcomes

Successful teaching for creative outcomes tends to require creative teaching. Guidelines for inviting creativity include the following:

- Believing students are capable of creative production
- Simply asking for creative responses
- Providing critical-constructive feedback
- Inviting and welcoming expressions of curiosity
- Illustrating and underscoring new twists on old patterns
- Teaching students how to give as well as receive critical-creative critiques
- Readying students for a much greater level of error or mistakes than most of us are used to experiencing
- Inviting contrary or opposing views
- Finding ways to grapple with authentic as well as academic issues (Manzo, 1998)

In addition to these classroom-based considerations, there is a need to build systemic support in the society at large for inventive thinking, especially for procedural and social solutions, for which society provides few incentives such as patents or royalties.

Much of what you will be reading and thinking about from this point forward is one of the quests or pioneering realms of content area literacy and professional education. Read ahead with the mindset of thinking both critically and constructively about how this might be done better in schools and, by extension, in society.

The NAEP Indicators of Higher Literacy

The National Assessment of Educational Progress (NAEP) is one of the major tools for documenting the efficacy of schooling in the United States. It samples students' academic progress in several areas and at several levels. In brief, scores are showing the most progress where we have concentrated resources, namely in the initial 3 grades of schooling. Soon we can expect the same levels of concern to reach the intermediate and high school level, or we will stall-out. But, here are some of the numbers.

The 1998 and 2002 NAEP results in the area of literacy are being heralded as showing "significant" progress over 1994. The new results from the 2002

NAEP (The Nation's Report Card, 2002), which has both national and state samples, indicate progress, most strikingly at the Basic achievement level. Sixteen states and three other jurisdictions show significant gains in fourth grade reading since 1998. The proportion of white fourth graders reaching the Proficient level in reading has grown to 41 percent. The proportion reaching Basic is 75 percent. By contrast, even with the gains they have made since 1992 and 2000, just 12 percent of black fourth graders reach the Proficient level, and just 40 percent read at the Basic level or above. For Hispanics, 15 percent of fourth graders reach Proficient, and 44 percent reach Basic. For these reasons, mean (average) scores have not improved as much as they need to. In addition, there is reason for concern that the growth in the lower categories has not been matched in the higher categories. If we used a normal distribution curve as a guide, there should be about the same proportion of students in the lowest category as in the highest, but there are many more in the lowest than the highest. It should also be noted that many who are in the "proficient" and "advanced" groups may have areas of need which these conventional tests do not measure and which, therefore, go unattended.

Unattended Needs of Even the Most Proficient Readers

Educators carefully note that there are subgroups of readers who are *dyslexic, remedial,* and *corrective.* However, when discussing *developmental readers,* or those on grade level and above, the implicit belief is that these students are a homogeneous group of students who are progressing as expected and need no further examination or assistance. Lack of attention to this issue masks several reading-thinking problems that need to be acknowledged before they can be addressed. Recent research is raising this veil of denial.

Four subtypes of otherwise proficient readers seem to be emerging. Each subgroup has strengths and weakness that content area literacy, and specifically the critical-creative thrust of this chapter, could be addressing. A recent study found that only one of the four subgroups seemed to be making real progress toward reading maturity, and even this group had a weakness in what could be called "entrepreneurial literacy"—again, the making as much as taking of jobs—arguably one of the strongest needs in contemporary life. (See Figure 8.2 for descriptions of the four subgroups identified). Two other subgroups of proficient readers had a decided gender-dominated bent, and the fourth appeared to have mastered the mechanics of language but not much of its subtleties' complex implications (Manzo, Manzo, Barnhill, & Thomas, 2000; Thomas, 2001). These subtypes, or *Reading Personality Profiles,* were deduced from a 148-item self-report inventory given to college level students. We do not yet know for certain when the characteristics identified had their developmental onset. However, one point seems logically supportable: Students are more likely to be "transformable," or guided toward a critical-constructive disposition, when younger than when older. Therefore, efforts to promote higher-order reading, writing, and thinking probably should be cultivated for all students, from the earliest grade levels, no matter how proficient they might appear on conventional measures of reading comprehension.

The Need to Cultivate Multiple Literacies
as Opposed to Merely More Reading

Jane Fell Greene, in a conference title for a presentation we have yet to hear, unpacks much of what concerns us in this tag line: "We Confused Literature with Literacy . . . So What Do We Do Now?" Higher-order literacy is not likely to be achieved merely by *more* story reading, nor by reading that is totally limited to one's narrow field of interest. Becoming more informed in a variety of fields and topics, or achieving multiple literacy, as in computer literacy and financial literacy and historical literacy, is the most basic and traditional way to enrich schema and broaden orientation. These *multiple literacies* amount to ingraining implicit questions, or quests, that engender the interests, motivation, and ability to use metaphors, and analogical thinking ("Oh, this is like that . . . ") to comprehend and reason beyond the lines. Real experts in any field are those who leverage their primary interest area to find more universal meanings and levels of meaning in

---

SUBTYPE I: DEVELOPMENTALLY MATURE
ANDROGYNOUS READERS

These most highly optimized subtype readers report that their reading is characterized by concentration, critical analysis, concept formation, inference, and interpretation. They think creatively with minimum prompts, and write fairly well. They have eclectic reading interests and seem confident and comfortable with traditional schooling. Since they did not have the strong, conventionalized male or female schema orientations noted in other subtypes, they are characterized as androgynous, or in touch with both their male and female sides. The only hypothesized characteristic of mature readers that these individuals lack is the entrepreneurial spirit that has become so necessary in contemporary life.

SUBTYPE II: CONVENTIONALIZED NONFICTION
MALE ORIENTATION

This subtype tends to have a conventionalized orientation that is most often associated with males in western cultures. They have an action stance and a fair transfer-of-training (the application level of thinking), and are disinclined to self-examination. They have conventional male interests in sports, outdoor life, business, gambling, social studies, and the mechanics of how things work. However, they indicated that they do not enjoy reading for pleasure, and even report some physical discomfort in doing so. They further indicate that they have trouble paying attention while reading, and suspect that they may be "learning disabled," to the point of being unable to stay attentive without active, pencil-in-hand, reading. They indicate that they are only moderately creative, and prefer repetitive tasks. Yet, they are critical and reflective: they engage in a great

---

Figure 8.2 Proficient-reader subtypes.

deal of active questioning while reading, attempting to convert what is read into action plans. Overall, they prefer to read in short spurts, and for pragmatic purposes.

SUBTYPE III: CONVENTIONALIZED STORY-READING FEMALE ORIENTATION

This subtype tends to have characteristics traditionally associated with females in literate cultures. They enjoy reading fiction, and report little interest in thinking deeply about what they read, and *no* interest in self-examination. They have virtually no interest in things mechanical, political, functional, or pragmatic. They have narrow, traditionalized female interests in fashion and children. They read for pleasure and escape with a self-declared tendency to be too literal, and to lack confidence in their understanding of what they read. Contrary to the image of the female diary keeper, they do not feel as if they learn from writing, and they find it very taxing. Overall, they are story-readers with solid literal comprehension and strongly expressed enjoyment of reading, but who see little connection between what they read and their own lives. Since it is the nature of fiction to unveil the complexities in understanding "relationships," it is possible that this is a desired, pragmatic goal.

SUBTYPE IV: DETAIL-DEPENDENT RULE FOLLOWERS

This subtype tends to be passive reader-learners with apparently good mastery of the mechanics of language, such as grammar and spelling, but who feel that they tend to get lost in details when they read or write. They have an expressed interest in magic, which suggests less emotional maturity and relatively unsophisticated patterns of thought for otherwise capable minds.

Figure 8.2 *(continued)*

various other knowledge areas. Further, they return from forays into other knowledge areas with new metaphors and analogies that excite clearer thinking in their areas of expertise. However, this transfer does not seem to occur naturally (Kirshner & Whitson, 1997). A study of mathematics majors had results similar to one found in the proficient reader study referenced previously. It showed that among those college students who had considerable experience with mathematics there was not a commensurate improvement in thinking that even vaguely resembled that of mathematicians (Stenger, 1999). The primary reason to study in any field is often said to be to learn how to "think in that subject." Current schooling does not seem to be accomplishing this objective to the extent that modern teaching and ancillary technologies suggest we could and should. The next section suggests some possible reasons for the difficulty of teaching toward this transfer of disposition and learning, and some viable classroom solutions that would be within the reach of content area teachers in middle and secondary schools.

The Problem of Inert Knowledge:
The Value of Connective Teaching-Learning

Traditionally, two of the highest objectives of literacy education have been to keep learning continuous or ongoing (Bruner, 1966) and to help students transfer learning from one situation or context to another—sometimes called the *evaluation/application level of thinking* (Bloom, 1976; McKeough, Lupart, & Marini, 1995). Fundamental to these interrelated objectives is the need to have knowledge rise above the level of the *inert*. The way this is done can be represented in a single word: *connections*. New experiences, ideas, and facts become usable, or transferable, only when they are connected with prior experience and knowledge. We have discussed several ways to do this in previous chapters under the labels of *schema activation, frontloading,* and *reading between the lines*. Addressed now are several other reasons and ways to *excite* acquired knowledge, making it more active and potentially attachable to other sources of incoming information.

It is now commonly held that the conversion of *inert* to *dynamic* knowledge is not best done merely through conventional *transmission* education—where information and knowledge is transferred from those who are "in the know" to those who are ignorant. Nor is it done merely through *transactional* education—where the object of teaching/learning is the individual's unique subjective, constructivist perceptions of experience and information. Achieving dynamic learning requires a certain level of *transformative* education—where learning and thinking are intended to change the learner's attitudes and dispositions, providing a more solid preparation for tomorrows that cannot be predicted. This form of learning is based on extensions of cognitive modeling or *cognitive apprenticeship* approaches that have been illustrated earlier in this text. These apprenticeships can be conducted in a variety of settings and from a variety of perspectives (Rogoff, 1990). Aiming these approaches toward transformative goals tends to require

- Problems that are stated in evocative ways
- Reciprocal interactions that shape the thinking of learners and the offerings of teachers
- Frequent, brief writing
- The environmental impact of the Internet on information sharing and our social images of literate people

To overlook the wrap-around effect of the Internet is to miss a developing opportunity to capitalize on its benefit to influence learning and thinking around the clock, around the home, in the community, in classrooms, and around the globe.

Writing in response to reading is a traditional means of teaching comprehension and developing thinking strategies. The types of responses students are guided toward reflect the teacher's theory of teaching-learning. The next section summarizes the primary schools of thought in this area.

Reader-Response Theories: Toward Transformational Turn Abouts, Tiny Rebirths, and Epiphanies

For some educators, the primary purpose of reading in school is to achieve cultural and historical *transmission* (Hirsch, 1987), or (again) the *orderly* transfer of knowledge from those who have it to those who would then be sufficiently informed to do likewise. For others, response to text largely should be a *transaction* (Harste, 1994; Rosenblatt, 1938), or a personal construction of meaning that is highly subjective and unguided by the teacher or some other higher authority. This can be somewhat disorderly, since it seems to imply that there are no limits to the number of different ways that text can be interpreted. For a growing number of educators, such as the previously mentioned English teacher from Brookline, Massachusetts, response to text has many, but not an infinite number of, possible interpretations. As such, responses to text should be, at least in school, based on certain grounded outcomes that are both informative and transformative. That is, students should become more willing to reformulate as well as formulate ideas through what have been called *reflective turnabouts* (Santa, Dailey, & Nelson, 1985) and *tiny rebirths* (Burke, 1950/1969), or changes in personal view. Such change may follow from receiving sound arguments and evidence contrary to their initial views (Manzo, Garber, Manzo, & Kahn, 1994; Manzo & Manzo, 1995) and from exchanges of different perspectives. In some cases, the change may come as a sweeping epiphany triggered by new experience, but it is more likely to be a gradual transformation, or *tiny rebirths* to more qualified thinking. These enlightenments seldom come about through argument. They tend to culminate from stories as much as from statistics. The challenge seems to be to impart a balance of intentional information that is "suasive," though not blatantly persuasive (more on this later), along with a continuing supply of stories and perspectives that encourage deeper sensitivity to the incongruities in language and common conceptions. Salibrici (1999) refers to these as "Burkean moments," a reference to the writings of Kenneth Burke on what we would characterize as the "implosive effect" on learning and thinking that can come from attempting to reconcile incongruities and paradoxes or seemingly conflicting stories and statistics.

A comparison study of the effects of each of these three approaches on measures of complexity of thinking and socioemotional adjustment showed that *transmission-type* teaching was the least effective, *transactive* (constructivist) was next best, and *transformative* teaching was by far the most effective (Garber, 1995). This finding has been richly supported in a second study with college students (Jackson-Albee, 2000). For a rhetorical picture of the distinctions among these three perspectives in terms of the role of the text, the reader, and the teacher, see Figure 8.3. For a more personal account, consider Mary Salibrici's (1999) anecdotal report. She describes how her students reacted to a unit of reading, writing, and discussion of the Rosenberg trial of the early 1950s. Julius and Ethel Rosenberg were the only Americans ever executed for treason during peacetime. They were instrumental in helping the then Soviet Union to gain access to secrets on how to build an atomic bomb. That which started as a topical unit in literature soon became almost indistinguishable from a unit in social studies on the mass psychology of fear. In this case, what would have been a mildly interesting story of an earlier era is converted to a potentially transformative reminder to think clearly about whatever time we are in just as you would try to rise above the preoccupations of a particular clique. (By the way, recent releases of previously secret Soviet files have confirmed that the Rosenbergs were communist spies.)

In simplest terms, the key element in transformative theory is a commitment to providing youngsters with some basic values, such as those associated with democratic life, without pedantically serving up unnecessarily biased views of

---

TRANSMISSION MODEL PERSPECTIVE *least effective*

Role of the Text: The text is a means of transmitting society's dominant historical, literary, and cultural canon. It has fixed meanings and values irrespective of the reader. The text remains virtually static over time.

Role of the Reader: The reader is expected to acquire the precise facts and ideas being conveyed by the author and reproduce these in the same formats in which they were presented. Little attention is given to the reader's personal or critical examination of the text. The reader is simply responsible for reconstructing the author's ideas.

Role of the Teacher: The teacher focuses classroom discussion on the author's biography, the historical and political context of the author, and the traditional literary elements.

TRANSACTION MODEL PERSPECTIVE

Role of the Text: The text means unique things to different readers regardless of what the author may have intended to communicate. There is no static or inherent meaning incorporated within the text itself. Instead, the text is viewed as dynamic and subjective.

Role of the Reader: The reader brings a host of associations and inferences to every reading experience. These reader-based conceptions are a chief consideration as the reader attempts to build meaning from the written words. The reader makes fresh and unmediated interpretations, which may reflect the emotional and aesthetic needs of the reader.

Role of the Teacher: The teacher focuses classroom discussion on the reader's feelings, associations, and personal interpretations of texts.

Figure 8.3 Theoretical perspectives on guiding students' responses to reading.

most effective [handwritten annotation]

TRANSFORMATION MODEL PERSPECTIVE

Role of the Text: The text is a tool for critical and constructive thought. It not only reflects the ideas and contexts of the author but also invites the thoughts and feelings of the reader. The text is a stimulus for critical-evaluative, or formative, thinking.

Role of the Reader: The reader examines the text critically with the goal of becoming a constructive thinker and solution-creator/implementer in the context of the surrounding society. The reader approaches each text consciously, separating what the author says from the reader's own thoughts and feelings. The reader suspends final judgment until the reader has developed legitimate and rational positions through a process of rigorously examining multiple interpretations. The reader sometimes reformulates thinking and/or becomes a producer of new knowledge and new texts as a result of this examination.

Role of the Teacher: The teacher focuses classroom discussion on generating and supporting varied interpretations with examples of multiple reader-response options. The teacher may ask students to make judgments about the author's intent, purpose, accuracy, logic, reliability, and literary form, or about others' responses to the same text.

Figure 8.3   *(continued)*

life's options. Needless to say, this isn't easy and we will all do it poorly sometimes. Therefore, we should judge ourselves by our long-term commitment more than our occasional lapses as all too human teachers. Writing and encouraging writing can be very useful in clarifying one's thoughts and message.

▶ CRITICAL READING-WRITING-THINKING: A TRADITIONAL AND EVOLVING GOAL

With a background now in place on the general idea of *critical–constructive* reading, writing, and thinking, and the transformational approach to teaching toward these ends, we turn to a review of *critical* thinking, including some new concepts and challenges in this field. We then will recombine critical-constructive reading, writing, and thinking into one more or less unifying concept and speak to several concrete methods for promoting this highest level of literacy. By the end of the chapter, you will have recapitulated much of the evolution of knowledge and art on these topics, from critical to critical-constructive to the, perhaps, coming age of constructive-creative reading, writing and thinking. Ideally, this story should be orderly, unambiguous, and without redundancies. In fact, helping to finish construct this story may be part of each reader's contribution to the science and art of professional education.

Critical Thinking

Critical reading-writing-thinking clearly is one of the most written and talked about topics in modern history. Nonetheless, it remains one of the least well understood. Critical reading is merely the use of critical thinking in the act of reading (Ennis, 1962). Hence, most anything said about one is likely to be true of the other. David Russell, writing over forty years ago, provides a most basic way for educators to understand critical reading and thinking. He says, essentially, that it is best defined as a three-factor ability, to which most contemporary educators would add a fourth, as shown here. Critical reading is

- An attitudinal, or dispositional, factor of effective questioning and suspension of judgment
- A functional factor of logical inquiry and problem solving, sometimes known as *dialogical* or *dialectical thinking*
- A judgmental factor based on some set of norms growing out of consensus, now called *cultural imperatives* (Russell, 1961)
- A matter of being able to imagine alternative perspectives often not represented (Lenski, Wham, & Johns, 1999; Paul, 1993), and which now we would more generically call *constructive-creative thinking*.

There are several paradoxes to overcome in teaching for and even talking about critical reading-thinking. For one, it is a *process*, the merit of which people tend to acknowledge based on whether or not the *product*, or conclusion reached, pleases them. In general, the term *critical* is only applied when the facts are incomplete or in dispute, and therefore where "right-thinking" people are likely to disagree. In other words, to teach critical thinking one must broach some controversial and even sensitive topics.

Critical Reading-Writing-Thinking Objectives

There are certain functions that sketch out the teacher's and students' rhetorical processes in achieving progress toward this higher level of literacy. Notice how later in this chapter these ideas begin to lean toward a more holistic concept of *critical-constructive* thinking rather than some kind of step-by-step process.

- Growth past reductionist thinking, or the tendency to oversimplify complex matters to black and white, either/or choices
- Overcoming the tendency to be deceptive and self-deceptive, as when sound information is disallowed because it does not suit one's purpose
- Learning to unpack one's own and a writer's intentions/motivations

- Learning how to read-write-think in ways that are not immediately comfortable to us, since various domains of learning and influence have their own characteristic ways of conducting discourse (e.g., science talk, literature talk, business talk)

- Achieving a certain measure of the goal of critical pedagogy/literacy, which is to increase insight into the ways in which one's reading-writing-thinking are bound to our cultural perceptions of race, gender, representations of self-image, and hence power

- Recognizing that language is "symbolic action" (Burke, 1950/1969), which implies a need to interrogate one's own and a writer's choice of words and positions in terms of their consequences to others

- Belief that one is responsible in some ways for the production or creation of knowledge and insight as well as for its consumption

There probably is no better, though no more disquieting, way to become a better critical-constructive reader-writer-thinker than to start with a thorough examination of one's own assumptions. This is especially urgent for teachers, ministers, administrators, and lawyers since assumptions guide the way we implicitly teach others to think critically.

Watch Your Assumptions

Most faulty conclusions can be traced back to faulty or unexamined assumptions. Of course, these seldom seem unexamined at the time. Some assumptions go unexamined because they are traditionally accepted givens. For example, the conclusion that one needs to have a college education to be successful in life is based on employment practices and cultural expectations that are changing rapidly. Other assumptions go unexamined because they too ride into town as innovations or movements that reveal the error or outdatedness of the old or traditional ways of thinking and/or acting. The other side of the example is the conclusion that the cost of a college education may now have exceeded its value. This conclusion, being reached by many young people who in prior times would never have raised the question, can be justified by numerous facts. However, it is based on the assumption that the primary benefits of a college education are financial in nature.

Examining assumptions involves a set of thinking strategies that form the core of insightful critical-constructive analysis. These include

- Asking a lot of relevant questions, even when the answers may seem self-evident

- Acquiring and objectively dealing with available information, whether or not it is personally "pleasing"

- Avoiding overly simplistic good/bad dichotomies

- Recognizing the persuasive effects of emotionally laden language

- Examining the author's motivation (Reformers' identities can get so tied up in the struggle that perpetuation of the cause becomes more important than its achievement.)

- Examining one's own motivation (This may involve coming to grips with that egoistic voice inside each of us and recognizing self-serving myths and convenient distortions of the truth; in other words, internalizing the spirit of the old saying, "If the truth is getting in your way, chances are that you're going the wrong direction.")

These habits of thought are fairly self-evident. Teaching them, however, requires some heuristics—or evocative actions—to stir them to action. The next subsection provides a set of questions for modeling critical thinking strategies on any issue.

Questions That Help Adolescents Think More Critically

- Has this been proposed before, and under what label or name?
- What are the credentials, background, and interests of the major advocates and adversaries?
- What assumptions are nested in the competing proposals?
- What factual evidence and logic supports and refutes this proposal?
- What other issues or matters are affected by accepting or rejecting this proposal?
- How might critics label or name this proposal?
- How do the choices affect me, and can I think clearly about this?
- Chances are that there is something of value and something needing correction in the competing proposals. Can these be reconciled?
- Is there more here than first meets the eye? A useful metaphor for critical reading/thinking is *pentimento,* a term used in art restoration for finding an (sometimes more valuable) oil painting underneath another one (due to the fact that canvases were expensive and artists often painted over their own works).

We'd now invite you to exercise *your* critical-constructive powers of analysis on some issues that are current in literacy and general education (see Figure 8.4, "Examples of Evocative and Critical Issues in Literacy Education"). Realize as you do this that the above is a set of thought-stimulating guidelines, and not a step-by-step formula. Nonetheless, like any set of ingredients, each may need to be folded in to achieve an optimal outcome. There also is an open invitation to add, though not to delete, considerations as long as the additions do not have the effect of altering something beyond recognition. For example, you cannot take the seafood out of paella, nor add a jar of peanut butter to the recipe for linguini with clam sauce, without altering the basic character and purpose of the dish. However, even this is allowable if it is declared that a new purpose or mission is being proposed, or a *new target* is raised. In fact, fertile minds regularly raise and hit targets that others have yet to identify. Being able to do this is almost a definition of the elevation of critical thinking to critical-constructive thinking.

- Never teach or drill anything in isolation.
- Graded books (written to be at a given difficulty level) are inauthentic and hinder learning at every level.
- The only way to improve reading is to read, read, read.
- Youngsters need to be taught to love reading.
- Education should be conducted so that it is a liberating force, rather than an indoctrination.
- Literature is literacy.
- Lecturing is bad teaching.
- Any subject can be taught through literature.
- Diversity is good, core culture is bad.
- Teaching declarative facts and consensual interpretations is bad.
- Teacher talk is bad, student talk is good.
- Constructivist philosophy is good for learning, traditionalist philosophy is bad for learning.
- Teaching phonics rules is bad.
- Teaching context clues is good.

Figure 8.4 Examples of evocative and critical issues in literacy education.

Critically Reading a Writer's Intent

In most print materials intended to inform, the writer has attempted to build an orderly progression of thought and information toward an unambiguous conclusion. Relevant examples and details are interwoven to add clarity and support. Depending on the author's intended or unintended purpose, however, the "facts" may be more or less complete and verifiable, and there may be more or less acknowledgment of alternative perspectives. Some theorists would argue that virtually everything written, from the Declaration of Independence to a cereal box, is intended to convince the reader of something, thereby shaping the reader's views and behavior. In the end, it is up to the reader to determine what to believe. There are several sets of lenses that can heighten critical analysis of a writer's intent and credibility.

The first aid in critical reading is to determine whether the author is attempting *knowledge telling* or *knowledge making* (Flower & Hayes, 1981). *Knowledge telling* typically is the attempt to articulate something one knows, or presumes to know, in the clearest and least ambiguous way possible. *Knowledge making* is that plunge into the murky unknown in an attempt to discover what the author is thinking or how he or she really feels about something. This also is the most transformative mode of writing. It tends to induce deeper thinking and result in more conclusions that influence, if not radically change, a great deal of subsequent reading, thinking, attitudes, and human behavior.

Another set of critical reading lenses involves recognizing and analyzing the nature of the claims used by the author to support a conclusion. A claim is a statement presented as truth when in fact it is open to question. Unrau (1997) details six types of claims which should alert critical readers to consider alternative propositions:

- What the writer believes to be true (*knowledge claims*)
- What or how something causes something else (*causal claims*)
- What is likely to result from current conditions (*predictive claims*)
- What is good and noble (*evaluative claims*)
- What is right and wrong (*moral claims*)
- What should be done (*policy claims*)

A final set of lenses for critical reading is awareness of the classical propaganda techniques that have evolved from marketing and politics. These techniques, detailed in Figure 8.5, provide a useful language for talking about critical reading as well as persuasive writing, debate techniques, and oral presentation.

Impediments to Critical-Constructive Thinking

A final consideration in melding a new focus on constructive reading-thinking with traditional and emerging concepts of critical analysis is to articulate why this is not already being done more systematically. Careful articulation of a problem is one way to overcome the human instinct to deny problems, avoid problems, or simply say that a problem is unsolvable. Furthermore, stating the question or problem often translates into 50% of the solution.

The human instinct to avoid problems is so deeply rooted that at one point in the late 1980s, it reached national concern. This led to an announcement by the Education Commission of the States of a large "Higher Literacies" project to look into state policies that either "constrain or promote" schools' efforts to teach "writing, problem-solving, critical thinking, argument, analysis, synthesis, interpretation and evaluation" (Tchudi, 1988). Here is a partial list of likely impediments to acknowledging and hence addressing problems.

- Textbooks tend to be inane and therefore fail to evoke critical thought.
- The printed word generates a "halo" effect: Because it is in print, it is true and therefore not worth questioning.
- Many school administrators and teachers are afraid to broach controversial subjects with students.
- There is a general emphasis on conformity in almost all aspects of life.
- Personal emotions and prejudices often tend to disrupt clear thinking.
- Critical reading-thinking is not routinely assessed and therefore is assumed to be less important than basic objectives.
- There is a lack of models (persons and programs) that epitomize or focus on constructive and critical thinking.

Critical reading often involves recognizing an author's use of propaganda, or selling techniques. These techniques are designed to convince, persuade, or move the reader/listener to action.

Bandwagon:	Everyone is doing a certain thing, so jump on the bandwagon and go along with the crowd. ("More kids want _____ than any other toothpaste.")
Testimonial:	A well-known person endorses a certain product or course of action even though he or she is not an authority on the subject. ("Take it from me, _____, this is the niftiest video game you can buy for the money.")
Plain folks:	People who appear to be "just plain folks," or "just like you and me," suggest that we think or act in a certain way. ("My family has been in farming for fifty years; you know I won't forget you when I get to Washington.")
Snob appeal:	The opposite of plain folks. ("These beautiful designer jeans were created for the with-it girl.")
Name-calling:	Applying a currently unpopular put-down to a person or movement without seeing if it really applies. ("That teacher is a geek—look at those ancient-looking clothes.")
Glittering generalities:	Words or phrases with favorable suggestions that lead us to favor a person or movement without examining the evidence (can also be used with unfavorable words). Such abstract words or phrases (e.g., "public spirit," "time for change," "patriotic duty," "fiscal responsibility") are used to make us support some person or idea with little further analysis. ("We need a leader who will guide us to greater fiscal responsibility, an improved standard of living, and a more fair system of taxation. It's time for a change.")
Transfer:	A commercial symbol that trades off our respect for something to which it really is not connected. ("Buy Red Cross shoes.")
Scientific slant:	Use of scientific terms and phrases to persuade us to accept something as being more than what it really is. ("The titanium light bulb burns for 7,000 hours"; "Four out of five dentists surveyed . . .")
False analogies:	Use of an analogy or comparison situation that is not really parallel, or simply is divergent on a critical point. ("Learning to read is a language process; it is no different from learning to speak.")
Confusing correlation with cause:	This deception amounts to attributing causation to things which may be related, but are not necessarily related in a cause-and-effect way. ("In the two years that I have been president we have had nothing but prosperity").

Figure 8.5 Propaganda techniques.

- Curriculum requirements generally do not include addressing or teaching specific critical reading-thinking strategies.
- There is a pervasive fear among students and teachers that criticism of *anything*, including introspective self-appraisals, ultimately unleashes criticism of *everything*, including schools, teachers, society, and self.
- It is a paradoxical fact that classroom questioning is used on the one hand to stimulate curiosity, reinforce knowledge, and ignite discussion and on the other to scold, embarrass, and test.
- Great ideas often are conceived and forged in passion, and we haven't quite figured out how to endure, let alone allow, passion in our schools and policy-making arenas.

The methods described next were designed to expose, circumvent, or even build on these innate human dispositions. *Intra-Act*, for example, capitalizes on adolescents' natural interest in predicting the opinions of their peers and in informal small group interaction.

Multiliteracies and Pop Culture: Contemporary Sources of Content, Critique, and Hybrid Culture

Multiliteracies involve modern age changes to communication, like the integration of various *designs, such* as visual, linguistic, and audio within one text (*New London Group,* 1996). The act of reading is no longer limited to the printed page, nor are texts perceived in the narrow sense of traditional print media. Virtually all systems of signing, from that employed by musicians and artists to that used by choreographers and television dramatists and comedians, are sending signals about what one might feel, believe in, or live by. This has led to two relatively new fields of study: *semiotics*, or the study of the history and impact of different signing systems, and *multiliteracies*. There also is a more didactic form, called *critical media literacy*, that makes use of popular culture texts and symbols in teaching, such as is done in advertising and story-based persuasive techniques, where the story, such as Pearl Buck's *The Good Earth*, sends a penetrating message.

The newest addition to *multiliteracies* is *fanfictions*. Kelly Chandler-Olcott and Donna Mahar report on the intriguing electronic exchanges of two teenage girls built around a new art form called *Anime*—a Japanese animation, also available as video, comics, and with memorabilia, and in this case entitled "The Shrine of Vegeta" (Chandler-Olcott & Mahar, 2003, p. 557). The researchers point out that while they do not consider that "cartoons in-and-of themselves are imperative for literacy educators to consider" (p. 558), they are, nonetheless, a primary influence on the writing that adolescents produce. There is a hub for such interactions and intertwined storylines. It can be found at the Anime Web Turnpike (*http://www.anipike.com*). This hub is part of a process that links and creates new meanings and new genres that is being called *hybridity*.

We find ourselves more fascinated by a slightly different meaning for this root term, *hybrid cultures* (Manzo, Manzo, & Albee, 2004). Our sense is that much of this play and interplay has even more significance than in the recent past. This is because it is not merely something to chat about, and claim as a *teen scene*, but that it actually is creating a hybrid culture that seems just as inviting to the youngest of children (think *Pokemon* and *Harry Potter*). It offers a common frame of experience shared by children from otherwise diverse linguistic and cultural backgrounds and an almost immediate foreground for social connecting. As such, a valuable goal is to find ways to harness this trend toward hybrid cultures to enhance content learning and student growth. Let's continue to speak of the values and possible traps of exploiting this trend with adolescents.

Reality TV shows, such as *Survivor*, are a poignant frame of reference for discussion before and in school. But while a sensible and resourceful teacher will use and accept such references, it is not without some risks. Lewis (1999) writes about *popular cultural studies* in a forward to a book on the topic by Alvermann, Moon, Hagwood (1999). She lists several interesting advantages, and at least one possible problem, to consider as one ventures out in the direction of popular cultural studies and references in English and social studies. She states that

- Popular cultural studies is inherently interdisciplinary.
- Popular cultural studies allows youth to self-examine the pop culture that may be strongly influencing their lives.
- Popular cultural studies tend to create a more student-centered classroom.

However, she notes—and we concur—that there is a certain degree of contradiction in teaching kids more about what they are expert in and about which we are relatively naïve. Pop culture, by its very name, is trendy and, as such, often quickly passing and hard to keep track of. There also is a strong likelihood that kids don't really want us in this, their nonadult world. This may be one of the reasons that they often carefully craft it to look, feel, and be different from whatever it is that their parents and their schools are embracing. During this, the greatest period of divorce and youth disorientation in modern history, kids also are still fully tuned into the sedate, traditional, and innocent, watching rerun shows like *The Brady Bunch* and the *Cosby Show* in record numbers. This all needs more careful examination and deeper consideration before we launch too many units and courses on pop culture and its transient icons. For the moment, we suggest that educators continue to monitor pop culture, but to use it sparingly. For all the difficulty associated with reading Shakespeare and Chaucer, these are still the coin of the realm and the source code for many referents and standardized test terms; though they do not, and should not, remain unchallenged. They, too, were once "pop culture."

▶ WRITING-BASED METHODS FOR GUIDING CRITICAL-CONSTRUCTIVE READING

One of the most effective ways to teach students to respond critically and constructively to what they read is through various forms of written response. This is traditionally done in the form of the research paper, a lengthy process in which students collect information from various sources and then synthesize it in their own words and toward their own points and conclusions. This process of "transforming text," according to Moffett (1989), is the highest level of writing. By translating information from the words of various authors to their own choices of words and phrases, the ideas and information become integrated into the students' personal knowledge bases. In this more personal form, it is less likely to be forgotten and more likely to grow into more sophisticated language and thought.

The challenge always has been in just how to teach the multiple perspectives and attitudes necessary to enable such transformation of text and *turn abouts* of student thinking. The methods in this section provide various ways to do this with reading materials of any type, any length, and in any discipline. The first method is something of a template for eliciting students' thoughts and reflections on a variety of possible topics, whether they be in pop culture, traditional literature, or wide-ranging ideas. It involves prompting students to make evaluative responses, predict the responses of their peers, and discuss the reasons for their judgments.

Intra-Act: Values-Guided versus Values-Driven Reading and Evaluative Thinking

The challenge to educators, and virtually all thinking people, is in how to be reasonably guided by a set of values but not so driven by these as to lose clarity and objectivity. One way that has been suggested by reflective educators is to provide more experience in school with the examination of authentic critical issues, and hence more experience with *evaluative thinking*, the cognitive psychology name for value-based reasoning. Intra-Act (Hoffman, 1977) is a teaching method that is representative of this class of methods and one that is especially compatible with content area literacy.

Intra-Act was designed to develop readers' ability to draw on their personal values base, which permeates and colors their sense of what they read and what they do with what is read. Intra-Act was influenced by the earlier work of Raths, Harmon, and Simon (1978) on "valuing process" and of Manzo and Sherk (1978) on "languaging," the process of using language to more deeply process complex issues. It involves group problem solving and cooperative learning. A study of the efficacy of the Intra-Act activity conducted by Hoffman (1977) concluded that the method was an effective means of teaching basic comprehension, that students were willing and able to "go beyond the material in projecting and perceiving personal values related to the content of the selections," and that "given an appropriately structured learning environment . . . students can and do learn from one another" (p. 63).

Steps in the Intra-Act Procedure

Preparation. Create two worksheets based on the reading selection. One is a set of non-fact-type questions, which could be answered, and argued, from several perspectives. The second is a set of related values-based (agree-disagree) statements (see example of the second kind of worksheet in Figure 8.6).

Step 1. Students read the assigned selection and individually answer the comprehension questions on the first worksheet.

Step 2. Form cooperative groups of four students each. A chairperson is appointed. (The chairperson's role is rotated each time the activity is performed.) Students compare their answers to the questions within their groups and *discuss the reasons* for their answers.

Your Name: _____   Date: _____
Group Chairperson: _____   Hour: _____

Directions: Circle A for "agree" or D for "disagree" to indicate your own responses to each statement. Then circle A or D to indicate how you think each other member of your group responsded to each statement.

		Me	*Group Members*		
		Me	*Mary*	*Jack*	*Helen*
1.	Men are usually better bosses than women.	A/D	A/D	A/D	A/D
2.	Once elected, a legislator should vote according to the wishes of the people he or she represents, not according to personal feelings.	A/D	A/D	A/D	A/D
3.	I would have voted the way the main character did in this story	A/D	A/D	A/D	A/D
4.	I probably would have reacted as negatively to the main character as her "constituents."	A/D	A/D	A/D	A/D

Figure 8.6   Sample valuing statement exercise sheet for Intra-Act.

Step 3.   The second worksheet is distributed, and students individually record their own responses to the values-based statements and predict the responses of the other members of their group (see Figure 8.6).

Step 4.   The chairperson reads the first statement, tells his or her response, and asks each group member to share his or her response. Students "check" their own predictions of their classmates' responses as the chairperson guides them through each item.

Step 5.   The teacher leads a whole-class discussion of students' personal judgments about the valuing statements and the accuracy of their predictions of the other students' judgments.

Sister to the valuing process, the next method is applicable from kindergarten to graduate school. It promotes reading, cognitive development, and even civics.

Polar Opposites Spur Higher-Order (Critical) Literacy

A new third grader once managed the complex wording that essentially said to us "Are we going to do more on what we think and feel about things, or do you have to explain *why* now that we're in third grade?" Evaluation and critique questions, presumably the highest order of thinking, are little more than tummy-level sentiments without careful reflection and reasoned thought. Thomas Bean (1981) developed a very sensible method for urging such thinking; it included stages of both scaffolding and fading to assist students with making evaluation-explanation responses, the implicit intent of higher-order questioning. Later the method was refined and further examples were added (Bean & Bishop, 1992). Bishop had high enthusiasm for the method from the beginning and has provided some touchstone examples of its worthiness down to the second-grade level (A. L. Bishop, personal communication, 2003). Here now is an abridged and edited version of Polar Opposites, largely from Bishop's Course Supplement (2003).

Polar Opposites: Rationale, Steps, and Examples

This method was designed to *spur students to higher levels of critical analysis.* The core idea is an adaptation of a means, called Semantic Differential, that originally was developed in the mid-1960s and often attributed to Murray Myron to assess possible shifts in attitudes pre- and post certain interventions. Polar Opposites consists of establishing some gritty adjectives at either end of a five- to seven-point scale, and having students indicate where on the scale they find their personal feelings and thinking.

Step 1. Select a book or article that is reasonably familiar to the majority of students. (*Example:* the book *The Day Jimmy's Boa Ate the Wash* (Trinka Hakes Noble/Puffin, Reprint Edition, 1992).

Step 2. Develop four to five polar opposites that address key characters, concepts, and/or events in the story. The following are illustrations from *The Day Jimmy's Boa Ate the Wash*:

> *A boa constrictor is a very _____ snake.*
> Small   *Large*
> 1.   2.   3.   4.   5.
> *The fight at the farm was started* . . .
> On Purpose   *Accidentally*
> 1.   2.   3.   4.   5.
> *It probably was a _____ idea that Jimmy brought his snake to the farm.*
> Bad   *Good*
> 1.   2.   3.   4.   5.
> *The girl telling the story found the field trip to the farm* . . .
> Unexciting   *Exciting*
> 1.   2.   3.   4.   5.

Step 3. Either orally read the book or selection to the class or have them read it silently. (It is best to read it to them in early trials. At the least, read an initial page or two before they continue silently.)

Step 4. Show and model how you would circle a choice for the first opposite. Defend your rating as a simple logical extension of saying anything evaluative. Explicitly state the importance of supporting one's position.

Step 5. Complete the second and possibly a third polar opposite as a group. Allow differences to be voiced, and encourage supporting evidence and logic. (Kids will quickly learn to challenge one another and therefore too, to think before they speak, and while they are speaking. *Self-editing is itself a higher level of metacognition and self-regulation.*)

Step 6. As students become more comfortable with this elementary process, it should be incorporated into most all class discussion as a seamless part of "saying what (and why) you think and feel as you do."

To further fade and pass along independent functioning, have students create one or two polar opposites for postreading discussion. To aid the deeper intent of this strategy as a *habit of mind* and way to do school and life, you might consider explicitly discussing why it is important to add the "whys" as well as the "whats" of evaluative thinking. This simple hook-up is one of the most fundamental requirements of sound critical analysis, antiprejudicial thinking, and civic responsibility. Writing in an analogous context, John McEneaney (2002) reminds us of how elementary this concern is to all social interactions with a reference to one of modern education's thought leaders: "It is not enough simply to assert, assertion must be *warranted* (Dewey, 1938, p. 9)" (p. 330).

Critical Discourse Analysis

More recently, Bean and Moni (2003) have stepped up and outside Polar Opposites by adding greater concern for Critical Discourse Analysis (CDA) (Fairclough, 1989). The point of such "critical literacy" is to further spur critical examination of the behind-the-scenes dimensions of text.

CDA, by the Bean and Moni (2003) account, "assumes that social conditions, particularly conditions of unequal power relationships, determine the properties of discourse" (p. 643). This suggests the need, at the very least, to add some Polar Opposites that might tap into this reservoir of hidden conditions, influences, and matters of judgment. In fact, in the story alluded to previously, Polar Opposites does just this when it asks

> *It probably was a _____ idea that Jimmy brought his snake to the farm.*
> Bad   Good
>   1.   2.   3.   4.   5.

To open this door to the behind-the-scenes conditions, the teacher might raise questions such as, *What could have led Jimmy to bring his boa to the farm?* And, with older students, this could be followed with some more poignant questions: *Was Jimmy being controlling, reckless, or just naïve in bringing the snake? How do you suppose others felt? Is this just another form of bully behavior? What may have happened before and after?* In other words, discuss unseen motives and possible circumstances. Most often, poor judgment can be traced back to displays of power, efforts to acquire it, or lack of thought. Such misdeeds become vicarious learning experiences with more careful reading and analysis.

Extended Anticipation-Reaction Guide

An extension of the Anticipation-Reaction Guide described in Chapter 4 is an effective way to encourage critical-constructive reading and responding. After students have recorded their responses to the A-R Guide statements before and after reading, they are directed to write an essay elaborating on their response to any one of the statements on the worksheet. Figure 8.7 presents an example of an A-R Guide and a related student essay from a class in economics.

Active interaction of the type generated by Anticipation-Reaction Guides promotes several key ingredients of critical reading-thinking:

- Conflict identification and resolution (Frager & Thompson, 1985)
- Metacognitive awareness of the strategies one is employing while reading (Brown, 1980)

Directions: Before reading, check Agree or Disagree for each statement. After reading, write a brief essay on one statement of your choice.

Agree   Disagree

_____ _____ 1. Supply-side economics favors the wealthy.

_____ _____ 2. You cannot be a Republican and be against supply-side economics.

_____ _____ 3. You cannot be a Democrat and be for supply-side economics.

STUDENT ESSAY

I think that supply-side economics favors the wealthy because it says that when profits go up, the number of suppliers will increase. This also is supposed to increase competition, and therefore reduce prices, since there would be more supply than demand.

The government, under this approach, is dedicated to helping create greater profits for suppliers. This, however, would tend to make the rich richer and leave the poor and middle class to be the perpetual shoppers, looking for oversupplies. In fact, though, whenever supply begins to exceed demand, the rich simply move their assets elsewhere, quickly reducing supply and competition.

Of course, supply-side thinking is basic to free enterprise. Without a profit motive, investors would not take risks. The role of government, however, needs to be balanced carefully so as to avoid unnecessarily crimping profits, but also avoiding measures that virtually guarantee profits. These include big tax breaks for industry or freedom to exploit the environment. When large corporations are legally permitted not to pay tax and/or to leave behind their industrial wastes, this amounts to a hidden surcharge on all the products bought and one that the rest of us, including future generations, eventually must pay.

Figure 8.7   Anticipation-Reaction Guide: Supply-side economics.

- Connections between one's knowledge of the world and comprehension of text (Waern, 1977a, 1977b)

Regarding the last point, Ericson, Hubler, Bean, Smith, and McKenzie (1987) point out that in the California Academic Partnership Program, in which professors used A-R Guides in working with teachers and junior high school students, students often would leave class at the end of the period still arguing the relative merits of their various points of view. This act of carrying the classroom out into the student's world may be the most powerful influence of all on learning and thinking. It extends the school day by increasing student time on task and reducing the sharp line of demarcation that often separates school learning from home and life experiences.

Opinion-Proof*

The Opinion-Proof method (Santa, Dailey, & Nelson, 1985) requires students to engage in four important aspects of higher-order literacy:

1. Evaluative thinking—forming an opinion
2. Verification—supporting an opinion
3. Persuasive articulation—writing about the opinion convincingly
4. Forming a consensus—cooperatively critiquing and reviewing an opinion

Steps in the Opinion-Proof Method

Step 1. Provide the students with an Opinion-Proof guide, either written on the chalkboard (or overhead, white board, or SmartBoard) or as a handout (see the example in Step 2).

Step 2. Have students write an opinion and supporting evidence for it from the text. Following is a guide for the short story "Old Horse," a popular selection about an elderly algebra teacher by Oliver Andersen:

Example:

Opinion Statement: Old Horse was sensitive.
Evidence to Prove My Opinion:

- Old Horse was sensitive.
- He was patient with Rabbit.
- He wanted Rabbit to belong.
- Old Horse forced Rabbit to dislike him.
- He put himself down for the sake of Rabbit.

Step 3. Students write a connected essay using their opinion and evidence as topic sentence and supporting details, respectively.

Example:

Old Horse was a very sensitive teacher. One reason I feel this way was because of his ability to understand Rabbit. Rabbit was not liked by the other students in his class because he was a friend of Old Horse's. In addition, Old Horse understood Rabbit's need to become a part of a group of friends, and Old Horse knew that he was part of the problem. Finally, Old Horse forced Rabbit to dislike him so much that he could become accepted by the other students. Therefore, Old Horse was a very sensitive man. He even sacrificed himself for the sake of his student.

Step 4. The final step is peer editing. In this step, students (1) develop specific criteria for evaluating their writing, such as the questions "Does my paragraph contain a main idea statement?" and "Do I have evidence to support my main idea?"; (2) divide up into pairs or small groups and read and react to one another's paragraphs; and (3) edit and/or revise their own paragraphs before submitting a final draft for teacher evaluation.

In addition to its role in reading and thinking, the Opinion-Proof process provides a useful sequence for organizing persuasive speeches, another important language art. It accomplishes this by having students state opinions and write out supporting and nonsupporting points. This often leads to the reflective turnabout that makes Opinion-Proof a good framework for teaching in the transformative mode.

Read-Encode-Annotate-Ponder

The Read-Encode-Annotate-Ponder (REAP) method (Eanet & Manzo, 1976; Manzo, Manzo & Albee, 2003; Manzo, 1973) was shown to be an effective tool for transformational teaching in two recent studies (Garber, 1995; Jackson-Albee, 2000). At its most basic level, REAP is a way to teach students to write (and think) from a variety of perspectives. It also was among the earliest strategies developed for students to use to improve study-type writing, thinking, and reading. The basic REAP formula is as follows:

R: *Read* to discern the writer's message.

E: *Encode* the message by mentally translating it into your own words.

A: *Annotate*, or make written note of, your brief responses from several perspectives.

P: *Ponder*, or further reflect on what you have read, thought, and written, through discussion of your own and others' responses to the selection and/or your and their annotations.

REAP introduces students to a variety of brief and poignant ways to critique or *annotate* what they have read. Annotation types range from simple summaries to highly challenging critical-constructive responses. Research on writing suggests that efforts to improve this type of critiquing, when taught concurrently with analytical reading and discipline instruction, result in enriched factual knowledge, conceptual development, writing improvement, vocabulary growth, and personal-social adjustment (Applebee, 1981; Bromley, 1985; Cunningham & Cunningham, 1976; Doctorow, Wittrock, & Marks, 1978; Eanet & Manzo, 1976; Garber, 1995; Tierney, Sorter, O'Flahavan, & McGinley, 1989).

Reap-Share: Achieving the Elusive Goals of a Community of Learners and Multiple Perspectives

Today, critiquing, annotating and discussing are part of several online services whereby readers can exchange views on a variety of subjects and books. This community of learners can be done asynchronously (online, but at different times) or through chat groups (online, in real time). In either case, the exchanges tend to be open ended and "hit and miss" in terms of pedagogic value. REAP-sharing is more disciplined. As indicated previously, it is a structured system designed over a generation ago to guide and teach reading and thoughtful reacting in a pedagogically sound way, easily applicable to online interactions (c.f. Thomas & Hofmeister, 2003). Students are introduced to the concept and value of writing from different perspectives in class. They then are led to discuss the merits of posting their annotations where they would be accessible to one another. Students easily spot one basic value, namely that they can read each other's critiques of certain works before they read the longer work and/or following reading. Through guided discussion, they come to appreciate other values in sharing annotations. Benefits include having multiple representations of different perspectives on a variety of materials to guide higher-level thinking; having model critiques to guide the craft side of writing; and having the option to reread or further read annotations during the time they are reading a difficult longer work like *Tale of Two Cities*, where it is easy to lose the thread of the plot. See the link provided at *www.LiteracyLeaders.com* for more information about Internet projects based on REAP-SHARE, also called REAP ANX, for REAP Annotation Exchange. In addition, as course-delivery software platforms such as BlackBoard and WebCT become more integrated into classroom practices at the K–12 levels, as they are currently in many higher-education settings, the availability of using asynchronous discussion boards will greatly increase opportunities (and illustrate the increased need) to apply the sort of disciplined reading-writing-thinking REAP-sharing techniques discussed here.

Stages in Using REAP as a Teaching Tool

The first stage in using REAP is to teach students how to write several of the annotation types described next and illustrated in Figure 8.8. Note that the annotation types represent a hierarchy from basic to higher-order levels of thinking, with the first four categorized as *reconstructive* level, requiring literal-level responding, and the next ten as *constructive* level, requiring reading and thinking between and beyond the lines. It is best to introduce students to three or four annotation types initially, provide practice with these, and then add additional annotation types gradually. Experience suggests that a good cluster to begin with is summary, attention-getting/heuristic, and critical.

Reconstructive Responses:

1. *Summary response.* States the basic message of the selection in brief form. In fiction, it is the basic story line; in nonfiction, it is a simple statement of the main ideas.

2. *Precise response.* Briefly states the author's basic idea or theme, with all unnecessary words removed. The result is a crisp, telegram-like message.

3. *Attention-getting or heuristic response.* Restates a snappy portion of the selection that makes the reader want to respond. It is best to use the author's own words.

4. *Question response.* Turns the main point of the story or information into an organizing question that the selection answers.

Constructive Responses:

5. *Personal view or transactional response.* Answers the question "How do your views and feelings compare with what you perceive the author to have said?"

6. *Critical response.* Supports, rejects, or questions the main idea, and tells why. The first sentence of this type of response should restate the author's position. The next sentence should state the writer's position. Additional sentences should explain how the two differ.

7. *Contrary response.* Attempts to state a logical alternative position, even if it is not one that the student necessarily supports. This is an especially important way to represent a minority view that can easily be overlooked.

8. *Intention response.* States and briefly explains what the responder thinks is the author's intention, plan, and purpose in writing the selection. This is a special version of the critical response that causes the reader/responder to try to think like the author or from the author's perspective.

9. *Motivation response.* States what may have caused the author to create or write the story or selection. This is another special version of critical responding. It is an attempt to discover the author's personal agenda and hence areas of writing or unwitting biases.

10. *Discovery response.* States one or more practical questions that need to be answered before the story or facts can be judged for accuracy or worth. This type of response to text is the mode of thinking that leads to more reading and research and occasionally to a reformulated position or view.

11. *Moral-ethical response.* Requires reference to values and beliefs that guide, or one believes should guide, attitudes and behavior; and hence, both reflects and influences character development and complexity of thinking.

12. *Discipline-connective (or interdisciplinary) response.* This is a conscious search for relevant ideas, facts, and factors that may seldom appear related to a topic because schooling, as opposed to learning, tends to have subject boundaries whereas ideas do not.

13. *Creative response.* Suggests different and perhaps better solutions or views and/or connections and applications to prior learning and experiences. Students usually need some guidance and/or examples to produce this type of response. Once they begin thinking in this way, however, the results can be remarkably constructive.

14. *Reading awareness (metacognitive) response.* Identifies or comments on a problem one may have had in reading and understanding a specific piece.

After students have had some practice in writing various types of annotations, these can be used in a variety of ways; a few are listed here:

- When giving a reading assignment, assign three annotation types for students to write and turn in.

- As students become more skilled at annotation writing, the assignment can be given with the requirement that, after they have read, students themselves decide which three annotation types to write in response.

- Assign each member of cooperative groups a different annotation type to write. When groups meet, encourage group members to offer constructive suggestions by offering extra credit points to the group with the best annotation of each type (judged by the teacher or the class as a whole).

- Introduce a new reading assignment by having students read annotations written by students in a previous year (or from a different section of the class).

- Provide incentive to read and write reflectively by posting exemplary annotations, signed by the author, on a bulletin board or Internet system.

- Encourage students to write from different disciplinary perspectives— "Write an annotation on *The Rainman* the way Mr. Kezlan your math teacher might, or like Mr. Willson your English teacher might write one." Expect some of these to be humorous, because they will be. (See item 12, "Discipline-connective responses" in Figure 8.8 for some representations that reduced the probability of humorous responses, should you wish to avoid these.)

REAP Responses as an Assessment System

To monitor student progress toward higher-order literacy, the teacher can use the preceding annotations listing as a rubric for reviewing student writings. The rubric can serve as a means of appraising the characteristic way in which a student or group of students responds to text. To use the REAP annotation types in this way, simply compare a student's writing to the preceding descriptions, and decide which annotation type it most closely resembles, keeping in mind that the annotations, as listed and illustrated here, already are roughly in order of difficulty: Lower numbers indicate more concrete thinking, and higher numbers more personal and abstract patterns of responding.

"Travelers and the Plane-Tree: A Fable"

Two travelers were walking along a bare and dusty road in the heat of a mid-summer's day. Coming upon a large shade tree, they happily stopped to shelter themselves from the burning sun in the shade of its spreading branches. While they rested, looking up into the tree, one of them said to his companion, "What a useless tree this is! It makes no flowers and bears no fruit. Of what use is it to anyone?" The tree itself replied indignantly, "You ungrateful people! You take shelter under me from the scorching sun, and then, in the very act of enjoying the cool shade of my leaves, you abuse me and call me good for nothing!"

Reconstructive Responses:

1. Summary response
   Travelers take shelter from the sun under a large tree. They criticize the tree for not making flowers or fruit. The tree speaks, and tells them that they are ungrateful people for taking shelter under her leaves and then criticizing her.

2. Precise response
   Travelers stop for rest and shade under big tree. Travelers say tree is useless. Tree tells them off.

3. Attention-getting response
   In this story, a tree talks back to people. The tree says, "You ungrateful people! You come and take shelter under me . . . and then . . . abuse me and call me nothing!"

4. Question response
   What tales might be told if inanimate objects could talk?

Constructive Responses

5. Personal view responses
   (a) We use resources like coal without thinking. Then we criticize the resource for damaging our lungs and dirtying our air
   (b) Kids sometimes use their parents the way the travelers used the tree, and then criticize them for letting themselves be used.

6. Critical response
   Not every word spoken in criticism is meant that way. The travelers were just a little grumpy from the long hard trip. The tree is being too sensitive.

7. Contrary response
   The travelers could be right. There are other trees that could produce something, as well as just providing shade.

8. Intention response
   The author wants us to be more sensitive to the people and things we depend on, especially those we see and use most often.

Figure 8.8 Examples of REAP annotations.

9. Motivation response
   It sounds like the author may have felt used, after having a bad experience with friends or family.

10. Discovery response
    I wonder how many of us know when we are being "users." It would be interesting to take an anonymous poll to see how many people secretly feel that they have been used, and how many honestly see themselves as users.

11. Moral-ethical response
    I think we should ask how some of history's enlightened moral thinkers would respond to this, say Jesus, Confucius, Augustine, Thomas Jefferson.

12. Discipline-connective responses
    (a) A poet would easily write an ode to such a tree; are there any?
    (b) A scientist might ask, "how does this tree manage to thrive where others cannot even manage to survive?"
    (c) A mathematician likely would want to calculate the probability of this tree's having rooted and found water before it was consumed by heat and drought; can that be done?

13. Creative response
    [Teacher guidance: What are some analogous situations this fable reminds you of?]
    (a) This fable reminds me of how Dobie Gillis uses and then abuses that nice, but plain girl who always hangs around him.
    (b) This fable made me think that teachers are sometimes used unfairly. They give us so much, and then we put them down if they make little mistakes. They're only human!
        [Teacher guidance: Having gotten the point of this fable, what should we do?]
    (c) We should put this fable on the bulletin board where it will remind us not to be ungrateful "users."
        [Teacher guidance: How would you retitle this fable if you were writing it?]
    (d) I'd call this fable "Travelers in the Dark," to show that we go through life without appreciating the many small "gifts" that come to us, while we're busy grumbling about what we don't have.

14. Reading awareness (metacognitive) response.
    (a) I feel like I'm beginning to better understand what the word "indignant" means from reading this, but I don't think I could define it yet
    (b) This fable is too short. My mind feels like it needs more words, or something to really get this.
    (c) I keep wondering how a fable is different from a parable.

Figure 8.8 *(continued)*

Acknowledging the Visceral Nature of Higher-Order Responding

One of the simplest ways to teach students to write constructively is to elicit quick personal responses to a piece they have read. Then the teacher should work with the class to form these initial highly subjective responses into more thoughtful critical and constructive ones. One way to do this is simply to ask students to give support for their positions—that is, to reconcile, or attempt to balance, their initial responses with the ethical and values-based positions that are fundamental to their communities and to higher ideals, such as liberty, as well as more practical ones such as how would their idea(s) be paid for or made workable. Again, students should not be forced to conformity here but should be encouraged to reprocess the rationale for societal goals and expectations. Where students' responses differ markedly from one another, divide them into groups that produce critiques of their varied viewpoints. See Figure 8.9 for an anecdotal example from an eighth-grade social studies class we observed.

Letters to the Editor

Another means of stimulating cogent writing in response to text is to refer students to good approximations of it in the form of model letters to the editor in newspapers and magazines. Notice how the sample letters to the editor in Figure 8.10 help one get a better grip on one's own thoughts and feelings about problems in China. This

---

Following silent reading of a selection on the exploits of Hernando de Soto, an eighth-grade teacher, rather than first seeking a summary of facts, asked the class, "What did you think of de Soto?" Reactions included "sick," "cruel," and "loser." When asked to explain why they felt this way, students recited a litany of facts and events that amounted to a summary. Then the teacher asked them to get together in groups and form their reactions and reasons into personal comments on the selection. The following critique was typical of the results:

> Hernando de Soto was a loser. After bringing gold back from Peru, the Spanish king encouraged him to go back to the New World by making him governor of Florida in 1539. He and 550 men looked for more gold. Even though some of them were priests, they mutilated and killed Indians in their search. After three years of this, de Soto died with nothing, and his men returned to Spain empty-handed.

In this case, students' visceral and somewhat "cranky" responses seemed to help them distinguish de Soto from other explorers of his time and recall important information. In this way, the purpose of writing following reading was well served: information was carefully processed, personalized, and stored for long-term recall. Further, the concept of "de Soto" and the context of the times replaced a collection of random facts about a vague historical figure named de Soto.

Figure 8.9 Encouraging higher-order responding.

> "How tragic it is that to cope with change, China's leaders felt they needed to kill their young."
>
> "The people of China will triumph. Deng Xiaoping and followers have forgotten their own history. It is impossible to repress an idea whose time has come!"
>
> "China had to crush the democratic resistance. The blood spilled in Tiananmen Square is a small price to pay to prevent a civil war that would consume thousands, if not millions."
>
> **_Ben Franklin on Tiananmen:_**
>
> "China is a sovereign state whose internal affairs we cannot intercede in under international law. However, if we trade with them, we will be their customers, and merchants always try to please their best customers."

Figure 8.10   Letters to the editor exemplify cogent response to text.

is a good place to invite interesting perspectives as may come from trying to write a letter as if it comes from a famous person, say Benjamin Franklin, one of our first foreign ambassadors (see "Ben Franklin on Tiananmen," also in Figure 8.10).

Less Can Be More

Brief response-type annotations, like letters to the editor, offer a challenge to sift through information and feelings and to struggle to take a thoughtful position. To this extent, such critiques can be more valuable than formal term papers and conventional book reports because they align more closely with student experiences and the faster pace of modern life. Additionally, this type of writing, because it is brief, provides more frequent opportunities for students to read, react, and write. On a very pragmatic level, such annotations can more easily be read and shared with peers and occasionally reviewed by a secondary teacher with an average load of more than 135 students per day, per semester.

▶ A FORMULA FOR PROMOTING CRITICAL-CONSTRUCTIVE THINKING

When the formula for teaching constructive reading, writing, and thinking is finally written, there is a good chance that it will contain at least these three factors: (1) respect for the past; (2) problem-based teaching; and (3) a collection of ways to invite creative production. See if the thoughts in the sections that follow meet these criteria.

Exploring Ideas—Past, Present, and Evolving

Once we heard a popular futurist speaker at an educational conference say that when you are traveling at the speed of light, as we are now in the modern age, you don't need a rear view mirror. We respectfully disagree. The past is always important. It is the way we are able to escape the limitations of personal experiences and connect to the continuum of efforts and solutions that have proven workable. The challenge of course is to recognize the difference between a road and a rut. A problem-solving orientation is one way to deal with this challenge.

Engagement with problem solving teaches respect for the past, or what has been learned. Tussling with problems also can be empowering because it helps us to tackle the daunting task of trying to have original thoughts, which it turns out we are more capable of than we ever realized. Teachers need to help students to discover that they are capable of being *ideators*, that is, idea makers, problem identifiers and problem solvers. Our collective tendency as teachers to almost never ask for creative production becomes a repeating, confirming lesson that this is hardly possible, let alone doable. For this problem, we are discovering some remarkably simple remedies with powerful implications for how kids will read, write, learn subjects, and otherwise think.

"Just Ask for It" Hypothesis and Mounting Evidence of Innate Capacity for Inventiveness

The door to creative thinking is opened by putting question marks where there are premature periods. Or, in other words, to *ask for* new twists, innovative approaches, fresh thinking, saying, and expressing. Ollman (1996) compared seven formats for promoting higher-level thinking. Reflecting on the results, she noted, "I could see clearly that if I wanted a particular kind of thinking, I needed to *ask students for it*" (p. 581). "Asking for it" begins with the teacher displaying his or her own enthusiasm for reading, learning, expressing, and inquiry; a sentiment nicely captured in this Indian bromide: *One who learns from one who is learning drinks from a running stream.*

There are some convincing clinical accounts and field studies suggesting that there is a great dormant force of creative energy waiting to transform the way in which we read and write in school, if teachers would "just ask for it." The question seems to impel the thinking and actions that follow.

One account, for example, tells of a professor of engineering's action research with his students. Students were randomly assigned to two groups and given identical plans to critique. However, one group was told to "critically" critique the plans, and the other to "constructively" critique them. The results showed that the "constructive" critiquers produced better criticisms and several very plausible, even creative, alternative solutions. The "criticisms" group offered weaker and more picky criticisms and virtually no constructive alternatives (in Baker & Schutz, 1972). Apparently, the capacities of the students in the "criticism" group to be constructive-creative simply remained dormant with no trigger mechanism to activate them.

If you are inclined to celebrate the wonders and unique capabilities of the human mind from such stories, you may need to consider deleting the words *unique* and *human* after reading this next account. Louis Herman, director of a marine mammal laboratory, had taught dolphins to respond to directions communicated through hand gestures. In some way, not explained in the news account, he taught them, or they learned, to comprehend a gesture meaning "creative." In any case, one day he signaled to two of them to perform in tandem and to do "something creative." With only that prompt, the dolphins submerged for a few moments, then swimming in tandem leaped into the air and simultaneously spit out jets of water before plunging back into the pool. On another occasion, given the same command, they performed a synchronized backward swim culminating in a simultaneous wave of the tails (*Time*, March 22, 1993, p. 54). Of course, almost as amazing as the creative nature of this feat is the wonder about how these sea mammals were able to comprehend the concept of creative and to communicate intentions to one another for a tandem effort.

Nonetheless, these anecdotes and some related empirical findings (discussed ahead) seem to give considerable creditability to the proposition that just asking for critical-constructive (i.e., creative) production is a solid way to begin to stimulate it. The simple logical explanation for this is the fact that higher levels of thinking tend to be *as much a matter of orientation and disposition* (Bereiter & Scardamalia, 1985)—or attitude, inclination, and focus—*as of aptitude*—or innate capacity which we apparently have, or we could not so easily answer this call to innovation.

Inviting Creative Production: Expressive-Artistic

A group of inner-city, once-failed-English, tenth-grade students were asked, as part of a *death and dying* literature theme, to try and create their own "communal poem"(Manzo & Martin, 1974). What they produced was called very worthy by several professors of literature, including the poet Dan Jaffe, who led this particular session. See Figure 8.11 for the Communal Poetry process and the poem.

Communal Poetry Process

1. The teacher asks questions designed to elicit fresh language and personal sensory responses about a chosen subject (e.g., "If death walked through that door, what would it look like?" "Who knows death best?").

2. Responses are recorded on the chalkboard. Clichés and other prosaic or hackneyed phrases are edited out as they occur.

3. Once the board is filled with raw material, students are asked to choose a beginning line from the material on the board.

4. The teacher writes the line and then aids students in selecting other phrases, helping them to establish rhythm and/or continuity of thought.

5. The teacher reads the recorded lines aloud again and asks students for additional choices from the board, allowing changes as the group indicates need.

6. When students are satisfied with the product, the leader reads the finished poem aloud.

7. A final copy is prepared with the names of the student participants, and copies are presented to the class.

Figure 8.11 Communal poetry process and poem.

Communal Poem

Somebody's Missing

Take a look around.
somebody's missing
   the dogs are howling
   somebody's going to sleep.

The grandfathers know
   what's going on:
   the air is polluted with grief.

Down on the corner, in the grocery store,
he's about to touch you on the arm
   with a silver knife
   a black guillotine
   a .38 pointed at your head.

Even the tough people are scared.

There I was slipping in the dark,
smelling the dumpyard,
   the wrinkled dirt,
   feeling so low I felt like getting high.

It's time
   to let life into this poem!
Time to take a bath,
   to pay death back with babies,
   to make even a policeman cry.

It's true
   not only an undertaker knows bodies.
Let's touch one another
   and send Death Nowhere.

Figure 8.11 *(continued)*

The Communal Poetry process is an excellent way to build group cohesiveness and collaboration. The topic and mood are easily set with just a few words. For example, on another occasion, we observed a teacher leading a session where she had conveyed a more humorous, "in-your-face" mood, and the class came back with a brief, rollicking poem that ended with a satisfying "Hurrah" for their effort (Manzo & Manzo, 1990a). While we have not tried it yet, it seems as if it could be convened and conducted online in real time or asynchronously. Please e-mail us to let us know if you pilot this possibility.

Inviting Creative Production: In the Realm of Idea Making (QuestMagnets)
Recently, we have begun to experiment with QuestMagnets (QM), a more wraparound, or surround-sound form of "Just Ask for It." QuestMagnets are heuristics, or specific self-discovery mechanisms that evoke fresh thinking and writing. They

are served up as an inviting variety of questions, problems, factoids, ideas, and musings that interrupt mundane thinking. Essentially, QMs essentially are open-ended questions and dialogues about a wide variety of things encountered in and out of school. They are one way to begin to *convert periods to question marks and question marks to wonder and original thinking.* The goal is to enrich students' inner speech—which continues outside class hours—with reminders of the mysteries and questions that anchor much of what is taught in school and of how much more needs to be discovered. For example, in science one might ask the question, "How does gravity really work?" If you have ever thought about this, and who hasn't, you will be interested to discover that the answer is, "We haven't but a clue." Ironically, discovering this seems to benefit attention and learning better than a lecture on the byplay between centripetal and centrifugal forces, words that more describe than explain how it is that the oceans don't empty into space.

There is no single way to stir and support higher-level reading, writing, and thinking, and yet there seem to be many ways. Clearly doing so must involve turning the attention of both teachers and students to the things about them that are worth pondering before being ingested as givens. Kristin Weissinger, a Manzo granddaughter, e-mailed us after a conversation on this subject with the contents of a poster she had told us was on the bulletin board of every classroom in her middle school:

- What if . . . ?

- How would it change if . . . ?

- Is there another way to solve, write, or say this?

- What's wrong here?

- Why can't we do that?

Her e-mail with these potentially stirring questions also contained a note that has us wondering, "What's wrong here?" Her note continued:

. . . but no one really pays attention to them. I think they're mostly there for the teachers. Love, Kristen

Though these questions contain the basis for imaginative thinking, creative writing, innovative problem solving, problem identification, and plausibility testing, they may be impotent when merely posted on classroom bulletin boards. Quest-Magnets are designed to be more participatory and to occur in a variety of ways and places. They are intended to "rouse minds to life" (Tharp & Gallimore, 1989).

QuestMagnets: Permission to Interrupt
Granted by Students and Parents

To optimize the positive effects of QuestMagnets, the first and most important thing to do is to explain to pupils and parents, in a note home, the value and purpose of these to learning, thinking, and discussion. In other words, ask for permission to interrupt, much as modern advertising is based on "permission marketing" (Godin,

1999), a means of not only gaining attention to a product but interest in hearing more about it because of the personal value that it brings. To extend the critical-constructive, reading-writing-thinking "ad campaign," QuestMagnets could be

- Posted on classroom bulletin boards, but also where one might not expect to find them, such as in locker rooms and on cafeteria walls
- Made into printed notes for the home refrigerator, where families can enjoy engaging and discussing them
- Invited from students, faculty, and parents (to further encourage thoughtful contributions, create blank post cards addressed to the school's Quest Learning Manager, and post names of submitters)
- Treated as brief critical/constructive writing assignments in classes where they might tie in with a curriculum topic
- Entered and dialogued on a class's or a school's Web site
- Possibly submitted to global Web sites, such as the Registry for Better Ideas, a site that hopes to raise funds to make awards to incisive new questions as well as solutions (see the link provided at *www.Literacy Leaders.com*)

Consider now some examples of QuestMagnets that might be used to stir REAP-like response writing and to generate additional submissions of like kinds. The following categories are not mutually exclusive.

QuestMagnets: Writing the Future

- Why are eyeglasses not engineered to more easily adjust to the facts that most people's ears are of unequal height and that long hours of pressure on any skin surface, such as the nose, is irritating?
- Why aren't we doing more to develop something like a Web-based universal voting system to complement and balance the influence of lobbyists on our current political system?

QuestMagnets: Factoids

- Deduce this: On what day are more take-out pizzas purchased than any other? (The day before Thanksgiving.)
- Southern California has fewer flying and crawling bugs per cubic foot of ground and space than the rest of the United States. Could this be the reason they also have less topsoil? Is topsoil largely bug guana and dead bug bodies?
- Females tend to see and remember more about what is in a room than do males; what can this mean?
- Single males are living home with their parents many years longer than single females, 29 years old versus 22.
- We're probably not all alike, and that may be our collective, adaptive advantage.

- Each U.S. acre contains an average of 400 lb. of insects, compared with only 14 lb. of people.

- It is frequently reported that the number of teen drivers killed in auto accidents is significantly greater than of urban teens killed by guns.

QuestMagnets: From the Heart

There are certain essential humanistic feelings that are not covered by law but that help us to keep our moral-ethical bearings. Sometimes these gurgle up within us as an urge or counterurge that says, "This doesn't feel right." On a purely cognitive level, observing, thinking, and puzzling over these "gnarlies" is a fundamental way to build higher-order thinking, interdisciplinary problem-solving, and a sense of moral rectitude. Here are some examples:

- Isn't there some more humane way to kill and cook lobsters than to slowly boil them alive?

- Shouldn't we think twice about adopting pets that require more care and attention than we are ready to provide?

- Should there be a web site where one can post and date the license plate numbers of reckless drivers?

QuestMagnets: By Subjects

(Math)	Why did it take such a very long time for humankind to discover and create zero (0)?
(Math)	What's all this business about "magic 9's"?
(Science)	Does anyone know how gravity really works? (Again, no they do not. For a fascinating new theory, see *http://amoureternal.com/oti/gravity/phen.htm*).
(Science)	How do electronic waves pass through the air and then recollect themselves in a radio or television set in the same patterns as they were sent?
(Social Studies)	If everyone has some money and they keep getting more, where did it first come from, and how does it continue to grow?
(Social Studies)	Why do some countries (like the United States) have "states" (which means independent countries, within the country as a whole), and doesn't this result in different laws and punishments in places that are separated only by an imaginary line?

QuestMusings: Wit and Wonder

School can be too serious and therefore a bit too confining. It can be liberating of the mind and spirit to think unseriously, and, ideally, wittily and amusingly. Invite such thoughts, more so than reactions, by sharing the wit and musings of some of the masters. Avoid heavy moralizing here; it's all in fun.

How come abbreviated is such a long word? (Steven Wright)

Why do scientists call it 're-search' when they are looking for something new? (Steven Wright)

QuestFinancial: Investing and Entrepreneurism

Making and keeping money is a fundamental need for most everyone. Help students to prepare for this life venture by orienting them early on to its obligatory demands. One way to do this is by raising it as a target, or orientation for reading, writing, and learning. (There is much more said on this topic in an online piece, *The 21 Century: Entrepreneurial Literacy*, available at *www.LiteracyLeaders.com.*) Minimally, however, have students read and react to articles and statements such as might be gathered under a title such as *$QUEST*, or *FinancialFutures*. Here are some evocative statements from a series of recent articles in a financial advisory magazine. Let a student chew on some of these before, during, and/or after reading such articles.

$Quest

- The key to having money is not in making a lot of it but in not spending so much of what you earn.

- You can be young without money, but you can't be old without it.

- The key to success in internet selling, according to one entrepreneur, is simply to be the first with a simple idea, such as he was with *www .golfballs.com,* a company that started by just selling and shipping golf balls but now is selling lots of related paraphernalia.

In general, questing is more a "search" than a "re-search" approach to reading-writing-thinking. It is the conscious effort to see what others are seeing but to see it freshly; to detect the signal through the static.

▶ CRITICAL-CONSTRUCTIVE DISCUSSION TECHNIQUES

Many teaching methods have a step called "discuss." Following are two classical methods and one newly developing method for promoting discussions that "rouse minds to life."

Developmental Discussion

The Developmental Discussion (Maier, 1963) and a rediscovered version called Guided Conversation (Gauthier, 1996) are intended to teach students about the full process of problem solving by involving them in all of its parts: identification and partitioning of the problem, collection of relevant data or information, generation of solutions, and appraisal of solutions. Most important, it emphasizes going beyond existing knowledge. As such, it should be basic to any program to improve creative thinking and problem solving. Much of this process can be shifted to an "asynchronous" system such as a Web site with a discussion board and/or an e-mail list serve.

Steps in Developmental Discussion/Guided Conversation

1. The teacher instructs students to try to identify certain conflicting points (rather than views) or problems inherent in material presented in text and lecture.

2. The teacher initially provides examples that can serve as models of problem identification (this usually requires comparing textual information to prior knowledge and experiences).

3. The teacher assists students in narrowing and partitioning the problem into manageable segments.

4. Students are divided into cooperative learning groups to solve the smaller parts of the problem. Each group is asked to jot down notes on individual and group members' answers using questions such as the following to guide their analysis:

    a. What do we know about this problem part?

    b. Which parts of the information we have are relevant to the problem?

    c. What more do we need to know to construct a possible solution?

    d. What are some possible solutions given what we now know?

    e. What additional information can we collect (and how) to formulate better solutions?

5. A large-group discussion is held to illustrate the different ways the problem can be viewed and solutions sought. The teacher reminds students to add to their notes during this discussion.

6. The class decides on a solution (usually a synthesis) or—in a significant departure from conventional school practices—may choose to table the matter until the class can collect additional information (see Figure 8.12 for an anecdotal account).

7. Students individually write out the solution as they see it and in the most convincing way possible. Then students exchange papers and give one another feedback on their essays. The teacher invites students and reviewers to read aloud phrases or sections that they feel were particularly well stated.

Devil's Advocate

One simple and direct way to encourage students to consider an issue from alternate perspectives is to get students into a discussion that evokes this type of reasoning. *Devil's Advocate* is an issues-based discussion that has a rich heritage (Alvermann, Dillon, & O'Brien, 1987; Roby, 1983). It was used by Socrates and Plato and is a common convention at synods of several religions around the world.

One of three things may happen in a Devil's Advocate discussion: Positions may be strengthened, modified, or abandoned. In any case, students involved in such a discussion tend to have a great many experiences with reflective turnabout. They learn about the enormous complexity of issues that initially appear clear-cut. They learn about the paradoxes involved in trying to solve a problem only to find that the best solution can sometimes be more disruptive than the existing problem. Finally, they learn to use language not merely to state what they believe but to discover what they *might* reasonably believe.

Mr. Freeble, a high school civics teacher, works with a group of average ability students for fifty minutes each morning. In a previous class session the students had read a five page textbook assignment and had completed the accompanying study guide. The assignment covered information about the Supreme Court—what it is, its purpose and charges, and its relationship to the entire governmental system.

Freeble began the developmental discussion by reviewing the previous textbook assignment for five minutes. From the review, students were reminded of the following key concepts: the Supreme Court is the highest court in the land, the individuals sitting on the Supreme Court are charged with interpreting the Constitution, and members of the Supreme Court may change a previous ruling by another branch of the government.

Next, Freeble asked the students to supply current information about events in the news concerning recent Supreme Court rulings. Elicited were facts about prayer in school and nativity scenes set up on public property. Freeble noted that the seasonal influence (it was close to Christmas) play [sic] a large role in students' interest in a local newspaper story about a controversial nativity scene. After ten minutes of discussing that story and its implications for local residents, the class decided on a problem that was text based but of immediate interest to them—should religious groups be allowed to erect nativity scenes on public property?

The teacher guided the students in breaking the larger problem (separation of church and state) into three smaller problems: (1) Does setting up a nativity scene on public property violate the rights of individuals who do not have the same religious beliefs?; (2) What information could the class add that would help solve the problem?; (3) What would be a reasonable way to share what was learned with the people involved in the controversy?

The students broke into smaller groups and began to work on the first part of the problem. Freeble supplied each group with a one page summary of the Pawtucket case involving a Supreme Court ruling on the display of nativity scenes on public property. Freeble circulated among the groups, observing and offering assistance when requested.

During the last fifteen minutes of the period, students participated in a large group discussion in which they reported on their reactions to the Pawtucket case and whether they believed the case had any implications for the local controversy.

Over the next two days, the students worked in small groups to tackle the remaining problem parts. Solutions to the overall problem included working with community leaders to foster improved communication among the dissident groups and writing letters to the editor of the local newspaper on the topic of how the Pawtucket case compared to the local one.

Figure 8.12 Anecdotal account of developmental discussion.

Source: Examples (pp. 38, 40–41) from Alvermann, Donna E., Dillon, Deborah R., & O'Brien, David G. (1987). *Using Discussion to Promote Reading Comprehension.* Newark, DE: International Reading Association. Reprinted with permission of Donna E. Alvermann and the International Reading Association. All rights reserved. © 1987 by the International Reading Association.

Steps in Devil's Advocate

1. The teacher poses an issue to the class.

2. Students are paired but asked to individually prepare written arguments using the text for essential information. Sometimes there are more than two positions.

3. Students are instructed to describe to their partners their best arguments for each position. They should discuss each argument to determine whether it contains faulty reasoning.

4. Still in pairs, students are asked to discuss with their partners whether the positions they originally supported have changed as a result of this activity and, if so, why and in what way. Then they revise their individual written statements accordingly.

5. A class discussion follows based on students' arguments for each side of the issue, any changes in attitude that occurred as a result of the activity, and sources of further information related to the issue.

6. Students are offered a final opportunity to revise and prepare a final form of their position statements.

See Figure 8.13 for an example of the Devil's Advocate method. Notice how this method emphasizes critical examination of the issue with the possibility of changing one's mind, or reformulating a position, rather than winning a debate.

Regression Equation Technique

The *Regression Equation Technique* (RET) is a method under development for increasing the likelihood that the discussion will detect the truth signal through the haze of social and semantic static, thus enabling participants to move more expeditiously toward sensible solutions. The method is based on a principle used in a statistical procedure of a similar name, the *multiple regression equation analysis*. The technique also draws on group process methods that encourage personal development of evaluative thinking, such as Hoffman's (1977) Intra-Act, and newer methods such as Moller and Bohning's (1992) *participatory ranking*, that are designed to get the best decision making out of diverse groups. These methods are built around some form of guided value voting, tallying, discussing, and revoting. Here is the useable core of RET as it now is conceived.

Steps in the Regression Equation Technique (RET)

1. Set up an equation that represents an item, or "independent variable," that you wish to explore or better understand. Start by simply writing the entity or factor to be examined on the left side of an equal sign.

2. Place all other factors, or "dependent variables," that seem to explain that factor on the right side of the equal sign. Be sure that one of these dependent variables is titled "unexplained portion." Invite the group to

Mr. Tennyson, a ninth grade social science teacher, used the Devil's Advocate strategy to structure a class discussion on banning nuclear testing. His students had read a section of their text that dealt with the horrors of nuclear warfare. As the discussion opens, Tennyson has just finished assigning the students to pairs.

"All right now, you and your partner find a place where you can talk quietly. Each of you should jot down why you believe the United States should stop testing nuclear weapons. Be sure to support your beliefs with evidence from the text. Then take the opposite stance (why the United States should not stop testing nuclear weapons) and again support your beliefs with evidence from the text."

(The students, working individually in pairs, take about ten minutes to complete this task.)

"Okay, now we're ready for the next step. Choose your best arguments and present them to your partner. Be certain that you discuss your beliefs with your partner; for example, seek your partner's ideas and evaluations of the pros and cons that you took on the issue. Is there evidence of any faulty reasoning on either one's part?"

(After approximately fifteen minutes, the noise level in the room drops, an indication that students have finished presenting the arguments they had with themselves.)

"May I have your attention. . . . There are two more things I would like you to do: (1) Think about how your ideas have changed on banning nuclear testing. For example, has your position shifted from your original one? If so, why? (2) Decide whether you have strengthened your original position, abandoned it completely, or only modified it. Then tell your partner your decision and see if he or she agrees."

(After approximately ten minutes, Tennyson drew the students into a whole class discussion by asking them to share some of their ideas on both sides of the issue.)

Figure 8.13 Example of Devil's Advocate method.

Source: Examples (pp. 38, 40–41) from Alvermann, Donna E., Dillon, Deborah R., & O'Brien, David G. (1987). *Using Discussion to Promote Reading Comprehension.* Newark, DE: International Reading Association. Reprinted with permission of Donna E. Alvermann and the International Reading Association. All rights reserved. © 1987 by the International Reading Association.

add or restate any factors, except the one to be examined. (Rewording the independent variable changes the exercise and should only be undertaken advisedly or as another comparative exercise.)

3. Have everyone in the discussion group independently distribute percentage weightings for each dependent variable to the right of the equal sign, including the "unexplained portion" (to total 100%).

4. Tally and record the range and average percent score for each factor.

5. Attempt to explain findings with briefly written personal notes and to reconcile differences through discussion.

Each time the researchers have used this basic discussion design in a domain in which the participants had real-life experience, they seem to have uniformly found their way back to some clearer signal (truth) and away from whatever static interference had been building around it. For example, the independent variable, or factor being analyzed, could be "academic success for inner-city youth," and the dependent variables or explaining factors could be elements like structured classrooms; direct instruction; reading of core literature; reading of nonfiction material; vocabulary study; academic aptitude; recitation; transactional (subjective) reacting; self-esteem; family reading habits; and multicultural curricula. In such cases, the results often come out sounding as they did in a radio ad for a new charter school that emerged in a district that was disaccredited for failing to meet every one of its state's eleven criteria. It had experimented for thirty years with almost all of the aforementioned dependent variables, though often by misassigning their respective weightings as explaining outcomes on conventional standardized tests (arguably one of the basic means of quality control of schools and learning). The charter school ad essentially said the following:

> What ensures school success? Is it diversity, attention to differences between boys and girls, campaigns to end violence, efforts to increase social responsiveness, attention to learning styles, cooperative grouping practices? Not really. Important as each of these may be to someone or even everyone, success in school is determined in greatest measure by a focus on reading, writing, and content area teaching and learning.

If you think you would like to join the effort to further develop this critical-constructive discussion technique, look at *www.LiteracyLeaders.com* for details as they develop. Ideally, try using the method in either a professional discussion or in a classroom situation where the independent variable can range from such traditional fare as "Rise of Labor Unions" or "Elements of Tragedy in Hamlet" to more contemporary issues such as "The Likely Power of Telecomputing in Modern Life" or " Factors Influencing Violent Behavior In Young Adults."

As you can see, this evolving technique is rigorous yet open ended. It brings several subtle points into focus that need to be better understood and dealt with in order to promote effective critical and constructive reading, discussion, and learning in school and in society. Some of these points are not immediately evident. For example, the person or group who gets to state the agenda or problem for review also has the greatest control over the discourse and hence the conclusions; therefore, teaching youngsters how to articulate problems may be as important as teaching them how to solve problems. At least half of the solution to any problem can be found in its identification and statement.

The critical-constructive value of RET is amplified by the Internet. An equation can be electronically published as a standing quest to which value can be added by each class and individual who reads, thinks, and writes about it over time. The equations would stand as QuestMagnets of their own, attracting relevant positive and negative experiences in life, literature, and varied content areas. This ongoing discourse should help teachers and students to make better sense of the overly compartmentalized structures of school curricular and the near-chaotic flow of information on the Internet. The process of framing the equations and the posting of them can serve as the shared quests that help solve the timeless educational problem of "Ungeared Minds" (Chase, 1926). These public quests can serve as the "motive ideas that call the will to action" (Chase, 1926, p. 196), and assist those able to read and write but somehow bewildered by answers to questions that they have not learned to raise.

► AFTER WORDS

A new target was raised in this chapter for content area literacy and education in general: to promote the constructive-creative process as well as critical reading-thinking. Proposed as the basic means by which to achieve this is to build content, reading, and writing instruction around a sense of wonder or quest to understand the questions as well as the answers that constitute the disciplines. The next chapter complements the ideas of this chapter by further addressing reading and writing to learn, across the grades and across the disciplines.

CHAPTER 9

READING AND WRITING TO LEARN ACROSS GRADE LEVELS AND CONTENT AREAS

The man who does not read good books has no advantage over the man who can't read them.

—Mark Twain

▶ FORE WORDS

This chapter addresses three complementary topic areas: emergent content area literacy, the use of literature and trade books to teach content at all grade levels, and the use of writing to enhance student learning across the disciplines. The section on emergent content area literacy discusses how we could be better preparing our secondary students for the challenges of content area literacies at the earliest of grade levels. Connected to this is the use of adolescent literature and trade books to enhance content learning during this stage of human development. The chapter concludes with some practical and creative ways to utilize writing as a thinking tool to enhance learning in all content areas.

- ▶ FORE WORDS
- ▶ EMERGENT CONTENT AREA LITERACY: HOW EARLY ELEMENTARY TEACHERS CAN BETTER PREPARE CHILDREN FOR READING TO LEARN
- ▶ EXTENDING EMERGENT LITERACY
- ▶ EMERGENT CONTENT AREA LITERACY: LEARNING FOR BEGINNERS
- ▶ NONPRINT ECAL METHODS
- ▶ PRINT RECORDS IMPORTANT INFORMATION AND WONDER RELEASES IT
- ▶ LITERATURE- AND THEME-BASED (INTERDISCIPLINARY) EXPLORATIONS INTO CONTENT, CONCEPTS, AND VOCABULARY
- ▶ WRITING TO LEARN
- ▶ AFTER WORDS

▶ EMERGENT CONTENT AREA LITERACY: HOW EARLY ELEMENTARY TEACHERS CAN BETTER PREPARE CHILDREN FOR READING TO LEARN

The goal of this section is to move wonder-driven learning down to the earliest stages of childhood. It appears that teaching children to read may actually interrupt the rather natural development of content and concept learning. This is no small point since it suggests that pressing for greater factual knowledge at an early age would not be another ramped-up incursion into early childhood education but more an attempt to utilize children's ways of knowing and being to foster rather natural states of knowledge and vocabulary growth, which are the lynchpins linking *learning to read* and *reading to learn*.

Secondary school teachers often bemoan the lack of preparation of children for the rigors of intensive discipline instruction. Just as the field of content area reading has developed largely in response to the concerns expressed by college professors about the underpreparation of students in high school, a similar movement now seems to be afoot to elicit the aid of elementary teachers to prepare kids for intermediate and high school.

The Jesuits are fond of saying, "Give me the child until age seven, and I'll give you the man." The wisdom in this educational plan should not be lost in public education, but it is not being heeded as fully as it might. Clearly, knowledge begets knowledge. But what if children are knowledge deprived? After all, elementary teachers are expected to be generalists who have a working knowledge of all disciplines from math to literature (El-Hindi, 2003) and fairly extensive knowledge of children's nonfiction trade books (Moss, 1991). This puts something of a cap on what can realistically be achieved by a single teacher, but it also cries out for further attention, because the need for early and continuing content and concept growth in the disciplines is clear.

An observational study revealed that on average, a mere 3.6 minutes per day was spent on reading and interacting on informational material in the early grades, and far less in lower socioeconomic status (SES) school districts (Duke, 2000). The early grades have a rich and sensible tradition of focusing on near-future needs of pupils: Children are taught to be good students by an emphasis on personal-social adjustment, language development, and teaching them to learn to read. However, primary school is not just preparation for life as a first, second, and third grader; it also must be a preparation for fourth grade and beyond. It is rather like Double A Little League: A team can win a lot of games by just hitting the ball to underdeveloped defensive players, but with hitting as its only focus, it isn't long before the other teams catch up in offense and games come to be decided by defense. In literacy terms, this means having a plan for better using this same period of development (between four and ten years old, and spanning five years of summers, after-school hours, and in-school time) to offer wonderfully enriching opportunities for gathering some of the rich factual and conceptual bases of human interests and knowledge. This can be done in ways that are compatible with children's developmental needs and experiential ways of knowing. To capture the value of this opportunity and to position it as a complement to the current early school curriculum and standards, we suggest that it should be called *emergent content area literacy (ECAL)* and be built on the foundation of content area literacy and emergent literacy, a branch of reading that attempts to impart attitudes, experiences, and skills that are simultaneously developmentally appropriate but that also accelerate immediate and subsequent learning. This is achieved essentially with what strikes us as *intentional-incidental* teaching-learning, as opposed to either a heavily didactic or a totally incidental teaching-learning approach. This sort of intentional-incidental teaching-learning requires vastly more planning than either of the other two approaches since it must be instructionally robust and yet have the character of teaching without appearing to teach. Of course, this approach does not exclude some direct teaching, but on balance the early grades need to remain child centered; not because it cannot be otherwise but because we value early childhood as a precious moment, especially in our affective as well as our cognitive development. This creates the challenge of not doing one at the expense of the other, but it also offers the opportunity of doing one in support of the other.

▶ EXTENDING EMERGENT LITERACY

Learning How to Read

The term *emergent literacy* is used most often to refer to the events and surroundings that need to be present to create a conducive environment for learning to read. The conceptual basis for this is that children's language acquisition—and interest in extending language to include reading and writing—is determined in large measure by the nature of their interactions with their environments. This idea often is attributed to Jean Piaget, the pioneer developmental psychologist, who showed that certain innate aptitudes and abilities would be substantially advanced in an environment that intentionally urged, more so than merely permitted, their "construction." In concrete terms, emergent literacy is made up of books, paper, and pencils and of people reading and talking about what they are reading, along with a teacher who reads to the children from "Big Books" that incidentally teach children about the concepts of print, left-to-right decoding of words across a page, recognition of letters and whole words and who imparts a sense of the fluency and the regard for punctuation that a reader needs to attain to derive meaning from the printed page. This strategy, along with direct instruction in phonemics and phonics, rapid word identification, and a good deal of storybook reading by children at ascending levels of difficulty, helps most children learn how to read.

Deceleration Requires Acceleration

Somewhere around fourth grade, however, children often reach a period of consolidation but also *deceleration*. From narrative material they typically have mastered rapid recognition of most high-frequency words. They also have acquired a fairly sound sense of character development, conflict resolution, the search for a moral, and other such aspects of story organization. However, children also appear to plateau as their rate of progress levels off, particularly in reading comprehension and fluency with informational text. There are many possible explanations for this deceleration, some of which are as healthy and explainable as the slight weight gain that seems to precede each spurt of growth in height. Such periods in normal physical development often are accompanied by longer periods of need for sleep—which, by the way, is the only time that growth can take place—and by a parallel need for more nourishment (as opposed to just calories) and increased exercise to support a larger, more agile structure. It has been noted that "instruction is, after all, an effort to assist growth" (Bruner, 1966, p. 1). While this may appear to occur rather naturally, it also requires an accelerated, but careful, preplanning and seizing of a propitious moment in early childhood development.

▶ EMERGENT CONTENT AREA LITERACY: LEARNING FOR BEGINNERS

Reading to Learn

Just as content area literacy developed essentially in response to the belief that intermediate and secondary teachers need to assist students in their continuing developmental process of learning to read, a new subfield of emergent content area literacy likely will develop essentially in response to the belief that primary and elementary teachers need to assist students in more securely launching and continuing their developmental process of reading to learn. ECAL, however, is not merely about beginning learning but about learning for beginners. Early learning is much more challenging than subsequent learning. It is more about promoting a particular mind-set, or habit of mind, that, in this case, values facts and information and their byproduct: an active interest in continuing the growth of knowledge. The philosopher Nietzsche is frequently attributed to have once noted that "a man [person] has no ears for that to which experience has given him no access." ECAL is about creating early *experiences* with the nature of knowledge and building an acquired taste for it. It's a way to alert the ear and eye to the sound and sense of *things worth knowing*. The need to support such early learning is furthered by Jerome Bruner's popular dictum that it is possible to introduce a child to most any complex adult concept in some "intellectually honest way." Bruner referred to this model as the basis for a "spiral curriculum"—that is, one that introduces ideas, content, concepts, and problem-solving challenges that are mapped into children's predominant modes of representation and then reintroduced with increasing complexity as the child matures (1966). It also has been noted that some questions and points of information should be raised even as some children may seem to ignore these points, because informational knowledge has a way "surfacing to consciousness at a later time" (Lee, Bingham, Woelfel, 1968, p. 31). But this raises the question of just what it is that children can understand and learn. *Pokemon* and other aspects of popular culture and modern media are providing some surprising and desirable (that is, serendipitous) clues to this perplexing developmental and philosophical question.

Reading Development May Be a Weak Indication of Cognitive Development

A sustained look at *Pokemon*, *Yu Gi OH*, and their now multiple variations speaks loudly to their significant complexity. These games and cards and stories would never have won approval as age appropriate from a curriculum committee. Yet children, largely boys, read and grasp the complex story lines and arcane games and guidelines for intelligently collecting and trading these inventive cards. Researchers are finding that boys are becoming literate "in spite of school instruction" and may end up better prepared for vocational careers because these skills are more useful than being able to write a narrative or analyze a work of fiction (Smyth, 2003). The lesson here is simple: Kids are more capable of understanding things of greater complexity than we have given them credit for. It seems that in the process of teaching youngsters to read, we have gathered a misimpression that their capacities to think are somehow tied to, if not arrested by, their rate of learning to read fluently, a two- to four-year process, on average. Now that we know otherwise, different implications present themselves. The challenge becomes one of asking, "What can we teach children about content and concepts and inquiry *while* they are learning to read?" because this will prepare them not merely for a smooth transition to reading to learn, but it will increase recognition of the complex ideas and factual information that our highly media-penetrating environment provides. In short, we may be seriously underestimating children's capacities to acquire knowledge, to think connectively, and to learn on their own.

Identifying and Promoting ECAL Curriculum and Practices

Soon there will be a new subfield that addresses *doing* emergent content area literacy. This is not going unnoticed by others, such as Barbara Moss (1991), who has written extensively about the value of non-fiction books in the elementary school, and Karen Wood (2002), who pointedly writes about the new dimensions of content area literacy that are not just for secondary teachers.

There have been essential elements identified for readers in today's world: Such readers must be code breakers, meaning makers, text users, and text critics (Luke & Freebody, 1997). We would add that they also must be more constructive-creative in their thinking than ever before simply to keep pace with a rapidly changing world and to be empowered and responsible for identifying its direction and its methods. Achieving these goals suggests several overlapping curriculum goals and objectives, gathered from several sources that seem to be leaning in this direction, some over 30 years old (Bean, 2000; Desmond, 1997; Lee, Bingham, & Woelfel, 1968; Moss, 1991; Wood, 2000, 2002):

- It must involve learning from more avenues than just reading;
- It must lay the experiential foundation for peer-based speaking, writing and discussion;
- It must teach youngsters to gain and cross-reference information from multiple sources—sometimes referred to as "multiple source literacy";
- It must require more higher-order thinking;
- It must teach empathy for others—that is, concern for the means as well as the end;
- It must teach and promote foundational understanding of key concepts;
- It must be reinforced and enriched by a suitably precise vocabulary—an often undervalued objective of early schooling;
- It must teach collaboration, but also the reality of competition;
- It must result in greater self-regulation and self-teaching from environmental options;
- It must teach youngsters to be question raisers, or inquirers, as well as question answerers, or information acquirers.

Again, this must all be served up in ways that are compatible with children's ways of knowing. Simply put, *these efforts can in no way negate or undermine the current social-emotional-developmental goals of early childhood education.*

Will Efforts to Stir Early Learning Really Work?

This question has not yet been fully tested, but there is a growing body of evidence suggesting that efforts to influence patterns of interests and learning result in different outcomes, almost immediately. One of the more telling of these is based on an observational study of identical twins, Alan and Gordon, who were four years old, together at home, and separated at nursery school. Alan's verbal expression is oriented mainly to purpose and planning, even as he talks about his favorite book, *Caps for Sale*. Gordon's verbal expression is more primitive but much richer in narration and imagination and very influenced by the then popular TV series *Batman* and a *Batman* deck of cards that he would play with at every opportunity (Lee, Bingham, & Woelfel, 1968). As you will see in the next section of this chapter in another broader study of verbal (i.e., questioning) behavior, children clearly are very sensitive to environmental cues, whether they be encouraging or discouraging of certain behaviors and underlying attitudes.

Here are our candidates for this emerging, emergent field of primary and early-intermediate-grades content area literacy development: (1) three simple methods that can be done before children can decode print; (2) one charting activity to help them to learn to extract information from reading and others sources; and (3) a cluster of means for tying content learning to children's literature, to the benefit of both.

▶ NONPRINT ECAL METHODS
Show and Question-Only (Gambit)

This instructional strategy probably qualifies as a *Cambrian method* since it has one of the essential features of this new type of teaching-learning: It prepares children to engage in public speech that ideally becomes inner speech and, hence, to engage in self-teaching, in and outside the classroom. At a practical level, it simply involves playing show-and-tell with an occasionally different flare that lays the foundations for

- Inquiry training;
- Self-guided purpose-setting in listening—the means by which 90% of new learning occurs—and soon reading;
- Aural-oral (listening-speaking) skills; and
- Collaborative learning

It also tends to be great fun. This is best launched with a little *gambit* (i.e., something done to open or focus conversation). It begins by demonstrating *Show and Question-Only* and then asking children to bring some things to class for student-led versions.

Steps in Show and Question-Only

1. Something interesting is shown to the class.
2. The class has 20 questions in which to discover what it is and what the presenter might wish to say about it.
3. The presenter may give some help by saying when they are getting "hotter" or "cooler."
4. The presenter finally tells all—usually to a very alert audience.

When this was done for the first time, as part of a study in the questioning behavior of kindergarten children, some remarkable things happened, immediately and thereafter (Manzo & Legenza, 1975). In this study a boy brought an old-fashioned hand-cranked coffee grinder to Show and Question-Only. The students gathered around and leaned forward, displaying the body language of attention and curiosity. At first they seemed to ask random questions but soon began to encourage one another to sequence their questions into a more orderly *inquiry*. Within about nine questions they deduced that they were looking at an old grinder, and probably of coffee beans (which they suspected quickly because small electric bean grinders were popular at the time of the study). They conceded after a few attempts that they could not guess what the presenter might want to say about it, but they did narrow it down to it being connected to his grandparents. (His story was that the coffee grinder was given to his mother by his grandparents, who had it in the family from when his mother's mother brought it west to Kansas City from Virginia many years ago.)

This slightly different form of show-and-tell tends to yield more knowledge-driven (epistemological) inquiry, as compared with the majority of questions that children raise, which are more along the lines of social banter. In this example, the discussion drew a bead on concepts like the westward migration and the intelligence in carrying coffee in the form of beans rather than preground, which would absorb moisture and grow stale.

Ideally, a *gambit*—or trial effort to stir interest and questioning—such as this one could be followed up with a brief reading from an appropriate book, much as is done in a conventional lesson, where the teacher would have introduced some artifact to raise curiosity and interest before reading. Show and Question-Only has intrinsic value in building curiosity and knowledge that are justifiable whether with or without pre- or follow-up reading. One of its chief values is that it is *experiential* and, therefore, likely to be remembered for a long time. To that extent, it is *schema* building, more so than would be just another piece of relatively isolated information. Schema, like Java Script in computer programming, is not merely a message but a vessel that prepares the mind to seek out and carry multiple packets of new information that may come its way. As such, artifacts are now being used widely to accompany storybooks; some books are sold with accompanying *realia*, another name for artifacts, which are more typically associated with archeological finds.

Such artifacts, or realia, may vary from a wand for a lead-in to *Harry Potter and the Sorcerer's Stone* to a bonnet to stir focused interest in a historical piece about the early pilgrims to America, or story reading, like *Little House on the Prairie*. We also have seen some very imaginative teachers use the disassembled parts of a wristwatch, a toaster, and a VCR to induce curiosity and examination of small machines. Attention often gets focused on the simple mechanical parts of these, since the electronic components can be rather mystifying even for adults to grasp. Nonetheless, the lessons are valuable in providing a certain content orientation, and especially so to girls, who tend to be less inquisitive about the mechanical world and, hence, less likely to pursue studies in engineering. Lack of knowledge and orientation to the mechanical world also can have more immediate and prolonged effects: Each new body of knowledge learned is a potential analog, or metaphor, for yet other complex content and concepts. Absent such knowledge, grasp of parallel, but different, concepts and content is considerably weakened.

This orientational issue alone may explain the lower proportion of females in applied mathematics, physics, chemistry, and, as mentioned previously, engineering.

▶ PRINT RECORDS IMPORTANT INFORMATION AND WONDER RELEASES IT

Teachers should wonder aloud about all manner of things that easily available print can quickly answer. Gestures as simple as these build an orientation toward, and respect for, the sheer utility and friendliness of print as a source of information.

- "I wonder how many crayons are in a box? Let's just read the box and see." (This can be followed by a count to see if there is the correct number in the box.)
- "I wonder what this color is called? It's a little red and a little purple. Let's see what it says on the crayon. Oh, it's called magenta!"
- "I wonder what all this writing is on this bottle of aspirin? Let's see if we can figure it out." (*Read aloud and discuss*)
- "I wonder if the child who fell in the well will be OK? Should I read the news story to you that tells about it?" (*Read aloud and discuss*)

Of course, today more so than ever, there are engaging informational books, like David Macaulay's 1988 bestseller *The Way Things Work.* But more on informational trade books ahead.

Reciprocal Questioning of Pictures Procedure

In the study of the questioning behaviors of kindergarten children reported earlier (Manzo & Legenza, 1975), the authors developed a measure of students' "manifest curiosity" as expressed through their questioning about pictures. This measure, called the *Reciprocal Questioning of Pictures Procedure (RQPP),* also now serves as a useful method for teaching and assessing youngsters engaged in a careful content analysis of a picture that nicely parallels the thinking processes necessary in content area reading. It simply goes like this:

Step 1. Select a book with lively, interesting pictures. Manzo and Legenza (1975) developed a method for determining the language-stimulation value of pictures that suggested three characteristics to be most stimulating to children's interests and exploration: (1) pictures of children of the same age; (2) action pictures; and (3) pictures containing complex and multiple activities.

Step 2. Say to the children that you and they will have one minute to study the picture, and try to recall all that is in it, after which, they, then you, will ask each other questions to see how many things each of you can remember as being represented when the picture is turned face down. After two or three rounds of this "recalling-retelling," the game is changed.

Step 3. Now say, "Let's take one turn asking others some interesting questions about this picture." The children go first. Most times they are uncertain as to what to ask, and say little, if anything. Oddly, this leaves them very attentive to the teacher's questions, since they are curious what these might be.

Step 4. The teacher then begins to ask a variety of who, what, where, and why questions and some inferential and conjectural questions having much the same form as these questions might if they were about something read: "Who/what is the main thing in this picture?" "What is happening?" "Why do you suppose mother put that cookie jar up so high?" "What do you suppose has happened before?" "What do you suppose will happen next?"

With this simple *teaching-without-teaching* procedure, children are taught how to exercise their own power of will and attention to increase recall—a fundamental function of content reading—and how to anticipate, and hence ask themselves the kind of questions that typically are asked of print material. Following are two lists of books, one without print and one stressing informational trade books, that can be used in the next stage of reading to learn. Further ahead you will find means of utilizing informational trade books in thematic ways that support, and in some instances out-do, the informational impact of standard textbooks, which sometimes can appear to be a stodgy litany of facts.

Picture Books. Books with particularly engaging pictures that enhance the theme, mood, and story line; encourage children to identify with characters and events; and heighten interest in the print.

Alexander and the Terrible, Horrible, No Good, Very Bad Day, by Judith Viorst, illustrated by Ray Cruz (K and up, 34 pp.)

Amelia Bedelia, by Peggy Parish, illustrated by Fritz Seibel (K–4, 24 pp.)

The Carp in the Bathtub, by Barbara Cohen, illustrated Joan Halpern (K–4, 48 pp.)

A Chair for My Mother, by Vera B. Williams (K–3, 30 pp.)

Curious George, by H. A. Rey (PP–1, 48 pp.)

The Cut-Ups Cut Loose, by James Marshall (K–2, 30 pp.)

The Day Jimmy's Boa Ate the Wash, by Trinka Hakes Noble (PP–2, 30 pp.)

An Evening at Alfie's, by Shirley Hughes (PP–2, 28 pp.)

Frog and Toad Are Friends, Arnold Lobel (PP–2, 64 pp.)

The Giving Tree, by Shel Silverstein (K–4, 52 pp.)

Goodnight Moon, by Margaret Wise Brown (P–K, 30 pp.)

Ira Sleeps Over, by Bernard Waber (K–6, 48 pp.)

Madeline, by Ludwig Bemelmans (P–2, 54 pp.)

Mike Mulligan and His Steam Shovel, by Virginia Lee Burton (K–4, 42 pp.)

The Napping House, by Audrey Wood, illustrated by Don Wood (P–K, 28 pp.)

Tintin in Tibet, by Herge (2–4, 62 pp.)

Where the Wild Things Are, by Maurice Sendak (K–3, 28 pp.)

Informational Books.   Nonfiction print satisfies and builds curiosity and re-inforces the information value of books.

Planes, by Byron Barton (P–2, 34 pp.)

Animals in the Country, by Kenneth Lilly (K–2)

Do Animals Dream?, by Joyce Pope (3–6)

Here a Chick, There a Chick, by Bruce McMillan (P–3)

How Much Is a Million?, by David M. Schwartz, illustrated by Steven Kel-logg (P–3)

How the Human Body Works, by Giovanni Caselli (5–9)

The Kids' Question and Answer Book, by the editors of *Owl* magazine (4–7)

Life through the Ages, by Giovanni Caselli (5–8)

The Milk Makers, by Gail Gibbons (P–3)

The Post Office Book: Mail and How It Moves, by Gail Gibbons (P–3)

Trucks, by Byron Barton (P–K, 16 pp.)

Wonder Charts

In a Wonder Chart, a space is provided for youngsters to tell about anything that "wonders" them. The purpose of these is to build interests and curiosity about the information in information trade books and textbooks. "Wonders" are recorded, by the teacher or the child and signed by the contributor. Space is provided for il-lustrating pictures or additional related information. Additional space is provided for "Answers"—or explanations, illustrations, pictures, or book titles that relate. In this way, children are taught to be question raisers as well as question answer-ers (see Figure 9.1).

The keenest part of Wonder Chart activities is that they not only broaden the circle of student participants but tend to include other teachers, library resources, newspapers, magazines, and parents. Every conceivable source of information soon becomes part of this cooperative learning activity. This activity also offers an-other opportunity for teachers to help children bring wonder and learning home to enrich family life:

"Dad, you're a mechanic, right? Well, we were wondering in school today how a car engine operates. Could you tell me how it works?"

"Mom, you said that you once worked in a fish canning factory in Seattle. We were wondering today how those little sardines get so neatly into every can."

Source: From *Teaching Children to be Literate, A Reflective Approach,* 1st edition, by MANZO/MANZO © 1996. Reprinted with permission of Wadsworth, a division of Thomson Learning. www.thomsonrights.com Fax 800-730-2215.

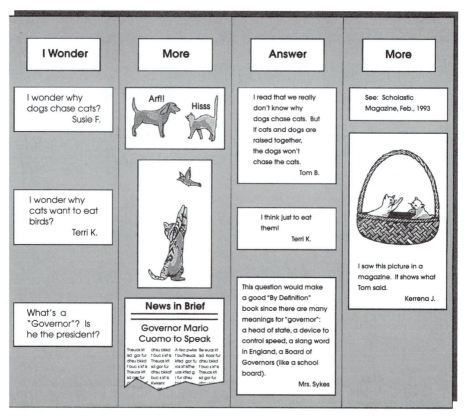

Figure 9.1 Wonder Chart.

Source: From *Teaching Children To Be Literate: A Reflective Approach*, 1st edition, by MANZO/ MANZO © 1996. Reprinted with permission of Wadsworth, a division of Thomson Learning. www.thomsonrights.com Fax 800-730-2215.

▶ LITERATURE- AND THEME-BASED (INTERDISCIPLINARY) EXPLORATIONS INTO CONTENT, CONCEPTS, AND VOCABULARY

Moss (1991) offers several sound reasons for promoting and using informational texts (trade books) in a thematic way, even where textbooks are the dominant medium. For example, textbooks tend to be written at a student's instructional level whereas trade books are often available on the same topic at a student's independent level. Further, trade books tend to be much more engaging, colorful, and detailed about a certain place and time—critical elements of children's ways of knowing. Beverly Korbin introduced *EyeOpeners* (1988) as a means of providing updates on available nonfiction children's books. Her first edition listed over 500 entries. Today there are several other sources, such as *The Horn Book Magazine* and the *Reading Teacher's* section on *Children's Books.* Trade books tend to have children reading and learning before, during, and after the bell (Moss, 1991). Many of the themes discussed next are available with videos (for example, Denise Fleming's *Animals, Growth and Change* [Pre K–1] is available from Weston Woods Videos: 800-243-5020).

Literature Base: *Landslide* (Veronique Day, Coward McCann, 1963) **Story Line:** Five children are trapped by a landslide while hiking. **Science Concepts:** What is erosion? What is the function of plants in maintaining a balance in nature? **Activity:** Construct a box that has two parts with a board separating those parts. Fill each side with dirt. Cover one side with grass seed. Let it grow. Then tilt the box and run water evenly down the two sides. Observe what happens to the dirt on the side without grass.	**Literature Base:** *Charlotte's Web* (E. B. White, Harper & Row, 1952) **Story Line:** A spider named Charlotte uses her web to not only catch insects for food, but also to save a pig's life. **Science Concepts:** How do spiders make their webs? How strong are spider webs? Why do spiders make webs? **Activity:** Have children carefully catch a spider (a large black and yellow garden spider is ideal), and place it in a large terrarium or similar container. The children can then observe the spider spin its web. Live insects are then placed in the container to see how the insects are caught in the web.
Literature Base: *The Tough Winter* (Robert Lawson, Puffin Books, 1979) **Story Line:** The story is about how animals work hard to survive a tough winter. **Science Concepts:** Why do we have seasons? What happens to plants during the winter? Where do animals spend the winter? What is hibernation? What foods can animals find during the winter? **Activity:** Collect some cocoons from tall grass during February and March. Bring them into the classroom. Put them in a widemouth gallon jar. Cover with flyscreen. Observe.	**Literature Base:** *Little Cloud* (Eric Carle, Puffin Books, 1998) and *The Cloud Book* (Tomie de Paola, Holiday House, 1985) **Activities:** Over a several-week period, read either of these pieces to primary grade children. Discuss the different shapes and density of clouds. Begin to note, and ideally photograph, different cloud formations outside. Help children to identify and properly name at least two of these formations. Read and discuss the second book. From this experience students would learn to be aware of the fact of and weather conditions associated with different cloud formations, and hence be open to the continuing growth of knowledge in this domain. Ideally, a few children may wish to build a relatively complete picture book of many formations.

Figure 9.2 Literature-based/themed science units.

Source: Pond, M., & Hoch, L. (1992). Linking children's literature and science activities. *Ohio Reading Teacher, 25* (2), 13–15.

Themed Science Units*

Pond and Hoch (1992, pp. 13–15) and Cerullo (1997) provide a number of examples to illustrate how literature can set the stage for activities that teach science concepts in meaningful ways. Four of these are detailed in Figure 9.2.

Children's literature is rich with books that can make science concepts richer and more understandable. Maggart and Zintz (1992, pp. 400–402) offer these examples for developing units on animals and weather:

Source: From *Teaching Children to be Literate, A Reflective Approach,* 1st edition, by MANZO/ MANZO © 1996. Reprinted with permission of Wadsworth, a division of Thomson Learning. www.thomsonrights.com Fax 800-730-2215.

Books for a unit on animals

- *Born in a Barn* (by E. Gemming)—primary grades
- *Panda* (by C. Curtis)—primary grades
- *Animal Superstars: Biggest, Strongest, Fastest, Smartest* (by R. Freedman)—intermediate grades
- *Here Come the Dolphins* (by A. Goudey)—intermediate grades
- *Born Free* (by J. Adamson)—upper grades
- *Whale Watch* (by A. Graham & F. Graham)—upper grades

Books for a unit on weather

- *Blizzard at the Zoo* (by R. Bahr)—primary grades
- *The Snowy Day* (by E. J. Keats)—primary grades
- *Listen to the Rain* (by B. Martin, Jr. & J. Archambault)—primary grades
- *The Cloud Book* (by T. dePaola)—intermediate grades

Literature-Based Mathematics Units*

For knowledge to be retained and transferred to other situations, it needs to be relevant and interesting to the student (Farris & Kaczmarski, 1988). Jamar and Morrow (1991) and Pauler and Bodevin (1990) have assembled integrated units for first and second graders. See the illustration in Figure 9.3 for a practical example of how "the natural language in good children's literature provides a vehicle that allows teachers to present interrelated activities in reading, writing, and mathematics" (Jamar & Morrow, 1991, p. 29).

Wood (1992) offers some additional examples of content area reading in mathematics that you might wish to examine. The methods she offers rely heavily on collaborative activities in reading, writing, and thinking aloud. One method, for example, uses a variation on "Big Books." Children produce enlarged versions of math word problems and then, using a pointer, show how they solved the problems (see Figure 9.4).

Other Literature-Content Ties*

Wooten (1992) gives several examples of how the Martin's books can be tied to subject area instruction. In one example, *Chicka Chicka Boom Boom* (Martin & Archambault, 1985), a colorful illustrated alphabet book typically used with kindergartners, was used with fourth-graders to release these "layers of learning" (see Figure 9.5).

Source: From *Teaching Children to be Literate, A Reflective Approach,* 1st edition, by MANZO/ MANZO © 1996. Reprinted with permission of Wadsworth, a division of Thomson Learning. www.thomsonrights.com Fax 800-730-2215.

Literature Base: *Cross-Country Cat* (Calhoun, 1979, NY: Morrow)	Literature Base: *Millions of Cats* (Wanda Gag, 1928, NY: Coward, McCann, Geohegan)
Story Line: Henry, a sassy Siamese cat, takes matters into his own "paws" when his family accidentally leaves him behind at a ski lodge. Henry skis home, meeting a variety of animals along the way.	**Story Line:** Includes a refrain children can join in on when the story is read aloud, about hundreds, thousands, millions, billions, and trillions of cats!
Mathematics Concepts: Counting by twos; one-to-one correspondence; comparison; sequencing; map-making and map-reading.	**Mathematics Concepts:** Place value, a mnemonic device for reading "big" numbers (a great motivator and confidence builder for young children)
Activity: Use cut-out pairs of skis to practice counting by two's; use items of ski-clothing to reinforce the concept of one-to-one correspondence (2 shoes for 2 feet; 1 scarf for 1 neck; 2 mittens for 2 hands; 1 hat for 1 head, etc.); reinforce the concept of sequencing by having children list the animals that Henry met on his journey home; have children create maps of Henry's journey, illustrating where he met each of the other animals; have children use a cut-out ski to measure the length of Henry's trip, and to spark a discussion with questions such as, "How long do you think Henry's trip took? How long did it take Henry to get as far as he did before the family found him? How did you decide this? What clues did you find in the story or the pictures?" The map-making activity can be extended to creation of a neighborhood map, and estimation of distances	**Activity:** Note and list on the board the names of the number places: hundreds, thousands, millions, billions, and trillions. Explain how to read each hundreds and tens place ("three hundred seventy-eight *million* . . ."). Then show children how they can use the *Millions of Cats* refrain as a way to remember how to read numbers with as many as fifteen places.
Source: Jamar, D., & Morrow, J. (1991). A literature-based interdisciplinary approach to the teaching of reading, writing, and mathematics. *The Ohio Reading Teacher*, 25 (3), 28-35.	Source: Pauler, S., & Bodevin, D. (1990). Book-specific response activities: Satisfaction guaranteed. *Georgia Journal of Reading*, 16 (2), 30-35.

Figure 9.3 Literature-based math units.

Indrisano and Paratore (1992) offer this other literature-to-content connection. The book is a nonfiction piece by Barbara Bash (1989) called *Desert Giant— The World of the Saguaro Cactus*. Indrisano and Paratore's graphic organizer for *Desert Giant*, shown in Figure 9.6, illustrates its potential for teaching science and ecology in an altogether engaging manner.

Children's literature is also full of natural connections with social studies. Select children's literature that illuminates the values of the people about whom the social studies text is written; books that teach something of the lives of the people, what daily living was like, what was fun, what games they played, what caused happiness and unhappiness, as well as fears and anxieties. Following are a few suggestions from Maggart and Zintz (1992, pp. 400–402):

- Biographies of historical figures, such as *Abe Lincoln Gets His Chance*, by Cavanah

Figure 9.4 Math word problems.
Source: From *Teaching Children To Be Literate: A Reflective Approach,* 1st edition, by MANZO/ MANZO © 1996. Reprinted with permission of Wadsworth, a division of Thomson Learning. www.thomsonrights.com Fax 800-730-2215.

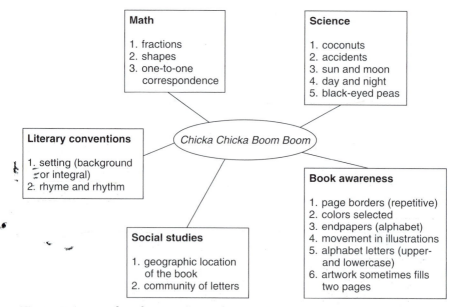

Figure 9.5 Interdisciplinary concepts through children's literature.
Source: Wooten, Deborah A. (1992). The magic of Martin. In B. E. Cullinan (Ed.), *Invitation to Read: More Children's Literature in the Reading Program* (pp. 72–79). Newark, DE: International Reading Association. Reprinted with the International Reading Association. All rights reserved.

How It Looks	How It Grows	How It Is Used
• Can grow as tall as 50 feet • Can weigh several tons • Has sharp spines • Has accordion-like pleats that expand when it rains to store water	• Begins under the canopy of a larger tree or "nurse plant" • After 50 years, it produces its first flowers • After 75 years, arms start to appear • At 150 years, it towers over the desert • Can live for 200 years	• Male woodpeckers make holes in the cactus for their mates' eggs • Elf owls and hawks live in them • Bats, doves, bees, and butterflies eat its flowers • Thrashers, lizards, and ants eat its fruit • Fruit is used for jams, candy, and wine • Hardened parts of dead cactus can be used for food containers • Termites feed on dead cactus • Snakes, geckos and spiders use the dead stalks as a home

Figure 9.6   Graphic organizer for *Desert Giant: The World of the Saguaro Cactus.*

Source: Figure from Indrisano, Roselmina, & Paratore, Jeanne R. (1992). Using Literature with Readers at Risk. In B.E. Cullinan (Ed.), *Invitation to Read: More Children's Literature in the Reading Program* (pp. 138–149). Newark, DE: International Reading Association. Reprinted with permission of Roselmina Indrisano and the International Reading Association. All rights reserved.

- Fictional accounts of historical periods, such as the Laura Ingalls Wilder series
- Books representing varied cultural worlds, such as *Fifth Chinese Daughter* (Wong), which reveals the conflict between parents and the children growing up as first-generation immigrants in San Francisco; and *Owl in the Cedar Tree* by Momaday, which presents a conflict between the culture of the Native Americans and the culture of the European settlers.

Theme-Based (Interdisciplinary) Units*

Once a teacher begins using literature as a springboard for content-based activities, the boundaries between subject areas begin to fade. A science lesson leads naturally to the introduction of a math concept, for example, and on to a social studies activity, and back to a writing activity. This is the height of excellence in teaching because it reflects the real world, where subjects do not exist as separate entities but as threads in a richly woven fabric. See Figure 9.7 for a lesson developed by Post (1992, pp. 29–35) as an illustration of how a single piece of literature can spark activities across the curriculum.

Source: From *Teaching Children to be Literate, A Reflective Approach*, 1st edition, by MANZO/MANZO © 1996. Reprinted with permission of Wadsworth, a division of Thomson Learning. www.thomsonrights.com Fax 800-730-2215.

Literature Base: *The Camel Caper* (Kristin Casler, Grand Rapids Press—see Post, 1992, for reprint)

Story Line: In this humorous article, Casler chronicles the escape of the camel, Roxanne, from the John Ball Zoo; her travels through the neighborhood; the reactions of stunned observers; and, finally, her capture.

Language Arts Activities:

- Introduction—Show a picture of a camel on an overhead, and have students brainstorm what they know about camels. Distribute the article for students to read.

- Getting the Facts—Distribute note cards, and have students work in pairs to jot down the basic "who, what, when, where, why/how's" of the article.

- Application 1—Distribute a map of the area in which the camel wandered, and have students trace the camel's route from the zoo to where she was captured. Have students compare their maps with those of a partner—where differences occur, reread for clarification. Show the map on an overhead, and have one or more students or groups share their results with the whole class.

- Application 2—Ask several students to volunteer to give an extemporaneous radio broadcast, using their "who, what, . . ." card as notes. Tape record the speaking exercises. The teacher begins each "broadcast" by saying,

  "Good evening. This is station WGRX, Grand Rapids, Michigan, here to bring you the latest news."

  Students speak into a real or pretend microphone. Replay each "broadcast," giving the speaker positive comments and constructive criticism. Later, transcribe these "broadcasts." Instead of writing them as a paragraph, list and number the sentences, and use these as the basis for teaching aspects of grammar.

Figure 9.7 Example theme-based (interdisciplinary) unit.

Source: Post, A. R. (1992). The camel caper: An integrated language arts lesson. *Michigan Reading Journal, 25* (2), 29–35.

In the Upper Grades: Using Literature and Trade Books in the Secondary Content Area Classrooms

It is commonly expected that literature will be found in English class and that in the other content areas, a textbook will be the primary source of print instruction. However, increasing attention is being paid to the value of using a variety of adolescent literature, trade books, and even picture books to teach in and across the content areas. In some ways, the rationale is simple: Textbooks are broad, encyclopedic, and have a lot of information, but through the ages, it is clear that people often learn best through stories. Through stories, students learn not just the historical, mathematical, or scientific facts of a field but also are able to *experience* vicariously diverse affective and social issues—namely, a fresh variety of human thoughts, emotions, and actions. As students get the chance to learn in this way through literature and other forms of trade books, they are provided increased scaffolding on which to learn more of the content area materials that are expected to be covered in our classes. This way of learning also allows students to experience more of the true interdisciplinary nature of knowledge, as they see how interrelated much of their content learning is with other disciplines and with the human experience in general.

Because of this, there is now an increasing interest in the use of adolescent literature and trade books to supplement the textbook and other traditional instruction more commonly expected in our content areas. This extension of the *reiterative reading* concept, which we introduced in Chapter 4 (Crafton, 1983), is now burgeoning into entire courses and textbooks dedicated to the topic. Therefore, what we've included here is designed only to serve as a mention and introduction to this important literacy subfield. See Figure 9.8 for a collection of resources that might help you find out more regarding adolescent literature and trade books for use in your content area teaching.

Textbooks	Textbook Chapters
Atwell, N. (1998). *In the middle: Writing, reading, and learning with adolescents* (2nd ed.). Portsmouth, NH: Boynton/Cook. Mueller, P. N. (2001). *Lifers: Learning from at-risk adolescent readers.* Portsmouth, NH: Heinemann. Hynds, S. (1997). *On the brink: Negotiating literature and life with adolescents.* New York: Teachers College Press. Nilsen, A. P., & Donelson, K. L. (2001). *Literature for today's young adults* (6th ed.). New York: Longman. Freeman, E. B., & Person, D. G. (1998). *Connecting informational children's books with content area learning.* Boston: Allyn & Bacon.	Chapter 9: "Literature-Based and Thematic Approaches to Content Area Teaching," in Roe, B. D., Stoodt, B. D., & Burns, P. C. (2001). *The content areas: Secondary school literacy instruction.* Boston, MA: Houghton-Mifflin. Chapter 12: "Developing Lifetime Readers: Literature in Content Area Classes," in Alvermann, D. E., & Phelps, S. F. (2002). *Content reading and literacy: Succeeding in today's diverse classrooms* (3rd. ed.). Boston, MA: Allyn & Bacon. Chapter 12: "Supporting the Textbook with Literature," in Richardson, J. S., & Morgan, R. F.(1997). *Reading to learn in the content areas* (3rd ed.). Belmont, CA: Wadsworth. Chapter 2: "Learning with Textbooks, Trade Books, and Electronic Texts," in Vacca, R. T., & Vacca, J. A. (2002). *Content area reading: Literacy and learning across the curriculum* (7th ed.). Boston, MA: Allyn & Bacon. Chapter 7: "Literature," in Readence, J. E., Bean, T. W., & Baldwin, R. S. (2001). *Content area literacy: An integrated approach* (7th ed.). Dubuque, IA: Kendall/Hunt.

Figure 9.8 Resources for learning more about using adolescent literature and other trade books in content area instruction.

Web Sites	Journal Articles
Science From the National Science Teachers Association: NSTA Outstanding Science Trade Books for Students K-12 http://www.nsta.org/ostbc From Reading Online, a review of thirteen trade books for use in the content area of science. http://www.readingonline.org/reviews/literature/andersen/ Outstanding Science Trade books for Children http://www.ucalgary.ca/~dkbrown/nsta98.html **Social Studies** From the National Council for the Social Studies---Notable Social Studies Trade books for Young People: http://www.ncss.org/resources/notable/2002.shtml **Math** Trade Books in Math: http://www.luc.edu/schools/education/csipdc/zbib.htm This site is a selected bibliography of books for kids that teach and reinforce math concepts, organized by topic: counting and numbers, number operations, large numbers, money, geometry, algebra, miscellaneous topics. Mathematician Biographies Online: http://www-groups.dcs.st-and.ac.uk/~history/BiogIndex.html This site contains biographical and historical information on hundreds of mathematicians from antiquities through the present. Great resource for reiterative reading in the math classroom. Mr. Brandenburg's Books about Math http://mathforum.com/t2t/faq/brandenburg.html This site contains an extensive collection of math-related trade books that can be used to supplement high school math instruction.	**Multiple Content Areas** Moss, B. & Hendershot, J. (2002). Exploring sixth graders' selection of nonfiction trade books. *The Reading Teacher,* 56(1), 6-17. Daisey, P. (1997). Promoting literacy in secondary content area classrooms with biography projects. *Journal of Adolescent & Adult Literacy,* 40(4), 270-278. Palmer, R.G., & Stewart, R.A. (1997). Nonfiction trade books in content area instruction: Realities and potential. *Journal of Adolescent & Adult Literacy,* 40(8), 630-641. Moss, B., & Noden, H. (1995). Resources for choosing and using trade books in the classroom. *The Reading Teacher,* 48(8), 724-726. **Science** Shackleford, B. (2003). Teaching through trade books: Seeing the seasons. *Science and Children,* 40(6), 14-16. Outstanding science trade books for students K-12: Books published in 2002 (2003, March). *Science and Children,* 40(6), 31-38. **Social Studies** Albright, L.K. (2002). Bringing the ice maiden to life: Engaging adolescents in learning through picture book read-alouds in contents areas. *Journal of Adolescent & Adult Literacy* 45(5), 418-428. **Math** Hellwig, S.J., Monroe, E.E., & Jabobs, J.S. (2000). Making informed choices: Selecting children's trade books for mathematics instruction. *Teaching Children Mathematics,* 7(3), 138. **Picture Books for Content Area Instruction** Carr, K.S., Buchanan, D.L., Wentz, J.B., Weiss, M.L., & Brant, K.J. (2001). Not just for the primary grades: A bibliography of picture books for secondary content teachers. *Journal of Adolescent & Adult Literacy,* 45(2), 146-153. Billman, L.W. (2002). Aren't these books for little kids? *Educational Leadership,* 60(3), 48-51.

Figure 9.8 *(continued)*

Web Sites	Journal Articles
Language Arts and Other Association for Library Service to Children: http://www.ala.org/ ALSCTemplate.cfm?Section=ALSC This extensive site's "Literary and Related Awards" link provides information on collections of the mostly highly regarded children and adolescent literature and trade books. Making Multicultural Connections Through Trade Books: http://www.mcps.k12.md.us/curriculum/ socialstd/MBD/Grade_index.html#top This site contains lists of trade books that can be used in making multicultural connections in teaching across the disciplines (grades K-6 emphasis). Bilingual Books for Children: http://www.ala.org/Content/NavigationMenu/ ALSC/Resources3/Book_Lists/ Bilingual_Books_for_Children.htm This site contains a bibliography of books currently available with bilingual text. Great Websites for Kids: http://www.ala.org/Content/NavigationMenu/ ALSC/Great_Web_Sites_for_Kids/ Great_Web_Sites_for_Kids.htm From the Association for Library Service to Children, this site has links to content area sites for Animals, Literature and Language Arts, Mathematics, Fine Art, Sciences, History, Social Science, and Reference.	

Figure 9.8 *(continued)*

▶ WRITING TO LEARN

This section takes a closer look at two instructional uses of writing: writing to learn, and writing papers. Guidelines are given for increasing the use of writing to learn—possibly the most underused teaching/learning tool at secondary teachers' disposal. The Writing Process is offered as a framework for guiding students' writing of various types of papers, from research papers to creative writing activities. The Writing Process is widely acknowledged as a means of teaching students how to write rather than simply grading the products of their writing.

Writing: Encouraging the Process and the Products

The process of simply writing something down—a note while reading, an item on a to-do list, a message to a friend, or an answer to a study guide question—adds a slight but significant element of commitment to that thought that it previously did not have. It becomes more real, more concrete, more likely to be remembered. Any form of writing prior to reading or listening tends to activate prior knowledge and experience and heighten the reader's anticipation of the author's focus and key points. This could be called *engaged* reading and listening. It is a more active, interactive, and memorable mode of operating than is the passive, or disassociated reading and listening that tends to occur in school. Additionally, each effort to write *after* reading also provides considerable benefits to learning. It requires active reconstruction of text and thereby increases sensitivity to the text's content, logic, and organization. Further, each effort to write in reaction to or evaluation of text constitutes that invigorating plunge into the unknown where language and thought trigger one another to discover and organize the "inchoate lump of meanings" (Henry, 1974) that we often are left with following typical passive reading.

Simply put, a routine requirement to write something—almost anything—before or after reading ignites more active thinking before, during, and following reading. In spite of these benefits, writing tends to be an underused tool in content classrooms. There are three primary reasons for this nonwriting orientation in school:

1. Most teachers have not themselves experienced a requirement for frequent writing as students, other than for an occasional book report or essay in English class and perhaps a research paper in social studies.

2. Relatedly, teachers are unaware of the many informal ways in which writing can be used as an aid to thinking.

3. Most teachers are reluctant to require frequent writing because of the time required to provide feedback.

Speaking to each of these three points now, let's see if we can become the generation of teachers that sets the example for others to follow. Our chances of accomplishing this goal are much improved over those who have preceded us. There is much that is new in the literature on writing, reading, and thinking to call on, in addition to the enabling possibilities inherent in use of the Internet in increasingly wired classrooms.

Righting Writing across the Curriculum: Road under Construction

The most important point to be made about writing as a thinking tool is that teachers should help students to distinguish between writing as a tool and writing as a product. When writing is used as a tool, *not everything students write has to be graded, or even read, by the teacher*. In the following suggestions, student writing may be followed by short cooperative group sharing of their writing, or added to a folder to be collected for "credit/no credit."

Before Reading

- *Timed prewriting:* Tell students the topic of a reading assignment, and give a short time (3 to 5 minutes) to write on what they think it will be about.

- *Prompted prewriting*: Give a specific prompt related to the content of a reading assignment, and have students write brief responses before reading.

While Reading

- *Main idea notes:* Give the reading assignment with directions to write the author's main points (in students' own words), with supporting details noted.
- *Factoids*: Direct students to look, while reading, for brief, interesting facts as might appear on CNN television, or set out in bold print to capture a reader's interest in a magazine or textbook.
- *Rewrite for different audiences*: Direct students to look, while reading, for a section to rewrite for a different audience (e.g., a younger person; a grandparent; corporate/ government leader).
- *Write the author:* Direct students to think, while reading, about how the material might be presented more clearly or interestingly, and to write a note to the author informing him or her of their ideas.
- *Add to it:* Direct students to write a paragraph or two that could/should be added to make the information clearer.
- *Write an example:* Direct students to look for points that remind them of relevant examples or stories that help make the author's point.

After Reading

- *Press release:* A public relations press release on a worthy idea or finding.
- *More information:* A letter of request to an author or other authority for more information.
- *Connections:* Tell about a related television program, Web site, book, article, idea, or related moral/ethical conflict.

Notice that most of these suggestions can be done quickly and with little preparation. However, they add considerably to a student's anticipation and/or deeper processing of most any fundamental set of information and ideas. It's a good bet that you can see yourself doing any of these. With another few moments of thought, you surely can come up with many similar and manageable writing-learning activities for almost any discipline, from the more obvious content areas such as English and social studies to some that at first blush may seem less amenable to writing, like physical education, music, and art.

Next, we turn to the nuts and bolts of guiding effective writing and thinking. Traditional efforts to teach writing have focused on the final *product*. More recently, an instructional framework for guiding student mastery of the *process* of writing has evolved. This instructional framework was designed to parallel the process one would reasonably go through in writing. Therefore, it has come to be called simply the *Writing Process*. The Writing Process framework is analogous to the three-step framework for planning prereading, guided silent reading, and postreading instruction—or *into, through,* and *beyond* reading. It indicates what should be done at each stage in general terms but leaves considerable latitude in just how to do it.

The Writing Process: A Framework for Guiding the Process of Paper Writing

It may be easy to request students to write, but writing is not easy to learn or to teach. It is a habit of mind, and often is hard work. The prolific writer and economist John Kenneth Galbraith has said it most sincerely: "There are days when the result is so bad that no fewer than five revisions are required. In contrast, when I'm greatly inspired, only four revisions are needed" (interview, CNBC, May 1996). For novice writers, the mere prospect of writing any type of paper is daunting. Traditionally, writing is a sink-or-swim proposition. A topic is assigned, and a due date is given. Sometimes a draft is critiqued by the teacher, but most of the real work of writing occurs before the initial draft is produced. The Writing Process framework is a way to provide guidance, from initial reflections through final editing stages.

Steps in the Writing Process

Step 1. *Prewriting: Getting It Together.* In the idea-building phase, the teacher prepares students for writing by
- Raising motivation and interest
- Calling up relevant prior knowledge and experiences
- Encouraging exploration of the topic and suggesting resources
- Reminding students to document sources of possible materials located in the library or on the Internet
- Eliciting additional details, reasons, or examples
- Providing basic expectations for the final product, usually in the form of a rubric

Step 2. *Drafting: Getting It Down.* In the drafting phase, students attempt to shape the unwieldy ideas, purposes, facts, personal feelings, and biases into the linearity of words and structure. This includes finding out what you really think and then how to say it best. During this phase, the teacher's role is to
1. Help students express initial thoughts and ideas on paper.
2. Remind students to refer to prewriting notes and experiences. Word processors are a tremendous aid at this stage. Notes can be copied and pasted quickly and easily.
3. Help students keep in mind the audience who will be reading their work, as a guide to the form and character of the composition.
4. Encourage the free flow of ideas by emphasizing content rather than mechanics or structure.

Step 3. *Revising: Getting It Organized.* Revising is an evaluative and reconstructive phase. It requires a good deal of introspection and willingness to critique oneself, to be critiqued, and, in several strategies described later, to think like an editor and to critique the work of others. In this phase, the teacher provides guidance by

1. Arranging for students to receive feedback from peers and/or various audiences. Draft copies can be e-mailed to a family member, an on-line tutor, or other willing helper.
2. Encouraging students to reorganize, rewrite, and revise as needed for fluency and coherence.
3. Guiding discussions that clarify and thereby point to specific areas of composition that require rewriting.
4. Encouraging redrafting as needed with an eye toward initial purpose and audience.
5. Helping students to consider how well others have understood and interpreted their writing.

Step 4. *Editing: Getting It Right.* In the final editing phase, the composition is reviewed for correct mechanics such as spelling, grammatical usage, and punctuation. The teacher assists by

1. Encouraging students to fine-tune their work. Here again, word processors are quite useful in checking spelling and grammar.
2. Noting common mechanical problems and providing class instruction in these areas.

Step 5. *Publishing: Going Public.* In the publishing phase, the final copy is shared with an audience. This can be done in a variety of formal and informal ways. The point is that writing becomes more real and serious when it is to be read by someone other than the teacher. The teacher aids in this process by

1. Employing methods that ensure that there will be readers for students' efforts. The Internet opens unlimited opportunities for creative ways of publishing student work.
2. Offering evaluative feedback based on a rubric for the assignment.
3. Offering opportunities for student papers to serve as a foundation for reading, discussion, or study.

▶ AFTER WORDS

This chapter has addressed three complementary topic areas: emergent content area literacy, the use of literature and trade books to teach content at all grade levels, and some practical ways to integrate the writing process to enhance student learning across the disciplines. The next chapter describes a variety of means and methods to assess and monitor specific educational needs, including the need to read, write, and think "beyond the lines," although you will not be surprised to learn that achieving the latter turns to out require more of a change of attitude than some breakthrough in psychoeducational testing.

CHAPTER 10

INTERACTIVE ASSESSMENT FOR ACTIVE SELF-MONITORING AND SELF-TEACHING

The examiner pipes and the teacher must dance—and the examiner sticks to the old tune.

—H. G. Wells, 1892

▶ FORE WORDS

Interactive teaching is characterized by interactive assessment. To achieve this, it is essential that assessment techniques be selected that invite a reasonably high level of student involvement. This is necessary for promoting self-teaching, the *sin qua non* of all instruction. The chapter details several such techniques that are both timely and have withstood the test of time. These include an informal textbook inventory designed to assess and teach students about the parts of their books, a rationale for portfolio evaluation of student progress, and a rubric system for easy evaluation of student writing. The chapter then addresses several simple ways to estimate the difficulty level, or readability, of textual material. Appropriate short-cuts and computer-based alternatives are noted along the way.

- ▶ FORE WORDS
- ▶ INTRODUCTION TO STUDENT ASSESSMENT
- ▶ TOOLS FOR ASSESSMENT OF STUDENT READING
- ▶ EVALUATION OF STUDENT WRITING
- ▶ PORTFOLIOS: RATIONALE, FUNCTIONS, PROMISE, PROBLEMS
- ▶ ASSESSING TEXT DIFFICULTY
- ▶ AFFECTIVE ISSUES AND MEASURES
- ▶ AFTER WORDS

▶ INTRODUCTION TO STUDENT ASSESSMENT

The Power of the Examiner

The power of the examiner is a long-standing and deeply rooted issue in education. In fact, the influence of testing may be greater now than at any time in our history. There are a variety of assessment movements with puzzling titles throughout the nation. In the past ten years, most states have first instituted and then dropped or redirected assessment procedures with names like *basic competencies, mastery learning, criterion-referenced* testing, and, more recently, *holistic, authentic, outcomes-based,* and *performance-based* assessment. One measure, however, remains a constant since federal law (NAEP: The National Assessment of Educational Progress) mandates it.

National Assessment of Educational Progress (NAEP)

As discussed in Chapter 8, the NAEP is one of the major literacy benchmarks. It was mandated by the Congress in 1969 and carried out on a mixed subject schedule every two or three years. Students in fourth, eighth, and twelfth grades receive 50 minutes to read graded passages and answer questions, both multiple choice and written. There are four possible levels of competency that one can achieve: *below basic; basic; proficient;* and *advanced.* Four sets of data are relevant: 1992, 1994, 1998 and 2002. The 1994 data were among the most shocking to the national conscience.

In that year, about 60% of adolescents, according to NAEP performance indicators, were able to read at a basic level. They could gather details, identify a main idea, and recognize connections among textually explicit ideas. Fewer than 5% of youngsters surveyed, however, were able to perform at *advanced* levels, where they were required to examine, extend, and elaborate meanings from representative fiction and nonfiction materials (Campbell, Donahue, Reese, & Phillips, 1996). Results of an NAEP *writing* assessment (Applebee, Langer, Mullis, Lathan, & Gentile, 1994) revealed that *most all* students in grades 4, 8, and 12 had difficulty with writing tasks that required higher levels of coherent thinking and the important capacity to provide details to support points made. Some have called this a national crisis (Vacca & Alvermann, 1998). We tend to see it as a growing awareness of one of the challenges inherent in the field of content area literacy: in addition to the need for systematic direct *instruction* in reading-thinking strategies across the disciplines, we need systematic ongoing *assessment* and feedback at the classroom level. Several basic formats for classroom assessment are described next.

Higher-Order and Performance-Based Assessment

Of the many recent efforts to reform educational assessment, the movement toward higher-order thinking and performance-based assessment, or the representation of real-life tasks in assessment, may be the most welcome (see Figure 10.1). The logic of mastery learning, which so strongly influenced teaching and testing in the past, now finally is being replaced with assessment more firmly grounded in interactive and integrated performance. Where mastery learning stressed the passive acquisition of facts and skills, newer interactive assessment models tend to emphasize the active role of readers and learners in using print to construct meaning and solve problems. Thus, there is a decreased emphasis on product outcomes of learning, such as information acquisition, and an increased emphasis on how well students are internalizing the thinking processes they will need to learn both in and out of school.

The goal of traditional assessment is to evaluate acquisition of information. The goal of performance-based assessment is to evaluate the processes for acquiring and using information. To do this, performance-based assessment is expected to have several of the following characteristics:

+ Is problem centered
+ Requires use of facts rather than recall of facts
+ Requires higher-order thinking along inferential and evaluative lines
+ Is more constructive in format than reconstructive
+ Does not necessarily have a single correct answer
+ Involves more hands-on doing than conventional knowledge testing
+ Is more authentic, or real-life
+ Reflects more fairly the diversity of perspectives in American cultures

---

Figure 10.1   Performance-based, or authentic, assessment: The current trend.

As more states move away from use of standardized test scores as the primary approach to evaluation of schools and school districts, it is expected that educators will feel less obliged to concentrate on simple fact acquisition and more committed to engaging students in authentic learning activities. Of course, this does not mean that standardized test scores are without value. See Figure 10.2 for an example of how such data can be used to suggest programmatic decisions.

For a more authentic and interactive means of assessing students' needs, consider the Informal Textbook Inventory. It is a means of introducing a textbook to a class, having students tell the teacher about their preparation for using it effectively, and seamlessly teaching them how to use it to full advantage. This technique sometimes is referred to as a Classroom Reading Inventory (CRI).

▶ TOOLS FOR ASSESSMENT OF STUDENT READING

The Informal Textbook Inventory

An Informal Textbook Inventory (ITI) essentially is a special type of open-book test designed to familiarize students with using one of education's most basic learning tools: the textbook. This "new idea" is over seventy-five years old. We have seen an excellent ten-question version of the ITI in a 1924 edition of a fifth-year reader (Walker & Parkman). Since most texts on the market do not contain such a ready-made inventory, you probably will need to construct your own. There are several good reasons for creating and using an ITI at the beginning of the school year:

- It is easily administered in group, paper-and-pencil format.
- It tests and teaches simultaneously.

The following standardized test score information was reported for a local high school in a major city. Of thirty-four high schools recently tested in the state, this high school was

First in mathematics
First in social studies
First in science
Second in narrative (story) reading
Sixth in expository (content area) reading

These data suggest the following conclusion. If the youngsters in this school are first in the three traditional areas of knowledge acquisition but sixth in ability to comprehend (i.e., think) in these subjects, then a program to further maximize application and content area reading in the disciplines is in order.

Figure 10.2 Local high school excels in knowledge but lags in reading.

- It draws the teacher's and students' attention to the processing strategies involved in using text parts, text aids, and related resources.
- It provokes active awareness and discussion of text features.
- It lends itself well to computer (hypertext) presentation and scoring.
- It is purposeful and well structured but nonthreatening.
- It reflects the highest current standards of performance-based assessment.

When used early in the school year, while student attitudes and expectations are still being formed, the ITI provides an excellent means of establishing a disciplined, well-managed classroom tone. By simply tallying the results of the inventory, the teacher can obtain a record of each student's ability to deal with the textbook as well as indications of some of the potential benefits and shortcomings of the textbook itself.

Such assessment can take time to prepare, but it also stores well and improves with age and use. It is the type of activity that is the mark of a professional teacher. Students appreciate the help, and supervisors rarely fail to take note. The second and subsequent times you use the ITI, you will be even more pleased because you will have refined it and will know better what to expect and how to better orchestrate the full activity.

Constructing the Informal Textbook Inventory
The following outline illustrates the general form of the ITI:

I. Organization and Structure of the Text
    A. Understanding the Textbook Organization
        Develop three to five straightforward questions about how the text is structured and how to use the comprehension aids provided within the text.
    B. Using the Text Organization Effectively
        Develop three to five questions that students can answer by referring to the index, table of contents, glossary, appendices, or other text sections and/or aids. *graphs, tables, pics*

II. Basic Comprehension
    Select a short portion of the text that contains an important concept with supporting details and at least one graph, chart, or picture. (The same selection can be used in the following section on applied comprehension.)
    A. Comprehending the Main Idea
        Develop one or two fill-in or multiple-choice questions that direct students to state or select the main idea of the material read.
    B. Noting Supporting Details
        Develop three or more fill-in, multiple-choice, or matching questions about specific facts or ideas in the selection.

    C. Understanding Vocabulary in Context

       Develop three or more fill-in, multiple-choice, or matching questions that direct students to state or select a definition for key terms used in the selection.

    D. Understanding Information Presented in Graphic or Pictorial Form

       Develop one or more questions requiring students to state or select an interpretation of a graph, chart, or picture that adds information not explicitly stated in the selection.

III. Applied Comprehension

Questions in these sections can be based on the same text selection used in Part II.

    A. Drawing Conclusions and Critical Thinking

       Develop one or more questions that require students to draw valid conclusions based on the information presented.

    B. Evaluating and Judging

       Develop one or more questions that require students to evaluate and apply information from the text in terms of their own experiences, values, and existing knowledge base.

IV. Specialized Options

    A. Assess special requirements of the discipline. This could mean understanding geographical directions in social studies, a section on understanding style or mood in literature, or a section on applying symbols in mathematical formulas. Examples are found in Chapter 12 on content-specific applications.

    B. Assess pupil abilities to deal with the linguistic features of the text with a Standard Cloze Passage test (described later in this chapter).

Administering and Evaluating the Informal Textbook Inventory

Before asking students to tackle the inventory, explain some of its features and purposes: It is not a test in the usual sense of the word; every text differs slightly from every other, and this is a way to find out how. Point out further that although answers will be discussed as a group, each student will need to complete the inventory independently as thoroughly and accurately as possible.

Once all students have completed the inventory, collect and score the results. For diagnostic purposes, any error is taken as a sign of need in that category.

Much of the diagnostic-teaching value of the inventory comes from the group discussion of the items when the tests are returned to the students. Compare and contrast student strengths and weaknesses among the various categories of questions. Review and discussion of the inventory with the class can take from one-half to two full class periods depending on individual students' abilities, the difficulty of the text, and the objectives the teacher may wish to achieve.

The next assessment instrument, the Standard Cloze Passage test, also can be constructed from a class textbook. It is much easier to construct, but it yields a more general account of a pupil's ability to handle a given textbook at the linguistic, or language and syntactic, level.

Standard Cloze Passage Test

The term *cloze* refers to a written passage with certain words blanked out to be filled in by the reader. Early studies of this task revealed that it is closely related to reading comprehension across age and most grade levels (Bormuth, 1965). Subsequent studies, however, indicated that cloze was not a direct measure of reading comprehension. Instead, it was a fairly accurate measure of one of the factors that contributes to comprehension, namely, familiarity with the language redundancy patterns, or repetitive sentence structures and phrases in prose (Culver, Godfrey, & Manzo, 1972; Weaver & Kingston, 1963). Technically speaking, this means that cloze and reading comprehension have relatively little in common with one another, but both are strongly related to a third thing (probably verbal reasoning), and therefore either can be used to infer the other.

This and related work added several points to our understanding of the potential values and possible shortcomings of cloze passage testing. These points are summarized in the following list:

1. Cloze is a good, quick assessment strategy for sampling students' ability to handle the language patterns common to different types of content material—and therefore is a good complement to an ITI.

2. Cloze will tend to underestimate the comprehension abilities of students with weak standard English backgrounds, since comprehension is inferred from familiarity with English language patterns. However, when compared with conventional measures of comprehension, this also makes it a fair measure of the degree to which English language learners are experiencing difficulty as a result of lack of familiarity with the new language.

3. Cloze tends to penalize students who are divergent thinking, impulsive, or perfectionistic, since the task is rather tedious, with an error rate higher than what students are used to.

4. Independent practice on cloze tasks does not contribute to improvement in reading comprehension; however, guided discussion of which words work best in each blank, and why, does result in improved comprehension.

The general cloze task can have many forms and purposes. The specific form of the cloze task described next, the Standard Cloze Passage test, is a useful assessment tool for content teachers.

Purpose of the Standard Cloze Passage Test

When constructed, administered, and scored as described next, the cloze test provides a fair indication of how a particular group of students will be able to read and understand a particular piece of reading material. Students' individual scores can be categorized to indicate whether the reading material used is at their own independent, instructional, or frustration level.

Preparation of the Standard Cloze Passage Test

To prepare a Standard Cloze test, select a passage of about 300 words from a textbook. The passage should be one that students have not yet read. Copy the first sentence with no deletions. Then select a word at random in the second sentence. Delete this word and every fifth word thereafter until fifty words have been deleted. Finish the sentence containing the fiftieth blank, and copy the next sentence with no deletions. The blanks should be typed as lines five spaces long and numbered from one to fifty. Students record their responses on numbered answer sheets.

Cautions for Administration of the Standard Cloze Passage Test

To administer the Standard Cloze test, first talk through a few sample cloze sentences. See Figure 10.3 for suggestions about how to do this. Tell students that the task is more difficult than what they may be used to, but that even if they miss half of the items they will have done very well (actually, 40% correct is still instructional level). You may also wish to assure students that their scores will not be part of their course grades but are an important means for teachers to better understand and provide for their reading needs. This introduction should encourage most students to do their best while reducing the problem noted earlier with this type of task.

Scoring the Standard Cloze Passage Test

To score the Standard Cloze Passage test, simply count the number of words filled in correctly. Count only exact words; do not count synonyms as correct. Multiply this number by 2 (since there are fifty items) to get the percent correct. Scores below 40% mean the material is at the students' frustration level: It is too difficult for them to read and learn from even with instructional support. Scores from 40% to 60% mean that the material is at these students' instructional level: They can read and learn from the material with some assistance and guidance.

Two elements must be considered for proper word replacement, *semantics*—or meaning—and *syntax*—or grammatical function. Demonstrate these by making choices available on the first two examples that make this point. Then increase the difficulty level of the examples to the actual testing task with two or three more deletions that offer no choices.

Example

Germany today is reunited, but its people still feel the differences from the period of Soviet domination. West Germans are highly (industrious/frivolous), in the tradition of (ancient/old) Germany. The East (Germans) feel less industrious and (are) given to reliance on (government) for their support.

Figure 10.3 Pointers on demonstrating cloze testing.

Scores above 60% generally indicate ability to read and learn with no special assistance, or the independent level.

Why Synonyms Won't Do

An understandable concern of teachers is the fact that only exact replacement words are counted correct in scoring the standard cloze test. Synonyms are not counted in such testing for three reasons. First, the assessment format was standardized according to exact-word scoring; therefore, the evaluation criterion cannot be used if synonyms are accepted. Second, the rank ordering of students does not change appreciably when synonyms are accepted; everyone simply has a higher score. Finally, if synonyms are allowed, scoring for the teacher becomes a much longer and more tedious process. You may, nonetheless, wish to use a more interactive version if you feel that the standard form is inappropriate for your students.

Interactive—Non-Standard-Cloze

For a more interactive version of cloze testing, consider these guidelines for a nonstandard form: Have students score their own papers with an allowance for synonyms based on class discussion of reasonable alternatives to the exact word deleted. Increase the independent reading level score to 70%.

To further encourage self-evaluation and strategic reading, ask pupils to write a sentence or two telling what they think their score indicates about their ability to read the material and what they think they should do to read better in the particular textbook from which the passage was taken.

Next, we turn to the topic of writing. Of all the things we attempt to evaluate in school, writing is one of the more difficult to assess satisfactorily. Nonetheless, it is an area of considerable interest in modern education.

▶ EVALUATION OF STUDENT WRITING

Teachers' enthusiasm for activities that involve student writing often is dampened by the prospect of piles of papers to be painstakingly graded. Fortunately, the recent renovation of an old idea called *rubric evaluation* of student writing cuts down on the paper load. As a result, it is making student writing a more attractive option for more teachers. Two types of rubrics are discussed next, one done essentially by teachers and one done by students.

Using Rubric Evaluation to Enhance Writing Activities

A writing rubric is a set of guidelines for holistic scoring of compositions. It is a teacher-constructed list of characteristics for ranking the quality of student papers, generally on a number scale or simply as *high, medium,* or *low.* The teacher uses a rubric to grade student compositions by simply determining which rubric level each composition best matches. Grading compositions thus becomes a speedy process of categorizing papers by level rather than a tedious chore of red-penciling each and every error and composing brief but time-consuming written comments on students' papers.

Ideally, the teacher gives the rubric for a writing assignment to students along with the topic. This encourages students to participate in self-evaluation, to internalize high standards and, hence, self-correct and self-teach. A partner-student reads a student's working drafts, using the rubric to make editorial suggestions. As teachers drop in on these peer-editing sessions, their suggestions become more meaningful to these works in progress than conventional written comments on a final product paper. Used in this way, rubrics are a valuable way of stimulating individual and peer revisions of school compositions.

Depending on the importance of the objective of the writing assignment, the rubric may be simple or quite complex. Figures 10.4 and 10.5 provide two sample rubrics: one addressing a specific writing objective and the other addressing content objectives of a particular writing assignment.

Evaluating Expression and Concepts

A persistent problem in evaluating student writing is that some compositions will be organizationally, structurally, and mechanically perfect but lack originality and richness of thought, while others may have distracting errors in form but contain striking expressions and/or fresh conceptual approaches. A popular solution to this problem has been a dual-grade system—one grade for ideas and one for mechanics. A rubric that combines mechanics and content, such as sample rubric 2 in Figure 10.5, provides guidelines for students to assist one another in working toward an effective combination of both aspects of a quality composition.

The initial planning time spent in preparing a rubric tends to enhance the quality of student products as well as to simplify grading. A rubric-guided writing assignment at the beginning of the school year can provide a valuable addition to the ITI.

3	The topic sentence is clearly written and strongly supported by lucid and interesting examples. Transitions tie the paper together in a fluid manner. Mechanical errors are slight.
2	The topic sentence is present, but support from the examples needs to be stronger and better organized. Transitions are used but need polishing. There are some mechanical errors.
1	The paragraph lacks a clear topic sentence. Examples are few in number and inadequately explained. Transitions are lacking, and mechanical errors are frequent.

Figure 10.4 Sample rubric 1: Using examples and illustrations.

Source: Adapted from P. Behle (Ed.) (1982), *The Double Helix: Teaching the Writing Process,* Florissant, MO, Ferguson-Florissant Writers Project. Copyright 1982 by Ferguson-Florissant Writers Project. Ferguson-Florissant School District, 1005 Waterford Drive, Florissant, MO 63033.

PAPER TOPIC: 1960s APPROACHES TO CIVIL RIGHTS IN THE UNITED STATES

High-Quality Papers Contain:

+ An overview of civil rights or their lack during the 1960s, with three specific examples

+ A statement defining civil disobedience, with three examples of how it was used and Martin Luther King, Jr.'s role

+ At least one other approach to civil rights, with specific examples, and a comparison of this approach with King's civil disobedience that illustrates differences or similarities in at least two ways

+ Good organization, well-developed arguments, few mechanical errors (sentence fragments, grammatical errors, spelling errors)

Medium-Quality Papers Contain:

+ An overview of black civil rights during the 1960s with two specific examples

+ A statement defining civil disobedience, with two examples of its use and Martin Luther King, Jr.'s involvement

+ One other approach to civil rights, with examples, and a comparison of it with King's civil disobedience by their differences

+ Good organization, few mechanical errors, moderately developed arguments

Lower-Quality Papers Contain:

+ A general statement defining civil disobedience with reference to Martin Luther King, Jr.'s involvement and at least one example

+ One other approach to civil rights and how it differed from civil disobedience

+ Fair organization, some mechanical errors

Lowest-Quality Papers Contain:

+ A general statement on who Martin Luther King, Jr. was, or a general statement on civil disobedience

+ A general statement that not all blacks agreed with civil disobedience

+ A list of points, poor organization, many mechanical errors

Figure 10.5   Sample rubric 2: A specific content assignment.

Source: Figure from Pearce, Daniel L. (1983, December). Guidelines for the use and evaluation of writing in content classrooms. *Journal of Reading,* 27(3), 212–218. Reprinted with permission of Daniel L. Pearce and the International Reading Association. All rights reserved. Copyright 1983 by the International Reading Association.

Self-Analysis of Writing Checklist

Recently, rubrics have been evolving into means of urging students to pay adequate attention to a chosen set of objectives in writing. The *Self Analysis of Writing*, or SAW (Figure 10.6), is a checklist-type rubric that is further intended to guide students in reviewing and self-improving their own work prior to submission.

Next, we discuss another form assessment that is growing in popularity. It is a means of incorporating and organizing many possible forms of assessment and is called portfolio collection and analysis.

▶ PORTFOLIOS: RATIONALE, FUNCTIONS, PROMISE, PROBLEMS

A portfolio is a collection of works intended to illustrate a range of abilities and possible special talents over time. The idea of a portfolio is to show what one can do and how one has progressed through various stages and periods.

Portfolios for students, in effect, are based on the proposition that pupils should be involved in assessing their progress and actively selecting and keeping samples of their best work for periodic review. There are two popular types of student portfolios: show portfolios, which include only a few selected samples of work, and working portfolios, which include a wide array of works in progress (Farr, 1992). Periodically, students should be helped to select pieces from their working portfolios to place in their show portfolios. The show portfolio should include the pupil's best current works, as well as some works that are representative of earlier stages of learning. The teacher's role is largely to serve as a consultant who councils students on the works that seem to reflect their progress in reading, writing, thinking, and content learning. The process of collecting, reviewing, and maintaining student portfolios tends to create interactions between teachers and students that can lead to greater empathy and a sense of common purpose.

Contents of Portfolios

Depending on the teacher's purposes, student portfolios may include any or all of the following types of entries:

- Quarterly writing samples from a variety of perspectives across genres: journal writing, personal narrative, fiction, nonfiction, poetry
- Evidence of progress in aspects of communications from phrasing to grammar and spelling
- Evidence of progress in comprehension and content knowledge
- Results from informal inventories
- Taped oral readings and presentations
- Drawings and other expressive works
- Photographs of special projects too bulky to store

Conventions (mechanics)	____	My work has been edited and proofread; it is easy to read.
	____	I used capital letters and punctuation correctly.
	____	I checked my spelling.
	____	You'd have to look hard to find mistakes in my paper!
Word Choice (vocabulary)	____	My reader will enjoy the words I chose.
	____	My words paint a descriptive picture.
	____	I think this is the best way to say it.
Ideas (topic)	____	It all makes sense, from title, to topic, to details.
	____	My reader will learn a lot.
	____	This is what I wanted to say.
	____	Details are adequate, but not overwhelming
Organization (sequence)	____	I love my beginning.
	____	I know where I am going; the middle nicely connects to the start.
	____	You can follow me.
	____	My ending is interesting and pulls things together.
Sentences (fluency & variety)	____	My sentences make sense.
	____	My paper is easy to read out loud.
	____	Some sentences are long and some are short.
	____	My sentences begin in several different ways.
Voice (overall impression)	____	This is what I feel, or believe.
	____	It makes you laugh, or cry, or even be angry.
	____	If you read my paper and it did not have a name on it, you would know that it is mine!
Rich Thinking (critical/	____	This is why I believe what I do.
	____	The paper rises above my personal feelings and beliefs.
	____	The paper gives a fair representation of other points of view.
	____	The paper seems to connect with certain other things we have learned.
	____	The paper raises some interesting questions that I will think about and perhaps write more about sometime.
	____	I'll bet I can find or think of a better idea or way to look at this.
Overall rating:	1 2 3 4 5 6 7 8 9 10	

Figure 10.6 SAW (Self-Analysis of Writing) checklist.

Source: Modified from a workshop handout of the Northwest Regional Education Laboratory, Shawnee Mission, KS, School District, May, 1998.

- Year-to-year photographs of self, the teacher, and other students
- Periodic anecdotal accounts and comments from teachers

Teacher and student comments give the portfolio depth and dimension. Here are some sample comments:

> Jack, your account of the religious basis for the civil war in Bosnia is enlightening. I read it to my wife at dinner the other night.
>
> Mr. Ahkim, 10/23/99

> Tamica, this algebra homework assignment tells me that you can read and follow word problems quite well. However, I think you should recheck your calculations.
>
> Ms. Toma, 11/10/99

Students can be asked to write short explanations of why they chose certain entries for their show portfolios. For example,

> I included this report on "Russia Today" because I think it includes my best work so far on using citations and references.
>
> Mark, 11/10/99

> This is a tape recording of me in the spring play. I was the narrator, and I thought I was pretty good. I'd like to listen to it again next year, and see how much I have changed.
>
> Nina, 5/12/99

The single most important value of portfolio assessment is that it shifts the emphasis away from the errors and the false starts kids make while acquiring knowledge and skill. Instead, the emphasis is placed on preserving, and periodically reviewing, completed pieces that youngsters value. Unlike grade books and permanent record files, which few have access to, the portfolio collection may be kept in an easily accessible part of the room for others to view, with proper permission. Maintaining portfolios is something youngsters do for themselves as well as for others. As such, the portfolio system helps to build and expand interests that lead to further reading (Ediger, 1992).

Disadvantages of Portfolios

The most serious disadvantage of portfolios is that they can quickly become complex and cumbersome. Portfolios were originally intended to provide a means of balancing other more standardized forms of assessment with a concrete record of a student's actual work. The student portfolio itself, however, is only the raw data on which this balancing is based. Evaluating these data should be a simple, subjective, and self-evident process. It can, however, be turned into a tedious, overly objectified, time-consuming one. According to one research report, some teach-

Figure 10.7 Assessing literacy through hypermedia portfolios.

Source: Duckworth, S. & Taylor R. (1995). Creating and assessing literacy in at-risk students through hypermedia portfolios. *Reading Improvement.* 32(1), 26–31.

ers view student portfolios as too demanding, and "yet another means of increasing and controlling teachers' work while appearing to empower them" (Gomez, Graue, & Bloch, 1991, p. 621). On the other hand, electronic technology is making portfolio collection and analysis somewhat easier. Computer programs are being written that guide collection, assessment, and interpretation, all with a click on an appropriate icon. See Figure 10.7 for an example (Duckworth & Taylor,

1995) of a computerized portfolio. On a further cautionary note, girls tend to enjoy this "scrapbooking" process much more than boys do.

Now that you know about several means of estimating students' abilities and progress in reading and writing about materials at different levels of difficulty, learn next how to estimate the difficulty level of the textual material they are asked to read. This, too, is a "new" technology that is about seventy-five years old.

►ASSESSING TEXT DIFFICULTY

Readability Formulas

The difficulty level of a text is referred to as the text's *readability*. Historically, junior and senior high school texts have been written with more concern for content than for difficulty level. A tenth-grade American history text, for example, might have a readability of grade twelve. This has begun to change in recent years as members of school district text selection committees have started including readability as a major criterion by which to evaluate potential textbook purchases.

Readability depends on a number of factors, including the influence of print size, number and quality of graphic aids, and an individual's level of interest and prior knowledge in the topic area. The greatest influence by far, however, comes from two simple factors: average length of sentences and word difficulty, which largely is a function of the frequency of use of a word in popular print. The most commonly used procedures for estimating readability are formulas that employ these two factors in one way or another.

One of the more commonly used readability formulas is detailed next. It is presented here to illustrate the process of estimating readability level rather than to suggest that teachers should regularly undertake even these abbreviated analyses by hand. However, it can be enlightening to do a text analysis by hand, especially if no other means is available.

Raygor's Readability Graph

The Raygor procedure, illustrated in Figure 10.8, uses the number of words containing six or more letters and the average sentence length of three passages of 100 words each to estimate a text's difficulty. Baldwin and Kaufman (1979) found the Raygor formula faster than and as accurate as the original Fry formula (1968, 1977), on which it is based.

Computer Programs for Readability Checking

Even simplified formulas for estimating readability are time-consuming to do manually. Fortunately, a wide variety of computer software now is available for obtaining readability estimates on textbook excerpts. This is much more realistic in terms of time and elimination of the human error inevitable with lengthy syllable/word counting and calculating. Microsoft Word 5.0 or higher has two readability formulas built in. For more information on commercially available computer readability programs, ask your local software dealer or school librarian.

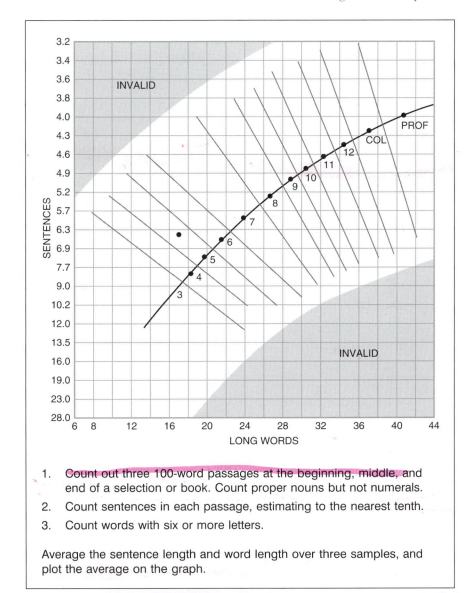

1. Count out three 100-word passages at the beginning, middle, and end of a selection or book. Count proper nouns but not numerals.
2. Count sentences in each passage, estimating to the nearest tenth.
3. Count words with six or more letters.

Average the sentence length and word length over three samples, and plot the average on the graph.

Figure 10.8   The Raygor procedure for estimating readability.

Source: From A. L. Raygor "The Raygor Readability Estimate: A Quick and Easy Way to Determine Difficulty" in *Reading: Theory, Research and Practice. Twenty-Sixth Yearbook of the National Reading Conference* (pp. 259–263), edited by P. D. Pearson, 1977, Clemson, SC: National Reading Conference.

There is another approach to evaluating readability that any veteran teacher can use effectively and that new teachers can use to increase their sensitivity to factors in a text that will influence the level of difficulty for students. It is called a readability checklist.

Readability Checklists

Checklists to guide readability estimates are totally subjective and do not necessarily yield a grade-level readability estimate. They do, however, indicate whether a given book is appropriate for a particular group of students. Checklists are most effective when several teachers rate the same material and then average (or otherwise compare) their judgments. A group of teachers from a given content area may wish to develop their own checklist that addresses specific content concerns.

One list includes the following items, to which the rater responds with a particular group of students in mind:

1. Are the concepts far beyond the students' direct experiences?
2. Are abstract concepts linked to examples and situations that are familiar to students?
3. Are technical terms defined in context as they appear?
4. Does one idea lead logically to another?
5. What does the author assume about the students' previous learning experiences?
6. Are textbooks aids provided?
7. Is the material appealing, or does it look too "textbookish"?
8. Is the writing brief, concise, and to the point? (Harker, 1977)*

Readability checklists can be adapted for use by students. To help students to become more independent and strategic readers, they need a greater capacity for self-appraisal of text difficulty, text aids, and personal ability to negotiate a given textbook. One way to help them to do this is the FLIP inventory, described next.

FLIP: For Student Analysis of Text Difficulty

FLIP (Schumm & Mangrum, 1991) invites students to judge how well they will be able to read and learn from a particular reading assignment by analyzing its friendliness, language, and their own interest and prior knowledge, using a FLIP chart (see Figure 10.9). Students are instructed to FLIP through the reading assignment and use the chart to record their judgments.

By adding the FLIP elements rated, students are able to evaluate the general level of the assignment. They then proceed to interpret their assessment to determine an appropriate reading rate and to budget reading and study time (see Figure 10.10).

*Source: Harker, W. J. (Ed.). (1977). *Classroom Strategies for Secondary Reading.* © International Reading Association. Used with permission.

Title of assignment _____ # of pages _____

General directions: Rate each of the four FLIP categories in a 1 to 5 scale (5 = high). Then determine your purpose for reading and appropriate reading rate, and budget your reading/study time.

F = Friendliness: How friendly is my reading assignment?

Directions: Examine your assignment to see if it includes the friendly elements listed below.

Friendly text features

Table of contents	Index	Glossary
Chapter introductions	Headings	Subheadings
Margin notes	Study questions	Chapter summary
Key terms highlighted	Graphs	Charts
Pictures	Signal words	Lists of key facts

1————2————3————4————5

No friendly text features	Some friendly text features	Many friendly text features

Friendliness rating = ____

L = Language: How difficult is the language in my reading assignment?

Directions: Skim the chapter quickly to determine the number of new terms. Read three random paragraphs to get a feel for the vocabulary level and number of long, complicated sentences.

1————2————3————4————5

Many new words; complicated sentences	Some new words; somewhat complicated sentences	No new words; clear sentences

Language rating = ____

I = Interest: How interesting is my reading assignment?

Directions: Read the title, introduction, headings/subheadings, and summary. Examine the pictures and graphics included.

1————2————3————4————5

Boring	Somewhat interesting	Very interesting

Interest rating = ____

Figure 10.9 FLIP chart.

Source: Figure from Schumm, Jeanne Shay, & Mangrum, Charles T., II. (1991, October). FLIP: A framework for content area reading," *Journal of Reading*, 35(2), 120–124. Reprinted with permission of Jeanne Shay Schumm and the International Reading Association. All rights reserved. © International Reading Association.

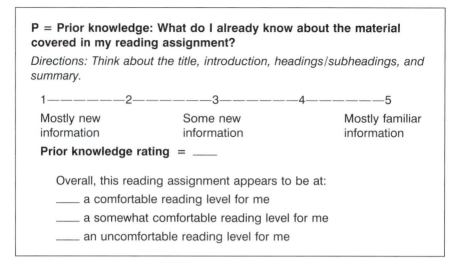

P = Prior knowledge: What do I already know about the material covered in my reading assignment?

Directions: Think about the title, introduction, headings/subheadings, and summary.

1————————2————————3————————4————————5

| Mostly new information | Some new information | Mostly familiar information |

Prior knowledge rating = ____

Overall, this reading assignment appears to be at:

____ a comfortable reading level for me

____ a somewhat comfortable reading level for me

____ an uncomfortable reading level for me

Figure 10.9 *continued*

My purpose for reading is (circle one):

A. Personal pleasure

B. To prepare for class discussions

C. To answer written questions for class assignment or for homework

D. To prepare for a test

E. Other _____

My reading rate should be (circle one):

A. Slow—allowing time for rereading if necessary

B. Medium—careful and analytical

C. Fast—steady, skipping sections that are about information I already know

Active reading time:

Chunk 1, pages _____–_____, estimated time: _____ minutes

Chunk 2, pages _____–_____, estimated time: _____ minutes

Chunk 3, pages _____–_____, estimated time: _____ minutes

Chunk 4, pages _____–_____, estimated time: _____ minutes

Total estimated time: _____ minutes

Figure 10.10 FLIP follow-up.

Source: Figure from Schumm, Jeanne Shay, & Mangrum, Charles T., II. (1991, October). FLIP: A framework for content area reading," *Journal of Reading,* 35(2), 120–124. Reprinted with permission of Jeanne Shay Schumm and the International Reading Association. All rights reserved. © International Reading Association.

Following is a valuable closing thought on readability. It uses the idea of student input in a way that may have occurred to you when you first read about cloze testing.

Matching Student Abilities with Text Difficulty through Cloze

The Standard Cloze Passage test described earlier is as much a readability strategy as it is a measure of students' reading ability. It does not yield a grade-level estimate of the difficulty of a given text, but it does predict how well a particular student or group of students will be able to read and learn from it. Hittleman (1978) pointed out that cloze measures readability, whereas other means predict text difficulty. He also noted that the cloze procedure is the only available procedure that can take into account, in a natural setting, the constraints of the language system of the reading matter, the reading ability and other characteristics of the reader, and the background information needed by the reader. In other words, there are two ways to compare your students' reading levels with your textbook's readability level. One is to compare some form of student reading test score to a formula-based readability estimate in the text. Another is simply to give a Standard Cloze Passage test constructed from a representative portion of the text. Hence, the Standard Cloze Passage test permits a direct comparison using a single measure. To improve the quality of the match, you have only to construct more than one sample for the text.

▶ AFFECTIVE ISSUES AND MEASURES

It is an axiom of professional education that to know others, you must first know yourself. To reach this island of self-knowledge, however, one must navigate through the reefs of self-doubt and self-examination. This can be particularly formidable because, as the German writer Herman Hesse put it, "Nothing . . . is so distasteful to man as to go the way which leads him to himself."

When you are up to facing this process, you might wish to look into some of the personality and temperament inventories that are available for popular consumption in most bookstores. These may not always have the same level of accuracy as norm-referenced personality tests, but they tend to be sufficiently accurate for getting a look at yourself, since most of them essentially are made up of the more telling items of traditional measures like the Minnesota Multiphasic Personality Inventory (MMPI).

▶ AFTER WORDS

This chapter offered a broad range of options for considering and conducting assessment in the context of the content area classroom. It described traditional and emerging options for assessing students' reading, text management, and writing. Finally, the chapter turned from student assessment to text assessment and provided a tour of available means for assessing the difficulty level of printed material.

CHAPTER 11

READING, LEARNING, AND REMEMBERING: STUDY METHODS AND MINDTOOLS

Study without reflection is a waste of time; reflection without study is dangerous.

—Confucius

▶ FORE WORDS

The term *study strategies* refers to the efficient use of time spent in learning and remembering. As such, it includes an array of diverse topics such as time management, techniques for active reading and listening, note taking, and test taking. Study strategies may be taught in mini-courses or as units in a regular class and/or integrated with the content of various classes. Each approach has merit. The content class approach is gaining in popularity as more teachers learn about the methods for imparting these strategies in their primary teacher training and in-service programs. Oddly, study strategies tend to be taught to academically motivated students but not to struggling students. The information ahead will help you to serve those with the greatest needs.

▶ FROM SKILLS TO STRATEGIES TO MINDTOOLS

Study skills have tended to track the educational trends of the times. McMurry wrote the first study skills text for classroom teachers in 1909. It was a no-frills book aptly called *How to Study and Teaching How to Study.* Its approach reflected the early-twentieth-century assumption that reading was a bottom-up process of mastering and applying a series of discrete subskills.

This skills-based approach continued through the popularization of self-directed study techniques during World Wars I and II. Armed services inductees needed quick training in how to read and master the contents of the manuals that accompanied increasingly sophisticated weapons and machines. Later, returning veterans willingly enrolled in study skills courses to improve their reading efficiency and grades in technical schools and colleges. By 1930, skills-based books with names like *Outlining as a Study Procedure* (Barton, 1930) were available at the college level.

The open admissions policies initiated in many colleges in the 1960s created a further need to assist underprepared students in meeting college-level reading, writing, and study requirements. By this time, many educators were realizing that effective study, like reading, was not something done to one, but something that one did. The emphasis on imparting study skills gradually evolved into the new emphasis on the learner as an active doer and strategy user.

Today, a new era is opening, one that is offering MindTools to students at every developmental level, and customizable to a variety of different learning styles and needs. These are especially compatible with Power Point and Internet usage, but they have their origins in the reading-thinking-study guides popularized by Herber (1978). MindTools take many forms. They can be formats for outlines, incomplete outlines, graphics, and even guides to thinking creatively, such as are provided by semantic/conceptual maps, charts, and graphs depicted in previous chapters. They are similar to formulas that guide financial investment, but in this case of human capital in dividend-rich reading and learning. The Internet offers the capability to search huge, worldwide databases for information and chat rooms on topics of interest and research. Let's go back for a historical look at one of the first and still most widely known MindTools for effective reading and study.

SQ3R: A Story unto Itself

The Survey-Question-Read-Recite-Review (SQ3R) technique is an early MindTool and the acknowledged granddaddy of study formulas. Developed by Francis Robinson (1946), its roots trace back to 1923. Robinson developed it into its current form in response to a need expressed by the U.S. Department of Defense during World War II (Stahl & Henk, 1986). As noted earlier, U.S. troops had a great deal of technical information to learn and little time in which to learn it. They needed a rigorous, self-guided technique that they could use with minimal instruction in field training situations. SQ3R stresses meticulous, step-by-step analysis of text, followed by repeated reviews to overlearn textual material to the point where key information can be recalled and recited with minimal cueing.

Steps in SQ3R

1. *Survey.* Survey a chapter before reading it closely.
    a. Read the title, and think about what it says or implies.
    b. Read the headings and subheadings.
    c. Read the summary if there is one.
    d. Read the captions under the pictures, charts, graphs, or other.
    e. See if there is a bibliography or a list of books related to the chapter.
2. *Question.* Ask yourself questions about what you are going to read.
    a. What does the title of the chapter mean?
    b. What do I already know about the subject?
    c. What did my instructor say about this chapter when it was assigned?
    d. What questions do the headings and subheadings suggest?
3. *Read.* Read actively.
    a. Read to answer the questions you raised while doing the survey/question routine.
    b. Read all the added attractions in the chapter (maps, graphs, tables, and other illustrations).
    c. Read all the underlined, italicized, or boldface words or phrases extra carefully.
4. *Recite.* Go over what you read in step 3 by either orally summarizing what you just read or making notes of some type.

5. *Review.* Periodically survey what you read and learned.
    a. Use your notes or markings to refresh your memory.
    b. Review immediately after reading.
    c. Review again periodically.
    d. Review again before taking an exam on the subject.

Efficacy of SQ3R for Independent and Content Class Use

The balance of opinion among specialists regarding the efficacy of SQ3R is positive but by no means unanimous. Several studies (Diggs, 1973; Donald, 1967; Gurrola, 1975; McNamara, 1977; Willmore, 1967; Wooster, 1958) found no significant differences between SQ3R and control (i.e., placebo) treatments. Thus, despite the popularity of SQ3R, evidence of its effectiveness as a self-guided reading–study formula still is uncertain.

We continue to endorse SQ3R for content classroom use, especially when each step is practiced under teacher guidance. Used in this way, SQ3R parallels the Directed Reading–Thinking Activity (DR-TA), which has been proven effective. We are also encouraged by the emergence of a new strategy which nicely fuses elements of both SQ3R and the DR-TA: SQP2RS (squeepers).

SQP2RS (*Squeepers*)

A historical footnote is necessary for appreciating this means of strategy instruction. Once a chemically or mechanically induced electrical impulse was combined with the function of a magnetic force that had mystified scientists for a thousand years, the electric motor and self-generating electric power were invented and made practical. Thereafter, two items formerly sitting on our collective shelf of interesting, but relatively inert knowledge began to change everything from fans to self-starting car engines. The same seems to be the case with SQP2RS, a relatively new entry from MaryEllen Vogt (Vogt, 2002) into guiding content area reading. It combines aspects of at least two legacy methods that despite being widely known, have suffered from problems with implementation: SQ3R—as just discussed, Robinson's (1946) intended *self-instructional* reading-study technique, and Russell Stauffer's (1969) more *teacher-directed* Read-Predict-Read formula for teaching thinking as well as reading (as discussed in the DR-TA material of Chapter 3 of this text). Vogt's new synthesis seems to be a better method to scaffold teaching for independent strategy acquisition. Consider how it combines these elements so as to achieve the goals of both more efficiently and surprisingly easily.

Steps in SQP2RS

1. *Survey*—have students scan the text to be read for 1–2 minutes
2. *Question*—have students generate likely questions to be answered by the text (teacher guidance should be greater at first, and faded thereafter to levels guided by class need and content density)
3. *Predict*—have students state 1-3 things that they *infer* that they likely will learn based on the questions generated

4. *Read*—silently search for confirming and disconfirming answers to predicted questions, with an eye to answers to questions not raised

5. *Respond*—orally answer questions raised, comment on questions that could/should have been raised, and formulate new ones for the next section of text that may be read in class or for homework

6. *Summarize*—add a quick written summary, personal response, and/or notes for later to further supplement and help consolidate the impact of step 5

The addition of this final summarizing step is of particular importance since it was shown in another methodology, KWL-Plus (Carr & Ogle, 1987; Ogle, 1989, 1996), which also added the summarizing step sometime after its initial trials—to have a very positive effect on reading comprehension outcomes, as discussed earlier in Chapter 5 of this text. The further addition of a self-recitation of notes can greatly insure study type reading and learning since it is one of the more research-supported aspects of SQ3R (Wark, 1964).

With this teacher and student friendly formula, SQP2RS provides instruction and content-based practice in self-guided surveying, questioning, predicting, inferring, enabled reading, oral language responding, writing and likely continuing-out-of-class thinking and self-instruction (the purpose of all teaching). It has great utility, as a *time-release* strategy to prime and guide required homework. In so doing, SQP2RS also meets most all of the criteria of *sheltered* instruction for English Language Learners. Four years of continuing research with SQP2RS largely with ELL students in grades 4–9 has been very encouraging both in terms of learning outcomes and teacher response. Teachers and students have given it the nickname *Squeepers*—often a sign of affection (Echevarria, Vogt, & Short, 2004).

Obstacles to Study Strategy Instruction— Habits Are Hard to Change

Teaching study strategies presents several unique challenges. At a basic managerial level, study strategy instruction is an additional layer of *content* to be taught and learned on top of existing demands.

The second challenge is the lofty goal of this type of instruction. The intent is to teach information, processes, and, even beyond this, to change habits of mind. And habits are notoriously difficult to change. Teaching students to use study strategies like SQ3R is analogous to teaching teachers to use instructional methods like the DR-TA. In each case, what is taught is a set of steps that teachers and students are expected to understand, remember, and then apply *on their own*. This requires preparation, guidance, and lots of practice. Even if students become convinced of the usefulness of a particular study strategy, they are likely to slip back into more accustomed patterns. To be effective, study strategies need to become new habits. Francis Robinson himself observed that SQ3R cannot possibly be effective until it becomes "automatic" and "subordinate to the task of reading" (1946, p. 21).

Another complicating factor is that people tend to resent being given advice, and most study strategies amount to advice. This problem persists even though the strategies and techniques are effective.

Finally, teachers tend to believe that what we do when we study is highly individual, and that no one strategy will work for everyone. While it is true that each of us tailors a particular strategy to our own personal style, fundamental principles of learning apply regardless of individual differences. In one of the early textbooks designed for college students with weak academic skills, Walter Pauk (1989) summarized much of what is known about effective learning and study in his "Eight Learning Principles." These research-based principles, shown in Figure 11.1, provide an excellent orientation to the field of developmental studies and a basis for evaluating any study strategies program.

▶ CONTENT AREA STUDY METHODS FOR IMPROVING LECTURE NOTE TAKING AND LISTENING

Palmatier's Unified Note-Taking System*

Students need instruction in how to learn from lecture as well as from text. Palmatier's Unified Note-Taking System (PUNS) urges students to review lecture notes immediately after class and supplement them with text information. The note-taking format also provides a built-in study system by separating key words from the body of the notes. PUNS is one of the few note-taking methods that has been validated through scientifically-based research (Palmatier, 1971, 1973; Palmatier & Bennett, 1974).

Steps in PUNS

1. *Record.* In a loose-leaf binder, use only one side of 8 1/2-by-11-inch notebook paper with a 3-inch margin on the left side. (Many college bookstores now stock this type of paper for this purpose.) Record lecture notes to the right of the margin. Use a modified outline form to isolate main topics. Leave space where information seems to be missing. Number each page as you record the notes.

2. *Organize.* As soon after the lecture as possible, add two sections to the notes. First, place labels inside the left margin. These should briefly describe the information in the recorded notes. Second, insert important text information directly into the recorded notes. If you need more space, you can use the back of the notebook paper.

3. *Study.* Remove the notes from the loose-leaf binder, and lay them out so that only the left margin of each page is visible. Use the labels as memory cues to recite as much of the information on the right as you can recall.

---

*Source: From Palmatier, R. A. (1973). A notetaking system for learning. *Journal of Reading, 17.* © International Reading Association. Used with permission.

1. **Principle of Motivated Interest.** We remember what interests us. Develop your natural interests, and try to create new interests by reading (e.g., magazine and newspaper articles) in diverse areas. If you find a subject boring, or irrelevant, try to find something in it of personal interest or use, and you will find it easier to learn.

2. **Principle of Selectivity.** Information must be grouped into units of a manageable size for efficient recall. In the nineteenth century, Hermann Ebbinghaus, one of the world's earliest experimental psychologists, found that it took fifteen times as many trials to memorize twelve nonsense syllables as the number of trials needed to memorize six nonsense syllables. One would predict that it would take only twice as many trials.

3. **Principle of Intention to Remember.** Prerequisites to efficient learning include careful attending, getting the facts right the first time, and striving to understand. Recall that this is the basic principle underlying the guided reading procedure, a total reading and study lesson design covered in Chapter 6. Active reading the *first* time saves time in the long run.

4. **Principle of Basic Background.** What we perceive (see, hear, taste, smell, feel, and read) depends in large measure on what we already know. Whenever you are trying to learn something new, connect it to something you know.

5. **Principle of Meaningful Organization.** George Miller, the eminent Harvard psychologist, found that the immediate memory span of the general population seems fixed at approximately seven bits of information, plus or minus two. For effective recall, therefore, information should be categorized into meaningful groups of no more than seven bits. The telephone company heeded this research when developing the telephone numbering system. The U.S. Postal Service, on the other hand, has challenged it by implementing a nine-digit Zip Code system.

6. **Principle of Recitation.** Study reading must be an active process. Recitation is analogous to exercising a muscle: it builds and embeds information in long-term memory. Pauk reminds us of how H. F. Spitzer's classic study compared the amount of information recalled by students seven and sixty-three days after learning. Students who reviewed immediately after learning remembered 83% after seven days and 70% after sixty-three days. Those who did not review immediately after learning remembered 33% after seven days and 14% after sixty-three days. Control groups of students who also did not review immediately after learning remembered approximately 55% after one day, 22% after fourteen days, 18% after twenty-one days, and 1% after twenty-eight days. Obviously, recitation-study works!

Figure 11.1 Pauk's eight learning principles.

Source: Pauk, Walter, *How to Study in College* (Fourth ed), Copyright © 1989 by Houghton Mifflin Company. Adapted with permission.

7. **Principle of Consolidation.** Information must be harbored in the mind for a certain period before a temporary memory can be consolidated into a more permanent one. Numerous records of accident victims show that a period of unconsciousness can erase the memory of events that occurred from fifteen to five minutes before the person lost consciousness. Spitzer's study, described in principle 6, further illustrates the effectiveness of an immediate review of new information.

8. **Principle of Distributed Practice.** A number of brief reviews are more effective than one long review session. Short sessions prevent physical and emotional fatigue and help sustain interest and motivation.

Figure 11.1 *continued*

The labels can be turned into questions stems, "What do I need to know about [insert label]?" Verify your recall immediately by lifting the page to read the information recorded to the right of the label. As you master the material on each page of notes, set that page aside in an "I already know" stack. For objective tests, the labels can be approached at random, simulating the format of multiple-choice, true/false, and matching tests. For essay tests, group information into logical units, formulate predicted essay questions, and practice writing answers. Figure 11.2 presents a sample PUNS format.

The notes students take during lectures are influenced as much by listening habits as by note-taking strategy. The next sections suggest ways to improve attention and active listening.

Enabling Questions

The Enabling Questions procedure is a student-initiated strategy developed by the authors. It is a prepared set of questions that students can use to tune in and reduce distraction during lectures. Using Enabling Questions puts the listener into an active, evaluative thinking mode and invites the teacher or speaker to talk a little less and welcome more interaction. Students should be urged to translate these questions into their own words.

Set 1: Questions that Help the Listener Organize and Clarify Information

1. What is/are the main *question(s)* you are answering by your lecture (or lesson) today?

2. Which key terms and concepts are most important for us to remember from what you have said (or will say) today?

3. What is most often misunderstood or confusing about the information or position you are presenting today?

Step 1: *Record.*
Use the right-hand
side of a specially
divided page,
leaving space to
add text notes.

Step 2: *Fill in labels.*
Write key word labels
in the left margin and
text notes in the
space provided for
lecture notes. Use
the back of the
previous page if
you need more
space.

Step 3: *Study key words.*
Lay out pages so
that only key words
show, and try to
recite information
from your notes.
Remove each page
as you master its
contents.

Figure 11.2 PUNS note taking.

Set 2: Questions that Help the Listener Get a Mental Breather

1. Could you please restate that last point in some other words?
2. Would you please spell ____ and ____ for us?
3. Would you please say which points you especially want us to note at this time?

Set 3: Questions that Invite Give-and-Take with the Speaker

1. How does what you have said compare with positions others have taken, and who might these others be?

2. Is there convincing evidence to support your position that you can share with us?

3. What do you think is the weakest part of the position you have taken?

4. How do you think this position (or new information) affects previously held beliefs?

5. What do you suppose would happen if you extended this point another step or two?

6. Would you mind pausing for a moment to see if there are other views on this in the class/audience? This would help us better understand and follow your points.

Any one of the latter set of questions likely would put the listener back into an active, evaluative thinking mode and reduce the sometimes excessive dominance of the speaker. It is important that the listener who wishes to use these types of questions does so with an eye toward using them for enriching comprehension, learning, and mature interaction, and not as a counteroffensive. One way to help students learn the value and become regular users of Enabling Questions is to *write these questions on index cards* and distribute a few to each class member. Then urge students to try to use the questions on their card(s) intelligently over a two- to three-day period. Schedule a day to discuss what happened and what students learned and what might need to be modified to make the Enabling Questions even more enabling.

Guided Lecture Procedure

The Guided Lecture Procedure (GLP) (Kelly & Holmes, 1979) is a teacher-directed method for improving listening.° It is the listening counterpart of the Guided Reading Procedure (Manzo, 1975).

Steps in the GLP

1. Students are directed to take no notes as they listen carefully to the lecture.

2. The teacher writes the objectives of the lecture on the chalkboard along with key technical terms.

3. The teacher lectures for about half the class period, then stops.

4. Students attempt to write down everything they can recall from the lecture.

5. Students form small cooperative learning groups to review and discuss their notes. This discussion, or language component, helps build related speaking, writing, and thinking strategies.

°*Source:* From Kelly, B. W., & Holmes, J. (1979). The Guided Lecture Procedure. *Journal of Reading, 22.* © International Reading Association. Used with permission.

The GLP has been used effectively with classes from middle school to college levels (Kelly & Holmes, 1979). The small-group activity that forms the latter part of the lesson is an excellent cooperative learning activity.

▶ CONTENT AREA STRATEGIES FOR TEST TAKING

Taking Multiple-Choice Tests

It is difficult to overstate the effects of test taking on the body and the ego. If test taking were a pill, it probably would never pass the Food and Drug Administration guidelines for benefit-to-risk ratio. The growing emphasis on writing and performance-based assessment has begun to decrease the use of multiple-choice tests in the classroom. However, most schools still use standardized multiple-choice tests for evaluation of their overall program. Students' scores on multiple-choice tests can be more a reflection of their test-taking savvy than their knowledge acquisition. See Figure 11.3 for a brief list of helpful hints for taking multiple-choice tests.

+ Block out a rough time plan for timed tests. Note what time it will be when half the time is up, and how many items you should have completed by that time.

+ Read slowly and answer quickly. Focus on the question instead of the answer choices. This prevents the frequent and irritating problem of misreading the question.

+ Answer the easy questions first, and skip the hard ones. Spending time on difficult questions raises anxiety and may cause you to forget information you knew when the test began. As you go through the test, you may find information that will help you remember answers to earlier difficult items.

+ Don't assume that the test is loaded with trick questions. This will cause you to read too much into the questions and spend too much time in needless internal debate. Read each question carefully, but concentrate on the main point rather than the details.

+ Avoid anxiety reactions that break concentration: glancing frequently at the clock or the instructor, polishing eyeglasses, examining fingernails, gazing at the wall or ceiling, excessive yawning or stretching.

+ Use all the time allotted. If you finish before the time is up, always check your work. Make sure you answered all the questions, but don't waste time reviewing the answers to easy questions. Change your answers if you have reason to. Research shows that contrary to common belief, three out of four times your changes will be correct. This may be because during a final check, the tension begins to lessen and thought processes are clearer.

Figure 11.3 Tips for taking multiple-choice tests.

PORPE: A Strategy for Taking Essay Tests

Predict-organize-rehearse-practice-evaluate (PORPE) was developed in response to students' anxiety about taking essay examinations (Simpson, 1986).° The method evolved from a review of the research literature to find practical ideas about how proficient readers prepare for essay-type tests. PORPE's five steps guide students to behave like "effective readers who have some awareness and control of their own cognitive activities while they read and study" (p. 408).

Steps in PORPE

1. *Predict:* Students are asked to predict essay questions that they might be asked. Teachers should make every effort to help students at this stage to raise synthesizing, analyzing, and application questions as well as more literal *what-* and *when-*type questions. One way to do this is to introduce students to a glossary of the most common words used in essay questions, such as *explain, criticize, compare, contrast, react, support,* and *elaborate.* As follow-up, teachers should model the thought process they go through in preparing (predicting) and phrasing essay questions on a previously studied body of information. Students then should prepare and share their predicted questions with classmates.

2. *Organize:* Students are encouraged to organize the information needed to answer predicted questions. Students are encouraged to use semantic maps and outlines for this purpose. Again, teachers should model this strategy.

3. *Rehearse:* This is the conventional study or recall and recite step. Students should be encouraged to use appropriate memory devices.

4. *Practice:* In this step students practice composing or answering essay-type questions. They should be reminded of the following in doing so:
    a. Work from an outline.
    b. Make sure your opening sentence rephrases the question and/or takes a clear position.
    c. Make the structure of your answer clear by using transitional words and phrases like *first, on the other hand, furthermore,* and *finally.*
    d. Give examples of major points.
    e. Reread what you wrote, and make appropriate editorial corrections.

5. *Evaluate:* This step continues logically from the latter portion of the last one but should occur after a brief pause. The idea simply is to consider how a teacher might evaluate your answer. It may be necessary to conduct several sessions where students listen to, read, and discuss the relative merits of various essay answers before they acquire the ability to get outside of themselves and review their own work.

°*Source:* From Simpson, M. (1986). PORPE: A writing strategy for studying and learning in the content areas. *Journal of Reading, 29*(5). © International Reading Association. Used with permission.

Notes on PORPE

PORPE has been found to be significantly more effective than question–answer recitation in improving comprehension and essay writing (Simpson, Hayes, Stahl, Connor, & Weaver, 1988). PORPE also makes a great deal of sense at an intuitive level. It incorporates attention to metacognitive development, content mastery, effective predicting, organizing, and test writing. Structurally, it progresses in logical movements from teacher instruction, modeling, and guidance to total student independence and control—the purpose of all study strategies instruction.

Study Journals

Keeping a study journal can make students more aware of their present study habits and attitudes. A study journal is simply a written record of thoughts and feelings about studying and about school. Students should be encouraged to make four or five brief journal entries each week, without undue concern for form or style. Guiding questions should be, "What am I doing when I study?" and "How do I feel about it?" Some categories for consideration include the following:

- *Classes*: participation or lack of it, difficulty paying attention, confidence level
- *Homework*: difficulty concentrating or getting started, organization of materials, strategies for studying
- *Tests*: thoughts before, during, and after tests; controlling anxiety
- *Time management*: difficulty getting everything done; setting priorities
- *Symptoms of stress*: fatigue, headaches, worry, apathy, guilt, problems in interpersonal relationships, insomnia, excessive snacking, and so on

Following are some sample study journal entries:

9/10: Algebra class always begins in English, but it soon becomes Greek. There must be something I can do to keep from getting lost about midway?

9/14: When I get home from school, I can't stand to face homework. Soon it's dinnertime, then the good programs are on, and then I'm too tired. When are you supposed to do homework anyway?

9/25: I hate tests. I never seem to study the right things.

10/2: I've been having trouble falling asleep, and I wake up two hours early thinking about that darn paper due next week. I also find it impossible to stay awake after lunch.

After students have made several entries in their journals, they should be encouraged to look back over what they have written. Are there noticeable patterns? Are there certain kinds of situations that tend to precipitate stress? What coping strategies did students try? How effective were these? We have found that study journals are more likely to be kept when they are combined with the next strategy, which offers a place and time for their use and reinforcement.

Problem-Solving Approach to Study Skills

The *Problem-Solving Approach to Study Skills* (PASS) (Manzo & Casale, 1980) is an interactive method designed to communicate the attitude that school, learning, and living present a series of typical study problems that generally are quite manageable and often solvable by critical, constructive analysis and personal resolve. PASS is a fundamental paradigm for teaching study skills since it is customized to each student's particular needs.

Steps in PASS

1. *Count:* The teacher presents students with a list of common study problems and asks them to check those that apply to them (see Figure 11.4).

2. *Characterize:* The teacher guides students in defining selected problems, and themselves, in specific terms. The teacher urges students to take inventories of learning style, temperament, skills, abilities, and attitudes in an effort to reach a firmer sense of themselves as learners.

3. *Consider:* Students consider how they typically have dealt with their particular needs and problems and the possible merit in these intuitive coping strategies.

—1. Taking good notes in class

—2. Completing reading assignments

—3. Finding the main ideas when reading

—4. Remembering details when reading

—5. Figuring out what the author/teacher means

—6. Staying relaxed when studying

—7. Concentrating while reading

—8. Paying attention in class

—9. Asking questions in class

—10. Vocabulary meanings

—11. Writing answers to questions

—12. Writing personal opinions about class topics

—13. Writing research papers

—14. Planning and completing class projects

—15. Taking notes while reading/studying

—16. Finding reference materials in the library

—17. Participating in class discussions

Other: _____

Figure 11.4 Checklist of common study problems.

4. *Collect:* The class discusses and judges standard techniques for dealing with reading/study problems on the basis of their compatibility with each student's style and character. Where these appear incompatible, the procedures are dismissed as inappropriate.

5. *Create:* Students seek inventive alternatives that match their personal styles. This step is best handled initially in small groups and then in larger group discussions.

Notes on PASS

PASS was evaluated in a case study approach and found to be a very sound means of improving study habits and positive attitudes toward learning (Casale [now Manzo] & Kelly, 1980). The content teacher's efforts to teach students how to study will be time well spent. Learning is as much attitudinal as it is intellectual. Teaching students how to study tells them that they are as important as the content.

► AFTER WORDS

This chapter suggested some ways in which the content area teacher might help students to build needed study strategies, attitudes, and habits. It focused on the things students do most: listening, note taking, personal problem solving, and test taking. The next chapter addresses some discipline-specific problems that students may encounter and the specific help that each subject teacher might contribute to a schoolwide content area literacy effort.

SECTION

IV

LITERACY APPLICATIONS, ISSUES FOR SPECIAL NEEDS STUDENTS, AND SCHOOL-WIDE CONTENT AREA LITERACY IMPLEMENTATION

Even now that you have established a solid understanding of how to promote reading/writing/thinking of between and beyond the lines, there is much more to learn about. The chapters in this section might be considered as important reference material for you going forward. Chapter 12 contains examples of applications of content area literacy in specific disciplines, Chapter 13 addresses special needs students, and Chapter 14 is designed to help you begin the process of becoming a literacy leader.

APPLICATIONS OF CONTENT AREA LITERACY TO DISCIPLINE-SPECIFIC KNOWLEDGE, INQUIRY, AND ACADEMIC LANGUAGE

Too much new information can drive knowledge out of circulation.
Knowledge is orderly and cumulative, an enduring treasure.

—Dan Boorstin

► FORE WORDS

This is something of a *reference* chapter; you cannot possibly ingest all that it contains. It is, nonetheless, important to your studies since schools, at this moment, are interviewing for enlightened educators to join their efforts to integrate the teaching of reading, writing, and thinking into discipline specific knowledge, inquiry, and academic languages. To do so means acquiring functional levels of professional knowledge in particular applications of content area literacy strategies and methods. This knowledge base is a technology that is just as refined, precise, and dynamically growing as any in the medical, legal or computer science fields. Here is your chance to read the past, or what we have learned about how to do this, and to write the ways in which we will do so in the future. Begin by looking ahead to the areas of application that are your current interests. Mark the rest for easier access as need presents itself.

- ▶ FORE WORDS
- ▶ DISTRIBUTED VS. UNIVERSAL RESPONSIBILITY FOR DISCIPLINE SPECIFIC ACADEMIC LANGUAGE AND SKILLS
- ▶ QUAINT OLDE ENGLISH
- ▶ FOREIGN LANGUAGE
- ▶ MATHEMATICS
- ▶ BIOLOGICAL-PHYSICAL SCIENCES
- ▶ SOCIAL STUDIES
- ▶ CONTENT AREA READING IN THE SUPPORT SUBJECT AREAS
- ▶ PHYSICAL EDUCATION
- ▶ VOCATIONAL ACADEMIC LANGUAGE & ORIENTATION
- ▶ CULTURAL LITERACY: ART, MUSIC, AND SPEECH
- ▶ BE CREATIVE AND ENCOURAGE CREATIVITY
- ▶ AFTER WORDS

▶ DISTRIBUTED VS. UNIVERSAL RESPONSIBILITY FOR DISCIPLINE SPECIFIC ACADEMIC LANGUAGE AND SKILLS

For some time, it has been the practice to educate teachers to the belief that it is each discipline's role to teach virtually all of the literacy skills that could possibly be employed in each subject area. This "everyone is responsible" approach sometimes tends to result in no one being responsible. To counter the downside effects of this unsuccessful policy, we suggest that you consider taking responsibility for some very specific skills that you would teach by special application. In addition, let all who teach also continue to feel responsible for reinforcing a focused and distributed part of the spectrum of literacy skills and strategies. To launch this relatively new approach, we have identified some basic skills to be distributed to four "major" subject areas, while keeping in mind that all subjects are important.

Distributed Parts of the Spectrum of Academic and Literacy Skills and Objectives by Major Disciplines

English

1. Story comprehension
2. Poetry comprehension
3. Language patterns
4. Creative writing

5. Summary writing

6. Systematic vocabulary

7. Literary reference books

Social Studies

1. Analytical discussion

2. Critical reading

3. Metaphorical thinking

4. Critique and reaction writing

5. Note taking

6. Social studies vocabulary

7. Almanac, encyclopedia, and related reference skills

8. Reading maps, charts, graphs, and cartoons

Science

1. Inquiry training

2. Thesis and detail writing from expository material and observation

3. Cooperative reading–learning

4. Accurate recall

5. Science vocabulary

6. Hypothesis formulations and testing

7. Abstract thinking

Mathematics

1. Recitation

2. Translation

3. Test taking

4. Mathematics vocabulary

5. Expository writing: What did this problem ask, and why did I solve it as I did?

6. Cooperative problem solving

This list could easily be extended to most all other subject areas. For example, Physical Education requires and teaches students how to *follow directions* and to *image body movements*, and complex games and sports. Music teaches and requires understanding and reading of an alternate means of coding sound (remember text print is just a means of coding the spoken word). Art teaches and requires visualization and sense awareness, a fundamental skill in story reading, and, for that matter, of nonfiction accounts of actions and sensations. Speech teaches and requires sensitivity to the way phonemes—the smallest sounds in words—are heard and formed; this is the basis of phonetic analysis. Speech also teaches composition and punctuation, the basis for all good thinking, successful communication, and persuasion. There is, too, one thing that all subject areas teach that improves student abilities to read: the specialized ways of thinking that each field brings to the mental table. Each teacher of a subject provides students with a specialized language and certain signature ways to see and reflect on the world about them. This alone is responsible for building a more powerful vocabulary and allied sets of concepts. Together these are known in the research literature on reading power as *prior knowledge*. And, this "what-you-know" factor alone is the best single predictor of reading comprehension, or the "what-you-have-learned" factor.

For these reasons it can correctly be said that every teacher is, in a sense, a teacher of reading, as well as a beneficiary of students' improved abilities to read. It is primarily through reading that students are able to be ready for continuing to teach themselves through reading, and for that matter listening and viewing, in each discipline, throughout their lives. Let's look in now on some of the disciplines and see how, in the particular, they are enhanced by and lend themselves to the advancement of reading, writing, and thinking.

▶ QUAINT OLDE ENGLISH

The English curriculum is the focal point for teaching language mastery. The term *English* is a quaint reminder of our colonial and cultural past. In fact, our language is Anglo-American and the discipline is Language Arts, or effective listening, speaking, reading, and writing. English clearly is the current language of choice on the Internet, at major airports throughout the world, and at global financial centers. The language may still be a little quaint and quirky, but it also is viable, and for those born speaking it, a great gift that keeps giving.

Reading and English

Student progress in reading receives its greatest emphasis in the English curriculum. English is the only discipline that traditionally has designated reading and writing improvement as a key objective. It also has traditionally provided direct and systematic instruction in vocabulary, writing, cultural literacy, and literary appreciation. Lately, it has taken to teaching mass media, and communications as well. As such, the English curriculum lays the classical and modern foundations for effective comprehension of text and for interpreting the contemporary experience. The English curriculum, however, remains primarily dedicated to ensuring that at least some explicit attention is given to receptive and expressive language in school. There are sound reasons for continuing this focus on language and literature up to and through graduate education. The most obvious is the fact that aural, written, and spoken language, along with reading, are developmental processes that can be refined and enhanced throughout one's lifetime. They are the mechanisms through which learning, as well as the capacity to learn, can be grown.

The English curriculum has some special requirements. The most difficult of these for pupils is the requirement to read anthologies of prose and poetry that often span hundreds of years in origins, context, and style. Finding value and meaning in story was and is the center of English class. To this end, we have discussed several means and methods in previous chapters, from plot mapping to character study. To this we now shall add a basic set of questions to guide literature study. Notice that the questions raised reveal a good deal about author craft and therefore can serve as aids in teaching creative writing. Keep in mind while reviewing this guide that it is just that, a *guide*. Literature is art, and art, like the life it imitates and the imitation of itself it evokes in life, does not lend itself to easy categorization and dissection. Realize, too, that this same guide can be used to unpackage a film or television presentation. It also can be used for general literature study, that is, as a postanalysis of several previously read and viewed pieces of fiction.

Guide to Literature Study[*]

Character Study

Who is the protagonist, or main character, and why?

Who is the antagonist, and why?

Does the author use common stereotypes or some inventive ways to introduce and picture the main characters?

Are there any minor characters who seem to have special appeal or possibilities for future development?

Setting

Does the story take place in a real or totally imagined place?

How does the author create mood through setting?

How do the characters react to the setting?

Plot

How does the author tell the story—through a narrator, a character, or some other way?

How does the point of view help readers to relate to the characters and to buy into the plot?

What information is given and when?

What information is held back from the reader for dramatic effect?

Theme

What type of conflict is depicted (e.g., person against person, person against nature, person against self)?

Can you detect some idea or attitude being conveyed through the story?

Are there subplots, and do they convey the same or different themes?

How do characters grow or change?

How do they deal with problems?

Style and Tone

Does the story contain elements of the unbelievable, and how is it made believable?

[*]*Source:* Liberally modified from Patricia O. Richards, Debra H. Thatch, Michelle Shreeves, Peggy Timmons, and Sallie Barker (1999), "Don't Let A Good Scare Frighten You: Choosing and Using Quality Chillers to Promote Reading," *Reading Teacher,* 52 (8), pp. 830–840. © (1999) by the International Reading Association.

How are facts, images, and words used to hook readers?

How is tension/humor built?

How is tension relieved?

What sensory images are used, and toward what effect?

Universal Truths

What ideas and values underlie the story or piece?

In your judgment, are the ideas and values mature or immature?

Are the ideas and values central to the piece or simply a mechanism for telling an entertaining story or tale?

Genre Comparisons

How would you characterize the story by literary type (e.g., fantasy, mystery, survival, science fiction, biography)?

What are the genre features of a given story?

How would you compare stories of a similar genre for distinguishing characteristics?

Author Comparisons

What are some of the distinctive style features of authors working in a similar genre?

What are some of the distinctive style features of authors working in the same theme but in different genre?

Can you describe different audiences that likely would be attracted to different author styles?

Which is/are your favorite authors/styles/genre and why?

Illustrations and Camera Work

Can you describe the style characteristics of the illustrations/camera work?

Are illustrations/camera work realistic or impressionistic?

What tends to be in focus, out of focus?

Beyond Literature Study to Academic Language

A newer view of the English/Language Arts curriculum says that a good job is being done with prose and poetry reading but that students need to be taught more about how to read specific academic or technical writing, something nineteen other industrialized nations already do. School reformer William Doggett maintains that America has moved on from being an industrialized society to one based on technologies and that our curricula are yet to catch up.

Much of the catch-up being called for, we believe, is occurring and will continue to occur at a lively pace largely due to the influence of the content area literacy movement, which emphasizes such, and the Internet, which is bringing terse, content-laden, hi-tech language into schools and homes via electronic text.

While almost all of the methods presented thus far would serve the English/Language Arts curriculum, two are highlighted here: specifications for English textbooks that could be added to the Informal Textbook Inventory (see Figure 12.1); and Cloze-Plus (Blanc, 1977), a method designed to improve poetry comprehension—a very special kind of academic language—more directly than do the reading guides previously described.

Cloze-Plus for Poetry

Cloze-Plus enhances comprehension of the meanings and techniques of poetry by dealing directly with the poem, using a cloze-type worksheet. Cloze techniques are most effective when they serve as the basis for an interactive discussion about language choices and forms. Used in this way, they also encourage peer teaching, urge students to generate their own guiding questions and serve as a readiness step for poetry writing activities.

Steps in Cloze-Plus

1. The teacher prepares a worksheet by writing the poem, deleting every fifth word beginning with the title (see Figure 12.2 for an example).

2. The teacher tells students that although they have not read the poem, they are to try to re-create it by filling in the deleted words as closely as possible to the exact words of the original. The teacher points out that the activity will be difficult, and students should rely on whatever clues they can find. Students then complete the poem individually.

3. Next, students work in small groups to discuss their word choices. The teacher stands back and lets it happen.

4. Once the groups have reconciled their choices, the teacher resumes a leader role, explaining terms such as *context, syntax,* and *rhyme* and asking students to express how they might have used these to fill in the blanks. (Further class discussion might include comments on poetic license, grammar, vocabulary, and style.)

5. The teacher reads the poem aloud, pausing at the previous blanks to give students time to correct their initial responses.

▶ FOREIGN LANGUAGE

No matter how the teaching of foreign languages is approached, its ultimate success depends on two rudimentary principles of learning that apply to all academic language learning: students must think *about* and *in* the language, and practice outside of scheduled lab and class times. For this reason, foreign language teachers have worked hard to network with English language teachers from around the world. In this way they have arranged for student pen pals and for students to visit one another's countries. This has been marginally successful. Now there is a new tool, the Internet.

Newby, Stepich, Lehman, and Russel (1996) describe this new dimension through the story of a Spanish teacher whose students now regularly chat by

I. *Use of Text Aids to Locate Information*
Construct 10 to 15 questions that assess student's ability to use parts of the textbook, such as:
A. What is the title of the book?
B. When was it published?
C. Who wrote the book?
D. How are the chapters arranged or grouped?
E. On what page does Chapter 8 begin?
F. In which chapter can you find something about Langston Hughes?
G. In which chapter can you find "Types of Humor in Modern American Literature"?

II. *Rate of Reading and Levels of Comprehension*
Choose a passage from the textbook that has not been read by students. Have students read the passage and record the time when they finish it. Help them to compute their rate of reading, or words per minute (number of words read divided by number of minutes spent = words per minute). Have students answer questions about the passage that require comprehension at literal, interpretive, and applied levels.

III. *Vocabulary Development*
A. *Contextual Analysis:* Choose sentences from the textbook that contain words that may be difficult for students. List these sentences, with the difficult words underlined. Have students predict the meaning of the underlined words, using clues from the context to make reasonable predictions (evaluate student responses in terms of "reasonableness" of prediction rather than accuracy of definition).
B. *Structural Analysis:* Select words from the textbook that are made up of affixes and recognizable English root words. Have students identify and explain the meaning or function of the root word, prefix, and/or suffix in each of these words.
C. *Dictionary Use:* Choose sentences from the textbook that contain a word or words that have multiple meanings. List these sentences, with the multiple-meaning word(s) underlined. Have students check a dictionary to select and write the appropriate meaning of each underlined word according to its use in the sentence. (From a term paper by Fengfang Lu, UMKC, 1986.)

IV. *Use of Reference Sources to Locate Information*
A. In our classroom dictionary, locate the origin of the word ("bonfire").
B. Using the library card catalog, find the names of two books written by (Judy Blume). Who is the author of (*The Great Gilly Hopkins*)?

Figure 12.1 Informal Textbook Inventory Questions for English.

Source: Sections IV and V from Criscoe, B. L., & Gee, T. C. Content Reading: A Diagnostic/Prescriptive Approach. Copyright © 1984. Published by Allyn and Bacon, Boston, MA. Copyright © 1984 by Pearson Education. Reprinted by permission of the publisher.

C. In the *Reader's Guide to Periodical Literature*, locate the journal and the year and month in which you find the short story entitled ("*Down the Down Staircase: A Sequel*").

D. In the *Essay and General Literature Index*, find the titles for three stories related to the theme of (family conflict).

E. In the *Current Biography*, locate information about (Ernest Hemingway's life).

F. In *Bartlett's Familiar Quotations*, locate the person credited with having written: ("One thorn of experience is worth a whole wilderness of warning.")

G. A thesaurus is a book of words grouped by ideas and used to locate precise words to express your idea. In *Roget's International Thesaurus*, locate at least three nouns that could be used instead of (cheerfulness.)

V. *Use of Graphic Aids to Interpret Meaning*

A. Study the cartoon on page ____ of your text. Describe what you believe to be the message of the cartoon.

B. Examine the timeline of major English literary periods on page ____ of your text. What years are considered to encompass the neoclassical literary period? List three prominent writers for this period.

C. The diagram on page ____ depicts the plot structure of Jackson's "The Lottery." After reading the story, briefly discuss the conflict, rising action, climax, and denouement of "The Lottery."

Figure 12.1 (*continued*)

Richard Cory

Whenever Richard ____ 1 ____ went down town,
We ____ 2 ____ on the pavement looked ____ 3 ____ him;
He was a ____ 4 ____ from sole to crown,
____ 5 ____-favored and imperially slim.

____ 6 ____ he was always quietly ____ 7 ____.
And he was always ____ 8 ____ when he talked;
But ____ 9 ____ he fluttered pulses when ____ 10 ____ said,
"Good-morning," and ____ 11 ____ glittered when he walked.
____ 12 ____ he was rich,—yes, ____ 13 ____ than a king—
And ____ 14 ____ schooled in every grace;
____ 15 ____ fine, we thought that ____ 16 ____ was everything
To make ____ 17 ____ wish that we were ____ 18 ____ his place.

So on ____ 19 ____ worked, and waited for ____ 20 ____ light,
And went without ____ 21 ____ meat, and cursed the ____ 22 ____,
And Richard Cory, one ____ 23 ____ summer night,
Went home ____ 24 ____ put a bullet through ____ 25 ____ head.

—Edwin Arlington Robinson

1. Cory; 2. people; 3. at; 4. gentleman; 5. clean; 6. And; 7. arrayed; 8. human, 9. still; 10. he; 11. he; 12. And; 13. richer; 14. admirably; 15. In; 16. he; 17. us; 18. in; 19. we; 20. the; 21. the; 22. bread, 23. calm; 24. and; 25. his.

Figure 12.2 Example of Cloze-Plus.

e-mail with a classroom in Seville, Spain. The future of foreign language educa-tion will be in cultivating the many dimensions and values in this new, rapid, and easy-access means of writing, reading and "speaking" in the vernacular(s) of other languages. Foreign language education need never seem as tedious again. To fur-ther advantage this chat environment, foreign language teachers could develop some common pieces of material for students to read and react to, such as in the REAP program described in Chapter 8. Every part of REAP seems to meet some part of learning a foreign language: especially the requirements that it be used in authentic contexts with native speakers.

▶ MATHEMATICS

Although some progress has been made over the past decade, reports of the Na-tional Assessment of Educational Progress and similar studies repeatedly reveal findings that are cause for concern about the state of mathematics proficiency in the United States (c.f. NCES, 2001, 2003).

- More than 30% of eighth-graders are below the most basic level, indicat-ing that they likely cannot handle elementary school arithmetic.
- Only 32% of fourth-graders perform at or above the proficient level.
- Only 29% of eighth-graders perform at or above the proficient level.
- U.S. 15-year-olds score lower than their peers in 17 other countries in mathematics literacy.
- Scores for Black and Hispanic students, despite modest gains, lag behind those of Caucasians.

The difficulties students experience in dealing effectively with word prob-lems and related mathematical concepts is unparalleled among current educa-tional dilemmas. Clearly there are more math illiterates than there are people who cannot read. Until recently, however, this problem has been among the low-est ranked national priorities. Weakness in dealing with math concepts, computa-tion, and word problems—i.e., academic language—is so pervasive that it tends to pass for a fact of life.

Mathematics More a "Second" Than an Academic Language

Improvement of mathematics and reading instruction has finally begun with the reconstruction of math books to conform more closely to conventional conversa-tional language. See Figure 12.3 for examples of the more conventional language found in modern math texts. Math itself is a system of reality coding that benefits from this more conversational approach.

Working within this theme, MacNeal (1994) referred to this need in a book he called *Mathsemantics: Making Numbers Talk.* Students can be taught to listen to and speak the language of mathematics in settings and situations that closely parallel the ways in which people successfully learn language, but especially sec-ond languages. Using the principles of second-language instruction, the reason, purpose, and value of mathematical systems can be more easily imparted, rein-

1. **Locating Information**
   Directions: Terms used in the book can be found in one of several places; preface, contents, appendix, and glossary/index. You will be able to locate each term on the right in one of the places on the left. Locate the term and then mark the place where you found it. Do this as quickly as you can.

Book Section		**Term**
A. Preface	_____	Using your income
	_____	Axes
B. Contents	_____	Individual differences
	_____	4 pecks = 1 bushel
C. Appendix	_____	Cubic units
	_____	Objectives
D. Glossary/Index	_____	Tables and graphs
	_____	1,760 Yds = 1 mile
	_____	Dividing fractions
	_____	Hourly wage
	_____	Measure your progress
	_____	Inch
	_____	Lesson organization
	_____	Overtime
	_____	Review

2. **Reading the Mathematics Textbook**
   Directions: Read p. 69. When you have finished reading, close your book and answer the following questions. Remember, once you have closed the book you may not open for any answers.

   Vocabulary: Mathematical and General

   a. Define *prime* first in the words of the text, then in your own words.
      What the text said: _____
      Your words: _____

   b. What did the author mean when he said, "a simple hunting and fishing existence . . ."?
      _____

   c. What does the term *signified* mean?
      _____

   Main Ideas

   d. How did the author explain that early humans needed a method of counting things?
      _____

   e. Why did the author include information about early counting methods in this chapter?
      _____

Figure 12.3 Mathematics Informal Textbook Inventory.

3. **Interpreting Graphs**
    Directions: Turn to p. 259 and read the section entitled "Reading Bar Graphs." Study Figure 199 and answer the following questions:

    a. How many students (total number) are represented on the bar graph? _____

    b. Circle the two categories below in which the same number of students is found:

    Poor   Fair   Good   Excellent   Superior

    c. Use the graph to determine an approximate answer to each of the following questions:

    How many students received "poor" grades? _____

    How many students received "good" grades? _____

    How many students received "excellent" grades? _____

    How many students received "superior" grades? _____

    d. Would you say that this test was a good test or a poor test? (Explain your answer.)

4. **Seeing and Using Text Markers**
    Directions: Read pp. 119–121. When you finish, close your book and fill in the missing parts of the following outline. Do this in pen.

    I. Units of Measurement
       A. Direct: measuring height with ruler
       B. _____
          1. Measuring temperature—thermometer
          2. _____—_____
          3. _____—_____
          4. Measuring air pressure—barometer
    II. Ancient Measurement Devices
       A. _____
          1. thumb
          2. foot
          3. hand
          4. forearm
          5. _____
       B. Difficulties of Ancient Measuring Devices
          1. _____
          2. _____

    Directions: Now that you have written in your first set of responses in pen, open your book and try to complete the outline in pencil.

Figure 12.3   *(continued)*

5. **Summarizing**
   Directions: You are going to read the section "The Metric System of Weights and Measures," p. 202. When you have finished this section about the consistency of the metric system, close your book. Write a summary of what you have read in four complete sentences.

   _____

   _____

   _____

   _____

6. **Where I Need Help!**
   Directions: Think back to all that you just read and the answers you gave. Indicate in no fewer than two sentences where you think you need help in understanding the information presented.

   _____

   _____

7. **What More?**
   Directions: Think again about what you have read. What are you most curious about? Write at least one sentence telling what you would like to learn more about.

   _____

   _____

Figure 12.3 *(continued)*

forced, and internalized. The simple idea is to *preteach* mathematics incidentally by making it a more common frame of reference in conversation. This allows the repeated exposures of previously unfamiliar terms to create a contextual lesson and an inclination to be attentive when direct instruction is offered on one of these terms. Another principle involves use of artifacts, or *realia*. This is some concrete thing that is identified with a culture or activity, such as a baseball glove is with baseball and sport. One often overlooked way to introduce the second-language learner to the culture and tools of the new language is through its literary artifacts, or books and writings. Math books are artifacts that represent math culture and serve as a math learning tool. Ideally, the math textbook should become a point of conversation and comfort, rather than fear and anxiety. To be sure, math, for all but a few, is an acquired taste: hence it may be necessary to create an interesting room and environment of other math artifacts, such as pictures and objects reflecting the past and present contributions of math to human history. The Internet, of course, is the other place to do some electronic-archeological digs. It also contains stories of modern efforts to do and teach math inventively. This need is greatest for females who continue to lag behind males on the SAT by a staggering 27 points (CNN news brief, 11/04/04). The more conversational and friendly use of math terms and text, as suggested in the Community of Language Approach in Chapter 7, seems an appropriate place to remedy this disparity.

Math Is a Trip: The Informal Textbook Inventory Is a Guide

Math is a trip, for some a good trip and for others a bad trip. Introducing students to their textbooks is a simple, sensible way to have them get to know and draw comfort from this well-informed travel companion. The math teacher should plan on spending a minimum of three days on this activity and giving two one-day refresher and extender sessions about two months apart. As students' skills and knowledge base in mathematics grow, so will their perceived need for, and therefore receptivity to, the helping features and value of the text.

The teacher should make an extra effort to conduct all sessions in a relaxed and supportive atmosphere. The Informal Textbook Inventory experience can be a nonthreatening, math-teacher-generated means of desensitizing and counter-conditioning math anxiety. The examples of Figure 12.3, especially questions 2, 5, 6, and 7, offer useful ways to help students converse in conversational terms about mathematical systems. Note especially question 7 for its possibilities for making math something to be curious about and interested in.

The next method for teaching mathematics and reading also imparts something more of the culture that is part of thinking and talking about math. The method addresses the persistent problem of reading and comprehending word problems. There have been many efforts to make math more friendly, such as with the lively and loosely connected quote and colorful names and problems. (See Figure 12.4 from a recent mathematics textbook for examples of both of these.) Nonetheless, word problems remain the most complex of academic languages. The one shown from the math book in the figure has five major parts and is difficult to translate into computational steps that most students know how to do.

The Dahmus Method for Word Problems

The Dahmus method for teaching word problems (Dahmus, 1970) emphasizes the translation of English statements into the academic language of mathematics. Recall from previous chapters that simple *translation* questions provide a bridge from literal to higher-order thinking skills.

Steps in the Dahmus Method

1. The statements and their parts in the translation must be in the same order as the verbal form.

2. No operations or substitutions should be performed until the translation is completed.

3. Students should read slowly and translate each idea and fact in the verbal form as it appears before reading. Dahmus recommends that students not read the entire problem beforehand.

4. All other facts suggested by the verbal form and required for the solution should be stated mathematically on students' papers. There should be no verbal forms of translation, only math notation.

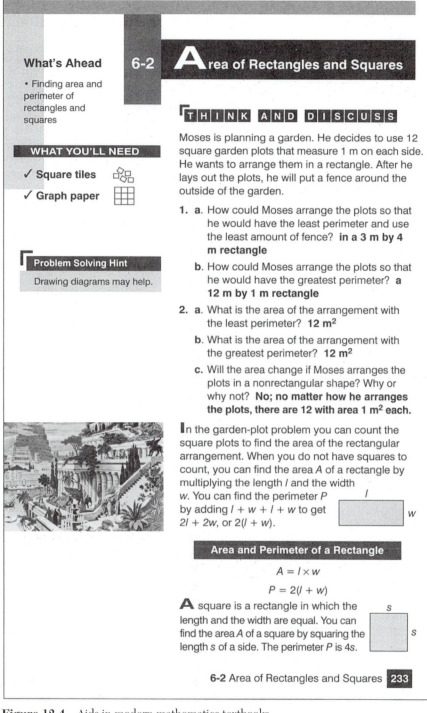

WHAT YOU'LL NEED

✓ Square tiles

✓ Graph paper

Problem Solving Hint

Drawing diagrams may help.

6-2 **A**rea of Rectangles and Squares

THINK AND DISCUSS

Moses is planning a garden. He decides to use 12 square garden plots that measure 1 m on each side. He wants to arrange them in a rectangle. After he lays out the plots, he will put a fence around the outside of the garden.

1. a. How could Moses arrange the plots so that he would have the least perimeter and use the least amount of fence? **in a 3 m by 4 m rectangle**

   b. How could Moses arrange the plots so that he would have the greatest perimeter? **a 12 m by 1 m rectangle**

2. a. What is the area of the arrangement with the least perimeter? **12 m²**

   b. What is the area of the arrangement with the greatest perimeter? **12 m²**

   c. Will the area change if Moses arranges the plots in a nonrectangular shape? Why or why not? **No; no matter how he arranges the plots, there are 12 with area 1 m² each.**

In the garden-plot problem you can count the square plots to find the area of the rectangular arrangement. When you do not have squares to count, you can find the area A of a rectangle by multiplying the length l and the width w. You can find the perimeter P by adding $l + w + l + w$ to get $2l + 2w$, or $2(l + w)$.

Area and Perimeter of a Rectangle

$$A = l \times w$$

$$P = 2(l + w)$$

A square is a rectangle in which the length and the width are equal. You can find the area A of a square by squaring the length s of a side. The perimeter P is $4s$.

Figure 12.4 Aids in modern mathematics textbooks.

Source: From *Middle Grades Mathematics: An Interactive Approach* by S. Chapin, M. Illingworth, M. Langauy, J. Masingila, and L. McCracken. © 1995 by Pearson Education, Inc., publishing as Pearson Prentice Hall. Used by permission.

Mark is twice as old as John. In two years, the sum of their ages
M   =   2×   J.   (M + 2) +   (J + 2)
will be five times as much as John's age was four years ago.
    =   5   ×   (J − 4)
How old is each now?
M = ?   J = ?

Figure 12.5   Example: The Dahmus Method
Source: Dahmus, M. E. (1970), *How to Teach Verbal Problems.* School Science and Mathematics.
© School Science and Mathematics Assn.

5. Students should use deductive reasoning on the translated and implied facts to obtain a solution.

Figure 12.5 provides an example of the Dahmus method.

▶ BIOLOGICAL-PHYSICAL SCIENCES

Bureaucratic reports are notorious for being dull and uninfluential. However, one written about 1945 by Vannevar Bush, Director of the U.S. Office of Scientific Research and Development, has become one of the most important documents in modern times. Called *Science, the Endless Frontier: A Report to the President,* this document was the major impetus for getting the massive and sustaining investments by the U.S. Congress in basic scientific research and, indirectly, in America's willingness to support the advancement of knowledge and the education of its students in the scientific method. This priority competes successfully year in and year out with the many other concerns and critical needs of the nation and is largely responsible for our continued program for the exploration of space.

It was in this spirit that science education, for over fifty years, has called for science to be taught as a narrative of inquiry with emphasis on self-discovery and hands-on learning. In fact, science education remains largely textbook dominated. On the plus side, a good deal of the influence of this revisionist view is now being reflected in published science materials and in a revised and more socially sensitive science curriculum in teacher training institutions. Accordingly, the stated goals of science education now include understanding self, appreciating (i.e., reading and following) technology, preparing for college, advancing modern culture, and understanding local issues. We would add the infusion of scientific language into everyday living to this list of goals.

Contribution of Science to Reading
& Reading to the Language of Science

The typical science curriculum, whether textbook or experiment based, already contributes naturally to growth in reading. Simply by teaching science well, the science teacher helps students to better grasp the fundamentals of systematic observation, scientific thinking, problem solving, science vocabulary, science concepts, and the physical world. These elements promote progress in reading by enhancing student schemata, as well as important related linguistic and thinking processes. For these reasons, science and reading have been called a "harmonic convergence" (Johnson, 1995).

The characteristics of an expert reader, such as described in prior chapters, strongly resemble and therefore are greatly compatible with the characteristics of those who are "scientifically literate" as defined by the National Science Teachers Association (NSES, 1998):

> Scientific literacy is the knowledge and understanding of scientific concepts and processes required for personal decision making, participation in civic and cultural affairs, and economic productivity. . . . Scientific literacy means that a person can ask, find, or determine answers to questions derived from curiosity about everyday experiences. It means that a person has the ability to describe, explain, and predict natural phenomena. Scientific literacy entails being able to read with understanding articles about science in the popular press and to engage in social conversation about the validity of the conclusions. Scientific literacy implies that a person can identify scientific issues underlying national and local decisions and express positions that are scientifically and technologically informed. A literate citizen should be able to evaluate the quality of scientific information on the basis of its source and the methods used to generate it. Scientific literacy also implies the capacity to pose and evaluate arguments based on evidence and to apply conclusions from such arguments appropriately (p. 22).

Problems in Reading Science

The problems students encounter in reading science material stem in large measure from five problem areas:

- Inadequate background of information
- Misconceptions about the physical world
- Inconsiderate or assumptive and inadequately explained text
- Difficulty in handling esoteric or technically overwhelming academic terms
- Inadequate preparation and orientation of teachers, particularly at the elementary level, in the basic sciences.

Consider some solutions to these problems as they bear on effective reading and study in science.

Using New-Generation Science Texts

Recently, science textbooks have been roundly criticized as being inadequate (Bradley, 1999). However, this criticism belies the fact that there is a new generation of science materials that offer great promise despite some rough spots that are not easily overcome because they are inherent to the discipline. The promise of the newer materials lies in their being better grounded in compellingly interesting issues, their attempt to stress scientific thinking, and the opportunities they offer for developing integrated reading, writing, and science skills. The inherent problem they pose is that issues-based materials tend to exceed the mental and social maturity levels of most students and can be controversial in some communities (e.g., the perceived conflict between theories and findings for evolution and beliefs nested in conservative religious views). Additionally, from a purely pedagogic perspective, *real issues cannot easily be disassembled and reassembled to meet a typical learning sequence.* These problems aside, the new materials do tend to do a better job of engaging students.

One of the reasons for higher levels of engagement in science texts may be traced to the casual use and reference to prose, poetry, and common experience as a known ground on which to build a sense of familiarity and a basis for new, less familiar knowledge (see Figure 12.6). Admittedly, these connections sometimes are a bit strained, but our sense is that students would rather have them than not. It would be even more effective if teachers could use the language of science across disciplines to provide more instances of intentional-incidental teaching of scientific academic language and ways of thinking.

Use of Science Texts

One ready means of learning how effectively students are using their science text while helping them improve usage is to prepare an Informal Textbook Inventory on the basic text. See Figure 12.7 for examples of science-oriented items to add to an ITI.

Using Media, Magazines, and Computers to Build Familiarity with the Academic Language of Science

One effective way to build your own as well as students' background knowledge in science is to read lay-science magazines, watch public television, and access a multimedia encyclopedia and texts on CD-ROM and the Internet. A new breed of lay-technical writers are turning out articles on such mind-boggling topics as quantum physics and string theory in crystal-clear language—which is not to say that these topics are easily comprehended even then. *Discover* and *Omni* are among the best written of these publications. There are also a multitude of project activities in progress on the Internet in the fun and collaborative ways inspired by the Web. An example of this is the *Mars 2030 Project.* Originally created by the White House Millennium Council, the United States through NASA has created a project for students, all ages and grades, to design a community for Mars for the year 2030. Kits are available (www.Mars2030.net).

Adaptations of the Guided Reading Procedure for Science

Two adaptations of the Guided Reading Procedure (Manzo, 1975) are especially appropriate for *Into* and *Beyond,* or pre- and postreading, activities using science material (Spiegel, 1980). The GRP-based *prereading procedure* has students identify clear purposes for study, become aware of specific gaps in their knowledge, and build the scaffolding necessary for forming new concepts. This is

5–2 The Excretory System

When the sixteenth-century English poet John Donne wrote that "No man is an island, entire of itself," he was actually talking about the human mind and spirit. However, this phrase can also be used to describe the human body: No human body can function without help from its surroundings. For example, your body must obtain food, water, and oxygen from its surroundings and get rid of wastes that may poison you. In order to do this, three body systems work together to provide a pathway for materials to enter and leave the body.

You have already learned about two of these systems: the digestive system and the respiratory system. The digestive system is the pathway for food and water to enter the body. The respiratory system enables oxygen to enter and carbon dioxide and water vapor to leave the body. The third system is the excretory (EHKS-kruh-tor-ee) system. **The excretory system provides a way for various wastes to be removed from the body.** These wastes include excess water and salts, carbon dioxide, and urea (a nitrogen waste). The process by which these wastes are removed from the body is called **excretion.**

You have just read about one of the organs of the excretory system: the lungs. Because the lungs get rid of the wastes carbon dioxide and water vapor, they are members of the excretory system as well as the respiratory system. The remaining organs of the excretory system are the kidneys, the liver, and the skin.

ACTIVITY
READING

❶

Reading Poetry

The first line of John Donne's poem entitled "Meditation XVII" was quoted in this chapter. Find a copy of this poem in the library and read it. Is there another line in this poem that is familiar to you?

The Kidneys

Have you ever made spaghetti? If so, you know that you have to use a strainer to separate the cooked spaghetti from the cooking water or else you will be eating soggy spaghetti! The strainer acts as a filter, separating one material (spaghetti) from the other (water). Like the spaghetti strainer, the **kidneys** act as the body's filter. In doing so, the kidneys filter wastes and poisons from the blood.

The kidneys, which are the main organs of the excretory system, are reddish brown in color and

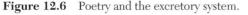

Figure 12.6 Poetry and the excretory system.

Source: From *Prentice Hall Science Human Biology and Health* by A. Maton, J. Hopkins, S. Johnson, D. LaHart, M. Q. Warner, and J. D. Wright. © 1994 by Pearson Education, Inc., publishing as Pearson Prentice Hall. Used by permission.

Using Resource Materials

The book *Through the Magnifying Glass* will tell you many ways to use scientific tools:

> How could you find who wrote the book?
>
> What is its library call number?
>
> Where in the library could you locate the titles of filmstrips that deal with ecology?
>
> In what library index could you locate the title of an article by Asimov?

Applying Theoretical Information

> How can the law of "centrifugal force" be proven?
>
> Describe an example of inertia that you might see every day.

Formulas and Symbols

> List the meaning of the symbols F and C.
>
> What do cm and ml stand for in measurement? (above three sections synthesized from Criscoe & G ee, 1984, pp. 124–125)

Using Graphics and Visual Aids

> What does the illustration on p. 202 (see below) say about the current flow in electricity?

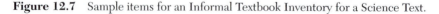

(Answer: Current flow requires a closed path)

Figure 12.7 Sample items for an Informal Textbook Inventory for a Science Text.

achieved by having students bring to mind what they already know about a topic and then organizing this information into an "advance outline" prior to reading. Then students read to test their preconceptions.

Steps in the Prereading GRP

1. The teacher identifies a unit or topic of study that is fairly narrow in scope, such as photosynthesis or spiders.

2. The teacher has students tell peer recorder(s) at the chalkboard (or overhead, whiteboard, or SmartBoard) everything they know about the topic prior to lecture or reading.

3. The class identifies conflicting information and areas in which no information has been provided ("Hey, we don't know what spiders eat!"; "Are very large spiders insects or animals?").

4. Students construct an outline with conflicting information listed side by side ("Spiders have six legs/eight legs[?]"). Areas in which no information is known are listed by headings in the outline.

5. The outline is displayed in the classroom throughout the unit of study.

6. The class is told to read to fill in or alter the outline (see Figure 12.8).

Other Science Application Methods

Several other methods covered in previous chapters have excellent application to the academic language and orientation of science. Chief among these are the Question-Only Strategy, which offers an effective means of inquiry training; the Oral Reading Strategy for giving direct assistance with science words and phrasing; and graphic organizers for imparting a "conceptual set" for numerous easily confounded details.

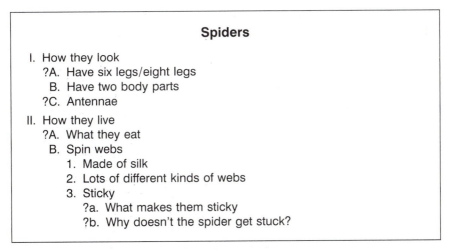

Spiders

I. How they look
   ?A. Have six legs/eight legs
   B. Have two body parts
   ?C. Antennae

II. How they live
   ?A. What they eat
   B. Spin webs
      1. Made of silk
      2. Lots of different kinds of webs
      3. Sticky
         ?a. What makes them sticky
         ?b. Why doesn't the spider get stuck?

Figure 12.8 GRP Prereading Outline.

▶ SOCIAL STUDIES

Executive Training

The Constitution gives enormous executive power to every citizen. Social studies is the fundamental school-based source of the sense of *agency* that every citizen needs in order to read, interpret, and vote on the streams of raw and prepared information emanating from newspapers, magazines, broadcast media, and now the Internet. The awesome responsibility facing all citizens with such executive power increases the responsibility of those of us who must agonize over what and how to teach them. Accordingly, today's social studies consists not merely of traditional fields like history, government, and geography but fields such as psychology, sociology, and philosophy and several conceptual approaches that can be applied across these fields, such as social inquiry, moral education, and values clarification (Peters, 1982). Indeed, one of the more welcome changes in the teaching of social studies is that it is more about people. Look, for example, at the page from a contemporary text (Figure 12.9) to see how immigration has been reduced to human scale in the story of Sacco and Vanzetti; it's not *People* magazine, but it's also not the antiseptic and decontextualized social studies of just a generation ago.

Contribution of Social Studies to Reading

The principles, precepts, and actual content of social studies underlie almost everything written. This may explain why social studies as a discipline is so highly correlated with general reading comprehension (Adams, 1982; Artley, 1944). Also for this reason, the social studies teacher is especially well situated to enhance students' understanding of how best to read and think about nearly all things written. This is done naturally as the teacher and textbook report to students how others think and feel about a variety of issues such as economics, politics, and culture and the consequences of these beliefs on individual liberties. Most important from the standpoint of the reading process, social studies imparts a rich fund of general information, a specialized academic but also general-purpose vocabulary, refined critical-relative thinking strategies, and the rudiments of cultural literacy, both about the "core" culture and the many diverse cultures within the American mainstream. It also is students' main source of information on our growing global awareness.

Obstacles to Reading and Studying in Social Studies

The major problems students encounter in reading in social studies stem in large measure from the very elements to which social studies ultimately contributes in general reading. Reading in social studies often requires conceptual and informational preparation. It also requires considerable assistance with objective reasoning and in connecting loose factual elements into a structure that subsequently can be used to read, grasp, and interpret still more.

Reasoning Guides

Reasoning Guides were developed and popularized in direct response to the aforementioned concerns. A Reasoning Guide is a specialized form of reading guide that strongly emphasizes interpretive and applied levels of reading and thinking

Sacco and Vanzetti
Millions of Americans mourned when Nicola Sacco and Bartolomeo Vanzetti were executed. They believed the immigrants were victims of prejudice. In this photo, the two men are shown handcuffed together as they await their fate. **Citizenship** *How did the Sacco and Vanzetti case fuel anti-immigrant feeling?*

Middle-class Americans worried that communists and anarchists would invade the United States.

Congress responded by passing the Emergency Quota Act in 1921. The act set up a quota system that allowed only a certain number of people from each country to enter the United States. "America must be kept American," said Calvin Coolidge.

The quota system favored immigrants from Northern Europe, especially Britain. In 1924, Congress passed new laws that further cut immigration, especially from Eastern Europe. In addition, Japanese were added to the list of Asians denied entry to the United States.

Immigrants From Latin America

Latin Americans and Canadians were not included in the quota system. In 1917, the Jones Act made Puerto Ricans American citizens. Poverty on the island led to a great migration to the United States. In 1910, only 1,500 Puerto Ricans lived in the mainland United States. By 1930, there were 53,000.

Farms and factories in the Southwest depended on workers from Mexico. By 1930, a million or more Mexicans had crossed the border. Most came to work in the vegetable fields, orchards, and factories of the Southwest. The pay was

low and the housing was poor. Still, the chance to earn more money was a very powerful lure. During the 1920s, more and more Mexicans began to settle in the large cities of the Midwest, too.

Solo in Chicago

Just before World War I, exciting news began filtering across the border into Mexico:

❝ In the early days . . . one heard only of the states of Texas and California. The few Mexicans that left Mexico went there and wrote back from there. After a while we heard of New Mexico and Arizona, but beyond that there was no more United States to us. I remember distinctly with what great surprise we received a letter in our pueblo from a Mexican who had gone to Pennsylvania. 'Oh, where can that be! That must be very, very far away.' **❞**

As news about jobs in the United States spread, young Mexican men made their way to El Paso or Laredo, Texas. There, they

Figure 12.9 Putting the story back in history.
Note: From *The American Nation* by J. W. Davidson and M. B. Stoff. © 1995 by Pearson Education, Inc., publishing as Pearson Prentice Hall. Used by permission.

(Herber, 1978). See Figure 12.10 for an example of the format and question types in a Reasoning Guide. Steps for using the Reasoning Guide are given next.

Steps in Using a Reasoning Guide

1. The teacher constructs a guide that draws focused attention to the key portions of a longer section (see Figure 12.11).

2. Students read the longer selection first before using the guide.

3. Students complete the Reasoning Guide, rereading the key portions of the text as necessary.

4. A class discussion in which students compare their answers and their reasons follows.

5. Students further discuss what they learned about their own thinking and about thinking in general; for example,
   a. In what way(s) can we discover what attitudes we and others hold other than by what we/they say? (By our/their actions)
   b. Is there really any value in trying to form generalizations without all the facts? (Life requires that we do, but any new piece of information may change all previous thoughts and conclusions)

Building Good Judgment to Accompany Increased *Agency*

Increased power, or *agency,* carries increased privilege and responsibility for making weighty decisions requiring good judgment. No one is born with good judgment. It is painstakingly acquired. An interesting format for promoting good judgment, or critical-evaluative thinking, in social studies was borrowed from experimental tests (Manzo & Manzo, 1990a) and further developed by ninth-grade teachers Susan Tarwater and the late Phyllis McConnel. McConnel and Tarwater used these formats in a team-taught core curriculum program combining social studies and English. The team approach permitted team members to relieve one another from classroom teaching duties to enable them to develop the necessary materials.

In the Critical Judgments Exercise, students first decide and then discuss their judgments of the relative *values* of certain pieces of information. The format can be used with general or background information or with items selected from a section of text that students read in class. Figure 12.11 presents examples of both general-information and text-based items.

▶ CONTENT AREA READING IN THE SUPPORT SUBJECT AREAS

Business, Physical Education, Vocational Technology, Art, Music, and Speech

The contemporary forces that have led to the information explosion in the core areas of the curriculum have profoundly influenced the support subjects as well. The evidence for this is readily apparent in even a casual inspection of any support area syllabus. In music, students now study jazz, rock, and hip-hop as well as choral,

Directions: Reread the sentences below taken from John F. Kennedy's inaugural address, which you just read in its entirety in your textbook. Then complete the exercises called for below.

A. The world is very different now.

B. For man holds in his mortal hands the power to abolish all forms of human poverty and all forms of human life.

C. . . . (T)he rights of man come not from the generosity of the state but from the hand of God.

D. United there is little we cannot do in a host of cooperative ventures.

E. To those people in huts . . . we pledge our best efforts . . . not because the communists are doing it, . . . but because it is right.

F. We dare not tempt them with weakness.

G. So let us begin anew, remembering on both sides that civility is not a sign of weakness . . .

H. Let both sides explore what problems unite us instead of belaboring those problems which divide us.

I. And so, my fellow Americans, ask not what your country can do for you, ask what you can do for your country.

Directions: Now consider each of the statements below, and decide based on the statements above whether JFK would have approved or disapproved of each. In column A, answer yes or no. In column B, write the letter indicating the quotation from JFK that influenced your decision. For number 10, write an original statement that you think JFK might have made. Quote some part of the address (in your text) other than the quotations listed above as evidence.

A   B

____ ____   1. The problems we are facing today are not much different than those that faced our forefathers.

____ ____   2. The oriental world is immensely different from our own.

____ ____   3. Our rights are given to us out of the goodness of humans' love for humankind.

____ ____   4. If we are to win over the threat of world communism, we must give money, supplies, and help to underdeveloped nations of the world.

____ ____   5. Let us demonstrate our goodwill to the world by disarming.

____ ____   6. Only the federal government can solve the complex problems of our society.

____ ____   7. We will never resort to violence.

____ ____   8. The events of the past have helped us to realize the truth of Washington's policy of isolationism. We should continue to heed the advice of our president.

____ ____   9. The greatest threat to humankind is not famine and sickness but the threat of world communism.

____ ____ 10. _____
                _____
                _____

Figure 12.10   Sample Reasoning Guide for social studies.

PART 1: GENERAL INFORMATION ITEMS

Directions: Using your best judgment, decide what you think would be the value to society in knowing each of the statements listed below. Consider each statement to be true. We shall discuss these momentarily.

$$
\begin{aligned}
1 &= \text{of no use} \\
2 &= \text{of little use} \\
3 &= \text{of moderate use} \\
4 &= \text{very useful} \\
5 &= \text{extremely useful}
\end{aligned}
$$

_____ 1. Mary Queen of Scots inherited the throne at the age of six days.

_____ 2. Simplicity and elegance in writing are more desirable than length or vocabulary.

_____ 3. The first European to sail into New York Harbor was Henry Hudson.

_____ 4. The tomato is not a vegetable but a fruit.

_____ 5. Left-handedness is a recessive genetic trait.

_____ 6. Mary Goddard was the only woman to have her name on the Declaration of Independence.

_____ 7. Diamond dust is black.

_____ 8. Red meats are high in fat content.

PART 2: TEXT-BASED ITEMS

Directions: Indicate your judgment of the relative values of the statements below taken from your text. Use the five-point scale—1 = lowest, 5 = highest value—that we have used previously.

A. _____ 1. The Nobel Prize is given at least once every five years.

_____ 2. The Nobel Prize is awarded for important discoveries or inventions in the five categories of knowledge.

_____ 3. No Nobel Prizes were given in 1940–1942.

_____ 4. The Noble Prize was founded by Alfred Nobel, a Swedish chemist and philanthropist.

_____ 5. Women as well as men have been awarded the Nobel Prize.

B. _____ 1. Oliver Cromwell was called "The Protector."

_____ 2. Cromwell was born in 1599.

_____ 3. Cromwell was a violent and persuasive speaker.

_____ 4. Cromwell expanded England's territories and increased her commerce.

_____ 5. Cromwell's court was frugal but dignified.

Figure 12.11 Critical Judgments Exercise.

orchestral, and symphonic works. Physical education now encompasses physiology and less popular sports such as badminton and soccer. In industrial arts, particularly automotive technology, there now is a strong emphasis on electronics. Family and Consumer Science (home economics) now addresses complex issues in nutrition, parenting, and diverse family relationships. Business education, which formerly meant typing and shorthand, now means word processing, inventory control, networking, purchasing and self-initiated appraisal of what may need to be done. In short, the traditional separation between academic subjects and what once were known as "minor" area subjects has all but vanished. These support areas involve complex technologies and require considerable and ongoing reading, research, and critical analysis. In some very real sense, the support area subjects are our best hope for a curriculum that is both authentic, in the sense of real, and interdisciplinary. Nonetheless, these subject domains are in jeopardy due to underfunding, and they should be appreciated and mainstreamed into the new emphases on academics.

Today's teachers of these subjects rarely need to be convinced that their subjects contain a heavy academic component. Thus, the support area teacher now has a heavy investment in, and commitment to, nourishing reading, writing, studying, language, and thinking strategies.

▶ PHYSICAL EDUCATION

"Reading is sport," wrote Gentile (1980). "It requires mastering the fundamental skills, sufficient practice, a well-balanced diet of literary experiences, and a lifetime of development" (p. 4). The artificial separation of physical and academic education that exists in most schools is unfortunate, unnecessary, and uncaring. Plato placed gymnastics at the highest level for training his philosophers.

The Physical Domain: Linking Physical and Academic Development

The relationship between physical and academic development is more than coincidental. As we noted in earlier chapters, all learning enters through and takes place in the body as well as in the mind. The linking of motor involvement with language and academic learning can be a "natural" for the P.E. class, as illustrated in a recent news report, which went something like this:

> In the gymnasium at the Jackson Avenue Elementary School of Mineola, New York, 8-year-olds ran through the pathways of a human circulatory system drawn on the parquet floor.
>
> Pretending they were blood cells, they grabbed oxygen molecules (bean bags) from a bucket, raced through the heart chambers (red and blue Hula-Hoops) and completed the circuit by exchanging the oxygen for carbon dioxide (crumpled waste paper). Their warm-up finished, the panting pupils checked their pulse rates.
>
> Watching them, Kathleen Kern, the school's physical education teacher, said, "You can't teach kids about aerobic fitness until they understand the circulatory system."

In the same vein, Gentile (1980) suggests an interesting "metacognitive" activity involving reading, appreciation of the physical domain, and provocative discussion: In gym class, have students read and discuss statements, such as one from Michener's *Sports in America*, which says, in effect, "If I had a child determined to be a writer, I'd expect that child to take two courses: one in ceramics so that he or she could feel form emerging from inchoate clay and a second in eurhythmic dancing so that child could feel within his or her own body the capacity for movement, form, and dramatic shifts in perspective."

The highest goal of the reading curriculum, as noted several times previously, is not merely to teach youngsters to read but to promote language, thinking, and social-emotional maturity. Here, in slightly paraphrased form, are a few methods recommended by Maring and Ritson (1980), professors of reading and physical education, respectively, for fostering content area literacy in gym classes.

Method 1: Reading to Reinforce Instruction

Make up one-page handouts that summarize and reinforce the physical education content and skills that have just been taught via lecture-explanation, demonstration, or charts and diagrams. Type key terms in all-capital letters, and underline portions of the text that explain their meanings. On the bottom or back of each handout, include a set of questions that relate to the main ideas in the lesson. After students have read the handout, have them form small groups to answer the questions (see Figure 12.12).

Method 2: Read and Do

Prepare "Read and Do" instruction sheets so that students will learn required content and at the same time improve their ability to follow written directions (see Figure 12.13).

THE BASIC RULES OF BASKETBALL

Directions: Review the underlined information about the capitalized key terms below. Then answer the questions that follow.

Key Terms

1. Each team is composed of five MEMBERS who play the entire court area.
2. A team scores 2 points when the ball passes through the hoop during regular play (FIELD GOAL).
3. A team may score additional points by means of free throws when a member of the opposing team commits a PERSONAL FOUL (hacking, pushing, holding, etc.).

Questions

1. Where on the court do team members play?
2. Explain in your own words what a field goal is.
3. Name two kinds of personal fouls.

Figure 12.12   Reading to Reinforce Instruction.

Source: Figures (pp. 27–30) from Maring, Gerald H., & Ritson, Robert. (1980, October). Reading improvement in the gymnasium. *Journal of Reading,* 24(1), 27–31. Reprinted with permission of Gerald H. Maring and the International Reading Association. All rights reserved. © (1980) International Reading Association.

MOTOR DEVELOPMENT EXERCISE

Single-heel click: Jump into the air, click heels together once, and land with feet apart (any distance). This can be turned into an amusing exercise in which students try to write out totally unambiguous expository directions for their peers to follow. You might invite an English teacher to cooperate with you on this project.

Figure 12.13 Read and Do.

Source: Figures (pp. 27–30) from Maring, Gerald H., & Ritson, Robert. (1980, October). Reading improvement in the gymnasium. *Journal of Reading,* 24(1), 27–31. Reprinted with permission of Gerald H. Maring and the International Reading Association. All rights reserved. © (1980) International Reading Association.

Method 3: Book Checkout
In the locker room or near your office, place a revolving bookrack displaying high-interest paperbacks with checkout cards pasted inside the back covers that relate to aspects of your physical education curriculum. Consult the school librarian and reading specialist for assistance in book selection. Have the class or team elect a librarian to be responsible for the lending and returning of the books.

Method 4: "Testlets"
Evaluate students' performance skills and knowledge by giving short tests that require students to read and follow directions (see Figure 12.14). Each test can be presented on an individual card. Students should be familiar with this format before being tested.

Method 5: Student Reports
Have students read and write a brief (half-page) report on any person making news in sports. Invite different students to give these reports in the opening five minutes of class. Tack up the best reports on a cork display board (Gentile, 1980).

▶ VOCATIONAL ACADEMIC LANGUAGE & ORIENTATION
Problems and Goals

Federal Public Law 98-524, also known as the Carl D. Perkins Vocational Act of 1984, has as one of its main purposes the goal of improving the academic foundations of vocational technology students. Simply put, the objective is to create a work force able to adjust to the "changing content of jobs." This act contains provisions to support schools willing to develop quality programming in reading, computing, and vocational areas.

The justification for such programming is well supported by several studies that have shown that the average workday for nonprofessional workers requires between 24 minutes and 4 hours of reading per day (Rush, Moe, & Storlie, 1986). Related research indicates that workers themselves underestimated by an average of 45% the amount of time they spent reading (Mikulecky, 1982). Furthermore, job-related reading is by no means easy. The materials essential to job compe-

---

Grapevine Test

Stand with heels together. Bend trunk forward, extend both arms down between legs and behind ankles, and hold fingers of hands together in front of ankles. Hold this position for five seconds. Failure: (a) to lose balance; (b) to not hold fingers of both hands together; (c) to not hold the position for five seconds.

Three-Dip Test

Take a front leaning-rest position. Bend arms, touching chest to the floor, and push body up again until forearms are in a straight line with upper arms. Execute three performances in succession. Do not touch the floor with legs or with abdomen. Failure: (a) to not push body up three times; (b) to not touch chest to floor; (c) to touch the floor with any part of the body other than hands, feet, and chest.

Full-Left-Turn Test

Stand with feel together. Jump upward, making a full turn to the left. Land at approximately the same place from where the test was started. (Feet may be separated when landing.) Do not lose your balance or move feet after they have touched the floor. Failure: (a) to not make a full turn to the left, (b) to move feet after they have returned to the floor; (c) to lose your balance.

Figure 12.14   Testlets.

Source: Figures (pp. 27–30) from Maring, Gerald H., & Ritson, Robert. (1980, October). Reading improvement in the gymnasium. *Journal of Reading,* 24(1), 27–31. Reprinted with permission of Gerald H. Maring and the International Reading Association. All rights reserved. © (1980) International Reading Association.

tency in 11 fields, ranging from account clerk to welder, have readability levels that rarely dip as low as ninth grade and typically reach as high as the sixteenth grade level. Secretarial reading is the most difficult, ranging from sixteenth to college graduate levels (Diehl & Mikulecky, 1980).

Not surprisingly, one of the nagging problems of vocational technology has been the difficulty level of school texts and the information and schematics that come up on computer screens. While this situation is changing, there still are plentiful examples of "inconsiderate" text. Derby (1987) offers examples from one vocational technology textbook:

- *This chapter is devoted to a study of the various ways in which the basic engine theory and parts are utilized to produce multicylinder engines of several types.* This, Derby explains, is an awkward way of saying, *This chapter is about the different kinds of engines that are used in today's cars.*

- In a second example, the same textbook states, *Although a number of three-rotor and four-rotor experimental engines have been built, common usage at this time employs either a one-rotor or a two-rotor engine.* A more "considerate text" version would read, *Although a number of experimental engines have been built with three or even four rotors, most engines being built today have just one or two rotors.*

Here are some services and functions vocational technology teachers can offer to help promote literacy in this domain.

Six Services Vocational Technology Teachers Can Provide

1. Work with students to use, and where necessary create, text aids such as Advance Organizers, pivotal questions, glossaries of terms, and concept maps.

2. Follow the simple steps of the Listen-Read-Discuss Method so that students will be better empowered for reading dense and often inconsiderate text.

3. Using the Informal Textbook Inventory, give students practice and instruction in using basic texts and reference books. For students of electricity, teach the use of the National Electrical Code; for health assistants, demonstrate the Physician's Desk Reference on diseases; and for automotive students, develop familiarity with the Chilton Repair Manual and other motor company services manuals.

4. Use the Question-Only procedure as a prereading and prelecture method: Instead of merely announcing a topic, show the class a vital engine part and have them conduct a systematic inquiry into its nature, functions, and most frequent failure points.

5. Vocational technology subjects offer abundant opportunities to use the Typical to Technical Vocabulary Approach, as discussed earlier in Chapter 7 (Welker, 1987). This strategy also can be used to concurrently improve abstract thinking. Here are some examples of automotive terms, suggested by Piercy (1976), for which students might have culled meanings from everyday life:
   - *Differential*—a set of gears that permit rear wheels to revolve at different speeds
   - *Differential*—peculiarity; distinction; feature; earmark
   - *Governor*—a device for automatically controlling the speed of an engine by regulating the intake of fuel
   - *Governor*—the elected head of any state in the United States
   - *Distributor*—a mechanical device for distributing electric current to the spark plugs of a gas engine
   - *Distributor*—a business firm that distributes goods to customers

6. Guiding a pre- and postreading analysis of diagrams and illustrations is a powerful way to promote strategic reading. This can be done in a survey fashion prior to reading and in a very careful way following silent reading. Where this procedure is followed routinely, students will be keyed into the supportive graphic material as they begin to read and anticipate further analysis following reading. This combination should increase the probability that students will use the illustrations, like the one in Figure 12.15, to grasp and clarify meanings when they read silently. It also should help them become better strategic readers for the time when they must read independently in school and on the job.

Text and Picture*

Current truck radiator installation design (left) requires flat front. Air resistance can be reduced by a streamlined design (right) where ducts bring sufficient cooling air to the radiator.

*Through design improvement, over-the-road trucks can function with radiator openings one-third as large as those used currently. Seating of ducts is necessary so that all cooling air is directed to the radiator. Applications of such truck designs have existed in the aircraft industry for many decades. Automotive engineers should examine aeronautical engineering practices in their quest for aerodynamic efficiency.

Figure 12.15   Using illustration to grasp and clarify meaning.

Source: Figure (p. 43) from Rush, R. Timothy, Moe, Alden J., & Storlie, Rebecca L. (1986). *Occupational Literacy Education.* Newark, DE: International Reading Association. Reprinted with permission of R. Timothy Rush and the International Reading Association. All rights reserved. © International Reading Association.

Career-Oriented Literature

Apart from textbooks and manuals, the vocational technology teacher needs a ready and readable supply of career-oriented literature (COL). Career-oriented literature refers to articles and stories about jobs and career areas. It tends to reflect how real people feel about their jobs and vocations.

COL materials tend to touch on matters that textbooks and manuals rarely address, such as apprenticeship programs and various employee benefit options. For publishers who offer other special, hard-to-find, human elements, see Figure 12.16.

Language Experiences

Most activities undertaken in career and vocational education can be performed better with student input. Language Experience Activities (LEAs) provide such opportunities. Here are a few LEA-type activities that are especially suitable for the vocational technology class.

1. *"Celebrity" Interview:* Have students interview working people as though the latter were celebrities. Ask concerned questions such as might be asked of celebrities: "How did you first get into this business?"; "Has this work been fulfilling for you?"; "Have you ever wished that you could have done something else?"; "Can you tell me an interesting or amusing expe-

The Globe Book Company has two books (*All in a Day's Work* and *It Happened on the Job*) containing true, brief anecdotal accounts of work situations which are unusual and sometime humorous.

Pitman Learning offers *Pacemaker Vocation Readers,* a set of ten high-interest, controlled-vocabulary books describing young trade-type people in challenging situations.

Scholastic Magazine has an Action Series that has a number of job-related storybooks like the *Plumber's Line, Rosina Torres, L.P.N., Demolition Man,* and *Paramedic Emergency.*

Vocational Biographies, Inc. offers *Project Earth* and *Project Explore,* describing jobs and careers in the context of scientific principles and actual vocational biographies highlighting real individuals.

Career World (formerly *Real World*) is a color newspaper, written in the vein of *USA Today.* It addresses the work-a-day world and contains actual reading-skill exercises (Derby, 1987).

Figure 12.16   Career-oriented Literature.

rience that you have had in this line of work?" Students could be instructed to watch television interview shows to get some ideas for "people questions." Discuss the questions they might ask before they ask them.

2. *Dialogue Journal:* As previously noted, have students keep a journal in which they write a sentence or two every other day regarding their career interests and experiences. Periodically, read and write a brief reaction to these: "Charlie, I didn't realize that your father is an electrician!"; "Mary, if you will see me after class, I can tell you where to get more information on summer jobs with the city."

3. *Vocabulary from the Workplace:* To help build respect and support for the vocational program throughout the school, have students interview friends and family about words and expressions that they use on the job but lay people would be unlikely to know. Ask English teachers, for example, to use the Vocabulary Self-Selection Strategy (Haggard, 1978) to include some of these words on English vocabulary lists. Vocabulary collections of this type can contribute to students' sense of accomplishment and make English teachers realize that many students who might not know what onomatopoeia means probably do know what a rocker-panel is (the name for the narrow shelf beneath all car doors). Terms such as these, which the English teacher probably doesn't know and which rarely can be found in most standard dictionaries, constitute a wider and richer language system than most academically oriented teachers have considered.

4. *Magazines:* Have students subscribe to a few quality news and trade magazines. These can be read in class or for homework. Assign groups to give well-organized reports on different articles.

5. *Computer Networks:* Browse the Internet for home-page sites that correspond to specific vocational technical interests.

▶ CULTURAL LITERACY: ART, MUSIC, AND SPEECH

Art, music, and speech teachers are important advocates and shapers of cultural literacy in the schools. Studies in art, music, and speech contribute to progress toward higher literacy in a variety of ways. Art and music raise students' level of cultural literacy; speech raises "phonemic awareness" (see Figure 12.17); and together they contribute to effective decoding and comprehension. Further, art, music, and speech offer a sheltering and enriching alternative to the sometimes harsh sounds and the challenges of life. As such, they enhance emotional well-being and simple joy in living. Art, music, and speech also tend to reflect diverse perspectives, dialects, and historical periods and therefore contribute to a broader and more multicultural outlook. They also provide pleasure and offer an outlet for more elevated expression. For these reasons, it is important to consider ways to gently weave together content area literacy and the art, music, and speech curricula, since each benefits the other.

The Challenging Academic Language of the Arts

Writing in art and music almost by nature tends to be an academic language that is esoteric and difficult to read. Sentences often contain complex syntax, unusual phrasings, assumptive references, sophisticated ideas, and names and words of foreign origin. It has been said that "One does not really read a music theory book . . . one grapples with it" (Duke, 1987). A typical passage even from a popular library book on music reads like this:

> In all of art's best periods, creative people were brought together, and thus we had Pericles' Athens, the Medici's Florence, Elizabeth's London, Goethe's (and later Liszt's) Weimar, Beethoven's (and later Brahms') Vienna, Emerson's Concord, Lowell's Boston and Monet's Paris. These were by no means smooth waters, but they were lively. (Bacon, 1963, p. 130)

One would need to be quite well informed in the areas of art, music, literature, and history and in the characteristics of several different cultures to take in the full significance of this almost casual observation by pianist and teacher Earnest Bacon.

Meeting the Challenge

The art, music, and speech teacher can help students meet and profit from the challenge of "inconsiderate text" in several ways. Some of these are specified next. Consider a suggestion to be applicable to all three subjects unless otherwise specified.

1. Use the Oral Reading Strategy to familiarize students with syntax, phrasing, proper breathing, enunciation, and pronunciations.

2. Ask frequent translation questions: "Can you say this in your own words?"

3. Add information as needed to enhance schema, or background knowledge: "Have you read or heard about the Medici family in world history class yet? They were a wealthy and influential Italian family in medieval Florence—a thriving seaport city in Italy. They were great patrons of the arts."

4. Use the Listen-Read-Discuss Method and Note Cue to guide reading and discussion in art, music, and effective speaking.

5. Have students use the Subjective Approach to Vocabulary with illustrations: Divide a page into quarters, and have students write the new word in quadrant I, write its dictionary meaning in II, draw a pictorial representation in III, and write out the subjective association in IV. Then the class discusses these and stores them in their notebooks.

6. The ambitious speech/theater teacher or speech pathologist can incidentally help youngsters to become better decoders of words by raising their phonemic awareness, or sense of the speech sounds represented in print. In fact, there is an approach to reading by the Lindamoods (1975) that is based on such training. The program, now called LIPS, originally used largely with adults, teaches students to feel and label various speech sounds, which are the basis for phonics in reading. The terms used for the speech sounds are descriptive, rather than the technical terms used in linguistics (e.g., fricatives, continuents, etc.). See Figure 12.17 for sample descriptive speech sounds that increase phonemic awareness. For more precise information on this technique, see Manzo, Manzo, and Albee (2004).

7. Work with science, literature, and social studies teachers to have students produce various forms of artistic representations of significant ideas.

8. Work with the school principal to use music in appropriate settings. Music has been shown to facilitate creative writing, mathematics, spelling, and art (Greenhoe, 1972; Maor, 1979; Taylor, 1980). While music sometimes can be distracting during reading, classical music has been found to be conducive to comprehension gains (Mullikin & Henk, 1985). The classical music played in the latter study was Pietro Mascagni's *Cavalleria Rusticana* "Intermeggio." A no-music condition produced better performance

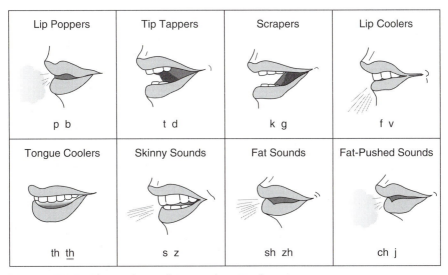

Figure 12.17 The Lindamood Approach to Reading.

Source: From *The A.D.D. Program, Auditory Discrimination in Depth* (Books 1 & 2) by C. H. Lindamood and P. C. Lindamood, 1975. Austin, TX: Pro-Ed. Reprinted with permission.

than did rock music, which is to say that rock is disruptive. Apparently, something soft, slow, and with methodical cadence is necessary to foster reading and thinking. The second author found this to be true while using taped music during "sustained silent reading" time with urban junior high school reading classes. Music was played during the first 10 minutes of class, during which time students who were caught up with class work had the privilege of reading anything of their choosing. I began the year with a few classical and "easy-listening" instrumental selections that I used for free reading time. Not knowing about Mullikin and Henk's finding, I succumbed several times to students' pleas to use rock music instead. It never worked: With a rock music background, students were more distracted than they would have been otherwise. When I eliminated rock music, however, they appreciated the more traditional melodic pieces enough to hush one another rather than lose the privilege.

9. Outstanding television shows are dramatized with music. Work with the English teacher to have students think through and try to score selections of literature with appropriate musical pieces and/or poignant oral readings. This takes a good deal of thinking and analysis. If you feel daring, ask students to select or compose theme tunes for the school and/or individual teachers.

▶ BE CREATIVE AND ENCOURAGE CREATIVITY

The last suggestion, to invite students to be creative, seems a good note on which to tie up this chapter. We urge you to use content area literacy to encourage creative thinking and problem solving *and* to be encouraged to be creative in your own thinking and teaching. Again, the three main ingredients encouraging creativity are to

1. Connect your students and yourself to creative thinkers whenever and wherever you can. Again, you might look up the Web page of the Foundation for Better Ideas and the Global Idea Bank on the Internet. It is one way to provide exposure to creative questions, creative answers, and even monetary and social incentives for creative production in a variety of disciplines and across disciplines.

2. Teach students to formulate appropriate guiding questions, or purposes, for which to read and listen, and list these on your actual and/or virtual classroom bulletin boards. A good question is half-way to an inventive answer.

3. Request and expect creative production from your students, and they will not disappoint you.

▶ AFTER WORDS

This chapter was intended to provide you with further possible in-depth knowledge of content literacy applications in individual areas of specialization. It also provided an overview of the specific values and problems of the other disciplines. Logically, now, you may wish to know a bit more about how to attend to students, as well as subjects, with specific or special needs in these same situations. The next chapter should equip you to better understand and provide for such needs.

CHAPTER 13

CONTENT AREA LITERACY SUPPORT FOR ENGLISH LANGUAGE LEARNERS, LEARNING DISABLED, AND OTHER STUDENTS WITH SPECIAL NEEDS

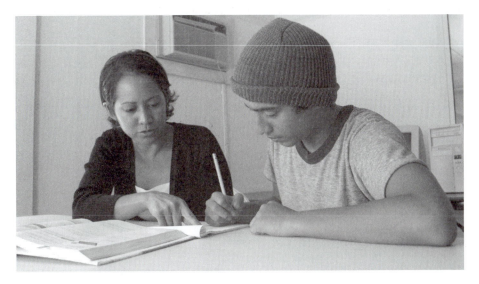

A helping word to one in trouble is often like a switch on a railroad track—
an inch between wreck and smooth-rolling prosperity.

—Henry Ward Beecher

▶ FORE WORDS

This chapter opens with a definition of special needs and then moves on to suggest two guiding principles. Since many of the problems addressed are social and values laden, the chapter necessarily had to address some rather weighty economic and philosophical issues and concerns. Discussion includes some concerns that touch several areas of special needs, including the sometimes radical throes of "normal" adolescent development, the gap in achievement test scores traditionally found among different racial and ethnic groups, gender issues, and particularly confusion about the sometimes competing sheltered and compensatory systems necessary to support youngsters who have to learn a new language while having to learn in a new language. The chapter urges that we reclaim some modest solutions, such as special remedial/corrective classes, that have lost favor in recent times, but perhaps for the wrong reasons. The chapter further details specific teaching methodologies ranging from means to improve basic word analysis (phonics) to techniques for enhancing exceptionally weak comprehension, thinking, writing, and classroom discussion. On a positive note, almost every teaching principle and practice covered in the preceding pages applies to the special needs focus of this chapter. In fact, content area literacy almost defines the ways and means of addressing diverse needs in a heterogeneous classroom.

- ▶ FORE WORDS
- ▶ SPECIAL NEEDS STUDENTS DEFINED
- ▶ KIDS ON THE CUSP: MOTIVATING THE UNMOTIVATED
- ▶ IMPROVEMENT OF BASIC DECODING AND WORD LEARNING
- ▶ OTHER INCLUSION METHODS
- ▶ LIMITED ENGLISH PROFICIENCY, ENGLISH LANGUAGE LEARNERS, AND CULTURAL DIFFERENCES
- ▶ AFTER WORDS

▶ SPECIAL NEEDS STUDENTS DEFINED

The term *special needs* is used here to refer to youngsters who are at risk of underachieving for a variety of reasons that are not typically provided for in a regular classroom setting. The chief approaches are a combination of *sheltered* and *compensatory education.* These approaches essentially are compatible and often identical to content area literacy methods and materials for helping students with special needs to make up, or compensate, for some developmental lag, deficit, or cultural-linguistic differences that may be putting them at increased risk to underachieve. Other reasons for special need might include limited English proficiency (LEP)—which includes English language learners (ELLs)—and those from sharply different dialect backgrounds, those who have been diagnosed with serious reading and learning disabilities, and those who simply lack the levels of academic motivation deemed necessary for successful progress in school. There are some underlying philosophical issues that deserve a word in order to fully justify and ensure the continued support of programs for those with special needs.

Philosophical Guidelines for Serving and Strategically Providing for Special Needs

President Franklin D. Roosevelt (1940), at the urging of first lady Eleanor Roosevelt, set the stage for shared concern for each individual in each new generation when he said, "We cannot always build the future for our youth, but we can build our youth for the future." In this statement he reminds us that all efforts to help youngsters must also be designed to make them stronger, more independent, and able to help themselves, as well as those who will follow them. In other words, there are no entitlements without corresponding responsibilities, and no certainty of continued support for programs and goals into the future without some shared values and understanding of the justification of additional costs. This is the job of *public education.* The extra costs in financial and human capital for those with special needs are best justified when those to whom they are granted are asked, in turn, to commit themselves to becoming givers as well as takers.

As long as resources are limited, there will be competition for them. Political conflict, and therefore diminished will to help one another, often follows from not making it clear to all who are asked to give that those with special needs (which, is most all of us at some time) understand that there is no such thing as a free lunch. Someone is paying for everything granted, and/or there likely is some other societal value not being adequately funded. Teachers, for example, cannot deliver special attention without great personal cost and considerably less attention to other students, who must be taught in larger classes, often with inadequate books and technologies or by teachers whose capacities are so stretched that they turn to other careers. Potential recipients probably need to be taught first to understand that they must be cooperating partners. "What will you do to help yourself?" and "How will you give back?" needs to be stated explicitly along with every statement and effort about "How can we help an individual or a group?"

Further, not everything that is unequal is the result of some intentional bias or inequity. It probably is no longer enough simply to argue that there are differences in achievement or opportunity. Strategically speaking, education, and especially special (additional cost) education, is likely to be more adequately funded as it shows its will and capacity to result in a greater good. National policies have stiffened, and there is now a common belief that we must reduce social welfare to a period of time rather than as long as need can be strung out. There also is a corresponding appreciation of the need to minimize corporate welfare, or the government's bailing out of failing businesses that should be allowed to fail and be replaced by more efficient ones under the principles of a free market economy. Of course, individuals and families who are unable to help themselves constitute a separate consideration. But, in the minds of many citizens, special considerations should be limited to the developmentally or physically disabled and those who clearly are too poor to participate in American society. Most everyone, however, has hidden thoughts of having a child with such needs and/or lapsing into such needs themselves with age or accidental disability. This tends to keep us all fairly humble and empathetic. With this as a backdrop, let's now consider a more universal period of critical need that any individual or family might experience during the tumultuous stage of adolescence. This common experience has created a universal sense of our fragile nature. It is not developed here merely to play on our emotions but because to grasp the challenges and risks inherent in this stage of development is real, humanizing, and relatively common across cultures, even where many surface features may otherwise appear distinctive.

All Adolescents Have Special Needs

The cry for support and special concern during adolescence essentially is based on the rapid shift in this stage from a life dominated by adults, who, by the definition of parenthood, protect and deflect pain, to a life less protected and more greatly influenced by other youth, who we quickly realize can be almost mindlessly unaware of the consequences of their actions. The realization of the power to act against the grain of childhood prohibitions at first feels liberating, but it also is frightening as youngsters see and experience how some of their peers deal with their new freedoms. It is at this time that adolescents begin to sense that a society can lapse into chaos and danger when external regulation begins to be replaced by immature, inexperienced internal self-regulation. This realization probably is one of the more fundamental reasons for heightened anxiety and angst in adolescents; they may appear protected in their own rooms and with their own televisions, but in truth they reside in a much less secure and much more fickle and peer punitive environment than do adults. Adolescence is characterized by an almost ceaseless and conflicted desire and effort simultaneously to be free from regulation and a wariness about what and how to replace it with some system of rules and regulations that provide a basic sense of security and safety. The school and its rules provide one set of stabilizing parameters, even though there is a certain ceremonious complaining about its rules and those of parents.

There is another *source* of support and value that every subject teacher can provide that is seldom appreciated for its longer term and more self-regulating place in adolescent development. It is the stability, culture, and connection to the past, and a heads-up introduction to the future that is implicit in the study of any subject area. The content teacher's world is orderly and, despite some groans to the contrary, interesting; why else would clusters of people across time have become interested and engaged by the discipline? But let's return for a moment to the nature of adolescent development to provide a sounder basis for this unusual point.

Kids on the Cusp: Special Concerns and Needs of All Adolescents

Generally speaking, it could be argued that the tumultuous nature of adolescence is largely due to its newness, not its inherent intensity. Much of adult life is a stream of trials and tests. This makes adolescence the beginning of what Nietzsche called "existential angst." With maturity we seem to learn better how to cope with life's throes, although a great deal of coping is blue smoke and mirrors; that is, appearances. This may be one of the reasons that dating back over many generations early maturing boys have been considered more positively and as having greater leadership ability (Jones & Bailey, 1950). Similarly, late maturing girls are more likely to suffer from anxiety about their physical development, social status, and, hence, ability to cope (Weatherly, 1964). It is an understatement to say that adolescents are very aware of how their physical development compares to their peers. In fact, adults who have been definitively early or late in their personal development are likely to attribute much of the rest of their social-emotional development and drive—or lack thereof—to this relatively slight period in time, which thereafter may be unrecognizable in adulthood.

The rapid changes that take place in physical characteristics during adolescence command a good deal of social attention, comment and shifts in the nature of interactions with and from most everyone encountered. The changes create a kind of unexpected celebrity; and most people don't deal well with celebrity. Not surprisingly, adolescents and celebrities deal with this intense attention in much the same ways: alternately overvaluing themselves above all others; withdrawal into comfortable cliques; periods of intense identity confusion; and so on. Above all else there is an almost exponential growth in self-consciousness. This leads to exaggerated comparisons with others in the age group, which should not be so surprising since the comparisons are anchored in rather vivid physical factors. For example, Gurian (1998) writes insightfully about the tensions in every male that arise from five to seven surging testosterone urges per day. In many ways, safe schools and eventual success in preparing youngsters to enter a competitive society are tied to our commitment to better understanding and managing the normal but challenging conflicts that arise from the collision of atavistic, or primordial, instincts to be active, aggressive, and sexually driven with the relatively passive, sedentary, and clerical nature of secondary schools. The underlying idea here resembles this book's theme of inverse teaching. It is to pay more attention to kids' needs on the *front end*, before trouble erupts. Our collective inability to address such periods probably explains the widespread diagnoses of clinical depression and social anxiety disorders and, with these, an exponential increase in students on potent psychopharmaceutical drugs.

For these reasons, it becomes essential to have plans in place to neutralize some of the considerable negatives that can haunt healthy personal-social adjustment in what otherwise might be a normal life phase. Literacy development can play an important role in healthy social-emotional development. Relatedly, however, educators will need to step up and explain that frustration, hostility, anger, insecurity, and resentment have long been, and will long be, the nature of common living. Pills can be a tragic deflection that artificially quench the desire to be a standout and to make a difference in the world. Drug company ads of confident restored selves give the false impression that with a pill or two a day, we can thrive cheerfully. The modern world clearly needs to address our generally high states of anxiety, despite our seeming affluence; but, in terms of net gain, pills may be keeping us from addressing some of the root causes, such as bureaucracies that drain rather than serve us and the ceaseless efforts to have us all function at peak performance at every moment. Teachers especially have been victims of this delusion. Again, ironically, it falls on us to bring relief if we are to win relief.

Literacy and Adolescent Development

The chief role of literacy in adolescent development is twofold: (1) It provides access to world literature with its many serious and humorous stories of coming of age; and (2) it provides diversion from self-absorption in related literature of adult trials and tribulations and moral dilemmas. It also connects developing adults with an array of human quests in the form of baseline knowledge of many areas of human study. Simply put, the content areas offer possible engagement not merely in what is known, but in the acquisition of new knowledge. Since all knowledge is connected in some way to all other aspects of knowledge and human experience, acquiring a taste for a certain subject or discipline adds a higher purpose to one's life and a lasting interest in reading and thinking about things of fundamental value to a host of others sharing and appreciating those same interests. It is like joining a club. This is no small benefit; in modern life it grants one membership in a tribe—an area of comfort and affiliation that seems fundamental to us, and especially to those who have begun to grow past the strictures, but also the comfort of guiding parents, with whom, by the quirks of genetics, we may share much or relatively little. Interest and inquiry in a subject can be life enriching both socially and in terms of cognitive development. It can, in fact, be as meaningful as shared interest in a sport, hobby, or church.

Subject Area Club Perks

At a practical level, these fundamental cognitive and social-emotional needs provide the opening for the teacher to invite each student into their subject area club, with perks such as signature occupations, language, and rituals. In adolescent development terms, engaging a new interest and area of continued reading and learning is equal to helping youngsters feel more capable, significant, powerful, and worthy, and to having a certain sense of group identity and purpose. This all equals higher levels of grounded self-esteem; that is, esteem based on real knowledge and a connection to, and affiliation with, some valued skills and, again, a larger sense of purpose. Good subject teaching and, implicitly, the selling of a life interest in certain disciplines and ideas can be therapeutic and life enriching. But let's turn now to the problem referred to as the *achievement gap*.

Minority Student Gap: A Qualified Crisis

On June 22, 2003, the Supreme Court, in a historic reversal of itself, essentially agreed that admissions policies at the University of Michigan School of Law could take race into consideration in order to improve diversity in the admission of minority students. There seems to be a national consensus that colleges and universities should continue to assist in dismantling the present effects of this country's past system of previously legalized apartheid. The prevailing sentiment also is that this need for racial preferences should last no more than 25 years. However, the court did not establish an ending date, as such. So the need to fix this problem, in a manner of speaking, has been made more urgent than ever before; 25 years is not much in bureaucratic and national trend years. Further, in related actions, the courts have upheld a provision that allows the top graduates from every high school (4% in Texas) to attend a state's leading research/prestige universities. The benefit in this is slightly nullified by the fact that it may indirectly support de facto segregation, as minority parents may be reluctant to move to predominately white areas, where a child may not finish in the top percents at graduation. So there are no easy answers to righting this need. This puts a greater burden on fixing the problem of underachieving schools.

Before attempting to fix anything, it is best to determine what is broken and how seriously so. The problem that is commanding the most concern in American schools is the gap in standardized test scores among Caucasians and Asians, on one hand, and African Americans and Latinos, on the other. The differences are considerable and remained fairly constant over time despite many experimental programs and large-scale efforts to narrow these margins. In general, the black–white gap is about 12 percentile points in the early grades and grows to 18 percentile points in the upper grades. While we have suggested earlier in the text that there is no general crisis in education, this is a national crisis with implications for how society is, and likely will continue to be, segregated and stratified. It requires unrestricted dialogue and reevaluation of everyone's pat answers and especially of certain socially driven educational experiments that may be aggravating the problem. This is not to say that the things that have been tried to date are of no value. Each prior effort has taught us much about what to question and possibly eliminate as a solution. One thing that the experiments of the last thirty years seem to be saying clearly is that programs, consultants, and strategies should not be put to social litmus tests but determined by substantive changes indexed to relatively standardized instruments, and ideally other more enlightened inventories and surveys as well. The past may even be telling us to think more deeply about social issues and answers but not to overburden the educational system with these. "Mission creep"—taking on multiple social dilemmas along with school-based needs—can nullify even that which could have been achieved with a clearer mission focus. Several leading black educators, such as Thaddeus Lott speaking to the Kansas City, Missouri school board, are saying things like, "[Educators] are hooked onto the latest classroom fad at the expense of methods already proven successful. They may even avoid things that they are opposed to philosophically even though they work" (White, 1998). The problems here are massive and complicated. One problem, however, is clear: Efforts to end segregation are not the same as making provisions for quality education. Let us see now what seems to work, philosophically and practically. After nearly thirty years of backsliding, it appears that board members, school administrators, community groups, and courts may finally be ready to address seriously this core school issue. Under affirmative action guidelines, individuals in both underachieving groups are making remarkable strides in achievement, power, and influence and hence lighting the path for others. This is one of the basic reasons why the courts and most Americans continue to support this partial solution. But let's now consider other means of support.

What Fleas Can Tell Us

Try this: Put some fleas in a glass jar with a lid, and observe. At first the fleas will try eagerly to get out, jumping all around and up and down in the jar. After just a few minutes, however, they will no longer hit the lid. Now take the lid off. The fleas will still jump now and then, but they never will jump out of the jar.

The lesson in this is obvious but bears stating: The content area teacher must be especially careful about inadvertently creating a glass ceiling of literal-level expectations for students, particularly those whom one might presume to be "too slow" to learn. This can be communicated in very subtle ways. The popularity, for example, of the "Matthew Effect" (Stanovich, 1986) has given rise to the misimpression that underachievement of some is somehow tied to the higher achievement of others, an attitude derived from a decontextualized biblical reference to the rich getting richer at the expense of the poor. This is not so where learning is concerned. Knowledge shared is not diminished nor taken at anyone's expense. For this and other reasons, it is just as important to "teach up" for remedial-level and struggling and English language learners as for those who are average and above. Several studies have definitively shown that teaching weaker students to read between and beyond the lines actually boosts their ability to read the lines, or at the literal level (Collins, 1991; Cooter & Flynt, 1986; Haggard, 1976). However, this is not the same thing as saying that those labeled slow are not slow, or that they can do anything if teachers would only challenge or teach them properly. Everyone does better when they are treated as if they are whole and unique rather than totally defined by a given deficiency or difference or, for that matter, even by a high proficiency, as in the cases of those who are academically gifted but may nonetheless have areas of specific need. Now prepare to tackle two related and intermingled messages that have come to be overstated and may need a modification of perspective, if we are to do what is best rather than what pleases us philosophically.

Two Overstated Perspectives: "Diversity Should Be Encouraged and Perpetuated," and "Remedial Reading Doesn't Work and Is Oppressive"

Two important aspects of schooling have taken an unfortunate turn where at-risk students are concerned. One is that cultural diversity and language differences must be perpetuated by being formally structured into the school curriculum, and the other is that remedial reading programs don't work and may even be oppressive. Our conclusions on both accounts are slightly different, less contentious, and we believe more workable.

Should Cultural and Language Differences Be Encouraged?

In the interests of open dialogue, let's now say what many people are thinking. Efforts to bring about greater tolerance of differences are always proper and reasonable. However, efforts to underscore, and hence exaggerate, cultural and language differences may be countereffective to the natural evolution of both and may be a something of disservice to individuals who may wish to be equipped to conduct most of life and business in a dominant culture and language different from their own. The dominant culture is ever evolving: It regularly shifts to be more like those who accumulate power to influence it; whereas excessive efforts to represent different cultures can perpetuate stereotypes that often have no life outside the representations presented in staged multicultural situations.

It is further notable that parents from America's diverse backgrounds overwhelmingly expect schools to prepare their children to speak, write, and acclimate to the mainstream as a means of becoming an influential part of it. The methods suggested throughout this text and in this chapter tend to have this as a predominant, though hardly exclusive, goal. Of equal importance, the methods described have the goal of empowering youngsters to influence culture and language by being highly competent and effective in telling their individual and collective stories. It is largely in this way that they can be expected to form the literary and intellectual bases from which to win empathy for their particular ways of thinking, speaking, behaving, and conducting business. This is the way diverse cultural and linguistic orientations traditionally have come to be considered legitimate entries into the competition for the conduct, curriculum, and character of the ever-evolving mainstream or dominant culture. Other means of fostering cultural equity may be more "fair" or philosophically preferable, but they are not proven. And, frankly, no means yet devised, short of creation of new, *hybrid cultures* (more on this ahead), have been totally successful in integrating even people who are physically indistinguishable, as are the northern and southern Irish and the factions in Bosnia who have been warring for hundreds of years, much less folks who look and sound differently. Nonetheless, America takes pride in its multicultural differences and hence in efforts to be tolerant of one another, unlike some countries, who find solace in homogeneity, such as do Japan and Korea. The arguments for diversity are many and layered. At an analogous level, many of the most important grasses, such as barley and emmer wheat, that support the globe's growing population are the byproducts of the rich diversity of grasses found only in the Fertile Crescent (largely current-day Iraq and Iran) and transplanted throughout the rest of the planet (Diamond, 1999). Nonetheless, it does not seem wise to press or dwell on differences; while intellectual enlightenment often runs ahead of baser instincts, it cannot seem to outrun it. So our approaches, detailed ahead, are pragmatic and blended from what have become competing camps. For example, we believe that youngsters who are learning a new language should be granted some special instruction and books in their heritage language during this long period of transition. But, first, let us address a more common issue.

Should Remedial Reading Continue in a State of Neglect?

The evidence is overwhelming that most remedial reading programs work well, although you might never know this by the criticisms and faint praise leveled at them even by certified literacy experts (Johnston & Allington, 1991). Remedial reading programs are proven to help many youngsters achieve at approximately twice the average rate in reading per semester and four times the prior pace of these same students (Klenck & Kibby, 2000; Manzo & Manzo, 1993; Spache, 1976). The fundamental reason that this goes unnoticed is because there have been a nearly irreducible number of students who do not make progress even with remedial assistance. Ironically, this number would be even smaller if remedial and early prevention programs and efforts were more fully supported rather than reduced and maligned, which has been the case now for over twenty years.

The disrepute into which remedial reading has fallen is part of a complex set of dynamics that have little bearing on the real efficacy of such programs. There appears to be a collection of at least three forces working against the potential values in remedial reading. Understandably, middle-class parents wanted a way to get help for their underachieving children without social stigma. In response, they seem to have created *learning disabilities (LD)*, a condition that clearly has some basis in reality though no educationally sound definition. In any case, some 80% of LD problems seem to be reading related (Alley & Deshler, 1980; Klenck & Kibby, 2000). These facts aside, legislative bodies have designated LD as a physically handicapping condition that otherwise is not the result of a socioeconomic deficit, cultural difference, or any apparent emotional problem. This entitled students with learning disabilities to receive special and personalized help in a least restrictive environment (i.e., in a socially acceptable fashion), with services and accommodations to continue through college. Accordingly, students so designated receive a great deal more in support than remedial readers ever did, including the right to have tests read to them and other such personalized assistance. This gain for students with learning disabilities has been at great cost to taxpayers and has overburdened states, teachers, and the entire federal system, which only funds about 17% of a need that the Congress, in effect, has itself created. These considerations are not unjustified, but in a world of limited resources, they have resulted in the loss of support for remedial reading programs and other such programs assisting the disenfranchised, which previously served a much larger population of those in need. Many colleges are now beginning to "jettison all remedial courses" (Cronholm, 1999) simply because they are bankrupting an already strained system. On a positive note, the means and methods for actually achieving such goals are well defined by the subdiscipline of this text, content area literacy (CAL). We have seen very few instances of methods or materials supporting LD and other in-class needs that did not emerge from this CAL movement. The methods presented in the prior chapters, along with those presented here, should be all that a content teacher should need to meet most expectations.

A second trend that has weakened belief and support for remedial reading, ironically, has been the overgeneralization of an argument in favor of content area literacy. The argument was that content teachers should provide a certain measure of help (i.e., instructional scaffolding) to all youngsters, especially those with special needs, and in a regular classroom setting. By a twist of fate, this regular class accommodation of readers came to replace remedial reading because the reading specialists who taught the remedial sections felt overburdened by the responsibility both to guide the school's content area literacy program and to teach the separate remedial groups. Of course, the logical thing to have done was to hire more reading specialists, but the funds went to create and hire more LD specialists, so that now there are very few literacy specialists in schools at any level.

Finally, important social activists, such as Paulo Freire (1985, 1987) and Ira Shor (Shor & Freire, 1987), have had their messages of *liberation education* convoluted to mean that remedial reading is oppressive. They have argued, as have most enlightened educators, that school should empower individuals to compete in society where the playing field often is not level. However, these social activists noticed that schooling, largely in developing nations, seemed to be designed to educate individuals only sufficiently to have them function as cogs in someone else's machine, but not to aspire to be, or to run, their own economic engines. This message became erroneously attached to remedial and corrective reading programs in the United States, which, due to the high percentage of enrollment of African American students, became viewed as another symbol of oppression. This connection was intensified by the concerns expressed about this by some well-meaning American educators and humanists, many of whom were "whole-language" enthusiasts who do not believe in heavy doses of direct instruction in any form. They further felt that underachievement was almost exclusively the result of social policies, lowered expectations, and poor self-esteem. Hence, they inadvertently sought social action solutions, often at the expense of relatively proven educational solutions, which in truth do take a generation or so to have significant impact.

In any case, as previously noted, even the most old-fashioned remedial/corrective reading programs tend to work well, with many youngsters achieving at two to four times their prior average rate per unit of time. However, we also must avoid becoming delusional in the sense of visualizing "remedial students in a kind of seamless progression, moving through their remedial classes, into college-level work, on to graduation, and then profitable postgraduate careers." (Cronholm, 1999, p. B6). Some forms of reading and learning disabilities clearly are anchored in lesser capacities for academic study and will not be easily or permanently fixed for each individual, but rather for one individual at a time. This suggests that remedial/corrective reading programs are sensible and necessary because content area teachers cannot reasonably provide explicit and intensive instruction to youngsters who are several grade levels below expected norms and hence unable to learn independently from most print sources. Ironically and sadly, efforts to make classroom teachers responsible for such dramatic differences in instructional need, without remedial/corrective reading support, may well have been the impetus behind so many teachers surrendering this career path and for causing some of them to further lower their expectations for many students and to pass and graduate youngsters who hardly read at all.

One way in which this is subtly communicated is by the number of mind-numbing ways that we try to avoid academic competition and to treat everyone as if they are so fragile that they will break if we were to emotionally challenge them. This, again, is part of our shared sense that normal life demands are excessive and that teens need to be further sheltered, sometimes into their early thirties.

Reconsider the Pain of Competition, Especially for Boys

Traditionally, 80% of remedial readers have been boys and about 80% of their teachers have been women. This inversion of gender cultures may require some rethinking. Populous author Michael Gurian puts it this way:

> Boys need to compete...to feel tested in the physical and interpersonal world.... Understanding boy society and its love of competition and performance ultimately requires us to give less weight to our victim-based relationship philosophies. The victim-based relationship philosophy says, "I'm set up to be a victim, so let's train everyone else not to victimize me."...This I've-been-abused philosophy impedes our ability to raise sons. It forgets that each of us care for ourselves. Especially as I grow up, no one else is responsible for me. (Gurian, 1998, p. 32)

A discussion on the CNN Book Channel (Oct. 2, 1999) by women authors Roth and Stolba of their new book, *Women's Figures*, confirms that an end may be in sight for the overgrowth of the "victim syndrome." They argue convincingly that *Western women* are no longer victims. They show convincingly that the statistical differences in income with men is less then 6% when even the most superficial factors are taken to account, such as comparing men and women in the same profession or doing the same work. Other differences are explainable by free decisions women make to work less and spend more time on personal matters, such as raising children or simply living less harried lives. Further, in the United States, and for the first time in human history, there are more women enrolled in postsecondary education than men. Clearly there are unresolved women's issues, and particularly so in other nations; but, at this moment, in this place (the United States), progress has been credible and admirable: Women are among the leading figures not only as interviewers on 24/7 cable business channels but as those being interviewed. There is a lot to celebrate, and time once again to perhaps consider some of issues of our sons and brothers and mates, such as determining just what is that might be keeping men from continuing their educations in the proportions necessary for them to provide for themselves and their families. Consider now just a few of the methods that can be used by content teachers to help youngsters with special needs. Frankly, most of these require somewhat to considerably more energy, effort, and direct intervention than the methods and general population of students discussed in previous chapters. But with few remedial/corrective programs still operating, it necessarily falls on content teachers to do whatever they reasonably can to accommodate special needs youngsters in the regular classroom. However, it is necessary to say again that teachers need more help than they (we) are getting. Most teachers are at the limits of what they can do.

Teaching Methods for Special Needs Students

The methods presented next focus on the needs of students who are said to have reading/learning disabilities, those with limited English proficiency, those with personal-social adjustment problems, and/or those who are culturally different.

Fortunately, most of the methodology and ideas developed for special needs students are of benefit to most typical students as well. This is because people are more alike than they are different. And almost all students, at one time or another, are likely to need some of the same kind of extraordinary thought, concern, and assistance that tend to be reserved for the different, the reluctant, and the chronic underachieving. In fact, we are coming to believe that by collapsing competing programs and extending the franchise of "special" attention to all—where *all* is defined as case-based, diagnostic-prescriptive teaching with support for teachers from tactical assistance groups—could create economies of scales that are cost effective and quite literally *leave no child behind.* But this is a developing story.

Throughout we have tried to select methods that are conducive to both teacher and student discovery and learning. Many of the ideas and practices advocated also are valuable in promoting tolerance, a multicultural outlook, and, again, the sensible goal of diversity and tolerance of others in education and society.

We have not directly addressed the gifted as a category of special needs students in this chapter, because many further issues confounding the definition of *giftedness* are well beyond the scope of this text. Also, you probably already have noticed that many of the methods presented in previous chapters, especially those on writing and higher-order literacy (such as REAP), serve the gifted nicely.

▶ KIDS ON THE CUSP: MOTIVATING THE UNMOTIVATED

Earlier chapters (notably Chapters 3 & 4) defined and developed the role of *engagement* theory in motivation. This section adds a few more thoughts and devices for reaching the reluctant, and occasionally resentful, reader. It begins with ideas for encouraging reading, discusses means and methods for dealing with disruptive behavior in the classroom, and concludes with techniques for improving basic word attack, comprehension, personal-social adjustment problems, and content-based mainstreaming efforts.

Encouraging Reading

Here are several methods designed to encourage reading. If you were to turn this section into a checklist and commit yourself to doing half of what is suggested for one full year, you would greatly help weak readers and contribute to creating a school environment conducive to higher-literacy and content learning.

1. **Establish a Sustained Silent Reading (SSR) program.** Once or twice a week, have students read anything they choose that is content related. Increase the time from seven to twenty minutes over a few months. This lengthening period of SSR can become an effective management tool as well as a means of teaching students how to read in an increasingly sustained manner. To be sure that everyone has something to read and to allay students' sense that this is an idle-time activity, it is best to store SSR materials in class and periodically to invite individual students to discuss what they are reading. This classroom-based activity can be broadened to include the entire school. It is most conducive if teachers, administrators, and all other personnel read for the sustained period as well. In our experience, doing this on a schoolwide basis provided a surprisingly settling effect in a school that frankly was rather chaotic. The sound of silence and an image of everyone reading produced a sense of peace, order, and purpose.

2. **Interesting materials.** Keep interesting newspaper and magazine articles, and make them available in the classroom for students to read before or after class or during downtime.

3. **Have students fill out a reading interest inventory, indicating the types of books they enjoy reading.** Invite the school librarian to help you select an appropriate inventory and to develop a list of suggested book titles related to areas of interest.

4. **Book clubs.** Encourage students to join a book club and/or subscribe to magazines in areas of special interest. Concerned members of the business community often will pay for these, as will community members who contribute books and magazines.

5. **Become a reading motivator.** Almost everyone likes to be read to. Set aside a few minutes of classroom time to read a poem, newspaper, or magazine article, or portion of a cherished book to the class. This simple gesture has been a staple of veteran teachers for generations.

6. **Collaborations.** Let two or more students read the same book for a book report to the class. Encourage them to discuss the book with one another.

7. **Use technology to encourage reading.** The school can buy multimedia CD-ROM disks or borrow them from libraries and/or hook up to the Internet to encourage reading for pleasure and expanded knowledge. There are many sites that contain wonderful books and excerpts that are no longer under copyright protection.

8. **Bulletin boards.** Cut out and display the weekly book review section of the newspaper. Add color pictures and captions from ads and reviews. Invite students to manage this in-class site.

9. **Media support.** Ask students to see a movie or television program either before or after reading a book on which one or the other is based.

10. **Have student groups create a book or article of the week poster.** Display books and articles with the caption "Read All About It." Invite students to share their books or articles with the class, noting the titles, authors, and sources of critiques.

11. **Local writers.** Invite local authors or poets to class to discuss and read their works. Perhaps call it the *Living (as opposed to Dead) Poets Society*.

12. **Give students incentives to read.** Students who read three or more books during a quarter or a semester can be rewarded with a donated gift certificate from a bookstore, record store, clothing store, or food store.

13. **Conduct reading conferences with students.** Personalized discussion and interest in a student's reading can be deeply motivating.

14. **Teach students to use the closed caption option on television to work incidentally on their own reading effectiveness** (Koskinen, Wilson, Gambrell, & Jensema, 1987). Similarly encourage weak readers to listen to books on tape while they follow along; however, this may have a slightly negative effect with above-average readers (Cloer & Denton, 1995).

The next section offers insights into dealing with behavioral issues, social adjustment, and literacy problems. The thrust of each of these methods is to help teachers and students deal with the sometimes corrosive effects of daily teaching and learning situations more than the explosive ones—a need poignantly expressed by the playwright Chekhov's observation that "Any idiot can face a crisis. It is this day-to-day living that wears you down."

Personal-Social Adjustment through Story, Biblio-Support, and Dialogue Journals

Story

Stories are one of the world's oldest tools for imparting values, guideposts, and enrichment of analogical thinking, the means by which minds establish parallel structures and understand the new from the previously learned. The archetypes of hero stories are not stereotypes but animated representations of good and bad in concrete, digestible form. Archetypes exist in relation to one another, serving as a map or record of the inner life of a single human and a society (Gurian, 1998). We are all a bit more complex and vulnerable than we are inclined to reveal.

Biblio-Support

For students who are inclined to read, biblio-support (Manzo, Manzo, & Albee, 2004) can be an effective means of aiding with personal-social adjustment. Biblio-support is based on bibliotherapy, which essentially means healing through reading (Edwards & Simpson, 1986). Generally, it entails redirecting students' perceptions and attitudes in a healthy direction by getting the right reading material to the right student at the right time.

The sources of problems students encounter as they grow and mature are varied: cultural differences, family relationships, moving, divorce, peer pressure, physical handicaps, racial prejudice, death of loved ones, gender identification confusion, and many others. Biblio-support is merely a means of becoming more broadly informed on and dealing with these personal-social and identity formation dilemmas so that schooling does not suffer irreversibly. Several authorities are contributing to this rapidly growing aspect of using literature and content texts to meet some of the complex challenges of adolescent development (cf. Allen & Ingulsrud, 2003; Bean & Moni, 2003; DeBlase, 2003; Maloney, 2003; Simmons, 2003).

Whenever possible, the teacher or counselor who recommends a book to a student should invite the student to retell the story, highlighting incidents and feelings that are relevant to the central situation. Changes in behavior, feelings, and relationships should be looked at closely to permit reasonable identification and empathy with the textual characters (Heaton & Lewis, 1955). Most important, the reader should have an opportunity to form a conclusion about the consequences of certain behaviors or feelings to determine whether or not these behaviors or feelings improve the human condition, as well as one's self-centered concerns or personal situation.

Reading and discussion are most fruitful when they are built around two questions, one that most everyone can answer easily, "What have you read that reminds you of someone you know?" and another that few of us can answer easily, "What reminds you of yourself?"

Dialogue Journals and E-mail

Biblio-support can be greatly enhanced by the addition of a writing component. The easiest way to do this is to have students keep personal journals in which they write brief reactions—at least one sentence—to whatever they read. Be careful not to overdo this however; the majority of boys and girls really do not like to write, and certainly not continuously in pensive, reflective terms (Manzo, Manzo,

Barnhill, & Thomas, 2000). That which is written can be stored in a box in the classroom or in a word processor, where, with students' prior approval, the teacher may read through them and write back personal notes and thoughts. Of course, notes and dialogue need not be limited to textual material; they can be extended to anything a student wishes to write or to anything a teacher may be interested in communicating. The idea of dialogue journals (Staton, 1980) is as old as conversation between caring friends. Teachers who use this approach regularly report touching insights revealed and warm relationships formed with students who at first appeared apathetic, hostile, or otherwise reluctant to learn (Kirby & Liner, 1981). In time, a teacher who uses this interactive means of teaching will learn a great deal about how to respond to many common complaints and potentially seething concerns of pre- and early adolescents. One teacher we know, for example, reminds teens, who frequently complain about the material things that they do not have, that even the poor today live better than the rich did 100 years ago, and infinitely better than did many kings and emperors 1,000 years ago. To dramatize the point, he has them list ten things that most of them have that the Czar of Russia did not have in 1900. Again, we all need a little reminder of our blessings to offset some of that existential (and real) angst of daily life. Adolescents especially appreciate these modest, little homilies; and, yes, they can be life saving to those who occasionally lapse into states of despair.

As classroom disruptions begin to diminish and participation starts to rise, it is necessary to begin closing gaps in the literacy levels of underachieving students. Failure to do so can inhibit progress and even foster a more embittered and hopeless attitude. The methods described next are particularly useful for helping to make quick-paced progress with and for those who may feel as if they have fallen hopelessly behind.

▶ IMPROVEMENT OF BASIC DECODING AND WORD LEARNING

The most essential facets of effective reading are decoding, or phonics, and comprehension. Poor readers, by definition, have difficulty with either or both. In fact, improving decoding is a fundamental way of improving comprehension. Upper high-school students who went through elementary schools in the mid-1990s are especially in need since this was a time when, frankly, schools were doing a poor job of teaching phonetic analysis. Here is a way for nonexperts to help with phonetic analysis, or phonics, and word learning.

Glass-Analysis Approach: Phonics Training, without Phonics Rules

There is an amusing scene in a Jack Nicholson movie (*Five Easy Pieces*) in which his character gets a waitress to make him a BLT sandwich, which she says they do not have, by starting with something else and removing this and that. Gerald Glass has done a similar thing to the teaching of decoding. In a stroke of ingenuity, he has taken the phonics out of decoding instruction, and somehow what remains is phonetic analysis without phonics instruction.

Glass-Analysis (Glass, 1973) is a simple procedure that enables virtually anyone who knows how to read to teach others how to do so. It can be used at opportune times as a whole-class method when introducing or reinforcing difficult content terms. Moreover, it takes some of the mystery out of dealing with the lowest readers. Teachers need *not* know about diphthongs, digraphs, and other phonic elements and rules. Teachers simply provide occasional assistance, based on their own ability to decode, as time and circumstances permit. This approach is developmentally appropriate for postelementary and English language learners since it takes up the challenge of hearing, seeing, and decoding complex words beyond the level of simple "onsets" (initial sounds) and "rimes" (final sounds). Struggling, postelementary students tend to have the greatest difficulty with "medial" sounds, and particularly so in multisyllabic words (e.g., *photosynthesis; bureaucracy*).

Glass-Analysis is a fairly directive method that boys especially can be induced into following as if it were a cadence for marching (remember that approximately 80% of remedial readers are boys). It is based on two or three verbal protocols, or cadence-like scripts. The scripts are designed to teach students to focus attention on the unrecognized word and increase their familiarity with the sounds of the most common letter clusters in the English language. Ideally, youngsters internalize this cadence and exercise it as an internal mediational system, or self-spoken and, therefore, self-teaching strategy for unlocking unfamiliar words. The sound for *ing*, for example, has a high frequency of occurrence and is more easily learned as a cluster than as three separate letter sounds that then must be synthesized. Following are some general guidelines and steps for teaching with Glass-Analysis.

Guidelines for Teaching Glass-Analysis

Students should continuously look at the word. Never cover part of the word or point to letters when presenting the word. Generally, the Glass approach discourages including definitions of words in the instruction unless a student asks. The idea is to keep students focused on word analysis and recognition. However, when Glass is used in a content class, word meanings should be discussed following the word identification, especially if they are central to the content. In either case, reinforce students for correct responses. If a student cannot answer a word attack question, state the answer and return to the same question before finishing with the word.

Steps in Glass-Analysis

1. Write the word to be taught on the chalkboard or a large card.
2. Pronounce the word. Then teach it using as many combinations of letter clusters as are sensible.
3. Use the following questions or verbal scripts:

    "What letters make the <ch> sound?"

    After you have used this question with the possible combinations, ask

    "What sound do the letters <c/h> make?"

Figure 13.1 illustrates how Glass would use this approach with a new word before silent reading. See Figure 13.2 for a listing of common letter clusters, grouped according to difficulty level.

The teacher writes the word *forgetfulness* in large letters on the chalk-board. Then the teacher uses the Glass-Analysis script as follows:

In the word *forgetfulness*, what letters make the *for* sound?

The *or* sound?

What letters make the *et* sound?

The *get* sound?

What letters make the *forget* sound?
In the word *forgetfulness*, what letters make the *ful* sound?

The *forgetful* sound?

What letters make the *fulness* sound?

What letters make the *getfulness* sound?

(Notice how many structures can be learned in just one word—all transfer-able to other words.)

In the word *forgetfulness*, what sound do the letters f/o/r make?

What sound do the letters e/t make?

The g/e/t?

The f/o/r/g/e/t?

What sound do the letters f/u/l/ make?

What sound does g/e/t/f/u/l make?

What sound does e/s/s make?
n/e/s/s?

In the word *forgetfulness*, what sound do the letters f/u/l/n/e/s/s make?

If I took off the letters f/o/r, what sound would be left?

If I took off the *ness* sound, what sound would be left?

What is the whole word?

Figure 13.1   Example of Glass-Analysis.

Uses of Glass-Analysis

Glass-Analysis can be used in three ways to create an effective schoolwide reme-dial/corrective decoding program:

- Content teachers can incidentally use this simple letter-clustering approach each time a new technical or content word is introduced: "This word (show-ing it) is *photosynthesis*. What letters make the *photo* sound? What letters make the *syn* sound? The *thesis* sound? What is the whole word again?" This can also be followed by letters-to-sounds questions if needed.

- Content teachers also can occasionally preview textual material assigned for reading and use Glass-Analysis to teach other challenging words, espe-cially foreign-language terms, that occur in text. "This is the Italian word *ciao*. Which letters make the *ch* sound in Italian? Which make the *ow*

STARTERS KIT			MEDIUMS KIT		
(Non-Reader, 1st grade decoding level, weak 2nd grade decoding level)			(2nd grade decoding level and/or weak 3rd grade decoding level)		
1. at	11. am	21. ash	31. ar	41. ame	41. ice
2. ing	12. un	22. ish	32. em	42. ape	52. ick
3. et	13. in	23. ed	33. up	43. ace	53. if(f)
4. it	14. ap	24. ig	34. ate	44. ang	54. ink
5. ot	15. and	25. ip	35. ent	45. ank	55. ob
6. im	16. ack	26. ud	36. est	46. ong	56. od
7. op	17. um	27. id	37. ake	47. all	57. og
8. an	18. ab	28. en	38. ide	48. aw	58. ub
9. ay	19. ag	29. ug	39. ock	49. el(l)	59. uf(f)
10. ad	20. old	30. ut	40. ade	50. eck	60. ush

HARDERS KIT			COMPLETERS KIT		
(3rd grade decoding level and above)			(Use after Harders)		
61. able	71. us	81. <u>ea</u>t	91. ave	101. eal	111. ure
62. ight	72. il(l)	82. as(s)	92. ove	102. <u>tea</u>	112. ur
63. is(s)	73. ite	83. ev	93. <u>folly</u>	103. ee	113. ir
64. on	74. es(s)	84. ind	94. age	104. <u>care</u>	114. ai
65. or	75. om	85. oss	95. er	105. <u>deaf</u>	115. au
66. ul(l)	76. oke	86. earn	96. air	106. <u>oa</u>t	116. oi
67. ac	77. ore	87. ost	97. ied	107. ue	117. tion
68. af(f)	78. <u>tow</u>	88. <u>rol(l)</u>	98. ew	108. s<u>oo</u>n	118. ture
69. ook	79. ast	89. one	99. ire	109. ou	119. al
70. <u>fowl</u>	80. ane	90. ale	100. ear	110. ound	

Figure 13.2 Letter Clusters (by difficulty level).

Source: Glass-Analysis for Decoding Only. ETL, Box 329, Garden City, New York, 11530. Used with permission.

sound? How is the whole word pronounced again?" All students especially appreciate this kind of assistance with words that may be cause for embarrassment, such as saying *chick* for *chic* when it is a French word that is pronounced *sheek*.

- Students with serious decoding deficiencies can be scheduled for one to five fifteen-minute sessions per week in which Glass-Analysis tutoring is provided. *Decoding Stations* can be set up in convenient, unobtrusive places throughout the school. These can be staffed by teachers serving a duty period and/or by volunteer paraprofessionals.

Cooperative Glossaries to Assist with Unfamiliar Word Meanings

A glossary is a handy mini-dictionary of terms used in a given book or field. Definitions are context specific and therefore concrete. Even proficient readers appreciate these when wading into a new field. Pupils spend each day wading through new fields. If there is not a glossary in the class text, or the particular book or novel being read, there is a relatively easy and instructive way to create one coop-eratively.

Steps in Constructing a Cooperative Glossary

1. The teacher constructs a simple glossary to a few pages of a longer selection or book.

2. Students are urged to use the cooperative glossary as they read.

3. Students are urged to read a few pages beyond those covered by the guide.

4. Discussion develops about how the guide helped and which additional words and/or phrases might need definition.

5. Each student is assigned to prepare a glossary for a few pages of the remainder of the text. Students should be told to note the page number for each word they select and to record *only* the dictionary definition that applies to the way the word is used in the selection.

6. Glossaries are compiled and reproduced for the entire class.

7. (Optional) The teacher adds a pronunciation guide. This step is optional because it is difficult to do; however, most students like—and need—one.

Figure 13.3 presents an example of a cooperative glossary.

▶ OTHER INCLUSION METHODS

Federal Public Law 94-142 mandates that youngsters with learning disabilities, developmental disabilities, and other physical handicapping conditions attend school in a least restrictive environment. This has been taken to mean that wher-

Page	Chapter	Word	Definition	Pronunciation
67	3	inscrutable	cannot be under-stood	in-screw-ta-ble
68		lamentation	cry out	la-men-ta-shun
70		opiate	a drug to help a person sleep	o-pee-ut
71		perpetuation	continuing	per-pet-chu-a-shun
72		specter	ghost	speck-tur
81	4	consignment	delivery	cun-sine-ment
83		disconcerted	confused	dis-cun-sir-ted
84		oblivion	complete forget-fulness	o-bli-vee-un
85		sonorous	loud praise	sah-nore-us
87		supplicatory	begging	suh-pli-cu-tory

Figure 13.3   Cooperative Glossary for *A Tale of Two Cities*.

ever possible such students will be mainstreamed or expected to attend and be accommodated in regular classes.

Most of the methodology of the content area reading movement is suitable for meeting this requirement. Maring and Furman (1985) have made an especially strong case for several whole-class, inclusion strategies for helping youngsters read and listen better in heterogeneous, content area classes.

1. Use the Oral Reading Method (described in Chapter 2) at least once a week to increase familiarity and comfortableness with the language of the text.

2. Use the whole-class graphic organizer called *pyramiding* (Clewell & Haidemos, 1983). This activity offers group assistance to students with learning disabilities in identifying, classifying, and properly subordinating terms and ideas found in text.
   a. Each student reads silently to identify and write down key facts and ideas.
   b. The teacher leads a discussion, using the chalkboard to pyramid, or group, facts and phrases into logical categories.
   c. The class decides on a sentence that answers the question, "What is the author saying about these ideas?" This sentence forms the base of the triangle (see Figure 13.4).

3. Enhance and review the informal textbook inventory described in Chapters 10 and 12, and add some easier questions to help make the course textbook more instructive and user friendly. For example,

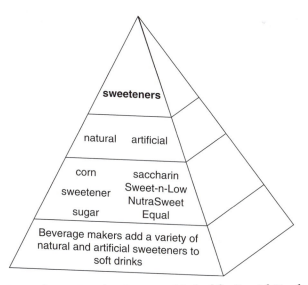

Figure 13.4 Pyramiding: A Graphic Organizer Method for Special-Needs Students.

Source: Figure from Maring, Gerald H., & Furman, Gail Chase. (1985, May). Seven "whole class" strategies to help mainstreamed young people read and listen better in content area classes. *Journal of Reading,* 28(8), 694–700. Reprinted with permission of Gerald H. Maring and the International Reading Association. All rights reserved. © [1985] The International Reading Association.

    a. How many pages are in the glossary?

    b. Where could you find more information about a term defined in the glossary? (Answer: the index.)

    c. What are the first and last page numbers of the index?

4. Use the Contextual Redefinition method, described in Chapter 7, to improve vocabulary while reading (Moore, Readence, & Rickelman, 1982).

5. Use Words on the Wall (J. W. Cunningham, Cunningham, & Arthur, 1981) as an uncomplicated means of providing students with learning disabilities and other students with an easily available set of key words from the text to which they can refer for meaning, significance, spelling, and increased familiarity. Simply write key words with a felt-tip marker on half-sheets of paper, and tape them on the walls during a given unit of study. (This can also be done with morphemes, as suggested in Chapter 7.)

6. Conduct the Guided Reading Procedure (see Chapter 6 for details) with the following specifications:

    a. Use the procedure every two weeks, and administer a delayed retention test in the intervening week.

    b. Try to get mainstreamed readers to contribute free recalls early in the lesson before the more able students contribute all of the easiest information.

    c. Reread the information on the board as students try to decide which items are main ideas, which are related details, and how to sequence the information.

7. Build further crutches, or scaffolding, into reading guides:

    a. Mark with asterisks those questions you feel are most necessary and appropriate for mainstreamed youngsters to answer. Tell them to answer these questions first.

    b. Put page, column, and paragraph numbers after certain questions to better guide those students who might have difficulty finding these (Wilkins & Miller, 1983); for example, "92, 2, 2" means page 92, second column, second paragraph.

▶ LIMITED ENGLISH PROFICIENCY, ENGLISH LANGUAGE LEARNERS, AND CULTURAL DIFFERENCES

Terminology

Generally speaking, the term *limited English proficiency* (LEP) is the larger category describing English dialect speakers and students for whom English is a second language (ESL). In recent times the ESL groups have come to be called English language learners (ELLs). This choice of terms remains fluid and not consistent across journals and scholars. However, ELL is the currently preferred term and the one that we have used in this text.

Learning Needs of ELL Students

If learning a new language while having to learn *in* a new language were not so common, it probably would be considered a serious form of learning disability since its impact on schooling can be considerable (Manzo, Manzo, & Albee, 2004). However, learning a new language while learning in a new language is not a learning disability, but a serious learning obstacle; youngsters generally learn the informal conversational aspects of language in about two years, but it can take five to seven years to acquire skill in formal and academic language. Understanding this distinction becomes a necessary step in reducing the likelihood of mislabeling students as "learning disabled" and therefore misdirecting their instructional needs. In fact, this happens too frequently. Many teachers have difficulty differentiating the normal phases of learning a new language from "learning defects." This mimicking effect has teachers overidentifying English language learners for special education (Cummins, 2001; Ordonz-Jasis, 2002). Accordingly, this is a solid reason to also be very cautious in judging how many ELL students are low functioning and very generous in saying how many probably are average and above.

The increasing numbers of youngsters pouring into our schools from foreign and diverse cultural backgrounds are once again hastening the need for all educators to be conversant with the precepts of teaching to those with limited English proficiency and/or are in transition as English language learners. Past efforts to accommodate non-English-speaking American youngsters have consistently resulted in a richer, more diverse, and stronger nation. To appreciate the nature of the challenge to ELL students is to begin to understand what needs to be done to accommodate them. Consider the challenges below. L1 refers to the students' first, or heritage, language, and L2 to the language (in this case, English) being learned.

Challenges of Learning a New Language While Having to Learn in a New Language:

1. There is no word form in L1 for one in L2.

2. Lack of familiarity with the grammatical and syntactical structures (or linguistic patterns that we use to fluidly predict the next word in a sentence) in L2.

3. Inadequate vocabulary and concept development in L1.

4. Confusions arising from seeming parallels in L1 and L2 from similarities in letter clusters and idioms that are, in fact, not parallel and, therefore, are misleading.

5. Lack of, and/or incongruous, background schemata, values, customs, and attitudes.

6. Lack of skills and knowledge in interpreting the communicative intent of a speaker/writer.

7. Inadequate and incongruous experience and knowledge of the acceptability of various forms of oral and written discourse.

The CAL Tool Box

As previously noted, many of the *tools*—methods and means—devised and developed for content area literacy have proven especially appropriate for use with linguistically and culturally different students. In many instances, these methods need not be modified but merely used as described. This certainly applies to methods that create a rich instructional conversation such as ReQuest, reported to be profoundly effective in English as a second language classes (McKenzie, Ericson, & Hunter, 1988), as well as other interactive methods such as Question-Only, the Cultural-Academic Trivia (knowledge) game, the Subjective Approach to Vocabulary, Vocabulary Development through Cooperative Learning, most variations on the cloze procedure, and the various response-to-text and discussion methods (such as REAP) presented in earlier chapters.

The most appealing feature of the general approaches presented next is that, in addressing second-language and limited English needs, they simultaneously account for certain universal needs shared by all students. Among the most prominent of these are the need for a multicultural outlook; the need to reconnect ourselves to certain traditional human values and wisdom; the need to think abstractly as a requisite to thinking adaptively; and the need to actively participate in class, that is, conduct ourselves in harmony with others while pursuing individual goals (a specific method for which is detailed ahead).

ELL and Culturally Diverse Methods

The methods described next can be used to aid language development and cultural diversity in almost any reading/language arts program and in almost any content class:

- Encourage students to watch captioned TV. This is a solid means of hearing and seeing new terms and customs of speech.

- Encourage students to comment on materials to be read by trying to predict what the selections in each unit of study might be about. Record students' predictions on a chart. At the end of a unit, encourage students to discuss whether or not their predictions were correct and why.

- Have as many books as possible available for students. Read the descriptions of books to them, encouraging them to select books from this list. In addition, select one book from each unit and orally read it to students to build familiarity with a content area's most frequent words and cadence.

- Have a variety of multiethnic literature available, including materials from the students' cultures and some in their native languages. Help them to build on their strengths, from a strong base of confidence and self-esteem.

- Exercise materials in any lesson should be read to students and discussed, not merely assigned.

- Read poetry aloud to students and discuss. If possible, record the poetry on a tape so students can hear the poet's language again and again.

- Read plays to students before they are asked to take character parts. If possible, provide audio or video recorders so students can practice their parts and hear (and see) themselves before they are asked to read aloud.

- Read postreading questions to students and discuss answers with them before having them write out their own answers.

- Have quasi-bilingual, or *transitional,* students read and write with aides, parents, and former ELL students who speak a student's first language.

- English language learners are likely to have a developmental gap between their ability to read and their ability to write in the second language. These students will benefit by working through stages of the Writing Process as a group activity. After a suitable prewriting activity and/or discussion, students should be asked to talk through the drafting stage, while someone records what they say on chart paper. Students then should be asked to reread the composition and make any needed revisions. The recorder should make these revisions while students observe and suggest any editing corrections that need to be made (spelling, usage, punctuation, and so on). Each student should then copy the finished work from the board so that he or she has a sense of ownership. As students gain a sense of confidence in their ability to write, pair students and have them write their compositions together. Move from this to having students write independently.

The next method presented can help teachers achieve the valued educational goal of independence in a highly structured way. It puts "training wheels" on classroom discussion. This method is most appropriate for early English language learners, but it also is suitable for reticent and shy students as well as for the unmotivated and occasionally disruptive student.

Note Cue: Training Wheels and Spotting for Class Discussion, Oral and Written Language, and Comprehension

Classroom listening and discussion remain the most fundamental means by which education is conducted. Nonetheless, students rarely are taught how to listen actively and participate in class discussion, that is, how to *ask, answer,* and make relevant and appropriate *comments.* English language learners, dialect speakers, and youngsters from culturally different backgrounds have traditionally found these social-academic strategies especially difficult to acquire. These, as well as some students from lower SES (socioeconomic status) backgrounds, sometimes are unfamiliar with the more subtle aspects of the English language, such as tempo and volume, and social protocols, such as waiting one's turn to speak, and speaking cogently.

Note Cue (Manzo & Manzo, 1987) is a form of highly scaffolded, or sheltered, practice designed to show students how a well-orchestrated literacy lesson might occur. In some ways it resembles training wheels on a two-wheel bike, and quickly thereafter, *spotting,* an independence-building technique used in physical education to guide initial attempts at tumbling (see Figure 13.5). Note Cue is a form of sensorimotor involvement in which the mind and the body learn complex new

(1)   (2)   (3)

Figure 13.5   Note Cue is like acrobatic spotting.

language, thinking, and social routines. The goal is to help students to become more proficient in text-grounded instructional conversation about books and ideas. It resembles a cue card system described by Brown and Cambourne (1987) as a linguist activity to aid recall, paraphrasing, and content area instruction.

Steps in Preparing for and Conducting the Note Cue Method

Teacher Preparation.   Prepare two sets of cards, one for prereading and one for postreading. On the prereading cards, write prereading questions (one per card), answers (one per card), and comments (one per card). Write the label "Question," "Answer," or "Comment" at the top of each card. Leave a few blank cards, initially just one, then one more blank each time you use the method until only 20% of the cards contain statements. Questions, answers, and comments should focus on predicting main topics, important events, and outcomes. Write in pencil, and remember to reread and edit your cards. Prepare the postreading cards the same way, but shift the focus from prediction to verification—what the passage actually states—and related evaluative questions and comments.

In preparing both sets of cards, be sure the answer card is phrased clearly enough to be easily matched to the question card (e.g., Q: Who followed Abraham Lincoln into the presidency? A: Andrew Johnson followed Abraham Lincoln into the presidency [not simply A: Andrew Johnson]).

Prereading Activity

1.   Instruct students to survey the reading material to try to predict what it will be about. Inform them that a brief written test will follow reading and discussion of the selection.

2.   While students are surveying, place one or more random or selected prereading cards on each student's desk.

3.   Instruct students to read their card(s) silently and think about when they should read it (them) and about whether they wish to add anything else.

4.   Instruct students with blank cards to think of a question, answer, or comment and, if time permits, write it on their cards.

5. Begin the prereading, or prediction, stage of the discussion by asking who has a question or comment that seems to provide a good idea of what the selection will be about. If a question is read, ask who has an answer that seems to fit it. This process continues until students have a sense of what the passage will be about. This should take no more than ten minutes; a brisk pace and aura of evolving a purpose for reading will convey to students that not all cards need to be read to establish a reasonable purpose for reading.

6. Instruct students to read the selection silently to test their predictions. Remind them to read their postreading cards, which will be placed on their desks while they are reading. Announce that you will come to the desk of any student who raises a hand for assistance.

Postreading Discussion

7. Ask, "Who has a good question to check comprehension of this selection?" then, "Who has a good answer to that question?" then, "Who has a comment that seems right to state?" and finally, "Who has reaction(s) or personal comment(s)?" The last question is intended to encourage extemporaneous statements as well as statements read from cards.

Follow-Up

8. Within the same class period, or later if preferred, give a test of five to ten questions that require brief written responses. Most questions should be taken directly from the cards to build an appreciation of the cooperative value in reading a cue card for all to hear and profit from.

Notes on Note Cue

If initial participation is slow to develop, try these options:

- Get things going by reading a question or comment card yourself.
- Simply call on students by name to read their card.
- Stimulate interest by inverting the process slightly: Request that an answer card be read; then ask, "What is the question?"
- Call on at least two students with question cards to read their cards aloud. Then, rather than immediately requesting an answer, ask, "Which question do you think should come first?"
- Have students write their names in pencil on the back of each card. Junior high teacher Betty Bennett says this heightens students' sense of ownership and accountability for the cards' contents and offers a good way to check afterward which students did not volunteer to read their cards.

To accelerate independence and transfer of learning, try these options:

- Reinforce high-quality extemporaneous responses by handing the student a blank card and saying, "That was very good. Would you please write it on this card for further use?"

- Divide the class into groups, and have them prepare the Note Cue cards for the next selections to be read.

- Once students are familiar with the activity, prepare some cards with prompts ("Try to ask a question to show that one should doubt what is being said") or an incomplete statement to be completed by students ("Make a comment by completing this statement: 'I enjoyed reading this story because . . .' or 'The reaction would have been different in my family or culture. We would have . . .'"). Other types of prompter cards can be personalized ("Come on, Fred, don't you have something you can say about this selection?").

To foster higher-level thinking, develop evocative comment cards, preferably ones related to students' experiences. One vivid example of this kind of bridging comes to mind from a lesson observed in an English class. The selection read had been excerpted from a popular book. It described how a fifteen-year-old boy set out on a solitary voyage across the Pacific in a small craft. The questions and answers the teacher had put on the cue cards were primarily from the teacher's manual for the text. One of the comments that she added, however, raised the class's interest and even indignation: "How in the world did this young man raise the money and supplies to do this, and why did his parents permit him to risk his life in such a silly venture?" A student might not have worded the comment quite like that, but such real reactions tend to invite equally real responses and lively discussion.

Finally, Note Cue, unlike many conventional lesson designs, is cumulative. The cards a teacher composes for today's lesson can be stored for future use. Through cooperative work and sharing, teachers can develop starter sets of Note Cues for most key selections of a text. More important, with each use, previously written cards can be modified following use, and new cards generated by students can be added. In this way, lessons can be kept fresh and current.

▶ AFTER WORDS

This chapter strongly endorsed the need for remedial reading programs and offered supportive methods to improve reading, oral language, thinking, and personal-social-cultural adjustment among special needs students in content classrooms. Methods included means of motivating the unmotivated; mainstreaming strategies; biblio-support and dialogue journals; Glass-Analysis to manage decoding problems; a cluster of methods and means to better understand and provide for the needs of dialect and English language learners; and Note Cue, a highly structured means of heightening active classroom participation and language experience. Most of these methods are applicable to broader student groups as well.

CHAPTER 14

LITERACY LEADERSHIP AND CONTENT AREA PROGRAMMING

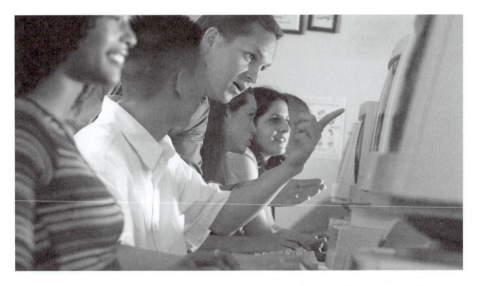

We know what we will have if we operate as we have in the past—and the prospects are not promising.

—Carl D. Glickman

▶ FORE WORDS

This chapter is structured to answer several organizing questions that a principal, classroom teacher, or literacy specialist would need to understand to be an effective participant in a school's content area literacy program at most any level of schooling.

1. What is meant by "literacy leadership," and how does it align with current views of "leadership"?

2. What do schoolwide content area literacy programs typically look like?

3. What are some newer directions for content area literacy programming and curriculum?

4. How do charter school and other educational reform movements reconcile with content area literacy methods and programming ideas?

Along the way in the chapter are invitations to the reader to join some of the more pioneering efforts in school programming, especially as these are finding expression on the World Wide Web.

- ▶ FORE WORDS
- ▶ LITERACY LEADERSHIP: PREPARE NOW TO LEAD LATER
- ▶ ESSENTIAL COMPONENTS OF CONTENT AREA LITERACY PROGRAMS
- ▶ ORGANIZATION, ROLES, AND RESPONSIBILITIES
- ▶ TOWARD A QUEST FUSION CURRICULUM
- ▶ QFLC DECLARES FOR DISCOVERY LEARNING AND SYNTHESIS OF FRAGMENTED THEORIES OF TEACHING/LEARNING
- ▶ AFTER WORDS

▶ LITERACY LEADERSHIP: PREPARE NOW TO LEAD LATER

Sara Van Horn spent the better part of her early adult life raising children and keeping her teaching career and credentials current. She did not anticipate that one day while still relatively young and with children still in school, and with little formal training, that she would find herself appointed as interim principal and then principal of a 600-plus-pupil middle school. Ironically, it turned out that her best preparation, and in fact her stepping stone to this new level of responsibility, was the precious, guarded time that she spent on the school's literacy committee, where she distinguished herself with her knowledge of this most basic aspect of curriculum and instructional planning.

The baby-boomer generation that is moving rapidly toward retirement is much larger than the generation behind it. This is creating a considerable leadership vacuum at every level of American life, and no less so in the nation's schools. For this reason it is useful to be informed about the latest thinking on leadership. It is in your personal interest and the nation as a whole in preparing to meet this great need. The primary source for this update is Linda Lambert's (1998) summative work.

Building School Literacy Leadership Capacity

Leadership does not begin or end with an appointment as designated leader. It starts with a sense of responsibility for a school's mission and a willingness to share one's limited energy and time toward some greater end. Older models of leadership were based more on charisma, core-culture features, connections, and status and, in more recent years, on being part of a previously underrepresented group enjoying some catch-up opportunity. With the gap now closing on underrepresentation of women and certain minorities, this issue is no longer a major consideration in determining who shall be selected to provide leadership. Organizations of all types, schools included, now are being assessed in terms of "bottom-line" effectiveness. For schools this means higher test scores, lower drop-out rates, improved school attendance, increased parent satisfaction surveys, and the like. Professional knowledge and skill are gaining new currency. Lambert (1998) offers a keen summary what leadership is evolving to in the new millennium.

1. Leadership is about learning together. It is about continuing conversations that inquire and generate ideas collaboratively, though not because this is sociable and nice, but because it is effective.

2. Leaders build leaders; they are not controlling, and sometimes even inspiring. They know when to follow someone else's lead. They build adult relationships that are not based on a "co-dependency" arrangement, where the leader is a benevolent authoritarian figure and all others are the "led," and therefore more likely to be "mis-led."

3. Leaders pose and constructively respond to questions that lead to reexamination of assumptions and beliefs.

4. Leaders raise a range of possibilities in order to avoid simplistic answers.

5. Leaders turn concerns into questions.

6. Leaders recognize that they sometimes will be wrong and do so with candor, grace, and humility.

7. Leaders also recognize that getting in front of a populist movement may win short-term support, but it is not the same as offering workable solutions; further, with the growing trend toward independent evaluators of progress, such political posturing will result in discredit to those who practice it.

There are five other notions, or awakenings, that are coming to be understood as influencing organizational change and school leadership. In summary, as noted by Glickman (1985), these are as follows:

1. What we have in education is *predicaments*, or recurring issues and needs, more so than one-time "problems" with final solutions (originally from Jerome Bruner).

2. Organizational effectiveness depends in great measure on the group buying into a *cause beyond oneself.*

3. Leadership styles can be roughly characterized as nondirective, collaborative, and/or direct. Directiveness need not be adversarial or capricious, but an honest regard for the different roles that may need to be played by school leaders and appointed supervisors.

4. The probability of achieving durable change can be predicted from situational factors, especially those that characterize the *maturity of the group as well as the designated leader.* According to the Hersey-Blanchard Situational-Leadership® Model (Hersey & Blanchard, 1977), group maturity can be characterized as high, medium, or low on three critical factors: (1) the *achievement* level or self-motivation of the group; (2) the sense of *responsibility* of group members to assume the various leadership roles necessary to keep an organizational goal on target despite competing and distracting events; and (3) the background, or *education* and experience, of the group to accomplish the subtasks comprising the larger goal.

5. To be effective change agents, leaders may need to adopt a leadership style that at least initially matches the culture or characteristic ways of functioning of the group. Even great leadership can be dissonance producing and inviting of resistance (see Figure 14.1, Matching on the Hersey-Blanchard Situational Leadership® Model).

Healthy change, or "developmental directionality" (Glickman, 1985), is an evolutionary more so than a revolutionary process. Old ways die hard. Nor do time and change pass evenhandedly across places and circumstances. At the moment, it is safe to say that there are few institutions run by enlightened executive thinkers working in "frictionless synchronicity" with fully competent and dedicated professionals. Institutions tend to be quirky (hence the need to actively develop *thought leaders*, or *informed advocates* who can help a school to identify, formulate, and hold to a set of mission-based guidelines).

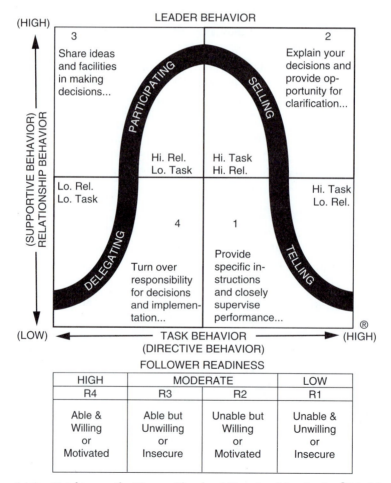

Figure 14.1 Matching on the Hersey-Blanchard Situational Leadership® Model.

Needed: Informed Advocates

Where content area literacy is concerned, leadership is urgently needed. Most postelementary teachers are trained to give optimal focus to subject learning or product over process learning. Similarly, most elementary teachers have little training or orientation in fusing reading, writing, and thinking to subject mastery. Both as a cause and a reflection of this situation, most school districts and state departments of education are muted on content area literacy objectives at elementary levels and silent at the postelementary levels. Hence, content area literacy often finds itself without informed advocates. This is different from the uninformed advocates, who sometimes spring up and can lead literacy programming into energized but ill-advised quagmires. While education greatly needs leadership, this should not be confused with the ungrounded leadership of the quirky types that often create something of a mega-mess. There are three common routes to developing informed advocacy or shoring up the literacy content knowledge of appointed school and state department administrators:

1. Have on-site or internal specialist(s) providing daily information and guidance. Be careful, however, not to appoint czars.

2. Develop a leadership committee.

3. Arrange for external consultants and reviews.

All of the preceding are necessary to initiate and sustain an effective school-based literacy program. The roles of principal and literacy specialist are discussed ahead in the section on essential components of a content area literacy program. The roles of committees and consultants are addressed next.

The Literacy Leadership Committee

Everything about newer concepts of leadership suggests the importance of building a bottom-up consensus for the content area literacy program. Leadership today is based on consensus building. The "chapters" on how to build consensus and get it pointed in the best direction are still being written. The idea of a *literacy leadership committee*, however, is looking like one fairly sound way to proceed. The confounding nature of group dynamics notwithstanding, a literacy leadership committee has merit for several reasons:

- It creates an advocacy group for an area of programming that otherwise tends to be underrepresented within the organizational structure of most schools.
- It allows leadership to emerge from within the organization.
- It provides a means of building consensus and systemic support over time.
- It creates responsible parties but is not vested in one individual and hence likely to rise and fall with that person's social influence.
- It tells faculty, students, community, and central administration that literacy is a valued goal, *a cause beyond oneself.*
- It almost always leads to seeking higher levels of expertise as issues are refined and important implementation decisions are pending.

For ongoing informational and personal support in organizing and guiding a content area literacy leadership committee, see www.LiteracyLeaders.com. Now consider the always-daunting issue of identifying appropriate consultants.

Consultants: Look for Certified Experts

External literacy consultants are a logical progression for most schools. It is unrealistic to expect school administrators and leaders, and even on-site literacy specialists and advocates, to know all they need to about this area of school programming. But this need for external assistance always raises the specter of who is an "expert" and "don't experts often disagree?" A broadly sampled research report says that over 50% of teachers do not know about proven, content area literacy methods, and of those who have been taught these in undergraduate and graduate school, few are using them (Spor & Schneider, 1999). There are a lot of predicaments inherent in this scenario, and they are not of leadership but of competent stewardship, attention to details, and lack of professional knowledge.

While schools of education are not blameless for such lapses in effective teacher education and training, they are most likely the best hope for fixing such problems in the near term. *Certified* (that is, college and university educated) *experts* tend to disagree much less than one would think and on fewer matters. Most of the seeming dilemmas of conflicting "experts" come from failure to establish who is certified and who is somehow self-proclaimed. While it is true that there are certified experts who might give less than the best advice, it is more common to receive misinformation and misdirection from self-made and populous types. In fact, as we mentally review some of the more high-profile fads and misdirections in literacy education of the last thirty years, not one of them was under the leadership of a university certified reading/literacy specialist; however, a few were people in higher education although working outside their areas of certified educational training. Without naming names (why further their notoriety?), here is a sample list of the "theses" and misguided interventions strategies that have been proposed by these self-made literacy leaders along with their true backgrounds.

- A heavily literature-based literacy program with little or no direct instruction or attention to science and mathematics or subject mastery. Leader: a psycholinguist, and, with slight variations on this theme, a professor of English literature with minimal training in any branch of education.

- An Individualized Reading program based on reading "self-selected" books and having little or no direct instruction. Leader: an elementary education specialist in language arts, and with no formal training in the teaching of reading.

- A highly prescriptive program of creeping and crawling to ostensibly correct underdeveloped brain connections and presumably most all reading problems. Leader: a school counselor and a generalist educator.

- A program to remedy dyslexia (severe reading failure) by correcting for undescended testicles in boys (with the help of a tuning fork...don't ask). Leader: osteopathic doctors in a Scandinavian country.

- A program of visual-perceptual training, and several variations that followed for vision (eye) training. Leaders: a child psychologist, several physicians, and many small town optometrists.

- A program that prescribes customized colored lenses that are said to improve reading and comprehension. Leader: a college remedial education program director with no formal training in any branch of education.

Many other programs and "experts" could be added to this list, as could the names of a flock of celebrities, corporations, and well-known foundations who have enthusiastically supported such ungrounded programs. (For a more complete listing with names, see Manzo and Manzo, 1993). Much of this misdirection could have been avoided or at least properly proportioned if more people had asked for the credentials of these charismatic, but somewhat misguided, "literacy leaders." For this reason, it is proper and necessary to check the credentials of school consultants and to challenge the credentials of internal administrators who may fancy themselves "universal leaders" in everything and everywhere strong leadership is recognized as a need. You will need to be especially watchful of reading programs that seek a "halo effect" by tying themselves to socially desirable goals and religious groups.

For a growing list of certified consultants, with brief biographies, and by geographic area and specialties see: www.LitearcyLeaders.com.

Use of Consultants

In general, a certified specialist in one realm can serve as commentator, or helpful guide, in framing the key questions and issues of a related area. This is because there are underlying principles of effective instruction, and certified professionals are more likely to be sensitive to what they do not know and cautious about claiming that they know how to deal with issues outside their realm of training. However, as a matter of course, expertise in one realm can not pass for expertise in another. Even subtle differences in the aim and purpose of seemingly related fields can be deceiving for all concerned. One frequent problem is acceptance of qualifications in learning disabilities or English education as preparation for guiding literacy programming. The literacy specialist may be trained to provide consultation to the LD and Language Arts program, but the inverse is not likely to be as true.

Evaluation of commercial programs is one area in which certified consultants are expected to be of most value. However, this often is problematic even for certified experts for several reasons:

1. There simply are too many commercial programs for the specialist to follow.

2. Schools typically are not willing to retain someone to do a careful analysis of a commercial program.

3. Schools often are not clear about what they intend to do with the program (e.g., use it as a supplement or primary program, and if the first, with precisely what other methods).

4. Schools will sometimes buy programs without training and technical support.

5. Schools are shy about discussing the political-social tie-ins of a particular set of practices or commercial program with a particular interest group.

6. Literacy programming is "rocket science"—it does not appear to be because most anyone can launch this rocket; however, with each distance it travels in space and time, it can move farther off its mark, launching a quality program not only requires proper pre-programming and stability, something commercial materials tend to do well, but also periodic course corrections.

Issues such as these can limit effective use of a consultant but also make it necessary, as can be seen in point 6 in the preceding list. In general, a consultant's value on arrival is determined by the preparation time that goes into that visit. If a particular decision is of great or long-lasting importance, it may be necessary to confer with more than one consultant. Finally, on this topic, do not confuse workshops with consultations. Workshops are organized presentations, or information sharing on a topic. A consultation is a focused analysis of a fairly specific problem, even if the problem sounds general, such as, "What might we be doing wrong in the area of (say, vocabulary) to be getting these marginal or weak scores?"

Finally, there is a way to judge a consultant's wisdom as well as knowledge. The wise consultant will offer solutions that are elegant more so than simplistic. The wise consultant will not have a long list of "don'ts," such as "never lecture," "never ask questions following reading only before," "don't use (unnatural) books with a controlled vocabulary." The wise consultant will support enlightened methods and approaches without damning more traditional methods: A new item on one end of the shelf need not shove a more traditional one off the other end, unless this has been fully justified. For the most part, logic suggests that unless there is definitive information on the countereffectiveness of a traditional practice, it is best to assume that the innovation offered is the "new kid" needing proof and "clinical" (classroom) testing. In other words, *traditional* should not be considered a bad word, although it may not be the last or best word. It should not be necessary to upset most working systems to install better ones.

In general, unless there is evidence of an imminent instructional crisis, changes sought in a professional or knowledge-based arena should be more evolutionary—as in requiring tweaking, elaborating and/or focusing—than revolutionary—as in radically altering direction or abandoning traditional practices.

▶ ESSENTIAL COMPONENTS OF CONTENT AREA LITERACY PROGRAMS

The term *program* here means any plan targeted at a stated goal or objective. Programs are necessary because day-to-day events can become random and even fragmented when unfolding in quasi-isolated classrooms. For this reason alone, it can be satisfying to get and have a place to refer back to the big picture. Another reason to try to gain a top-down perspective is its value in giving the professional educator an opportunity to exercise a more assertive role in defining, refining, and aligning classroom practices with larger school goals and objectives.

Successful content area literacy programs, typically, are built around nine key elements that together equal the big picture:

- Leadership
- A grounded ideology or philosophy
- Objectives and goals
- Clear roles and responsibilities
- Special services for various segments of the student body
- Ongoing needs assessment and program evaluation
- A curriculum plan
- A staff development program that provides consultation, in-service training, and sharing opportunities
- Activities that are results-oriented and promote collaboration and cooperation

The following sections show how some of these elements might be or are being implemented in actual school programs. The examples and discussions include some optional as well as essential elements.

Ideology, or Guiding Ideas

The term *ideology* is used here not in its more recent connotation of *blinding beliefs*, but rather in its stricter sense of a set of professionally accepted *ideas* and proven practices, or guiding philosophy. It usually is expressed in the form of a unifying theme or focus that serves as the conceptual basis or organizing principle(s) for programming.

Several philosophies have held sway in recent years. Most notable among these has been the mastery learning perspective, which emphasizes heavy doses of direct instruction, a strong dose of testing for transmission of knowledge, and a skills-based orientation. In counterpoint is the *whole-language* orientation, which emphasizes indirect teaching; transactional, or constructionist, subjectivity in reading; virtually no testing; and the integration of content mastery, reading, writing, and speaking largely through literature-based learning.

The most popular philosophy, however, is an eclectic one. *Eclecticism* is a philosophy that permits one to pick and choose parts, principles, and practices from all others. Our own choice is a form of eclecticism that has been labeled the *New, or Informed, Eclecticism* (Manzo & Manzo, 1997b). This philosophy differs from conventional eclecticism, or "balanced" programming (Duffy & Hoffman, 1999), which often means a "little of this and that." There are three distinguishing characteristics of *Informed Eclecticism:*

- Every effort must be made to reconcile (seemingly) competing ideas and political crosscurrents, since there is a good chance that these will enhance rather than displace each other.
- Instructional decisions should be guided not merely by subjective judgments and equal proportions but rather by assessment of student needs

and reference to research findings that support or fail to support given practices and their degrees of value.

- There must be an emphasis on critical-constructive or inquiry-based learning, since this is the fundamental purpose of schooling. See the section titled "Quest Fusion Literacy Curriculum" (pp. 384–387) for a current attempt to formulate such a focus.

The chief value of these simple guidelines is that they encourage attention to innovation but help schools to resist fads and hollow buzzwords, even when the new buzzwords are *balance* and *eclectic*.

Objectives and Goals

Attempts to state specific goals and objectives represent the first fleshing out of an ideology or philosophical bent. School districts are very good at cranking out hair-splittingly specific objectives and/or goals that may be socially significant and appropriate to be represented but not necessarily central to school learning. It is important to take this exercise seriously. The words chosen are an institution's public declarations and logically the basis for the development of strategic planning and allocations of resources. Since resources are almost always limited, this is where priorities and compromises should be negotiated. Everything cannot be a top priority.

Here are some examples of sentences and phrases that align with the themes in this text and that can be combined into descriptive statements to guide content area literacy programs and curricula:

- Promoting progress toward reading-language-thinking-content-social/ emotional maturity as opposed to mere reading competence
- Promoting higher-order literacy, or working to assess and remedy shortfalls in critical-constructive thinking, among the academically proficient as well as those reading below age-grade expectations
- The improvement of reading, writing, speaking, listening, and thinking
- Promoting multiple literacies, including knowledge of diverse cultures and backgrounds
- Fusing literacy, content teaching, Internet technology, and diverse cultures
- Creating an inquiry, or quest-based, multiple-literacy and learning curriculum
- Fusing content, literacy, and thinking to the demands of the New (Entrepreneurial) Economy"

"Best" Literacy Practices Can Be a Tough Sell

Realistically speaking, the preceding words and themes may not always play well in a particular school or community, even though they should be an integral part of the school's philosophical or ideological goals. For example, it might be fairly easy to get a faculty committee to say that the school literacy program should include attention to the higher literacy needs of the three near dysfunctional sub-types of "proficient" readers identified previously in Chapter 8; in practice, how-ever, there likely would be several objections. Objections would range from limited resources to lack of knowledge about what to do. In such situations, it is more practical first to express the focus for the school program in more traditional terms, such as the following:

- Advancing comprehension and vocabulary
- Promoting efficient reading and study habits
- Increasing reading and writing to learn
- Preparing for standardized tests

Ironically, the most concrete-looking item, "preparing for standardized tests," may best open the door for attention to higher literacy since questions on such tests can tend to be of a more abstract nature than on conventional classroom tests. As such, the standardized test will show which students have been receiving much higher grades in class than is perhaps justified by the quality of their ab-stract thinking. In most cases, the ideology of the school program will be ex-pressed in a combination of the preceding terms with some locally recognized need. Examples of specific local needs might include functional literacy for job flexibility, college preparation, or effective reading and use of technology. See the section titled "Implementing Sustainable Programs" (pp. 377–78) for further thoughts and strategies for advancing important objectives like higher literacy.

▶ ORGANIZATION, ROLES, AND RESPONSIBILITIES

The chief element in translating program ideals into practice is the assignment of role responsibilities. Following are the most commonly acknowledged responsi-bilities of the school administrator, reading specialist, and classroom teacher.

The School Principal

The school principal has the primary responsibility for initiating and supporting the development and implementation of the goals, objectives, curriculum, and design of the literacy program. In this capacity, the principal is the one who needs to know enough to initiate schoolwide survey testing, program evaluation, and on-going literacy-related faculty development programs. It also is the principal's re-sponsibility to cultivate a positive school climate. It is important to note, however, that "a poor climate can inhibit learning, but a positive climate does not guarantee success" (Hoffman, 1991, p. 926). In other words, the highly vaunted objective of "team building," while truly important to faculty morale, should not become a pri-mary goal since it is not easily translated into improved student performance. As one leading educator confided in a private conversation regarding the evaluation of principals, "We've got them by the data now." Overall, leadership/supervision should not be viewed as quite so glamorous, because it is not. Administrative leadership is like glue on a chair; largely unrecognized or appreciated when work-ing, but evident and faulted when it is not (Glickman, 1985).

Team Can Be Overdone

In school design something has got to be secondary, and even tertiary, and this "team building" stuff may be it. Gilbert and Sullivan created some of the most durable and lyrical musicals of the early twentieth century, yet they so intensely disliked one another that they did virtually all of their collaboration by mail. They were competent and even creatively productive (that is, they produced great synergies), but they were never a "team"—they simply recognized a goal greater than themselves. Working as a team, or *synergizing,* does not require holding hands and loving your leader and even one another; it requires competency and even the suspension of personal goals in favor of larger, professional goals. This is not to say that good feelings are not important to one's sense of personal worth and the overwhelming human need for affiliation, but it is not why professionals are hired—unless of course, they are professional psychologists and counselors brought in to help prevent or correct social dysfunctionality that is spilling over into the deterioration of duties.

We will do much of our collaborating in this new century through various forms of Internet communication that result in fewer conventional teams and fewer leaders to guide us. However, we will have more information and better critiques than ever before, and fewer leaders controlling our access to it. It is true that myth makers have greater access to promoting ill-advised programs, but so too will they have to weather the scrutiny of de-myth-making information, Web sites, and perspectives. Chat groups and interactive Web sites are helping everyone not merely to access more information but to get help in processing and digesting it. Much of this open access should keep professionals at every level current but grounded. More than ever, authority will be determined by good sense and ability to stand up under cross examination. Easy access to hordes of Internet-based information should not diminish the importance of college and postgraduate education, as many fear, but further validate it as people and institutions seek more analytical help, as well as mere access to largely ambiguous information.

The Literacy Specialist

Literacy specialists essentially are people who not only have information, or data points, but *knowledge,* which is the grasp of potentially unifying concepts that make it possible to connect those dots varying different arrangements as required by a given predicament or sets of circumstances.

As a rule of thumb, an intermediate and secondary school should have one full-time reading/literacy specialist for every 250 students. Reading specialists are expected to serve as resource persons in the development of the goals, objectives, curriculum, and design of the literacy program. They typically are responsible for coordinating and interpreting schoolwide survey testing to assist in the ongoing evaluation of the literacy program and for administering additional diagnostic tests as needed based on survey test results and/or referrals. Reading specialists provide ongoing assistance to teachers in a variety of forms: determining their felt needs, helping them to better understand the nature and implications of those needs, planning in-service activities, evaluating and/or preparing instructional materials, and demonstrating new methods. In addition, they should be responsible for eliciting and coordinating the contributions of other support services, such as librarians, counselors, outside consultants, and parents.

The Content Area Teacher

The ultimate power and responsibility for the overall literacy program rests with classroom teachers. A vital content area literacy program enlists teachers' participation in the identification and development of the goals, objectives, curriculum, design, and evaluation procedures for the schoolwide literacy program. This participation helps to ensure whole-hearted implementation of the program.

There is a growing belief that teachers may be the chief agents for change in literacy programming. For a solid *source* book on supporting this movement, see Lawrence G. Erickson's (1995) *Supervision of Literacy Programs—Teachers as Grass-Roots Change Agents*. It is important to note that durable results are not possible without scheduled time for classroom teachers to make their contribution (Glickman, 1985).

Special Services Component

In the context of schoolwide programming, *special services* means assistance available for students with special needs that cannot easily be met in a regular class situation. This typically involves pull-out programs, elective or mini-courses, resource rooms, and drop-in help. It now also can include e-mail and phone "hotline" help. At this time, the authors among others are attempting to develop online special services in the form of digital tutor and mentoring programs. These should assist teachers in providing a virtual form of "up close and personal" support to students in reading, writing, and thinking to higher levels. The chief benefit of such programs is that they would increase the amount of *engaged* time students spend in reading and writing with feedback and encouragement. The program that the authors are embracing uses the REAP annotation exchange system, described in Chapter 8, as its primary delivery vehicle. This type of programming resembles conventional pull-out services, but it is asynchronous, or not occurring in real time, but rather as tutor and tutee are able and willing to engage tasks.

Pull-Out Services

In *pull-out programs*, a reading/literacy specialist offers diagnostic and/or remedial/corrective tutoring for youngsters who cannot be adequately provided for in regular classes. This component is intended to ensure that

1. No remedial-level reader falls between the cracks and leaves school quasi-literate after thirteen years in our charge.

2. Students whose first language is not English and language-handicapped students receive special attention where this appears necessary.

3. Assessment and treatment are provided for other difficult, different, or sometimes overlooked problems (e.g., higher-order literacy needs,

cultural differences, study skills deficiencies, and reading-related writing, grammar, and spelling).

4. Ideally, consultation is provided for all teachers in selecting and using appropriate methods and materials.

In general, pull-out programs create a safety net, where a member of the faculty becomes responsible for the subject that no one seems to think that they teach. It also tasks someone with providing attention to literacy needs that may require out-of-class conferences with parents and the marshalling of available resources, in the school, and in the community, for those youngsters at risk of becoming school dropouts or social graduates.

Elective Courses

Content area literacy specialists in upper elementary, middle, and high schools frequently offer exploratory mini-courses or full elective courses on topics such as study strategies, reading rate, critical reading, and vocabulary enrichment. This type of short-term, focused instruction reinforces and builds on the ongoing content reading instruction provided daily in content classrooms. It also extends the services of the literacy specialist and committee to a fuller complement of the student body.

Learning Centers

The learning center usually is the hub out of which a reading or literacy department may operate. Bernice Bragstad (1985), an International Reading Association award-winning content area literacy specialist, says that her former high school's learning center provided these three services:

1. Individualized or small-group tutoring in any subject or skill, provided by a select cadre of proficient student-tutors or the reading specialist

2. Individualized help with writing, provided by several English teachers who served their duty periods in this way

3. A preventative biweekly summer tutoring program conducted by high school students for middle and junior high students

In addition to these services, learning centers can offer walk-in assistance with almost any pressing homework or academic problem. The Kansas City Public School District has extended this concept to a homework hotline. The hotline is available after school hours and is staffed by volunteer teachers.

Needs Assessment and Evaluation

Information about students' academic status and about the effects of the school program on this basic school obligation is essential to determining what needs to be done and how best to do it. This type of information should be collected regularly by school leaders and cross verified by an independent audit from an outside team of consultants about every three to five years. Surveys guided by outside consultants help identify problems that have a way of cropping up in virtually every operation in which day-to-day pressures erode educators' sensitivity to basic flaws in policy and procedure. Most effective businesses routinely budget for such periodic surveys and reviews. It is a fundamental form of quality control. One often overlooked aspect of evaluation is to look at student progress in terms of key "process variables" that tend to support prevention or program failure. One key variable that should be monitored is in-school "engaged time on task." There needs to be clear evidence that sufficient time (we estimate, no less than 30 to 40% of the total school day) be spent on "basics" such as these:

- Organized presentation of information
- Frontloading, or preparation for guided silent reading
- Discussion and supervised study
- Frequent, brief periods of additional help to students with special needs

Most everything else, including popular issues such as diversity, use of cooperative structures, gender concerns, character education, and meeting learning style differences, will be more attainable with full commitment to monitoring and nurturing these fundamental programming requirements.

Another important part of needs assessment is determination of areas of suboptimal, though not necessarily failing, levels of literacy development. This would include informal assessments of factors such as study habits, writing, listening, and higher literacy.

Implementing Sustainable Programs

The literacy leadership committee can facilitate program implementation in a variety of ways. However, it typically has no authority but serves only in an advisory capacity. Therefore, a full implementation cycle may need to be measured in years, not weeks or semesters. The committee will win respect for its purposes largely by the quality of its information and recommendations and by patient construction and introduction of its programming ideas. Achieving these goals requires a great deal of "prioritizing" and decision making. Methods such as the Regression Equation Technique (see Chapter 8) or similar decision-making structures (cf. Erickson, 1995) can be of considerable assistance in converting a literacy leadership *deliberative* committee into a literacy leadership *action* committee. The basic strategy of an *action committee* should be to TNT, or specify the *tasks*, *names*, and *times* of people responsible for getting strategically important things done in a timely manner (Erickson, 1995).

Launching a sustainable new program also tends to require a special level of monitoring for "allergic reactions." These generally can be traced to anything that upsets existing routines or social structures. These can be subtle and difficult to detect. For example, an effort to increase reflective reading and writing of literature (i.e., stories) will easily win the support of the English department. However, efforts to identify those who read too much story literature and who do not connect their reading to real-life situations will almost surely induce an allergic reaction from that same English department, because this is something that literature majors generally do not do well. When reading beyond the lines is connected to real-life problem solving, or action planning, it amounts to a culture clash, or introduction of a foreign substance into the literature major's environment; literature majors routinely have low scores on psychological measures of pragmatism, the essence of applied thinking. Go back and read the profiles of four proficient reader subgroups in Chapter 8 (pp. 190–192) for further verification of this point.

One manageable way to anticipate and establish readiness for such allergic sensitivity is to provide "allergy shots," which amount to small quantities of exposure to the offending element, and then monitor for reactions. One way to do this is to nest information and stratagem into a periodic newsletter, electronic billboard, and Web site with hyperlinks to appropriate sites. In general, the most tangible and discussion provoking of these is the one-page newsletter. By the way, our given example, literature majors have other affective characteristics that make them inclined to be persuaded to do what is best for their students—namely, high empathy, compassion, and capacity to be influenced by personal stories.

To begin to construct a newsletter that is professional and authoritative, the committee need only decompose a text such as this one into a series of one-page summaries of content area literacy methods. The burden of selecting and editing can be shared with other schools in the district, or outside the district, with similar goals and objectives.

Curriculum Implementation Plan

Apart from the obvious effort to infuse each content subject with the necessary reading-related teaching methods and student strategies, each discipline can be designated, by common agreement, to give special attention to specific features of the content area literacy curriculum. Distribution and assignment of reading and literacy-related objectives to each subject area proceeds best when school units volunteer to play designated roles. This horizontal distribution also can be detailed vertically by age/grade level (see beginning of Chapter 12 for a distribution of literacy skills and objectives by major disciplines).

Staff Development

A well-planned staff development program is an important means of ensuring that programs endure and evolve over time in an institutional setting that undergoes frequent changes in administration and staff. An effective plan for staff development should include four basic components:

1. A means of enlisting teacher support in program development and an ongoing sense of program ownership
2. A way to provoke program review and renewal
3. A means of fine-tuning a program and accommodating individual teacher's needs

4. Attention to innovation and resistance of fads and hollow words

Four means are discussed next for addressing some of these components.

Determining Training Needs

The first question that a staff development program should ask, according to Marzano (1997), is, "What part of the learning process needs to be improved?" This question then is converted into consideration of the various possible resources—from books, to Web sites, to workshops—that could be brought to fill those needs for the school, subgroups within it, or for individuals. See www.mcrel.org, a federal teaching-learning laboratory, for Marzano's excellent "Framework for Planning Staff Development."

Beware of Bad Currency

There is one precaution that should be exercised in the use of the Internet in inservice education. It is the currency of its data banks. Things that are "current" by definition are time tested. They may become gold-plated standards, but they also may prove to be unsupportable. In any case, most online journals and touted programs do not reach back prior to 1990, yet the knowledge bases for most fields extends much farther back. In the case of content area literacy, its "golden age" of development was between 1969 and 1990. Much of value has occurred since, but much was created prior to this dawning of the Internet. So consult textbooks and look for sites that reference these classic works.

Action Research

Classroom experimentation is a proven way to change instructional routines. It has been pointed out that by involving teachers in planning, conducting, and reporting classroom research, teachers greatly increased their sense of ownership of ideas while providing hands-on evidence of the value of several basic content area literacy methods (Santa, Isaacson, & Manning, 1987).

The process of involving teachers in action research projects is more manageable today than ever before. Assistance with research design and statistics usually can be had for a small fee or even free from a school district's own office of research, from advanced degree-seeking teachers, and/or from nearby university campuses. Action research need not be limited to doing, but can involve searching, as in Web and textbook questing for certain types of information. For example, teachers might go on a *Great Paradigm Quest* to find and identify some very basic structures for teaching in specific CAL areas. In this text that would include the Directed Reading-Thinking Activity for text comprehension and the Frayer model for teaching vocabulary and concepts. There are several others; see if you can find a paradigm for inquiry-based learning, and one for teaching writing, and… you get the idea. Activities such as these tend to increase feelings of ownership and to stimulate a good deal of creative problem-solving.

The idea of teacher-scholars has a rich history in education (Chall, 1986). No doubt you have noticed that several of the methods and ideas presented in this text were suggested by classroom teachers and other school practitioners.

In-Service Education

In-service education, or staff informing and transforming, is a key feature of successful school programming. This can take several forms. The action research model just discussed is one means of broadening horizons. The most practical methods, however, involve direct in-service training.

There are no clear formulas for conducting in-service teacher training. Nonetheless, there has been a good deal of research on the efficacy of various generic approaches. A meta-analysis (broad-summary analysis) of many studies (Wade, 1984–1985) and our own more recent research (Manzo & Manzo, 1995) support the following conclusions:

- Regardless of who conducts in-service sessions (trainers come under many different job classifications), teachers are more likely to benefit when they use methods that permit learning by doing.

- Move beyond *doing* to discovery learning workshops that are built around *heuristic* tasks, actions and activities that result in penetrating insights. See Figure 14.2 for suggested in-service discovery workshop activities.

---

1. Make informal textbook diagnostic tests.
2. Create a reading-study-thinking guide.
3. Identify key questions that underlie a course's content.
4. Search for instructional paradigms that virtually define the most complete way to teach something that is fundamental. Three such paradigms include the Directed Reading–Thinking Activity (a design for teaching a complete content literacy lesson), the Frayer model (for teaching vocabulary and concepts), and the "writing process" (for teaching all phases of effective writing).
5. To further ensure that teachers are becoming investors in a school program, invite them to participate in identifying and solving instructional problems. (See Chapter 8 on critical-constructive teaching and learning for relevant ideas.)
6. Recommend the Listen-Read-Discuss method from Chapter 1 as an initial offering. This *time-release* method was designed to stimulate professional discussion and to invite increasingly more sophisticated discussion among the professional staff.
7. Administer instruments that tend to uncover areas of suboptimal literacy development, for example, *The Informal Reading–Thinking Inventory* (Manzo, Manzo & McKenna, 1995), for middle grades.

Figure 14.2 Suggested in-service heuristic/discovery workshop activities.

- There is no magical combination of methods for successful in-service education. Nevertheless, in-service programs that use observation, microteaching, auditory and visual feedback, and practice, either individually or in some combination, are more effective than programs that do not use these methods.

- Contrary to recent populist trends, in-service education is most successful when led by an expert but organized to encourage participant involvement and contributions. Increasingly, in the future, the Internet will play an important role in in-service and pre-service education. It provides a platform for dialogue, information, and demonstration lessons.

Evaluation

Quality control must be a fundamental part of every intervention effort. It begins with a careful perusal of the literature in a field and extends into field tests. Chapter 10 on assessment, provides a solid array of options for preassessing need and evaluating outcomes. *Your effort to learn the contents of this and other such textbooks is the best preparation for learning the literature and guiding concepts of the field.*

Content Area Literacy and Educational Reform

There are several larger reform movements in education that are proving to be meaningful and durable. Unfortunately, each of these tends to function in relative isolation of all others. It seems reasonable to begin to fuse these collateral movements to the content area literacy's highly refined principles and procedures. This would be a fortunate merger since content area literacy is well grounded in teaching practices. As such, it would "put legs under" many of the reform programs that are steeped in an enlightened philosophy but light on specific practices. Conversely, these reform programs tend to be recognizable to most school administrators and boards but not to most teachers and literacy specialists. Technology transfer and sharing across related fields are a logical next step to the great increase in availability of information. To date, issues in policy studies, school decision making, reform, and just what constitutes "best practices" are matters that have proceeded on relatively parallel and therefore non-interacting paths.

School reform in general is not without problems. Reform movements vary widely in purpose, method, and degree of development. They can be political in purpose, or just quirky as when they reflect a particularly well-leveraged person's or group's special interests. In fact, there is a reaction growing to the large and overleveraged abilities of some reforms and reformers. The 29 superintendents of Orange County, California voted unanimously to call for a moratorium on state legislative reforms. They say the barrage of laws passed in almost every session are willy-nilly and picayunish—they have mandated something as specific as teaching about the Irish potato famine. In general, these interferences are causing chaos and financial strain, and the legislatures almost never appropriate new funds to implement their quirky laws and regulations (based on a news story in the *Los Angles Times*, 5/29/99). A quick summary of school reforms and reformers is found at our Web site, www.literacyleaders.com.

As noble and influential as these reform efforts have been, none is likely to have the impact of the Charter School Movement. It will affect every educator's work and career even if they never teach in a charter school.

Charter Schools

What are charter schools, once you get past anecdotal headlines like "Gritty Harding High Charter: A Place Where Kids "SUCCEED"? Essentially, charter schools are public schools that are licensed to operate with many of the same freedoms as private schools, with no additional charges to parents allowed. Generally, this means that teachers need not meet the same credential requirements, and hundreds of lesser rules and regulations either do not apply or are more liberally interpreted. Most charter schools are allowed to have up to 20% of teachers that have no teaching credential whatsoever. To get a feel for what this means, think of what you have learned about content area literacy this semester, and realize that one-fifth of the teachers in these schools may not have a clue that these options even exist.

Almost anyone can apply to the state to operate a charter school; this includes parents, teachers, organizations, and even religious groups as long as they do not operate as a sectarian institution. If approved, they receive state funding on the same per-pupil basis as other public schools (about $7,100 per year on average, although the figure varies widely from Maine to Mississippi). Charter schools also may qualify for additional support from county and local municipal governments. They are not exempt from most state criterion-based tests but may be exempt from nationally normed, standardized tests.

These common factors aside, charter schools are very different from one another. Some are built around themes, such as art or foreign language, others around an idea, such as operating schools through most of the summer or meeting kids' learning styles. The nation's first charter school, City Academy, was founded by teachers in St. Paul, Minnesota. They felt they could attract and provide for kids who felt alienated by conventional education. Other charter schools are founded by concerned parents, such as one in Oakland, California, started by parents frustrated with lack of attention to the special needs of Latino students.

Teacher groups are split on charter schools. Some feel that they have diminished the status of teachers and teaching; others see them as a way to curb excessive bureaucracy and top-heavy administration. Clearly, both of these are reasonable objectives. However, each time a district or new administrative grouping tries to eliminate workers, they tend to reduce the number of curriculum coordinators and master teachers with release time to work with others, a move that seems to have little negative effect immediately but that eventually stalls progress. To counter this impact, schools try to import whole plans from elsewhere. These franchise operations seldom are able to sustain themselves, even when done by the same people in a different location. There also is a history of eventual collapse of alternate schools. The reasons vary, but certain intrinsic factors tend to sabotage the best efforts.

Alternative Schools and Their Sometimes Naïve Experiments

Alternative schools often are based on some unsupportable premise or principle. For example, one (called the KIPP program in New York City) has a school day that begins at 7 A.M. and lasts until 5 P.M. It also goes through the summer and pays teachers the same as more conventional schools—this apparent "solution" flies in the face of recent findings by William Demont, of the Sleep Disorders Center of Standford University, that most kids can't fall asleep before 11 P.M. and require 9 full hours of sleep. With school days starting at times between 7 and 7:45 A.M. and lasting past 2:30–5:00 P.M., it is no wonder that their initial grade increases are unsupportable. Other researchers, such as Mary Carskadon of Brown University, are finding that about half of youngsters living in this pattern are so chronically tired and unfocused that their brains will lapse into deep, REM sleep–like states within three to four minutes in tests done at different periods during the day.

For quirky reasons such as these, experimental schools seldom are able to continue to attract stalwart students. Most alternative schools must first play up and then live down the mark of being different, this at a time in adolescent life when being like one's peers is the driving emotional state. At first they have fewer instructional administrators, but in time recruitment becomes their administrative overgrowth and advertising and public relations their cost overrun. Eventually, schools based on reform cannot even attract students that previously would have gone to its alternative program. These students shy away as the school's reputation becomes tarnished by its nontraditional bent, and also because such schools begin life without a local tradition and alumni, an advantage initially but a recruiting and public relations problem thereafter. Alternative schools also tend to operate under some "new" idea about curriculum or approach to teaching that is, by definition, outside the mainstream and often unproven and undeveloped. As a result, they must constantly be engaged in a heavy level of research and development and extraordinary efforts to explain and justify themselves, something they are seldom equipped to do.

The last time something like charter schools happened on a mass scale was in the mid-1970s. It was called experience-based career education (EBCE). By 1978 it covered over 250 secondary schools in almost every state. It came about through an unlikely marriage of the counterculture movement and massive federal spending. It was commonly held that the spending was insincere and largely prompted by an effort to use the schools to quell revolutionary thinking by institutionalizing it. EBCE was not a total disaster, but it did fizzle essentially for the reasons noted previously and for one other that does not quite fit the charter school movement: EBCE programs tended to become the place that administrators sent their lowest performing and most difficult students (Meyer, 1988). It is everyone's hope, even those who are the most skeptical, that charter schools will do better. Charter schools do have one thing in their favor: They are helping to reestablish urban neighborhood schools; home values in cities that have been so affected already are soaring. Finally, charters could be instrumental in having people finally admit that the large homes of suburbia are mausoleum-like structures, and suburban towns, with no sidewalks and no place to walk to—not stores, parks, or libraries—are something of a failed twentieth-century experiment.

▶ TOWARD A QUEST FUSION CURRICULUM

No effort to bring about syntheses of loosely associated parts, such as of content mastery and reading, writing, and thinking processes, is likely to gain strength without some overarching concepts and metaphors to guide thinking into a unifying action plan. With this in mind, we have begun to set out some concerns, principles, and practices that we are calling the *Quest Fusion Literacy Curriculum* (QFLC). In concert with its inquiry-based theme, we invite the reader to consider the forming tenets of this "curriculum" and to join the effort to further refine and specify it as it evolves on our Web site into guidelines and practices (although several of the latter have been detailed in previous chapters). One goal is to help teachers to value and use the content area literacy methods that Spor and Schneider (1999) found to be so underutilized. This open-ended approach to learning and creating together is the essence of the "community of learners" approach to education that has been given such great currency and meaning by telecomputing.

Quest Fusion Literacy Curriculum: Basic Idea

The QFLC is a cluster of largely content area literacy methods selected to advance curiosity, inquiry, and creative thinking. The curriculum has a strong constructivist orientation but also seeks to find value in traditional educational goals and practices and to build on these rather than to reject all that came before modern constructivism. To be more precise, it is based on constructive thinking more so than the philosophy of constructivism. The goal of collectively constructing a more dynamic curriculum aimed at creative reading, writing, and thinking serves as the quest, or cause beyond oneself, that is so important to supporting durable and sensible changes in current educational practices. This Quest Literacy Curriculum also attempts to address a number of problems and issues in contemporary education. See Figures 14.3 and 14.4.

---

1. Curriculum impediment to creativity: neither art nor science seems to invite innovation in training minds to think creatively. Art tends to treat it as springing from mysticism or the muses; and science as commonly practiced sees it as nearly contradictory: ". . . it is impossible to devise rules [of logic and science] that would enable one to infer new hypotheses from observations" (Longino, 1990, p. 24).

2. School progress can be slowed more than advanced by the demands of a "never-ending stream of new curricular initiatives" (Labbo & Ash, 1998, p. 181) that tend to be played out as competing with traditional theories and practices.

3. There is a need for a cohesive, coherent, and stable body of knowledge and objectives that remain open to new perspectives, but are not easily or overly swayed by every new or revisited challenge and educational fad.

Figure 14.3 Summary of problems, predicaments, and needs addressed by the Quest Fusion Curriculum.

4. Many sensible school solutions do not achieve a significant level of sustained value because they cannot break through one form or another of political barriers that bias discourse of their efficacy (e.g., the sometimes/someplace excesses of radical multiculturalism, bilingualism, feminism, LD-ism, pop-psychology overemphasis on self-esteem and/or religiosity).

5. Few politically inspired reform themes have addressed the fundamental need to change how teachers teach and how students learn in the classroom. Nonetheless, a revolution has taken place in pedagogy, one that few outside of education are aware of. Educators have shown that they can increase the performance of remedial-level students by four grade levels in twenty days of instruction, and methods based on these cognitive science approaches have resulted in some sixth-graders understanding Newtonian physics as well as do high school students (Bruer, 1993).

6. Our relative ignorance of pedagogical content knowledge has been called "the missing research program." (Bruer, 1993, p. 282, citing Shulman).

7. Schools need to be restructured to better align with human physiology and consequently psychology. They need to be made more conducive to the sprint-and-rest nature of the human attention span and to the circadian rhythms of adolescent sleep needs being reported at several sleep disorder centers—(high school kids need nine hours of sleep per day and cannot be expected to fall asleep much before 11 P.M.).

8. Means must be engineered to expose more students to the "influential teachers" who are able to tap internal motivation that stimulates intellectual curiosity and the desire to solve problems, deal with predicaments, and use clearly formulated teaching methods (Ruddell, 1999).

9. Educators must figure out how to induce more of transformational learning; alternately known as *peak learning experiences* (Bloom, 1981), FLOW (Csikszentmihalyi, 1991) and *manifest curiosity* (Manzo & Sherk, 1978).

10. Schooling must be redesigned so as to gear minds to overcome what sociobiologist E. O. Wilson in his recent book, *Consilience* (1998), notes as the mind's remarkable inability to see the world as an integrated whole, despite our great need to do so.

Figure 14.3 (*continued*)

AQFL would be achieved simply by selecting and routinely using content area literacy methods that already fuse reading, writing, thinking, and content mastery to "questing," or inquiry-based learning. Selecting from the methods covered in previous chapters, these might include the following:

Question-Only method

ReQuest procedure

K-W-L plus

Enabling Questions

Note Cue

Problem-solving approach to study skills

What others might you add, and to what purpose? See our Web site to join the quest for a practical and effective way to build a more seamless, interdisciplinary, and inquiry-based content area literacy curriculum.

Figure 14.4 Examples of the methods that combine to form a Quest Fusion Literacy Curriculum (QFLC).

▶ QFLC DECLARES FOR DISCOVERY LEARNING AND SYNTHESIS OF FRAGMENTED THEORIES OF TEACHING/LEARNING

In brief, the feeling is that teaching toward attributes such as wonder, curiosity, and constructive thinking-responding are more likely to be sustainable parts of school practices when they are *declared* purposes of education. Achieving this is difficult, perhaps because of the absence of a metaphor or synthesizing construct to guide education out of the room-for-only-one-theme-or-conflict-at-a-time kind of thinking. Strictly speaking, this should not be so difficult. It is not like trying to create a unified theory of macro and quantum (or atomic) physics. It is more like a manageable engineering feat, like the Hoover Dam, that simply needs our collective attention and resources. Much of what we need to know to do this is known. It simply is unintegrated, intermittent, and diluted by passing interests, fads, and special interest groups. The only way to avoid another 30 years of the Reading Wars (between "whole-language" and "skills" advocates) is to set integration of theories and parts of educational process as a goal for every graduate of every school of education and every conference on education, everywhere.

The Quest and Fusion Metaphors

To help individual minds and institutions become more able to address this complex task, two working metaphors are offered: the multilevel value in the terms *quest*—which conjures the *wonder* and *invent* part of learning—and *fusion*—a term that speaks to the melding of dissimilar parts into new entities that complement rather than compete. Where this has occurred in the past there often has been a release of energy and spirit that is greater than would be suggested by the simple sum of the parts. Beyond the obvious example of the power released in nuclear fusion is Fusion Cooking, or the unique blending of ethnic and American cuisines into dishes that not only fuse styles of cooking but the art and science of food preparation into dishes that further fuse haute cuisine with home cooking. Two concrete examples that almost any amateur chef could duplicate, and be inspired by, will help you to see the metaphor. Take old-fashioned (packaged) beef barley soup and add "five star oriental spices" (available in most grocery stores), and you have a spectacular new flavor that is capturing supporters everywhere it is tried. Another, which is slightly more difficult, starts with a plate of pasta with fresh tomatoes. To this is added a ladle of rich chicken broth and, ideally, a link of chicken sausage with apple (your local butcher will not only make it up for you, but you can expect to see him or her offering it and variations on it in short order), and voilá, you have a Sacramento Hilton Hotel treat.

Seeing and knowing about innovations such as these inspire and teach in ways that transcend our best efforts to teach in conventional ways. As noted in Chapter 8, we tend to disbelieve our capacities to be inventive, and hence do not ask for it in school, but as you have seen throughout this text, it is increasingly becoming part of life beyond the classroom, where being creative now is ranked as the number one survival skill. See www.LiteracyLeaders.com for more details and to participate in the further development of the *Quest Fusion Literacy Curriculum*, now spanning preschool to high school.

▶ AFTER WORDS

We feel that the next chapter in the saga of content area literacy will include attempts to peer into the future by addressing two contemporary themes that appear to be taking on the force of megatrends: interdisciplinary units and entrepreneurial literacy—or teaching youngsters how to make as well as take jobs. Both have strong implications for the way content teaching is likely to be conducted and the way we conduct commerce in ideas as well as dollars in the future. These topics also are good examples of literacies that are fusing themselves into education and our collective future. We invite you to visit www.LiteracyLeaders. com to read more about this and to help us shape the future of education. Thanks for joining us on the journey thus far; we'll look forward to hearing from you.

MODEL PROFESSIONAL PORTFOLIO RECORDER AND PLANNER

A professional portfolio, begun early in your career, can be an invaluable lifelong resource. To construct a model portfolio, you will need the following materials:

- A three-ring binder (you may want to begin with a one-inch binder and transfer materials to a larger-size binder as your collection grows)
- Nine three-hole notebook pockets for storing materials in various sections of the portfolio (see below)
- Attachable index tabs to mark each section (attach these to the pockets, since these extend farther than regular-sized sheets)
- Section titles (described next), copied onto separate sheets for insertion into the notebook, between pockets

With these simple materials, and a bit of reflection on your past, present, and future, you are ready to assemble a model portfolio that will grow with you through your professional career.

Section I: Guiding Thoughts

In this section, record relevant quotations you run across that strike you as worth remembering and that can serve to keep your thinking and instructional decision making on track.

A. Thoughts and perspectives on careers in general

Examples

- Successful careers don't just happen; they are the result of vision, planning, and effort.
- Most successful careers are beset by occasional setbacks. Expect these, and be ready to push on.
- When truth stands in your way, you are headed in the wrong direction.

B. Thoughts and perspectives on teachers and teaching

Examples

- The art of teaching is the art of assisting discovery.
- The enthusiastic teacher is a lifelong student.
- The finer the instruction, the more it invites; the poorer it is, the more it compels.

    C.   Thoughts and perspectives on schools and schooling

Examples

- Nowadays, school heads are chosen to run a school rather than lead it.
- The school's task is to take a lot of live wires and see that they get well grounded.

Section II: Employment Record

In this section, keep a running record of both teaching and nonteaching experiences, and store an updated resume.

    A.   Nonteaching job experiences
    B.   Educational job experiences
    C.   Other

(Pocket: current resume)

Section III: Personal History (Birth to High School)

In this section, make relevant notes about your family and early school background, and store related documents.

    A.   Family background
    B.   Medical/health factors
    C.   Social, athletic affiliations
    D.   Academic record, K–12
    E.   Hobbies and interests
    F.   Significant memories

(Pocket: birth certificate, passport, school records, early photos, letters, memorabilia)

Section IV: Personal History (Postsecondary)

In this section, make notes about your college life and education, and store related documents.

    A.   Academic record (degrees, majors, minors)
    B.   Activities (extracurricular; organizations, religious, athletic)

C.   Social life (personal and family)

D.   Intellectual development (books, magazines, ideas)

(Pocket: transcripts, letters of reference, other records)

Section V: Material Accounting

In this section, keep notes about your financial standing and store related documents.

A.   Gifts, trusts, support

B.   Income history

C.   Loan history

D.   Assets (stocks, car, furniture, property)

E.   Approximate net worth

F.   Prospects (likely legacies and/or opportunities)

(Pocket: financial records, photos, memorabilia)

Section VI: Professional History

In this section, make notes about your teaching career, and store related documents.

A.   Certificates

B.   Evaluations/recommendations

C.   Memorable teachers and colleagues

D.   Teaching experiences: subjects, grade levels, situations

E.   Related nonteaching roles and experiences

F.   Memorable in-service sessions, conferences, sabbaticals

G.   Memorable articles, books, papers

H.   Membership and roles in committees and professional organizations

I.   Grants, travel, awards

J.   Summer activities and employment

(Pocket: teaching certificates, letters, articles or summaries)

Section VII: Self-Appraisals

In this section, keep notes on an ongoing self-assessment, and store related records.

A.   Attitudes

B.   Interests and abilities

C.   Temperament/personality

    D.   Teaching/learning style

    E.   Personal assessment of strengths and weaknesses as a person and as a teacher

(Pocket: records)

Section VIII: Occasional Notes

In this section, make additional notes of memorable events and experiences, and store related records.

    A.   Notes on memorable personal events (marriage, deaths, births, friendships)

    B.   Notes on memorable professional experiences (significant mentor relationships, special students)

(Pocket: records)

Section IX: Blueprints

In this section, keep notes about long-term career plans, and store related documents.

    A.   Personal career goals

    B.   Objectives that might contribute to your professional education

(Pocket: related articles, notes, and documents)

Section X: Teaching Competence

In this section, keep notes about your experiences in using various teaching approaches and methods, and store related materials.

    A.   Teaching methods you have mastered

    B.   Teaching methods you intend to try

(Pocket: related articles and notes on each method)

REFERENCES

Aaronson, E., Blaney, N., Sikes, J., Stevan, C., & Snapp, N. (1975, February). The jigsaw route to learning and liking. *Psychology Today*, 43–50.

Aaronson, E., Stephan, C., Sikes, J., Blaney, N., & Snapp, M. (1978). *The jigsaw classroom*. Beverly Hills, CA: Sage.

Adams, E. K. (1982). What research says to the disciplinarian. In G. H. McNinch (Ed.), *Readings in the disciplines, Second yearbook of the American Reading Forum* (pp. 109–111). Athens, GA: American Reading Forum.

Adams, M. J. (1990). *Beginning to read: Thinking and learning about print*. Cambridge, MA: MIT Press.

Adler, M. J. (1982). *The paideia proposal*. New York: Macmillan.

Allen, K., & Ingulsrud, J. E. (2003). Manga literacy: Popular culture and the reading habits of Japanese college students. *Journal of Adolescent & Adult Literacy* (46)8, 674–683.

Alley, G., & Deshler, D. (1980). *Teaching the learning disabled adolescent: Strategies and methods*. Denver, CO: Love.

Alvermann, D. E., & Boothby, P. R. (1983). A preliminary investigation of the differences in children's retention of "inconsiderate" text. *Reading Psychology, 4*, 237–246.

Alvermann, D. E., Dillon, D. R., & O'Brien, D. G. (1987). Using discussion to promote reading comprehension. Newark, DE: International Reading Association.

Alvermann, D. E. & Hagood, M. C. (2000). Fandom and critical media literacy.

Alvermann, D. E., Moon, J. S., & Hagood, M. C. (1999). *Popular Culture in the Classroom: Teaching and Researching Critical Media Literacy*, Newark, DE: International Reading Association.

Anders, P. L., Bos, C. S., & Filip, D. (1984). The effect of semantic feature analysis on the reading comprehension of learning-disabled students. In J. A. Niles & L. A. Harris (Eds.), *Changing perspectives on research in reading/language processing and instruction. Thirty-third yearbook of the National Reading Conference* (pp. 162–166). Rochester, NY: National Reading Conference.

Anderson, R. C., & Nagy, W. E. (1989). *Word meanings*. (Tech. Rep. No. 485). Cambridge, MA: Bolt, Beranek and Newman.

Ankney, P., & McClurg, E. (1981). Testing Manzo's Guided Reading Procedure. *The Reading Teacher, 34*, 681–685.

Applebee, A. N. (1981). *Writing in the secondary school*. Urbana, IL: National Council of Teachers of English.

Applebee, A., Langer, J., Mullis, I., Lathan, A., & Gentile, C. (1994). *NAEP 1992 Writing Report Card*. Washington, DC: U.S. Department of Education, Office of Educational Research and Improvement.

Artley, A. S. (1944). A study of certain relationships existing between general reading comprehension and reading comprehension in a specific subject-matter area. *Journal of Educational Research, 37*, 464–473.

Aschner, M. J., Gallagher, J. J., Perry, J. M., Afsar, S. S., Jenne, W., & Farr, H. (1962). *A system for classifying thought processes in the context of classroom verbal interaction*. Champaign: University of Illinois, Institute for Research on Exceptional Children.

Athanses, S. (1988). Developing a class-room community of interpreters. *English Journal, 77*, 45–48.

Ausubel, D. P. (1960). The use of advance organizers in the learning and retention of meaningful verbal material. *Journal of Educational Psychology, 51*, 267–272.

Bacon, E. (1963). *Notes on the piano*. Syracuse, NY: Syracuse University Press.

Baer, M. (1998). Smart kids? Who needs 'em. *Wired Magazine. 6:9*, 123–127.

Baines, L. (1998). The future of the written word. In J. S. Simmons & L. Baines (Eds.) *Language study in middle school, high school and beyond: Views on enhancing the study of language*. Newark, DE: International Reading Association.

Baker, L., & Brown, A. L. (1984). Metacognitive skills and reading. In P. D. Pearson (Ed.), *Handbook of reading research* (pp. 333–394). New York: Longman.

Baker, R. L., & Schutz, R. E. (Eds). (1972). *Instructional product research*. New York: Van Nostrand.

Baldwin, R. S., & Kaufman, R. K. (1979). A concurrent validity study of the Raygor readability estimate. *Journal of Reading, 23*, 148–153.

Baloche, L., Mauger, M. L., Willis, T. M., Filinuk, J. R., & Michalsky, B. V. (1993). Fishbowls, creative controversy, talking chips: Exploring literature cooperatively. *English Journal, 82*, 43–48.

Barrett, T. C. (1967). *The evaluation of children's reading achievement*. Newark, DE: International Reading Association.

Barton, J. (1995). Conducting effective classroom discussions. *Journal of Reading. 38*, 346–350.

Barton, W. A. (1930). *Outlining as a study procedure*. New York: Columbia University, Teacher's College.

Baumann, J. F., & Kameenui, E. J. (1991). Research on vocabulary instruction. In J. Flood, J. M. Jensen, D. Lapp, & J.

Squire (Eds.), *Handbook of research on teaching the English language arts* (pp. 604–631). Upper Saddle River, NJ: Prentice Hall.

Bean, T. W. (1981). Matching materials and strategies for comprehension. In V. Pesqueira & C. Boling (Eds). *Reading: A Foundation for Success*. Fourth Yearbook of the Arizona State University Reading Conference, Tempe, Arizona.

Bean, T. W. (2000). Reading in the content areas: Social constructivist dimensions. In Kamil, M. L., Mosenthal, P. B., Pearson, P. D., & Barr, R. (Eds.), *Handbook of reading research, volume III*. (pp. 629–644). Mahwah, NJ: Erlbaum.

Bean, T. W., & Bishop, A. (1992). Polar opposites: A strategy for guiding students' critical reading and discussion. In E. Dischner et. al (Eds.) *Reading in the Content Areas*. Dubuque, IA: Kendall/Hunt.

Bean T. W., Bean, S. K., & Bean, K. F., (1999). Intergenerational conversations and two adolescents' multiple literacies: Implications for redefining content area literacy. *Journal of Adolescent and Adult Literacy, 42*, 438–448.

Bean, T. W., & Moni, K. (2003). Developing students' critical literacy: Exploring identity construction in young adult fiction. *Journal of Adolescent & Adult Literacy, (46)*8, 638–648.

Bean, T. W., & Pardi, R. (1979). A field test of a guided reading strategy. *Journal of Reading, 23*, 144–147.

Behle, P. (Ed). (1982). *The double helix: Teaching the writing process*. Florissant, MO: Ferguson-Florissant Writers Project.

Bereiter, C. & Scardamalia, M. (1985). Cognitive coping strategies and the problem of inert knowledge. In S. F. Chipman, J. W. Segal, & R. Glazer, (Eds.) *Thinking and learning skills,*

Vol. 2: Current research and open questions (pp. 65–80). Hillsdale, NJ: Erlbaum.

Bintz, W. (1997). Exploring reading nightmares of middle and secondary school teachers. *Journal of Adolescent & Adult Literacy, 41*, 12–24.

Bishop, A. (2003). Course supplement for Reading 508. (Available from School of Education, P.O. Box 6868, California State University—Fullerton, Fullerton, CA 92834).

Blanc, R. A. (1977). Cloze-plus as an alternative to "guides" for understanding and appreciating poetry. *Journal of Reading, 21*, 215–218.

Bloom, B. S. (Ed.). (1956). *Taxonomy of educational objectives: The classification of educational goals. Handbook 1. Cognitive domain*. New York: Longman, Green.

Bloom, B. S. (1976). *Human characteristics and school learning*. New York: McGraw-Hill.

Bloom, B. S. (1981). *All our children learning*. New York: McGraw-Hill.

Bormuth, J. R. (1965). Validities of grammatical and semantic classifications of cloze test scores. In J. A. Figurel (Ed.), *Reading and inquiry. International Reading Association Conference Proceedings* (Vol. 10, pp. 283–286). Newark, DE: International Reading Association.

Bradley, A. (1999). Science group finds middle school textbooks inadequate. *Education Week, 19*:6, 5.

Bragstad, B. (1985, March). *Mapping: Using both sides of the brain*. Lecture handout, International Reading Association State Council Meeting. Orlando, FL.

Braught, L. R. (1992). Student operated bookshops: A program to encourage middle-grade literacy. *The Reading Teacher, 45*, 438–444.

Bromley, K. D. (1985). Pre′ cis writing and outlining enhance content learning. *The Reading Teacher, 38*, 406–411.

Brown, A. L. (1980). Metacognition development and reading. In R. J. Spiro, B. C. Bruce, & W. F. Brewer (Eds.), *Theoretical issues in reading comprehension* (pp. 453–481). Hillsdale, NJ: Erlbaum Associates.

Brown, H. & Cambourne, B. (1987). *Read and retell*. Portsmouth: Heinemann.

Brozo, W. G., & Simpson, M. L. (1999). *Readers, teachers, learners: Expanding literacy across the content areas* (3rd ed.) Columbus, OH: Merrill, an imprint of Prentice Hall.

Bruer, J. T. (1993). *Schools for thought: A science of learning in the classroom*. Cambridge, MA: A Bradford Book of MIT Press.

Bruner, J. S. (1966). *Toward a theory of instruction*. Cambridge, MA: Harvard University Press.

Burke, K. (1950/1969). *A rhetoric of motives*. Berkeley, CA: University of California Press.

Bush, V. (1945). *Science—the endless frontier: a report to the President by Vannevar Bush, Director of the Office of Scientific Research and Development, July 1945*. Washington, DC: U.S. Government Printing Office.

Calfee, R. C., Dunlap, K. L., & Wat, A. Y. (1994). Authentic discussion of texts in middle school. *Journal of Reading, 37*(7), 546–556.

Campbell, J., Donahue, P., Reese, C., & Phillips, G. (1996). *NAEP 1994 reading report card for the nation and the states*. Washington, DC: U.S. Department of Education, OERI, 1996.

Camperell, K. (1982). Vygotsky's theory of intellectual development: The effect of subjectmatter instruction on self-regulated cognitive processes. In G. H. McNich (Ed.), *Reading in the disciplines. Second yearbook of the American Read-*

ing Forum (pp. 33–35). Athens: University of Georgia.

Carr, E. M., & Ogle, D. M. (1987). K-W-L Plus: A strategy for comprehension and summarization. *Journal of Reading, 30,* 626–631.

Carver, R. P. (1985). Is the Degrees of Reading Power test valid or invalid? *Journal of Reading, 29,* 34–41.

Casale, U. P. (1985). Motor imaging: A reading-vocabulary strategy. *Journal of Reading, 28,* 619–621.

Casale, U. P., & Kelly, B. W. (1980). Problem-solving approach to study skills (PASS) for students in professional schools. *Journal of Reading, 24,* 232–238.

Casale, U. P., & Manzo, A. V. (1983). Differential effects of cognitive, affective, and proprioceptive approaches on vocabulary acquisition. In G. H. McNinch (Ed.), *Reading research to reading practice. Third yearbook of the American Reading Forum* (pp. 71–73). Athens, GA: American Reading Forum.

Cassidy, J., & Cassidy, D. (2001–2002). What's hot, what's not for 2002. *Reading Today* 19(3), 1, 3.

Cassidy, J. & Cassidy, D. (2003–2004). What's not, what's not for 2004. *Reading Today,* 21(3), 34.

Caverly, D. C., Burrell, K., & McFarland, J. (1992, November). *Evaluation results of a whole language TASP reading program.* Paper presented at the annual conference of the Conference on Academic Support Programs, Fort Worth, TX.

Caverly, D. C., Mandeville, T. F., & Nicholson, S. A. (1995). PLAN: A study-reading strategy for informational text. *Journal of Adolescent and Adult Literacy, 39,* 190–199.

Cerullo, M. (1997). *Reading the environment: Children's literature in the science classroom.* Portsmouth, NH: Heinemann.

Chall, J. S. (1986). The teacher as scholar. *The Reading Teacher, 39,* 792–797.

Chandler-Olcott, K., Mahar, D. (2003). Adolescents' anime-inspired "fanfictions": An exploration of multiliteracies. *Journal of Adolescent & Adult Literacy, 46*(7), 556–566.

Chapin, S., Illingworth, M., Landau, S., Masingila, O., & McCracken, L. (1995). *Middle Grades Mathematics: An Interactive Approach.* Upper Saddle River, NJ: Prentice Hall.

Chase, R. H. (1926). *The ungeared mind.* Philadelphia: F.A. Davis Company, Publishers.

Ciardiello, A. V. (1998). Did you ask a good question today? Alternative cognitive and metacognitive strategies. *Journal of Adolescent and Adult Literacy. 42,* 210–219.

Ciardiello, A. V., & Cicchelli, T. (1994). The effects of instructional training models and content knowledge on student questioning in social studies. *The Journal of Social Studies Research, 19,* 30–37.

Clewell, S. E., & Haidemos, J. (1983). Organizational strategies to increase comprehension. *Reading World, 22,* 314–321.

Cloer, T., Jr., & Denton, G. R. (1995). The effects of read-along tapes on the comprehension of middle school students. In K. Camparell, B. L. Hayes, & R. Telfer (Eds.), Linking literacy: past, present, and future. *American Reading Forum Yearbook* (Vol. 15, pp. 85–92). Logan, Utah: American Reading Forum Yearbook.

CNN Book Channel (1999, October 2). Roth and Stolba interview on their book, *Women's Figures* [Television broadcast]. Atlanta, GA: CNN.

Collins, C. (1987). Content mastery strategies aid classroom discussion. *The Reading Teacher, 40,* 816–818.

Collins, C. (1991). Reading instruction that increases thinking abilities. *Journal of Reading, 34,* 510–516.

Commeyras, M. (1993). Promoting critical thinking through dialogical-thinking reading lessons. *The Reading Teacher, 6,* 486–493.

Condus, M. M., Marshall, K. J., & Miller, S. R. (1986). Effect of the key-word mnemonic strategy on vocabulary acquisition and maintenance by learning disabled children. *Journal of Learning Disabilities, 19,* 609–613.

Cooter, R. B., & Flynt, E. S. (1986). *Reading comprehension: Out of the ivory tower and into the classroom.* Unpublished paper, Northwestern State University, Natchitoches, LA.

Crafton, L. K. (1983). Learning from reading: What happens when students generate their own background information? *Journal of Reading, 26,* 586–592.

Criscoe, B. L., & Gee, T. C. (1984). *Content reading: A diagnostic/prescriptive approach.* Upper Saddle River, NJ: Prentice Hall.

Cronholm, L. (1999). Why Baruch ended remedial classes. *The Chronicle of Higher Education.* September 24.

Csikszentmihalyi, M. (1991) *Flow: The psychology of optimal experience.* New York: Harper Perennial.

Culver, V. I., Godfrey, H. C., & Manzo, A. V. (1972). A partial reanalysis of the validity of the cloze procedure as an appropriate measure of reading comprehension [Research report summary]. *Journal of Reading, 16,* 256–257.

Cummins, J. (2001). Language, power, and pedagogy: Bilingual children in the crossfire. Clevedon, UK: Multilingual Matters.

Cunningham, D., & Shablak, S. L. (1975). Selective Reading Guide-O-Rama: The content teacher's best friend. *Journal of Reading, 18,* 380–382.

Cunningham, J. W., Cunningham, P. M., & Arthur, S. V. (1981). *Middle and secondary school reading.* New York: Longman.

Cunningham, P. M., & Cunningham, J. W. (1976). SSSW, better content-writing. *The Clearing House, 49,* 237–238.

Cunningham, P. M., Moore, S. A., Cunningham, J. W., & Moore, D. W. (1983). *Reading in elementary classrooms: Strategies and observations.* New York: Longman.

Dahmus, M. E. (1970). How to teach verbal problems. *School Science and Mathematics, 70,* 121–138.

Daly, J. (1999, October). *Business 2.0.*

Davey, B. (1983). Think aloud—Modeling the cognitive processes of reading comprehension. *Journal of Reading, 27,* 44–47.

Davidson, J. W., & Stoff, M. B. (1995). *The American Nation.* Upper Saddle River, NJ: Prentice Hall.

DeBlase, G. (2003). Acknowledging agency while accommodating romance: Girls negotiating meaning in literacy transactions. *Journal of Adolescent & Adult Literacy, 46*(8), 624–635.

Derby, T. (1987). Reading instruction and course related materials for vocational high school students. *Journal of Reading, 30,* 308–316.

Desmond, R. (1997). Media literacy in the home: Acquisition vs. deficit models. In R. Kubey (ed.). *Media literacy in the information age* (pp. 323–343). New Brunswick, N.J.: Transaction Books.

Diamond, J. (1999). *Guns, germs, and steel: The fates of human societies.* NY: W.W. Norton & Co.

Diehl, W. A., & Mikulecky, L. (1980). The nature of reading as work. *Journal of Reading, 24,* 221–227.

Diggs, V. M. (1973). The relative effectiveness of the SQ3R method, a mechanized approach, and a combination method for training remedial reading to college freshmen (Doctoral dissertation, West Virginia University, Morgantown, 1972). *Dissertation Abstracts International, 33,* 5964A. (University Microfilms No. 74-4, 786)

Doctorow, M., Wittrock, M. C., & Marks, C. (1978). Generative processes in reading comprehension. *Journal of Educational Psychology, 70,* 109–118.

Dodson, S. (1997). *The mother daughter book club.* New York: Harper Perennial.

Donald, M., Sr. (1967). The SQ3R method in grade seven. *Journal of Reading, 11,* 33–35, 43.

Dortch, S. (1995). Talking with fewer words. *American Demographics.* (April) http://www.demographics.com/publications/.

Drucker, P. (1989). *The new realities: in government and politics, in economy and business, in society, and in world view.* Oxford: Heinemann Professional Publishing.

Duckworth, S., & Taylor, R. (1995). Creating and assessing literacy in at-risk students through hypermedia portfolios. *Reading Improvement, 32*(1), 26–31.

Duffelmeyer, F. (1994). Effective anticipation guide statements for learning from expository prose. *Journal of Reading, 37,* 452–457.

Duffelmeyer, F., Baum, D., & Merkley, D. (1987). Maximizing reader-text confrontation with an extended anticipation guide. *Journal of Reading, 31,* 146–151.

Duffy, G. G., & Hoffman, J. V. (1999). In pursuit of an illusion: The flawed search for a perfect method. *The Reading Teacher, 53:*1, 10–16.

Duke, C. R. (1987). Integrating reading, writing, and thinking skills into the music class. *Journal of Reading, 31,* 152–157.

Duke, N. K. (2000). 3.6 minutes per day: The scarcity of informational texts in first grade. *Reading Research Quarterly, 35*(2), 202–224.

Durkin, D. (1978–1979). What classroom observations reveal about comprehension instruction. *Reading Research Quarterly, 14,* 481–533.

Eanet, M. G., & Manzo, A. V. (1976). REAP—A strategy for improving reading/writing/study skills. *Journal of Reading, 19,* 647–652.

Echevarria, J., Vogt, M. E., & Short, D. (2004). *Making content comprehensible for English learners: The SIOP model* (2nd ed.). Boston: Allyn & Bacon (Ch. 5, pp. 92–93).

Ediger, M. (1992). The middle school student and interest in reading. *Journal of Affective Reading Education, 10*(2), 9–13.

Edwards, P. A., & Simpson, L. (1986). Bibliotherapy: A strategy for communication between parents and their children. *Journal of Reading, 30,* 110–118.

El-Hindi, A. E. (2003). Integrating literacy and science in the classroom: From ecomysteries to readers theatre. *The Reading Teacher, 56*(6), 536–539.

Embracing the persecuted: Park College kept Japanese-Americans out of detention camps (1999). *The Kansas City Star,* August 16.

Ennis, R. H. (1962). The concept of critical thinking. *Harvard Educational Review, 32,* 81–111.

Erickson, L. G. (1995). *Supervision of Literacy Programs: Teachers as Grass-Roots Change Agents.* Boston: Allyn and Bacon.

Ericson, B., Hubler, M., Bean, T. W., Smith, C. C., & McKenzie, J. V. (1987). Increasing critical reading in junior high classrooms. *Journal of Reading, 30,* 430–439.

Estes, T. H. (1991). Ten best. In E. Fry (Ed.), *Ten best ideas for reading teachers* (p. 59). New York: Addison-Wesley.

Fairclough, N. (1989). *Language and Power.* London: Longman.

Farr, R. (1992). Putting it all together: Solving the reading assessment puzzle. *The Reading Teacher, 46*(1), 26–37.

Farris, P. J., & Kaczmarski, D. (1988). Whole language: A closer look. *Contemporary Education, 59*(2), 77–81.

Feathers, K. M., & Smith, F. R. (1987). Meeting the reading demands of the real world: Literacy based content instruction. *Journal of Reading, 30,* 506–511.

Flower, L., & Hayes, J. R. (1981). A cognitive process theory of writing. *College Composition and Communication, 32,* 365–387.

Fogarty, R. (1992). Beyond test scores: Tracking significant outcomes. *Cogitare,* 6:3, 2.

Fogarty, R. & McTighe, J. (1993, Summer). Educating teachers for higher-order thinking: The three-story intellect. *Theory into Practice, 32:3,* 161–169.

Frager, A. M., & Thompson, L. C. (1985). Conflict: The key to critical reading instruction. *Journal of Reading, 28,* 676–683.

Freire, P. (1985). *The politics of education: Culture, power, and liberation.* South Hadley, MA: Bergin & Garvey.

Freire, P. (1987). Literacy: Reading the word and the world. South Hadley, MA: Bergin & Garvey.

Friedel, G. (1976, September). *Instant study skills.* Workshop handout, University of Missouri–Kansas City.

Fry, E. (1968).A readability formula that saves time. *Journal of Reading, 11,* 513–516, 575–578.

Fry, E. (1977). Fry's readability graph: Clarification, validity, and extension to level 17. *Journal of Reading, 21,* 242–252.

Furchtgott-Roth, D. F., & Stolba, C. (2000). *Women's figures: The economic progress of women in America.* Arlington, VA: Independent Women's Forum.

Galbraith, J. K. (1996, May). Interview on CNBC [Television broadcast]. New York: NBC.

Garber, K. S. (1995). *The effects of transmissional, transactional, and transformational reader-response strategies on middle school students' thinking complexity and social development.* (Unpublished doctoral dissertation, Kansas City, MO: University of Missouri–Kansas City.)

Gardner, H. (1983). *Frames of mind: The theory of multiple intelligences.* New York: Harper and Row.

Gardner, H. (1985). *The mind's new science.* New York: Basic Books.

Gauthier, L. R. (1996). Using guided conversation to increase students' content area comprehension. *Journal of Adolescent & Adult Literacy, 39,* 310–312.

Gee, T. C., & Rakow, S. J. (1987). Content reading specialists evaluate teaching practices. *Journal of Reading, 31,* 234–237.

Gentile, L. M. (1980). *Using sports and physical education to strengthen content area reading skills.* Newark, DE: International Reading Association.

Gerber, S., & Finn, J. D. (1998). Learning document skills at school and at work. *Journal of Adolescent and Adult Literacy, 42,* 32–44.

Geyer, J. J. (1972). Comprehensive and partial models related to the reading process. *Reading Research Quarterly, 7,* 541–587.

Gilbert, J. C. (1989). A two week K-6 interdisciplinary unit. In H. H. Jacobs (Ed.) *Interdisciplinary curriculum: design and improvement* (pp. 46–51). Alexandria, VA: Association for Supervision and Curriculum Development.

Gipe, J. P. (1978–1979). Investigating techniques for teaching word meanings. *Reading Research Quarterly, 14,* 624–644.

Gipe, J.P. (1998). *Multiple paths to literacy: Corrective reading techniques for classroom teachers.* Upper Saddle River, NJ: Prentice Hall.

Glickman, C. D. (1985). *Supervision of instruction: A developmental approach.* Newton, MA: Allyn & Bacon.

Glass, G. G. (1973). *Teaching decoding as separate from reading.* Garden City, New York: Adelphi University Press.

Godin, S. (1999). *Permission Marketing: Turning strangers into friends, and friends into customers*. New York: Simon & Schuster.

Gomez, M. L., Graue, M. E., & Bloch, M. N. (1991). Reassessing portfolio assessment: Rhetoric and reality. *Language Arts, 68:8,* 620–628.

Goodman, K. S., Bird, L. B., & Goodman, Y. M. (1991). *The whole language catalog*. Santa Rosa, CA: American School Publishers.

Gough, E. B., & Cosky, M. J. (1977). One second of reading again. In N. J. Castellan, Jr., D. Pisoni, & G. Potts (Eds.), *Cognitive theory* (Vol. 2, pp. 271–288). Hillsdale, NJ: Erlbaum.

Gray, D. (1988, Summer). *Socratic seminars: Basic education and reformation. Basic Education: Issues, Answers, and Facts, 3, 14.* Washington, DC: Council for Basic Education.

Gray, W. S. (1946). *On their own in reading*. Chicago: Scott, Foresman.

Greenewald, M. J., & Wolf, A. E. (1980). Professional journals in secondary education: Which ones do teachers recommend most? *The Clearing House, 53,* 349–350.

Greenhoe, M. L. (1972). Parameters of creativity in music education: An exploratory study (Doctoral dissertation, The University of Tennessee, Knoxville). *Dissertation Abstracts International, 33,* 1766A.

Guinier, L., Fine, M., & Balin, J. (1997). *Becoming gentlemen: Women, law school, and institutional change.* Boston: Beacon Press

Gurian, M. (1998). *A fine young man: What parents, mentors and educators can do to shape adolescent boys into exceptional men.* New York: Jeremy P. Tarcher/Putnam.

Gurrola, S. (1975). Determination of the relative effectiveness and efficiency of selected combinations of SQ3R study method components (Doctoral dissertation, New Mexico State University, 1974). *Dissertation Abstracts International, 35,* 6938A. (University Microfilms No. 75-10, 822)

Guthrie, J. T. (1984). Lexical learning. *The Reading Teacher, 37,* 660–662.

Haggard, M. [Ruddell]. (1976). *Creative Thinking-Reading Activities (CT-RA) as a means for improving comprehension.* Unpublished doctoral dissertation, University of Missouri-Kansas City, Kansas City, MO.

Haggard, M. R. (1978). The effect of creative thinking-reading activities (CT-RA) on reading comprehension. In P. D. Pearson & J. Hansen (Eds.), *Reading: Disciplined inquiry in process and practice. Twenty-seventh yearbook of the National Reading Conference* (pp. 233–236). Clemson, SC: National Reading Conference.

Haggard, M. R. (1982). The vocabulary self-collection strategy: An active approach to word learning. *Journal of Reading, 27,* 203–207.

Haggard, M. R. (1986). The vocabulary self-collection strategy: Using student interest and world knowledge to enhance vocabulary growth. *Journal of Reading, 29,* 634–642.

Harker, W. J. (1972–1973). An evaluative summary of models of reading comprehension. *Journal of Reading Behavior, 5,* 26–34.

Harker, W. J. (Ed.). (1977). *Classroom strategies for secondary reading.* Newark, DE: International Reading Association.

Harmon, J. M. (2002). Teaching independent word learning strategies to struggling readers. *Journal of Adolescent & Adult Literacy, 45*(7), 606–616.

Harste, J. (1978). Instructional implications of Rumelhart's model. In W. A. Diehi (Ed.), *Secondary reading: Theory and application. The 1978 Lilly conference on secondary reading* (Monographs in Teaching and Learning No. 1, pp. 21–23). Bloomington: Indiana University, School of Education.

Harste, J. C. (1994). Whole-language assessment. In A. Purves (Ed.), *Encyclopedia of English studies and language arts* (Vol. 2, pp. 1262–1263). New York: Scholastic.

Haven, K. (1999). "Good to the last drop": Making the most of stories to enhance language arts learning. *The California Reader, 32:2*, 5–9.

Heaton, M. M., & Lewis, H. B. (1955). *Reading ladders for human relations* (3rd ed.). Washington, DC: American Council on Education.

Henry, G. H. (1974). *Teaching reading as concept development: Emphasis on affective thinking*. Newark, DE: International Reading Association.

Herber, H. L. (1978). *Teaching reading in content areas* (2nd ed.). Englewood Cliffs, NJ: Prentice Hall.

Hersey, P., & Blanchard, K. H. (1997). *Management of organizational behavior: Utilizing human resources*. Englewood Cliffs, NJ: Prentice Hall.

Hirsch, E. D. (1987). *Cultural literacy: What every American needs to know*. Boston: Houghton Mifflin.

Hittleman, C. (1984, Spring/Summer). Peer response groups: The writing process in action. *Language Connections: Hofstra University Newsletter, 4.*

Hittleman, D. K. (1978). Readability, readability formulas, and cloze: Selecting instructional materials. *Journal of Reading, 22*, 117–122.

Hoffman, J. V. (1977). Intra-Act: A languaging in the content areas teaching procedure (Doctoral dissertation, University of Missouri-Kansas City). *Dissertation Abstracts International, 38*, 3248A.

Hoffman, J. V. (1991). Teacher and school effects in learning to read. In R. Barr, M. Kamil, P. Mosenthal, & D. P. Pearson (Eds.), *Handbook of reading research* (Vol. 11, pp. 911–950). White Plains, NY: Longman.

Hori, A. K. O. (1977). *An investigation of the efficacy of a questioning training procedure on increasing the reading comprehension performance of junior high school learning disabled students*. (Unpublished master's thesis, University of Kansas, Lawrence.)

Indrisano, R., & Paratore, J. R. (1992). Using literature with readers at risk. In B. E. Cullinan (Ed.), *Invitation to read: More children's literature in the reading program* (pp. 139–149). Newark, DE: International Reading Association.

Jackson-Albee, J. A. (2000). *The effect of Read-Encode-Annotate-Ponder annotation exchange (REAP AnX) on the complex thinking of undergraduate students in children's literature courses*. (Unpublished doctoral dissertation, Kansas City, MO: University of Missouri–Kansas City.)

Johnson, A. P. (1995). Science in reading: A harmonic convergence. *Iowa Reading Journal, 8*(1), 12–13.

Jamar, D., & Morrow, J. (1991). A literature-based interdisciplinary approach to the teaching of reading, writing, and mathematics. *The Ohio Reading Teacher, 25*(3), 28–35.

Johnson, D. D., & Pearson, P. D. (1984). *Teaching reading vocabulary* (2nd ed.). New York: Holt, Rinehart & Winston.

Johnson, D. D., Toms-Bronowski, S., & Pittelman, S. D. (1982). *An investigation of the effectiveness of semantic mapping and semantic feature analysis with intermediate grade students* (Program Report 83–3). Madison: University of Wisconsin, Wisconsin Center for Education Research.

Johnston, P. H., & Allington, R. (1991). Remediation. In R. Barr, M. L. Kamil, P. B. Mosenthal, & P. D. Pearson (Eds.), *Handbook of reading research* (Vol. 2, pp. 984–1012). New York: Longman.

Jonassen, D. H. (1985a). Generative learning vs. mathemagenic control of text processing. In D. H. Jonassen (Ed.), *The technology of text: Principles for structuring, designing, and displaying text* (Vol. 2, pp. 9–45). Englewood

Cliffs, NJ: Educational Technology Publications.

Jonassen, D. H. (Ed.). (1982). *The technology of text: Principles for structuring, designing, and displaying text* (Vol. 1). Englewood Cliffs, NJ: Educational Technology Publications.

Jonassen, D. H. (Ed.). (1985b). *The technology of text: Principles for structuring, designing, and displaying text* (Vol. 2). Englewood Cliffs, NJ: Educational Technology Publications.

Jones, M. C., & Bailey, N. (1950). Physical maturing boys as related to behavior. *Journal of Educational Psychology, 41,* 129–148.

Kagan, S. (1994). *Cooperative Learning.* San Clemente, CA: Kagan Cooperative Learning.

Kay, L., Young, J. L., & Mottley, R. R. (1986). Using Manzo's ReQuest model with delinquent adolescents. *Journal of Reading, 29,* 506–510.

Kelly, B. W., & Holmes, J. (1979). The Guided Lecture Procedure. *Journal of Reading, 22,* 602–604.

Kibby, M. W. (1995). The organization and teaching of things and the words that signify them. *Journal of Adolescent and Adult Literacy, 39,* 208–223.

King, C. M., & Parent Johnson, L. M. (1999). Constructing meaning via reciprocal teaching. *Reading Research and Instruction, 38:3,* 169–186.

King, A., & Rosenshine, B. (1993). Effects of guided cooperative questioning on children's knowledge construction. *Journal of Experimental Education, 61:2,* 127–148.

Kirby, D., & Liner, T. (1981). *Inside out: Developmental strategies for teaching.* Montclair, NJ: Boynton/Cook.

Kirshner, D., & Whitson, J. A., Eds. (1997). *Situated cognition: Social, semiotic, and psychological perspectives.* Mahwah, NJ: Lawrence Erlbaum Associates, Publishers.

Klenck, L., & Kibby, M. W. (2000). Re-mediating reading difficulties: Appraising the past, reconciling the present, constructing the future. In Kamil, M.L, Mosenthal, P.B., Pearson, P.D., & Barr, R. (Eds.), *Handbook of reading research, volume III.* (pp. 667–690). Mahwah, NJ: Erlbaum.

Konopak, B. C., & Williams, N. L. (1988). Using the key word method to help young readers learn content material. *The Reading Teacher, 41,* 682–687.

Konopak, B. C., Martin. S. H., & Martin, M. A. (1987). Reading and writing: Aids to learning in the content areas. In E. K. Dishner, T. W. Bean, J. E. Readence, & D. W. Moore (Eds.), *Reading in the content areas: Improving classroom instruction* (3rd ed.) Dubuque, IA: Kendall/Hunt.

Korbin, B. (1988). *Eyeopeners! How to choose and use children's books about real people, places, and things.* New York: Penguin.

Koskinen, P. S., Wilson, R. M., Gambrell, L. B., & Jensema, C. J. (1987). *Using the technology of closed-captioned television to teach reading to handicapped students.* (Performance Report, U.S. Department of Education Grant No. G-00-84-30067). Falls Church, VA: National Captioning Institute.

Krathwohl, D. R., Bloom, B. S., & Masia, B. B. (Eds.). (1956). *Taxonomy of educational objectives: The classification of educational goals. Handbook 2. Affective domain.* New York: Longman, Green.

Kruger, J. (1999). Touched by an Angel. *Bloomberg Personal Finance,* June, 46–51.

Labbo, L. D., & Ash, G. E. (1998). What is the role of computer-related technology in early literacy? In S. B. Neuman & K. A. Roskos (Eds.) *Children achieving: Best practices in early literacy.* Newark, DE: International Reading Association.

Lambert, L. (1998). How to build leadership capacity. *Educational Leadership,* 7(55), 17–19.

Lance, J. (1981). Practicing for touchdowns. *Journal of Physical Education, Recreation, and Dance,* 5, 38.

Laws, K. (1984). The physics of dance. New York: Macmillan, Inc.

Lee, D. M., Bingham, A., & Woelfel, S. (1968). *Critical reading develops early.* Newark, DE: International Reading Association.

Legenza, A. (1978). Inquiry training for reading and learning improvement. *Reading Improvement, 15,* 309–316.

Lenski, S. D., Wham, M. A., & Johns, J. L. (1999). *Reading and learning strategies for middle and high school students.* Dubuque, IA: Kendall/Hunt Publishing Company.

Levin, J. R., Morrison, C. R., McGivern, J. E., Mastropieri, M. A., & Scruggs, T. E. (1986). Mnemonic facilitation of text-embedded science facts. *American Educational Research Journal, 23,* 489–506.

Lewis, C. (1999). Forward to *Popular culture in the classroom: Teaching and researching critical media literacy* (Alvermann, Moon, & Hagood, authors). Newark, DE: International Reading Association.

Lindamood, C. H., & Lindamood, P. C. (1975). *The A.D.D. program, auditory discrimination in depth* (Books 1 & 2). Hingham, MA: Teaching Resources.

Lipson, M. Y., & Wixson, K. K. (1997). *Assessment and instruction of reading and writing disability: an interactive approach.* 2nd edition, New York: Longman.

Longino, H. E. (1990). *Science as social knowledge.* Princeton, NJ: Princeton University Press.

Lovett, M. B. (1981). Reading skill and its development: Theoretical and empirical considerations. In G. MacKinnon & T. Waller (Eds.), *Reading research: Advances in theory and practice* (Vol. 3, pp. 1–37). New York: Academic Press.

Luke, A., & Elkins, J. (1998). Reinventing literacy in "new times." *Journal of Adolescent and Adult Literacy, 42,* 4–7.

Luke, A., & Freebody, P. (1997). The social practices of reading. In S. Muspratt, A. Luke, & P. Freebody (Eds.), *Constructing critical literacies: Teaching and learning textual practices* (pp. 185–225). Cresskill, NJ: Hampton Press.

Maier, N. R. E. (1963). *Problem solving discussions and conferences: Leadership methods and skills.* New York: McGraw-Hill.

MacNeal, E. (1994). *Mathsemantics: Making numbers talk sense.* New York: Viking.

Maggart, Z. D., & Zintz, M. V. (1992). *The reading process: The teacher and the learner* (6th ed.). Dubuque, IA: W. C. Brown & Benchmark.

Maloney, W. H. (2003). Connecting the texts of their lives to academic literacy: Creating success for at-risk first-year college students. *Journal of Adolescent & Adult Literacy, 46* (8), 664–673.

Manthon, A., Hopkins, J., Johnson, S., Lahart, D., McLaughlin, C., Quon Warner, M., & Wright, J. (1994). *Human Biology and Health.* Upper Saddle River, NJ: Prentice Hall.

Manzo, A. V. (1969a). Improving reading comprehension through reciprocal questioning (Doctoral dissertation, Syracuse University, Syracuse, NY, 1968). *Dissertation Abstracts International, 30,* 5344A.

Manzo, A. V. (1969b). The ReQuest procedure. *Journal of Reading, 13,* 123–126.

Manzo, A. V. (1970a). Reading and questioning: The ReQuest procedure. *Reading Improvement, 7,* 80–83.

Manzo, A. V. (1970b). CAT—A game for extending vocabulary and knowledge of allusions. *Journal of Reading, 13,* 367–369.

Manzo, A. V. (1973). CONPASS English: A demonstration project. *Journal of Reading, 16,* 539–545.

Manzo, A. V. (1974). The group reading activity. *Forum for Reading, 3,* 26–33.

Manzo, A. V. (1975). Guided reading procedure. *Journal of Reading, 18,* 287–291.

Manzo, A. V. (1977). *Recent developments in content area reading.* Keynote address, Missouri Council of Teachers of English, Springfield, MO.

Manzo, A. V. (1980). Three "universal" strategies in content area reading and languaging. *Journal of Reading, 24,* 146–149.

Manzo, A. V. (1983). "Subjective approach to vocabulary" acquisition (Or ". . . I think my brother is arboreal!"). *Reading Psychology, 3,* 155–160.

Manzo, A. V. (1985). Expansion modules for the ReQuest, CAT, GRP, and REAP reading/study procedures. *Journal of Reading, 28,* 498–502.

Manzo, A. V. (1998). Teaching for creative outcomes: Why we don't, how we all can. *The Clearinghouse, 71:5,* 287–290.

Manzo, A. V. (2003). Literacy crisis or Cambrian Period? Theory, practice, and public policy implications. *Journal of Adolescent & Adult Literacy, 46*(8), 654–661.

Manzo, A. V., & Casale, U. P. (1980). The five C's: A problem-solving approach to study skills. *Reading Horizons, 20,* 281–284.

Manzo, A. V., & Casale, U. P. (1985). Listen-read-discuss: A content reading heuristic. *Journal of Reading, 28,* 732–734.

Manzo, A. V., & Garber, K. (1995). Study guides. In A. Purves (Ed.), *Encyclopedia of English studies and language arts* (pp. 1124–1125). New York: Scholastic.

Manzo, A. V., & Legenza, A. (1975). Inquiry training for kindergarten children.

Journal of Educational Leadership, 32, 479–483.

Manzo, A. V., & Manzo, U. C. (1987). *Asking, answering, commenting: A participation training strategy.* Paper presented at the annual meeting of the International Reading Association, Anaheim, CA.

Manzo, A. V., & Manzo U. C. (1990a). *Content area reading: A heuristic approach.* Upper Saddle River, NJ: Merrill/Prentice Hall.

Manzo, A. V., & Manzo, U. C. (1990b). Note Cue: A comprehension and participation training strategy. *Journal of Reading, 33,* 608–611.

Manzo, A. V., & Manzo, U. C. (1993). *Literacy disorders: Holistic diagnosis and remediation.* Fort Worth, TX: Harcourt Brace Jovanovich.

Manzo, A. V., & Manzo, U. C. (1995). *Teaching children to be literate: A reflective approach.* Fort Worth, TX: Harcourt Brace College Publishers.

Manzo, A. V., & Manzo, U. C. (1997a). *Content area literacy: Interactive teaching for active learning,* 2nd edition. Upper Saddle River, NJ: Merrill.

Manzo, A. V., & Manzo, U. C. (1997b). A new eclecticism for literacy education. *Journal of Reading Research and Instruction, 37:2,* 94–100.

Manzo, A. V., & Manzo, U. C. (2002). Mental modeling. In B. Guzzetti (Ed.) *Literacy in America: An encyclopedia of history, theory, and practice.* Santa Barbara, CA: ABC CLIO.

Manzo, A. V., Manzo, U. C., & Albee, J. J., (2004). *Reading assessment for diagnostic-prescriptive teaching* (2nd Ed.). Belmont, CA: Wadsworth/Thompson Learning.

Manzo, A. V., Manzo, U. C., Barnhill, A., & Thomas, M. M. (2000). Of different minds: Possible proficient reader subtypes—implications for literacy and gendered theory and practice. *Reading Psychology, 21,* 217–225.

Manzo, A. V., Manzo, U. C., Lang, A., & Barnhill, A. (1996). World wide web: Six enterprises connecting schools to authentic commerce in literature, ideas, humanitarianism, and the free market. Paper presented at the American Reading Forum, Sanibel Island, FL.

Manzo, A. V., Manzo, U. C., & McKenna, M. (1995). *The informal reading-thinking inventory*. Fort Worth, TX: Harcourt Brace College Publishers.

Manzo, A. V. & Martin, D. C. (1974). Writing communal poetry. *Journal of Reading, 17*, 638–643.

Manzo, A. V., & Sherk, J. K. (1971–1972). Some generalizations and strategies for guiding vocabulary acquisition. *Journal of Reading Behavior, 4*, 78–89.

Manzo, A. V., & Sherk, J. K. (1978). Reading and "languaging in the content areas": A third generation approach. *The New England Reading Association Journal, 13*:1, 28–32.

Manzo, A. V., Garber, K., & Warm, J. (1992). *Dialectical thinking: A generative approach to critical/creative reading*. Paper presented at the National Reading Conference, San Antonio, TX, 1992.

Manzo, A. V., Garber, K., Manzo, U. C., & Kahn, R. (1994). *Transmission, transaction, and transformation: Response to text perspectives*. Paper presented at the National Developmental Educators Conference, Kansas City, MO.

Manzo, U. C., Manzo. A. V., & Riley, B. A. (1996). Concepts, content, and cohesion: Impact of concept-based interdisciplinary instruction on the literacy and learning of at-risk fourth graders. Paper. Society for the Scientific Study of Reading, San Francisco, CA.

Maor, E. (1979). A unification of two famous theorems from classical geometry. *Mathematics Teacher, 72*, 363–367.

Maria, K., & MacGinitie, W. (1987). Learning form texts that refute the reader's prior knowledge. *Reading Research and Instruction, 26*, 222–238.

Maring, G. H., & Furman, G. (1985). Seven "whole class" strategies to help mainstreamed young people read and listen better in content area classes. *Journal of Reading, 28*, 694–700.

Maring, G. H., & Ritson, R. (1980). Reading improvement in the gymnasium. *Journal of Reading, 24*, 27–31.

Martin, D. C., Lorton, M., Blanc, R. A., & Evans, C. (1977). *The learning center: A comprehensive model for colleges and universities*. Grand Rapids, MI: Central Trade Plant.

Marzano, R. J. (1997). *Designing standards-based districts, schools, and classrooms*. Alexandria, VA: ASCD.

Marzano, R. J., & Marzano, J. S. (1988). *A cluster approach to elementary vocabulary instruction*. Newark, DE: International Reading Association.

McEneaney, J. E. (2002). Prologue to an object-agent theory of literacy. In D. Schallert, C. Fairbanks, J. Worthy, B. Maloch, & J. Hoffman (Eds.), *51st Yearbook of the National Reading Conference* (pp 321–332). Oak Creek, WI: National Reading Conference.

McFadden, C., & Yaeger, R. E. (1993). *Science plus*. Austin, TX: Holt, Rinehart & Winston.

McKeon, R. (Ed.). (1947). *Introduction to Aristotle*. New York: The Modern Library.

McKeough, A., Lupart, J., & Marini, A., Eds. (1995). *Teaching for transfer: Fostering generalization in learning*. Mahway, NJ: Lawrence Erlbaum Associates, Publishers.

McKenzie, J. V., Ericson, B., & Hunter, L. (1988). *Questions may be an answer*. (Unpublished manuscript, California State University at Northridge.)

McMurry, F. M. (1909). *How to study and teaching how to study*. Boston & Houghton Mifflin & Co.

McNamara, L. P. (1977). A study of the cloze procedure as an alternate group instructional strategy in secondary school American government classes. (Doctoral dissertation, Northern Illinois University, DeKalb). *Dissertation Abstracts International, 39*, 216A.

McNamara, T., Miller, D., & Bransford, J. (1991). Mental models and reading comprehension. In R. Barr, M. Kamil, P. Mosenthal, & P. D. Pearson (Eds.), *Handbook of Reading Research* (Vol. 2). White Plains, NY: Longman.

Meichenbaum, D., & Asarnow, J. (1979). Cognitive-behavioral modifications and metacognitive development. In P. C. Kendall & S. D. Hollan (Eds.), *Cognitive-behavioral interventions: Theory, research and procedures* (pp. 11–35). New York: Academic Press.

Metzger, M. (1998). Teaching reading: Beyond the plot. *Phi Delta Kappan, 80*(3), 240.

Meyer, B. J. E. (1975). *The organization of prose and its effect on memory*. Amsterdam: North-Holland.

Meyer, L. (1988). Research on implementation: What seems to work (pp. 40–57). In S. J. Samuels & P. David Pearson (Eds.), *Changing School Reading Programs: Principles and Case Studies*. Newark, DE: International Reading Association.

Mikulecky, L. (1982). Job literacy: The relationship between school preparation and workplace actuality. *Reading Research Quarterly, 17*, 400–419.

Miller, W. E., & Dollard, J. (1941). *Social learning and imitation*. New Haven, CT: Yale University Press.

Minton, S. C. (1984). Modern dance: Body and mind. Englewood, CO: Morton.

Minton, S., & Beckworth, B. (1986). Dance and sport—the elusive connection. *Journal of Physical Education, Recreation, and Dance, 57*:5, 26, 54.

Missouri Department of Elementary and Secondary Education. (1986). *Core competencies and key skills for Missouri schools: For grades 2 through 10*. Jefferson City, MO: Author.

Mitchell, D. C. (1982). *The process of reading: A cognitive analysis of fluent reading and learning to read*. Somerset, NJ: Wiley.

Moffett, J. (1989). *Storm in the mountains: A case study of censorship, conflict, and consciousness*. Carbondale, IL: Southern Illinois University Press.

Moje, E. B. (1996). "I teach students, not subjects": Teacher-student relationships as contexts for secondary literacy. *Reading Research Quarterly, 31*:2, 172–195.

Moje, E. B., Young, J. P., Readence, J. E., & Moore, D. W. (2000). Reinventing adolescent literacy for new times: Perennial and millennial issues. *Journal of Adolescent and Adult Literacy, 43*, 400–410.

Moller, G., & Bohning, G. (1992, Spring). Setting reading program priorities. *Journal of Reading Education, 17*:3, 22–28.

Moore, D. W., Readence, J. E., & Rickelman, R. J. (1982). *Prereading activities for content area reading and learning*. Newark, DE: International Reading Association.

Moore, D. W., Readence, J. E., & Rickelman, R. J. (1983). An historical exploration of content area reading instruction. *Reading Research Quarterly, 18*, 419–438.

Moss, B. (1991). Children's nonfiction trade books: A complement to content area texts. *The Reading Teacher, 45*(1), 26–32.

Mountain, L. (2002). Flip-a-chip to build vocabulary. *Journal of Adolescent & Adult Literacy, 46*(1), 62–69.

Mulliken, C. N., & Henk, W. A. (1985). Using music as a background for reading: An exploratory study. *Journal of Reading, 28*, 353–358.

Murry, C. (2003, April). Tablet computing: The "next big thing" in school computing has arrived. *ESchool News, eSN Special Report*. Retrieved from http://www.eschoolnews.com/resources/reports/TabletSpec403/

Nagy, W. E. (1988). *Teaching vocabulary to improve reading comprehension*. Newark, DE: International Reading Association.

Naisbitt, J. (1982). *Re-inventing the corporation: Transforming your job and your company for the new information society*. New York: Warner Books.

National Assessment of Educational Progress. *Report in brief:NAEP 1996 trends in academic progress*. Washington, DC: NAEP, 1997.

The Nation's Report Card (2002). *NCES National Center for Education Statistics, Reading*. Retrieved January 31, 2004 from http://nces.ed.gov/nations reportcard/reading/results 2002/

NCES (2001). U.S. Department of Education, National Center for Education Statistics. *Outcomes of Learning: Results From the 2000 Program for International Student Assessment of 15-Year-Olds in Reading, Mathematics, and Science Literacy*, NCES 2002-115, by Mariann Lemke, Christopher Calsyn, Laura Lippman, Leslie Jocelyn, David Kastberg, Yan Yun Liu, Stephen Rocy, Trevor Williams, Thea Kruger, and Ghedam Bairu. Washington, DC: 2001.

NCES (2003). U.S. Department of Education. Institute for Education Sciences. National Center for Education Statistics. *The Nation's Report Card: Mathematics Highlights 2003*, NCES 2004–451, by J. S. Braswell, M. C. Daane, and W. S. Grigg. Washington, DC: 2003.

Newby, T., Stepich, D., Lehman, J., & Russel, J. (1996). *Instructional technology for teaching and learning*. Englewood Cliffs, NJ: Prentice Hall.

New London Group (1996). A pedagogy of multiliteracies: Designing social futures. *Harvard Educational Review, 66*, 60–92.

Niles, O. (1965). Organization perceived. In H. L. Herber (Ed.), *Developing study skills in secondary schools* (pp. 57–76). Newark, DE: International Reading Association.

Nilsen, A. P., & Nilsen, D. L. F. (2003). Lessons in the teaching of vocabulary from September 11 and Harry Potter. *Journal of Adolescent & Adult Literacy, 46*(3), 254–261.

NSES (1998). *National Science Education Standards*. Washington, DC: National Academy Press.

Ogle, D. (1989). Study techniques that ensure content area reading success. In D. Lapp, J. Flood, & N. Farnam (Eds.), *Content area reading and learning* (2nd ed.). Boston: Allyn & Bacon.

Ogle, D. M. (1996). Study techniques that ensure content area reading success. In D. Lapp, J. Flood, & N. Farnan (Eds.), *Content area reading and learning* (2nd ed.). Boston: Allyn & Bacon.

Ollmann, H. E. (1996). Creating higher level thinking with reading response. *Journal of Adolescent and Adult Literacy, 39*, 576–581.

Ordonz-Jasis, R. (2002) Latino families and schools: Tensions, transitions and transformations. Unpublished Doctoral Dissertation, University of California-Berkeley.

Otto, W., & Hayes, B. (1982). Glossing for improved comprehension: Progress and prospect. In G. H. McNinch (Ed.), *Reading in the disciplines. Second yearbook of the American Reading Forum* (pp. 16–18). Athens, GA: American Reading Forum.

Padak, N. D. (1986). Teachers' verbal behaviors: A window to the teaching process. In J. A. Niles & R. V. Lalik (Eds.), *Solving problems in literacy: Learners, teachers, and researchers*.

Thirty-fifth yearbook of the National Reading Conference (pp. 185–191). Rochester, NY: National Reading Conference.

Paley, V. G. (1986, May). On listening to what the children say. *Harvard Educational Review, 56:2*, 122–131.

Palincsar, A. S., & Brown, A. L. (1984). Reciprocal teaching of comprehension monitoring activities. *Cognition and Instruction, 1*, 117–175.

Palmatier, R. A. (1971). Comparison of four note-taking procedures. *Journal of Reading, 14*, 235–258.

Palmatier, R. A. (1973). A notetaking system for learning. *Journal of Reading, 17*, 36–39.

Palmatier, R. A., & Bennett, J. M. (1974). Notetaking habits of college students. *Journal of Reading, 18*, 215–218.

Pauk, W. (1989). *How to study in college* (4th ed.). Boston: Houghton Mifflin.

Paul, R. W. (1993). *Critical thinking: How to prepare students for a rapidly changing world*. Santa Rosa, CA: Foundation for Critical Thinking.

Pauler, S., & Bodevin, D. (1990). Book-specific response activities: Satisfaction guaranteed. *George Journal of Reading, 16*(2), 30–35.

Pearce, D. L. (1983). Guidelines for the use and evaluation of writing in content classrooms. *Journal of Reading, 27*, 215.

Perry, M. (1971). *Man's unfinished journey*. Boston: Houghton Mifflin.

Peters, C. W. (1982). The content processing model: A new approach to conceptualizing content reading. In J. P. Palberg (Ed.), *Reading in the content areas: Application of a concept* (pp. 100–109). Toledo, OH: University of Toledo, College of Education.

Phelps, S., & Smith, L. (1989). Microcomputer applications for content area vocabulary. *Reading Horizons, 29*, 103–109.

Piercy, D. (1976). *Reading activities in content areas*. Boston: Allyn & Bacon. Pol-

lution of the Caesars (1998). *Discover, 19:3*.

Pond, M., & Hoch, L. (1992). Linking children's literature and science activities. *Ohio Reading Teacher, 25*(2), 13–15.

Post, A. R. (1992). The camel caper: An integrated language arts lesson. *Michigan Reading Journal, 25*(2), 29–35.

Postman, N. (1969). *Teaching as a subversive activity*. New York: Dell Publishing Company, Inc.

Pressley, M. (2000). What should comprehension instruction be the instruction of? In Kamil, M. L., Mosenthal, P. B., Pearson, P. D., & Barr, R. (Eds.), *Handbook of reading research, volume III*. (pp. 545–561). Mahwah, NJ: Erlbaum.

Pressley, M., Johnson, C. J., & Symons, S. (1987). Elaborating to learn and learning to elaborate. *Journal of Learning Disabilities, 20*, 76–91.

Pressley, M., Levin, J. R., & MacDaniel, M. A. (1987). Remembering versus inferring what a word means: Mnemonic and contextual approaches. In M. C. McKeown & M. E. Curtis (Eds.), *The nature of vocabulary acquisition* (pp. 107–129). Hillsdale, NJ: Erlbaum.

Pressley, M., Levin, J. R., & Miller, G. E. (1981). How does the keyword method affect vocabulary comprehension and usage? *Reading Research Quarterly, 16*, 213–225.

Putnam, L., Bader, L., Bean, R. (1988). Clinic directors share insights into effective strategies. *Journal of Clinical Reading, 3*, 16–20.

Rakes, S. K., & Smith, L. J. (1987). Strengthening comprehension and recall through the principle of recitation. *Journal of Reading, 31*, 260–263.

Rasinski, T. V. (1989). Fluency for everyone: Incorporating fluency instruction in the classroom. *The Reading Teacher, 42*, 690–693.

Ratekin, N., Simpson, M. L., Alvermann, D. E., & Dishner, E. K. (1985). Why teachers resist content area reading instruction. *Journal of Reading, 28,* 432–437.

Raths, L. E., Harmon, M., & Simon, S. B. (1978). *Values and teaching* (2nd ed.). Columbus, OH: Merrill.

Raygor, A. L. (1977). The Raygor readability estimate: A quick and easy way to determine difficulty. In P. D. Pearson (Ed.), *Reading: Theory, research, and practice.* Clemson, SC: National Reading Conference.

Reeve, R. A., Palincsar, A. S., & Brown, A. L. (1985). *Everyday and academic thinking: Implications for learning and problem solving* (Journal of Curriculum Studies Technical Report No. 349). Champaign: University of Illinois, Center for the Study of Reading.

Rhoder, C., & Huerster, P. (2002). Use dictionaries for word learning with caution. *Journal of Adolescent & Adult Literacy, 45*(8), 730–736.

Richards, P., Thatch, D., Shreeves, M., Timmons, P., & Barker, S. (1999). Don't let a good scare frighten you: Choosing and using quality chillers to promote reading, *Reading Teacher, 52*(8), 830–840.

Robinson, F. (1946). *Effective study.* New York: Harper Brothers.

Robinson, E. A. (1897). In M. D. Zabel (Ed.) *Selected poems of Edwin Arlington Robinson.* (1965) London: Macmillan.

Roby, T. (1983, April). *The other side of the question: Controversial turns, the devil's advocate, and reflective responses.* Paper presented at the annual meeting of the American Educational Research Association, Montreal.

Rogoff, B. (1990). *Apprenticeship in thinking: Cognitive development in social context.* New York: Oxford University Press.

Rosenblatt, L. (1938). *Literature as exploration.* New York: Appleton-Century.

Rosenshine, B. V. (1984). Content, time, and direct instruction. In P. L. Peterson & H. J. Walberg (Eds.), *Research on teaching: Concepts, findings, and implications* (pp. 102–106). Berkeley, CA: McCutchan.

Rowe, M. B. (1974). Wait time and rewards as instructional variables, their influences on language, logic, and fate control: Part One—Wait time. *Journal of Research in Science Teaching, 11,* 81–94.

Rowe, M. B. (1986). Wait time: Slowing down may be a way of speeding up! *Journal of Teacher Education, 37,* 43–50.

Rud, A. G. (1997). The use and abuse of Socrates in present day teaching. *Education Policy Analysis Archives, 5:20.* (http://olam.ed.asu.edu/epaa).

Ruddell, M. R. (1993). *Teaching content reading and writing.* Boston: Allyn & Bacon.

Ruddell, M. R. (1997). *Teaching content reading and writing,* (2nd ed). Boston: Allyn & Bacon.

Ruddell, M. R., & Shearer, B. A. (2002). "Extraordinary," "tremendous," "exhilarating," "magnificent": Middle school at-risk students become avid word learners with the vocabulary self-collection strategy (VSS). *Journal of Adolescent & Adult Literacy, 45*(5), 352–364.

Ruddell, R. B. (1999). *Teaching children to read and write: Becoming an influential teacher* (2nd ed.). Boston: Allyn & Bacon.

Ruddell, R. B., & Ruddell, M. H. (1995). *Theoretical processes and models of reading* (3rd ed.). Newark, DE: International Reading Association.

Rush, T., Moe, A., & Storlie, R. (1986). *Occupational literacy education.* Newark, DE: International Reading Association.

Russell, D. (1961). *Children learn to read* (2nd ed.). New York: Ginn.

Sage, G. H. (1977). Introduction to motor behavior: A neuropsychological approach (2nd ed.). Reading, MA: Addison-Wesley.

Salibrici, M. (1999). Dissonance and rhetorical inquiry: A Burkean model for critical reading and writing. *Journal of Adolescent and Adult Literacy, 42,* 628–637.

Samuels, S. J. (1977). Introduction to theoretical models of reading. In W. Otto, N. A. Peters, & C. W. Peters (Eds.), *Reading problems: A multidisciplinary perspective* (pp. 7–41). Reading, MA: Addison-Wesley.

Sanders, P. L. (1969). Teaching map reading skills in grade 9. *Journal of Reading, 12,* 283–286, 337.

Santa, C. M., Dailey, S. C., & Nelson, M. (1985). Free-response and opinion proof: A reading and writing strategy for middle grade and secondary teachers. *Journal of Reading, 28,* 346–352.

Santa, C. M., Isaacson, L., & Manning, G. (1987). Changing content instruction through action research. *The Reading Teacher, 40,* 434–438.

Schell, L. M. (1988). Dilemmas in assessing reading comprehension. *The Reading Teacher, 42,* 12–16.

Schumm, J. S., & Mangrum, C. T., II (1991). FLIP: A framework for content area reading. *Journal of Reading, 35,* 120–123.

Shepherd, D. (1978). *Comprehensive high school reading methods* (3rd ed.). Upper Saddle River, NJ: Merrill/Prentice Hall.

Shor, I., & Freire, P. (1987). *A pedagogy for liberation: Dialogues on transforming education.* South Hadley, MA: Bergin & Garvey.

Shore, B. (1999). *The cathedral within: Transforming your life by giving something back.* New York: Random House.

Shulman, L. S. (1987). Knowledge and teaching: Foundations of the new reform. *Harvard Educational Review, 57,* 1–22.

Simmons, J. (2003). Responders are taught, not born. *Journal of Adolescent & Adult Literacy, 46*(8), 684–693.

Simpson, M. (1986). PORPE: A writing strategy for studying and learning in the content areas. *Journal of Reading, 29,* 407–414.

Simpson, M. L., Hayes, C. G., Stahl, N. A., Connor R. T., & Weaver, D. (1988). An initial validation of a study strategy system. *Journal of Reading Behavior, 20,* 149–180.

Singer, H. (1976). Theoretical models of reading. In H. Singer & R. B. Ruddell (Eds.), *Theoretical models and processes of reading* (2nd ed., pp. 634–654). Newark, DE: International Reading Association.

Singer, H., & Dolan, D. (1980). *Reading and learning from text.* Boston: Little, Brown.

Singer, H., & Ruddell, R. B. (1976). *Theoretical models and processes of reading* (2nd ed.). Newark, DE: International Reading Association.

Sizer, T. R. (1984). *Horace's compromise: The dilemma of the American high school.* Boston: Houghton Mifflin.

Smith, R. J., & Dauer, V. L. (1984). A comprehension-monitoring strategy for reading content area materials. *Journal of Reading, 28,* 144–147.

Smyth, J. (2003, January 23). Study says boys do read, they just don't read books. *National Post.* Retrieved January 23, 2003 from http://www.nationalpost.com and now available for order from the archive at http://www.infomart.ca.

Spache, G. D. (1976). *Diagnosing and correcting reading disabilities.* Boston: Allyn & Bacon.

Spiegel, D. L. (1980). Adaptations of Manzo's guided reading procedure. *Reading Horizons, 20,* 188–192.

Spor, M. W. & Schneider, B. K. (1999). Content reading strategies: What teachers know, use, and want to learn. *Reading Research and Instruction, 38*:3, 221–231.

Stahl, N. A., & Henk, W. A. (1986). Tracing the roots of textbook study systems: An extended historical perspective. In J. A. Niles & R. V. Lalik (Eds.), *Solving problems in literacy: Learners, teachers, and researchers. Thirty-fifth yearbook of the National Reading Conference* (pp. 366–374). Rochester, NY: National Reading Conference.

Stahl, S. A., & Fairbanks, M. M. (1986). The effects of vocabulary instruction: A model-based meta-analysis. *Review of Educational Research, 56,* 72–110.

Stanovich, K. E. (1986). Matthew effects in reading: Some consequences of individual differences in the acquisition of literacy. *Reading Research Quarterly,* (21) 4, 360–407.

Staton, J. (1980). Writing and counseling: Using a dialogue journal. *Language Arts, 57,* 514–518.

Stauffer, R. (1969). *Directing reading maturity as a cognitive process.* New York: Harper & Row.

Stenger, C. (1999). *A characterization of undergraduate mathematical thinking.* Paper presented at the Fourth Annual Conference on Undergraduate Mathematics Education. Chicago, IL.

Stevens, K. C. (1982). Can we improve reading by teaching background information? *Journal of Reading, 25,* 326–329.

Stieglitz, E. L., & Stieglitz, V. S. (1981). SAVOR the word to reinforce vocabulary in the content areas. *Journal of Reading, 25,* 48.

Strickland, D., & Morrow, L. (1990). Integrating the emergent literacy curriculum with themes. *The Reading Teacher, 43,* 604–605.

Suarez, R. (1999). *The old neighborhood: what we lost in the great suburban migration, 1966–1999.* New York: Free Press.

Tan, A., & Nicholson, T. (1997). Flashcards revisited: Training poor readers to read words faster improves their comprehension of text. *Journal of Educational Psychology, 89*(2), 276–288.

Taylor, G. C. (1980). Music in language arts instruction. *Language Arts, 58,* 363–367.

Tchudi, S. (1988). Invisible thinking and the hypertext. *English Journal, 77*:1, 22–30.

Tharp, R. G., & Gallimore, R. (1989). *Rousing minds to life: Teaching, learning, and schooling in social context.* New York: Cambridge University Press.

Tharp, R. G., & Gallimore, R. (1990). *Rousing minds to life: Teaching, learning, and schooling social context.* New York: Cambridge University Press.

Thomas, M. M. (1998, May). *Furthering higher-order literacy using the internet.* Paper presented as part of a full-day seminar with others entitled "Higher-Order Literacy: Redefining Remedial, Developmental, and Proficient Readers" at the 43rd Annual Convention of the International Reading Association, Orlando, Florida.

Thomas, M. M. (2001). Proficient reader characteristics: Relationships among text-dependent and higher-order literacy variables with reference to stage theories of intellectual development. *Dissertation Abstracts International* (UMI No. 3010626).

Thomas, M. M., & Hofmeister, D. (2003). Moving content area literacy into the digital age: Using online discussion board interactions. *Journal of Content Area Reading, 2*(1), 61–80.

Thomas, M. M., King, A., & Cetinguc, T. (2004). My first year with a Tablet PC: Has literacy found a means to ubiquitous computing at last? *Proceedings of the 2004 Society for Information Technology in Teacher Education Conference.*

Thorndike, E. L. (1917). Reading as reasoning: A study of mistakes in paragraph reading. *Journal of Educational Psychology, 8,* 323–332.

Tierney, R. J., Readence, J. E., & Dishner, E. K. (1990). *Reading strategies and practices* (3rd ed.). Needham Heights, MA: Allyn & Bacon.

Tierney, R. J., Soter, A., O'Flahavan, J. F., & McGinley, W. (1989). The effects of reading and writing upon thinking critically. *Reading Research Quarterly, 24,* 134–137. *Time* (March 22, 1993). 54.

Unrau, N. J. (1997). *Thoughtful teachers, thoughtful learners: A guide to helping adolescents think critically.* Scarborough, Ont: Pippin Publishing.

Unrau, N. J. (2004). Content area reading and writing : Fostering literacies in middle and high school cultures. Upper Saddle River, NJ: Prentice Hall.

Vacca. R. T. (1998). Forward. In D. E. Alvermann, K. A. Hinchman, D. W. Moore, S. F. Phelps, & D. R. Waff (Eds.). *Reconceptualizing the literacies in adolescents' lives* (pp. xv–xvi). Hillsdale, NJ: Erlbaum.

Vacca, R. T., & Alvermann, D. E. (1998). The crisis in adolescent literacy: Is it real or imagined? *NASSP Bulletin, 82:*600, 4–9.

Vacca, R. T., & Vacca, J. L. (1986). *Content area reading* (2nd ed.). Boston: Little, Brown. Vaulting Vampires (1998). *Discover Magazine, 19:*3.

Vogt, M. E. (2002). *SQP2RS: Increasing students' understandings of expository text through cognitive and metacognitive strategy application.* Paper presented at the 52nd Annual Meeting of the National Reading Conference, Miami, FL.

Vygotsky, L. S. (1978). *Mind in society: The development of higher psychological process.* Cambridge, MA: Harvard University Press.

Wade, R. K. (1984–1985). What makes a difference in inservice teacher education? A meta-analysis of research. *Educational Leadership, 42*(4), 48–54.

Waern, Y. (1977a). Comprehension and belief structure. *Scandinavian Journal of Psychology, 18,* 266–274.

Waern, Y. (1977b). On the relationship between knowledge of the world and comprehension of texts. *Scandinavian Journal of Psychology, 18,* 130–139.

Walker, A., & Parkman, M. (1924). *The study readers: Fifth year.* New York: Merrill.

Walker, B. J. (1985). Right brain strategies for teaching comprehension. *Academic Therapy, 21,* 133–141.

Wark, D. M. (1964). Survey Q3R: System or superstition? In D. M. Wark (Ed.), *College and adult reading.* Third and fourth annual yearbook of the North Central Reading Association (pp. 161–70). St. Paul: University of Minnesota, Student Counseling Bureau.

Watkins, J., McKenna, M., Manzo, A., & Manzo, U. (1995). *The effects of the listen-read-discuss procedure on the content learning of high school students.* (Unpublished manuscript.)

Weatherly, D. (1964). Self-perceived rate of physical maturation and personality in adolescence. *Child Development, 35,* 1197–1210.

Weaver, W. W., & Kingston, A. J. (1963). A factor analysis of cloze procedure and other measures of reading and language ability. *Journal of Communication, 13,* 252–261.

Welker, W. A. (1987). Going from typical to technical meaning. *Journal of Reading, 31,* 275–276.

White, T. (1998, November 6). Bypass of school woes in KC urged focus on teachers, students, not trouble with leaders, man says. *The Kansas City Star,* p. C8.

Wilkins, G., & Miller S. (1983). *Strategies for success: An effective guide for teachers of secondary-level slow learners.* New York: Teachers College Press.

Williams, J. P. (1973). Learning to read: A review of theories and models. *Reading Research Quarterly, 8,* 121–146.

Willmore, D. J. (1967). A comparison of four methods of studying a college textbook. (Doctoral dissertation, University of Minnesota, 1966). *Dissertation Abstracts, 27,* 2413A.

Wilson, E. O. (1998). *Consilience: The unity of knowledge.* New York: Knopf.

Wood, K. D. (1992). Fostering collaborative reading and writing experiences in mathematics. *Journal of Reading, 36*(2), 96–103.

Wood, K. D. (2000). Asset building in the classroom: An instructional perspective, research into practice. *Middle School Journal, 31*(3), 53–56.

Wood, K. D. (2002). Aiding comprehension with the imagine, elaborate, predict, and confirm (IEPC) strategy: Research into practice. *Middle School Journal, 33*(3), 47–54.

Wooster, G. E. (1958). Teaching the SQ3R method of study: An investigation of the instructional approach (Doctoral dissertation, The Ohio State University, 1953). *Dissertation Abstracts International, 18*, 2067–2068.

Wooten, D. A. (1992). The magic of Martin. In B. E. Cullinan (Ed.), *Invitation to read: More children's literature in the reading program* (pp. 73–79). Newark, DE: International Reading Association.

Worthy, J. (1998). On every page someone gets killed! Book conversations you don't hear in school. *Journal of Adolescent and Adult Literacy, 41*, 508–517.

Zola, J. (Host). (1998). How to conduct successful Socratic seminars [Video recording]. Alexandria, VA: Association for Supervision and Curriculum Development.

CHILDREN'S BOOKS CITED

Adamson, J. (1960). *Born Free.* New York: Pantheon.

Bahr, R. (1982). *Blizzard at the Zoo.* New York: Lothrop.

Barton, B. (1986). *Planes* New York: Crowell.

Barton, B. (1986). *Trucks.* New York: Crowell.

Bash, B. (1989). *Desert Giant: The World of the Saguano Cactus.* Boston: Little Brown.

Bemelmans, L. (1939). *Madeline.* New York: Viking.

Brown, M. W. (1988). *Goodnight Moon.* New York: Harper & Row.

Burton, V. L. (1939). *Mike Mulligan and His Steam Shovel.* Boston: Houghton Mifflin.

Calhoun, M. (1979). *Cross-Country Cat.* New York: Morrow.

Carle, E. (1998). *Little Cloud.* New York: Philomel Books.

Caselli, G. (1987). *How the Human Body Works.* New York: Grosset & Dunlap.

Caselli, G. (1992). *Life Through the Ages.* New York: Darling Kindersley.

Cavanah, F. (1978). *Abe Lincoln Gets His Chance.* New York: Scholastic.

Cohen, B. (1983). *The Carp in the Bathtub.* Illustrated by Joan Halpern. New York: Lothrop.

Curtis, C. (1978). *Panda.* New York: Delacorte.

Day, V. (1963). *Landslide.* New York: Coward McCann.

dePaola, T. (1975). *The Cloud Book.* New York: Holiday.

dePaola, T. (1975). *The Cloud Book.* New York: G.P. Putnam's.

Freedman, R. (1984). *Animal Superstars: Biggest, Strongest, Fastest, Smartest.* New York: Prentice Hall.

Gag, W. (1928). *Millions of Cats.* New York: Coward, McCann, & Geoghegan.

Gemming, E. (1974). *Born in a Barn.* New York: Coward, McCann, & Geoghegan.

Gibbons, G. (1982). *The Post Office Book: Mail and How It Moves.* New York: Crowell.

Gibbons, G. (1985). *The Milk Makers.* New York: Macmillan.

Goudey, A. (1961). *Here Come the Dolphins.* New York: Scribner's.

Graham, A., & Graham, F. (1978). *Whale Watch.* New York: Delacorte.

Herge. (1975). *Tintin in Tibet.* New York: Little Brown.

Hughes, S. (1985). *An Evening at Alfie's.* New York: Lothrop.

Keats, E. J. (1967). *The Snowy Day.* New York: Viking.

The Kids' Question and Answer Book, by the editors of *Owl* magazine. (1988). New York: Putnam.

Lawson, R. (1979). *The Tough Winter.* New York: Puffin Books.

Lilly, K. (1982). *Animals in the Country.* New York: Simon & Schuster.

Lobel, A. (1970). *Frog and Toad Are Friends.* New York: Harper & Row.

Macauley, D. (1988). The Way Things Work. New York: Penguin.

Marshall, J. (1987). *The Cut-Ups Cut Loose.* New York: Viking.

Martin, B., Jr., & Archambault, J. (1985). *Chicka Chicka Boom Boom.* Illustrated by T. Rand. New York: Simon & Schuster.

Martin, B., Jr., & Archambault, J. (1988). *Listen to the Rain.* New York: Henry Holt.

McMillan, B. (1983). *Here a Chick, There a Chick.* New York: Lothrop, Lee & Shepard.

Momaday, N. S. (1975). *Owl in the Cedar Tree.* Flagstaff, AZ: Northland Press.

Noble, T.H. (1984). *The Day Jimmy's Boa Ate the Wash.* New York: Dial Press.

Parish, P. (1989). *Amelia Bedelia.* Illustrated by Fritz Seibel. New York: Harper & Row.

Pope, J. (1986). *Do Animals Dream?* New York: Viking.

Rey, H. A. (1973). *Curious George.* Boston: Houghton Mifflin.

Schwartz, D. M. (1985). *How Much Is a Million?* Illustrated by Steven Kellogg. New York: Lothrop, Lee & Shepard.

Sendak, M. (1985). *Where the Wild Things Are.* New York: HarperCollins.

Silverstein, S. (1987). *The Giving Tree.* New York: HarperCollins.

Viorst, J. (1987). *Alexander and the Terrible, Horrible, No Good, Very Bad Day.* Illustrated by Ray Cruz. New York: Macmillan.

Waber, B. (1973). *Ira Sleeps Over.* Boston: Houghton Mifflin.

White, E. B. (1952). *Charlotte's Web.* New York: Harper & Row.

Williams, V. (1982). *A Chair for My Mother.* New York: Greenwillow.

Wong, J. S. (1963). *Fifth Chinese Daughter.* New York: Scholastic.

Wood, A. (1984). *The Napping House.* Illustrated by D. Wood. San Diego: Harcourt Brace Jovanovich.

PHOTO CREDITS

Chapter 1
Page 3: Photodisc Red./Getty Images.

Chapter 2
Page 23: PhotoDisc, Inc./Getty Images.

Chapter 3
Page 43: Photodisc Green/Getty Images.

Chapter 4
Page 69: Digital Vision.

Chapter 5
Page 103: Photodisc Green/Getty Images.

Chapter 6
Page 125: PhotoDisc, Inc./Getty Images.

Chapter 7
Page 155: PhotoDisc, Inc./Getty Images.

Chapter 8
Page 185: Digital Vision.

Chapter 9
Page 233: Image 100 Ltd./Corbis Images.

Chapter 10
Page 259: Photodisc Red/Getty Images.

Chapter 11
Page 281: Photodisc Blue/Getty Images.

Chapter 12
Page 299: Royalty-free/Corbis Images. Page 313: Bettmann/Corbis Images.
Page 321: Bettmann/Corbis Images.

Chapter 13
Page 335: Thinkstock/Getty Images.

Chapter 14
Page 363: Brand X Pictures/Getty Images.

INDEX